FIRST EDITION

SUSTAINABILITY
GLOBAL ISSUES, GLOBAL PERSPECTIVES

EDITED BY Astrid Cerny

cognella®
academic publishing

Bassim Hamadeh, CEO and Publisher
Michael Simpson, Vice President of Acquisitions and Sales
Jamie Giganti, Senior Managing Editor
Jess Busch, Senior Graphic Designer
John Remington, Senior Field Acquisitions Editor
Monika Dziamka, Project Editor
Brian Fahey, Licensing Specialist
Allie Kiekhofer, Interior Designer

First published in the United States of America in 2016 by Cognella, Inc.

Cover image copyright © 2012 by Depositphotos / 1xpert.
Interior image copyright © by Depositphotos / smarques27.

Printed in the United States of America

ISBN: 978-1-63487-895-1 (pbk) / 978-1-63487-896-8 (br)

www.cognella.com   800-200-3908

TABLE OF CONTENTS

CONTENTS

LIST OF TABLES AND FIGURES

TABLES

FIGURES

Preface

BY ASTRID CERNY

A KAZAK WHO LIVES WITH HIS FAMILY AS PART OF A LARGER COM-munity of Kazak livestock herders in western China knows his place in the grand scheme of things. He is required to know from memory his lineage and the names of his ancestors for seven generations into the past.

Kazak hospitality is very distinct and practiced across several Central Asian cultures in a similar way. When a guest arrives, the women rush to put out a tablecloth, a *dastarqan*, and to lay it with what the household has to offer that day. Hot black tea with milk or cream and butter is served, and the tablecloth is laid with *borsaq*—deep-fried dough pieces, dried fruits, nuts, and candies. Guests help themselves and the host asks the predictable questions: whose child are you? What is your family line? What is your lineage? The guest answers, and host and guest enjoy the conversation to look for common ancestors that will strengthen a deeper bond between them.

The Iroquois confederation of North America also traces its place in time by the power of seven. The Iroquois think and make decisions according to the idea of seven generations into the future. No decision should be made in self-interest, says article 28 of the Iroquois Nations constitution, but always under consideration of the needs of coming generations, even those as yet unborn.[1] Oren Lyons, Faithkeeper of the Onondaga Council of

---

1 In fact, the original language (modern version) is as follows: "In all of your deliberations in the Confederate Council, in your efforts at law making, in all your official acts, self-interest shall be cast into oblivion. … Look and listen for the welfare of the whole people and have always in view not only the present but also the coming generations, even those whose faces are yet beneath the surface of the ground—the unborn of the future Nation." Gerald Murphy, "About the Iroquois Confederation." *Modern History Sourcebook* accessed October 27, 2014, http://www.fordham.edu/halsall/mod/iroquois.asp.

Chiefs, speaking at the Association of American Geographers conference in New York in 2012 said, "Look to the seventh generation. When you do that, you yourself will have peace."

It is no coincidence that the Kazak herders and Iroquois are peoples of Asia and North America who still today are deeply aware of the land they inhabit. Their historical and customary rights to land and territory were diminished by the encroachment of new settlers who asserted their own stakes on property. Today, remaining Native American and other native populations seek strength in numbers through the identification as indigenous people, for which they fought 30 years to get recognition at the United Nations. This recognition came in the form of the Declaration of the Rights of Indigenous Peoples, on September 13, 2007, adopted at the General Assembly of the United Nations in New York. Their unique, distinct cultures have been recognized, and their voices speak from another kind of wisdom—about what it means to live an honorable life, with respect for traditional knowledge from the generations of the past still present in their actions today.

The length of a generation is commonly understood as 20 years. Thus, the Kazaks know their lineage at least 140 years into the past, and the Iroquois consider the needs of people 140 years into the future. The idea of intergenerational equity, that which binds generations together in consciousness and responsibility, is slowly gaining ground.

In 1987, a seminal document was published, also at the United Nations, which considered environment and development as inexorably linked with each other. Officially called *Our Common Future*, it is also referred to as "the Brundtland Report" after its chairwoman, Gro Harlem Brundtland (United Nations General Assembly, *Report of the World Commission on Environment and Development: Our Common Future*, 1987). The effort to write this report was monumental for its day, to select and bring to words the most pressing issues of the time, and to articulate the anticipated wishes and needs for all of humanity on a finite planet Earth into the future. Officially registered as a UN document bearing the classification A/42/427, it generated many important new international debates, and it is today, like the Constitution of the Iroquois Confederacy, a document circulating in its entirety in the public domain of the Internet.

Our Common Future articulated the moral and ethical obligation to make significant changes in how we treat our oceans and atmosphere, and how we regulate to ensure equity among generations and nations. Its most quoted statement is the definition of sustainable development in chapter two: "Sustainable development is development that meets the needs of the present without compromising the ability of future generations to meet their own needs" (United Nations General Assembly, "A/42/427").

This definition became somewhat normative to the international development and environmental communities from that point forward, and it helped to stimulate the many articulations of what it means to be sustainable, to pursue sustainable development, sustainable agriculture, sustainability, and many other ideas. Significantly, the legacy of *Our Common Future* has helped shape the way we see, promote, and delimit the three pillars of sustainability—environment, economy, and society.

A new paradigm wants to emerge in our time, but it is fighting with an old one. The old one is the paradigm of capitalism as a universal force of growth and development for positive change in the world. We are taught in schools about the wonders that the Industrial Revolution unleashed and how post-World War II development has connected us through transportation, trade, and new communication technologies, seemingly into a global village. Capitalism did stimulate and pay for many important advances, notably in health and human longevity, but capitalism may now have gone too far in serving itself. It can no longer be understood only as our benefactor.

The current paradigm, which encourages us to support the economy as our friend and protector, teaches us to spend and consume. It teaches us to indulge ourselves, buy ourselves new objects, those trending, luxuriously packaged ones, or those imprinted with a certain brand name or logo. We are encouraged and even intentionally misled into believing that it is all about us, our individual self, me.

Media and technology both now converge on this message: here, right now, it is about this moment, me and my newest latest gadget and its apps, on Facetime, Facebook, texting, tweeting, or just plain staring into the screen that gives the illusion of endless choice and access to anything on the big wide world of the Internet. Yet this is not the whole truth. Gadget fixation teaches self-centeredness, short-term thinking, and denial of technology's consequences—such as environmental pollution in someone else's backyard and human isolation even in congested cities. All because the stimulation of the distracting message on the screen right now, in this instant, feels. So. Good.

Limited at first to the economically richest countries in the world, gadgets like laptops and iPhones have changed the world we live in, in many ways for the better. It is true that technology, in the form of handheld gadgets, is increasingly becoming available to people in poorer nations and even in the most remote regions like the Himalayan plateau and sub-Saharan Africa is somewhat of a game changer. Cell phones allow farmers to make deals with middlemen to buy the new harvest, just as these phones allow Wall Street traders to reach their most important customers for rapid and convenient transactions.

We appreciate the convenience of these technologies, but increasingly we are also bearing the costs of their existence. More and more people can see a new truth emerging. This truth is still diffuse, arising in the consciousness of individuals such as Chief Lyons, in global political forums such as the General Assembly at the United Nations, and in research across the sciences and social sciences.

This understanding is that humans have gone too far in taking natural resources from Earth, and too far in putting back into the air, soil, and water only our wastes and innumerable forms of contamination.

This book builds on the emerging understandings of sustainability as a holistic endeavor for humanity, and that embracing sustainability, indeed changing the paradigm of what we mean by development, is the only way we have of handling the massive geophysical changes we are already beginning to experience under climate change.

In this book we examine a few of the major topics of concern for students and professionals from the Environment with a capital E, to the very loaded term sustainability. We take a global perspective, though of course we had to limit our scope to a reasonable page limit. This is the first edition of a book we will expand to include more topics and perspectives. The goal of this textbook is to provide the interested reader with a snapshot of the dominant concerns, even major crises that we all face together, whether they are visible to us in our immediate location or not. Intended for classroom use and personal enjoyment in introductory environmental, sustainability, or global studies courses, the authors share their many years of research and their professional perspectives from a range of academic disciplines and activist practice. In this edition, the authors write about Mali, Mauritania, and Africa as a whole, the United States at the state and national level, and select examples from many Latin American, European, and Asian locations.

We discuss the major topics for sustainability, and we also introduce important components for a new paradigm. We are perhaps not revolutionary in our concepts, but we are part of the new paradigm emerging. We posit a holistic perspective. In this book we question the legacy of globalization and promote ideas of inclusion of people and acceptance of responsibility to create the change we want to see in the world, whether that is in our immediate surroundings, in our country, or for global equity.

What will people seven generations from now say about us? In a way, this edition lays the foundation for understanding where we are at, and what choices are already available for us to make, for the common good.

Astrid Cerny
Editor

REFERENCES

Murphy, Gerald. 2014. "About the Iroquois Confederation." *Modern History Sourcebook*. Available at http://www.fordham.edu/halsall/mod/iroquois.asp.

United Nations General Assembly. 1987. *Report of the World Commission on Environment and Development: Our Common Future.*

INTRODUCTION

SECTION 1

Chapter 1

AN INTRODUCTION TO ENVIRONMENTAL THOUGHT

BY BETH KINNE

THE CONCEPT OF THE ENVIRONMENT AS A SUSTAINING FORCE FOR human life is not new. Hundreds of years of study have steadily increased our scientific understanding of the role of the greater environment in maintaining the human species and all we depend on for life. However, despite our ever-increasing understanding of the interrelatedness of species, ecosystems, and geophysical, chemical, and biological processes, most of us live with less tangible contact with the world that supports us than did our grandparents of just two generations ago. Most students can name the three pillars of environmental sustainability: economic, social, environmental. Many are concerned about the impacts of climate change on fresh water availability, food production, and sea levels. Few people in the developed world have any direct experience raising the food they eat whether animals or vegetables. And only a slightly greater number have ever spent more than one night outside in the woods camping or hiking.

Chances are, if you are reading this chapter, you have a greater-than-average interest in the environment, but you may still not know where the water comes from at the home where you grew up, or where your garbage goes after the truck picks it up at the curb.

You are probably similar to most Americans, indeed most people in the developed world, in the lack of awareness of physical connection between your daily life and the natural systems that support it. Most of us regularly consume meat and vegetables at cafeterias and restaurants, purchase groceries regularly at the local market, and take showers and flush toilets, seldom giving a thought to where that food or water came from or where it will go after we are finished with it. The popularity of environmental science and environmental studies as a respectable area of academic pursuit is growing, but our individual connections to the environment are arguably weakening as people—particularly in the developed world—live in increasingly dense populations of humans and their man-made artifacts: buildings, sidewalks, airports, shopping malls, houses. It is ironic that as our scientific knowledge of the state of the environment grows increasingly sophisticated, our personal relationship or direct experience with that environment grows increasingly limited.

This is not to say that the value of individual experiences is more important than having a theoretical, big-picture understanding. It is impossible to make good long-term policy decisions based solely on individual experiences over short periods of time. For example, our understanding of climate change is based on data collected over many decades in many locations around the globe. Individual experiences of weather in the short term—such as the abnormally cold winter in North America in 2014–2015—seem to contradict the longer trend of global temperature increase, and without a more comprehensive picture could lead us to a very different conclusion. Nevertheless, the short-term, immediate experiences such as weather are still important. We have to survive today's hurricane or tornado, this year's winter, in order to survive the coming century. It is the challenge of sound environmental thinking to take both into consideration—the immediate and the relatively far-off welfare of ourselves, future generations, and our environment.

Like science and art, the concept of environment is not static but changes with time, place, and individuals or groups. History, culture, and social norms impact how people think of "the environment" and how they perceive their relationship to it.

An appreciation for the natural world as "the environment" or "nature" has led to innovations such as national parks. The US national park system is a model for national park systems around the world. National parks are areas set aside for the preservation of ecological diversity, shielded from human intervention. But national parks are managed by people who effectively stop natural processes from occurring in them. Park managers halt the march of invasive species; preserve specific habitats through controlled burn regimens, and cull or encourage various populations of animals and plants in particular places. Human intervention is still there, then, but it is carefully prescribed and culturally shaped. Historically, people lived in the forests, until we regulated them out. Wolves were part of the forest as well, until they were hunted to extinction in most of the United States. The lack of people and wolves in the forest is a result of policy and legal decisions created in a cultural context that defined the relationship between humans and the environment. The development of this relationship has changed over time, through applications of philosophies that as often as not are contradictory, in tension with one another.

This chapter introduces some of the individual people—philosophers, scientists, farmers, politicians, and activists—who have contributed to the evolution of environmental thought and "environmentalism." Indeed, the myriad ways in which humans around the world perceive of their relationship to the non-human world gives rise to multiple "environmentalisms," not simply one all-encompassing version. Limitations on time and space do not allow us to mention every influential movement or person in the history of environmental thought. Moreover, this text will not even do justice to the contributions of those we mention here. Therefore, this chapter should serve as a place from which your study and understanding of environmentalism can begin, rather than one where it both begins and ends.

KEY CONCEPTS: WILDERNESS, PRESERVATION, AND CONSERVATION

Environmental thought is shaped by conceptions we have in our minds, and how we distinguish distinct ideas about nature, the environment, and wilderness. We then find a long-standing separation between nature and that which our ancestors considered civilization or the human world. For example, the Oxford English Dictionary defines wilderness as "an uncultivated, uninhabited, and inhospitable region," a definitively negative connotation. Early references to wilderness also impact our historical concepts of the environment. In the Judeo-Christian tradition as illustrated in the Old Testament, for example, the wilderness is a place of uncertainty, exile, danger, and testing,[1, 2] but it is also a place of transformation and renewal.[3] These two competing ideas about wilderness as something that

---

1   God led the Israelites out of Egypt and into the wilderness in Exodus.
2   See Matthew 4:1, where God led Jesus into the wilderness to be tested by the devil.
3   The Israelites formed a new relationship with God while in the wilderness, for example.

needs to be tamed and controlled continue to permeate Western literature and even legal policies toward the environment. These concepts, which have parallels in the conflicting roles of humans as both rightful recipients of the earth's bounty and stewards of its future, shape our attitude towards everything non-human in our world.

In the early and mid-1800s, thinkers Ralph Waldo Emerson and Henry David Thoreau contributed to the development of a new American cultural identity, one that included Emerson's intellectual understanding of a divinity that is within everything and Thoreau's reverence for the value of nature.[4] In the late 1800s and early 1900s, a generation of advocates for the environment continued to build on Thoreau's seminal work, promoting the concept of the *value* of wilderness and therefore preservation of that wilderness. They would leave an indelible mark on Western ideas of environmentalism. Among them, Edward Abby and John Muir promoted a concern for the loss of wild areas in the American West, in stark contrast to the widely held political support for the rapid growth of California and "progress," which meant a definite taming of that "Wild West."

A pioneering thinker on conservation, John Muir (1838–1914) reportedly once described himself as a "poetico-trampo-geologist-botanist and ornithologist-naturalist etc. etc.!!!!"[5] Muir's writings and advocacy greatly influenced President Theodore Roosevelt and spurred the creation of some of the first US National Parks. In 1892, he and others founded the Sierra Club, and he served as the club's first president.[6] Muir considered the experience of nature and wilderness as critical to the moral and spiritual development and well-being of people, and he advocated for preservation of nature as part of our natural heritage. His success in helping to create Yosemite National Park in 1890 and his legacy of connection to the environment inspire many environmental activists and outdoor enthusiasts to this day.

The resource conservation movement became institutionalized at the turn of the twentieth century with the installation of Theodore Roosevelt as US President and subsequent appointment of Yale University graduate Gifford Pinchot as Chief Forester.[7] Roosevelt and Pinchot realized that

---

4   Emerson's writings include his seminal essay "Nature" (1836).
5   "The John Muir Exhibit," *The Sierra Club*, http://vault.sierraclub.org/john_muir_exhibit/about.
6   For a chronology of John Muir's life, see "Chronology (Timeline) of the Life and Legacy of John Muir," *The Sierra Club*, http://vault.sierraclub.org/john_muir_exhibit/life/chronology.aspx .
7   For more on Pinchot, see his autobiography, *Breaking New Ground* (New York: Island Press, 1998).

US forests, which had seemed so vast to early European settlers as to be indomitable, were in danger of being destroyed by indiscriminate use.[8] As first head of the US Forest Service, Pinchot's vision for the national forests was one of conservation.

The concept of "conservation" is often used interchangeably with "preservation," and in many modern examples, this is appropriate. In fact, the National Wilderness Act, signed by Lyndon B. Johnson in 1964, provided an avenue for the protection of several hundred millions of acres of land under the National Wilderness Preservation System (NWPS).[9] National parks, national forests, national wildlife refuges, and Bureau of Land Management (BLM) lands are all part of the NWPS.[10] However, some of these places (national wildlife refuges) are largely protected from human encroachment while others (national forests and BLM lands) are open to logging, mining, and grazing, among other activities. In some cases, preservation includes active maintenance of certain ecosystems to support wildlife, or specific forms of wildlife.

In spite of the common usage of the terms, the distinction between conservation and preservation is worth maintaining because in theory they can point to very different managerial approaches and to a very different relationship between humans and the natural environment. Conservation includes use and harvesting of natural resources at a sustainable rate, meaning one that will allow renewal of the resource.[11] Non-renewable resources such as fossil fuels require conservative use so as to maximize the length of time those resources can support the human population.[12] Conservation practices have been applied to forests, fisheries, and rangelands with some success. The key, of course, to effective conservation, is accurate prediction of what the maximum yield is. Historically, natural resource managers and industry, and even fishermen and farmers, have often overestimated that number, causing precipitous declines in species we would like to maintain in perpetuity.

---

8   Note that freshwater and ocean fisheries also fell victim to the same fate, but were arguably less easy to remediate.

9   For a map of areas protected under the NWPS, see http://www.wilderness.net/map.cfm.

10   "National Wilderness Preservation System," *The Wilderness Society*, http://wilderness.org/article/national-wilderness-preservation-system.

11   One could argue that all resources are renewable, but the time frame over which that occurs may or may not be useful to humans. A forest that regrows in 25 years is renewable from a human perspective; coal that might be formed millions of years from now from the remains of these trees is not, in all practicality, renewable.

12   See "Conservation," *The US Department of Agriculture: Forest Service*, http://www.fs.fed.us/gt/local-links/historical-info/gifford/conservation.shtml.

In contrast, preservation means setting aside valued resources and preventing their use or change. National parks are probably the regions in the United States most closely governed by the preservation ethic. The Grand Canyon, Yosemite, and Yellowstone are examples of how unique characteristics in landscape and wildlife led to their geographic area being considered valued resources and thus enclosed and protected within the National Park System.

In practice, complete preservation is very difficult and seldom applied. People need to be kept out, which is not easy, but easier than managing migrating wildlife, pests, and invasive species. This is a big challenge to true preservation—maintaining the dynamic and authentic character of natural systems over time. The trouble is that preservation in a steady state actually requires a great deal of active management—which is done by people. For example, the US National Park Service employs Invasive Plant Management Teams, which are involved in the extirpation of invasive species.[13] Pine beetles, leaf borers, and other insects do not observe the toll gates to the parks, but pursue their activities inside and outside the park just the same. Wildfire management has also been a contentious issue over time, as wildfires do occur naturally and can leave unsightly devastation behind, as with the 1988 fires in Yellowstone. People are divided on the issue of when and what to preserve in the case of wildfires.

Finally, we need to remember that maintaining the parks in a more "natural" state is based on a baseline or standard set at some point in historical time. This point was chosen by an expert manager of ecosystems in a particular political context that was favorable to protecting land and water resources. When signing the Wilderness Act of 1964, Lyndon B. Johnson stated, "If future generations are to remember us with gratitude rather than contempt, we must leave them something more than the miracles of technology. We must leave them a glimpse of the world as it was in the beginning, not just after we got through with it."[14] Heroic words for an ongoing act of protection of some unique and beautiful places. But let us not forget that the "beginning," in this instance, is really the post–World War II period.

---

13 "Invasive Species: What Are They and Why Are They a Problem?" *National Park Service*, http://www.nature.nps.gov/biology/invasivespecies.
14 Quoted in "National Wilderness Preservation System," *The Wilderness Society*, http://wilderness.org/article/national-wilderness-preservation-system.

THE ECOLOGICAL ETHIC

Environmentalism has long included an "ecological ethic," the idea that there is some intrinsic value in the earth and its ecosystems that cannot, and perhaps should not, be monetized or reduced to some economic value. The ecological ethic is rooted in the belief that there is value in the natural world that is yet unknown and, due to the limitations of the human mind, may never be known. However, regardless of whether the value is known, it is believed that the natural world should be protected to the best of our abilities. The next section introduces some of the key thinkers in American environmentalism who contributed to this philosophy.

In 1933, US forester Aldo Leopold[15] published "The Conservation Ethic,"[16] an essay in which he advocated a different way of thinking about nature. Leopold argued that humans should treat land—which for him included vegetation, animals, and everything that inhabited the land—as a community to which humans belong, and therefore should extend to the land the same ethics and respect we extend to people.

In that same year, he published the first textbook on wildlife management, *Game Management*, in which he asserted that people could interact with nature to restore populations of game and manage them for productivity in perpetuity through wise use and planning and human intervention.[17] Leopold managed US forests in Arizona and New Mexico before being transferred to Wisconsin in 1924, where he purchased a rundown farm and began restoring ecosystems on it through active management. He continued to write about these experiences in his book of essays, *A Sand County Almanac*, which was published a year after his death and is widely considered a seminal text in American environmental thought. Leopold's land ethic advocates for respect and appreciation for the land and its intrinsic value, but like Pinchot, he also advocated active management of ecosystems.

Harvard Professor E. O. Wilson, an entomologist who studied the social and biological behavior of ants, also fundamentally altered our understanding of and conversation about the environment. Wilson's work introduced the concept of biodiversity into environmental discourse. The

---

15 Leopold lived from 1887–1948, had a degree in forestry from Yale University, and served with the US Forest Service in Arizona; then as Associate Director of the US Forest Service Product Laboratory (from 1924) and professor at University of Wisconsin, Madison. See "Aldo Leopold," *The Aldo Leopold Foundation*, http://www.aldoleopold.org/AldoLeopold/leopold_bio.shtml.

16 A. Leopold, "The Conservation Ethic," *Journal of Forestry* 31, no. 6 (1933): 634–643.

17 A. Leopold, *Game Management*, (Madison: University of Wisconsin Press, 1986).

importance of understanding the close interactions that maintain complex ecosystems is now integrated into conservation programs, development planning, and even environmental legislation. Wilson pioneered the discipline of socio-biology, the principle that the social interactions of animals and humans have biological underpinnings.[18]

FROM CONCERN WITH OVERUSE TO CONCERN WITH POLLUTION

The 1960s brought an era of increased concern for the deleterious impacts of pollution created by modern-day chemical fertilizers, pesticides, and warfare. Scientists at Johns Hopkins published the "Baby Tooth Study," in which they showed that baby teeth exhibited uptake of Strontium 90 emitted from nuclear testing in the US West. Author Rachel Carson released her timeless, best-selling book, *Silent Spring*, which awakened a generation of Americans and others to the existence and harmful effects of radioactivity and pesticides in the food chain and human bodies. In spite of harsh critique by the agricultural and pesticide manufacturing lobbies, the John F. Kennedy administration initiated a federal study that eventually supported much of what Carson concluded in *Silent Spring*— that industrial contaminants, chemical pesticides, and pharmaceuticals could have significant negative health impacts if not carefully regulated. Nearly a decade before the era of environmental lawmaking of the 1970s, the political and social groundwork for increased legislation for protecting the environment from man-made impacts of the industrial world was being laid.

In the late 1960s, the Cuyahoga River Fire in Cleveland, the Santa Barbara oil spill, and other environmental disasters stirred widespread popular demand for better regulation of pollution for the sake of human health. On the eve of 1970, US President Richard Nixon signed the Environmental Protection Act, and early in 1970 he created the Environmental Protection Agency (EPA). These laws and the decade of environmental legislation to follow laid the groundwork for a fundamentally different way of documenting and addressing environmental impacts.

---

18 For more on E. O. Wilson, see the E. O. Wilson Foundation at eowilsonfoundation.org.

The 1960s and '70s also brought the beginning of radical environmentalism, which would, if nothing else, create room for more progressive mainstream policies. The way this occurred is through the "flanking principle." The flanking principle is at work when certain groups taking extreme actions change the metric by which extreme is measured, the very way in which broad swathes of society understand "extreme." In doing so, radical groups broaden the space for more moderate responses, which may still be far more progressive and beneficial than the status quo. In the same way in which the advent of many people over seven feet would redefine what "tall" means, thereby allowing many six-foot-tall people to seem more moderate height, the advent of extreme responses to environmental problems—such as blowing up dams and spiking ancient trees—makes policy decisions like protesting logging and lobbying against dams seem quite reasonable.[19]

The personalities of environmental radicals grew out of true appreciation for the environment combined with frustration with the government's general disregard for the environment. Their understanding inspired their followers as much as the radical non-standard behaviors they participated in and advocated for.

Edward Abby's writings on the intricacies of southwestern desert ecology inspired many who had never even seen this region of the world. His individualistic personality and advocacy for disobedience, as a mechanism for halting the destruction of the natural world, is embodied in his comic 1975 novel *The Monkey Wrench Gang*.[20] This radical environmental activism contributed to an increasing awareness of the inability of the regular political process to fairly weigh the value of the environment in policy decisions. Later, Dave Foreman, co-founder of the radical environmental group Earth First!, would continue in this vein. His book, *Confessions of an Eco-Warrior*, is an autobiography of a Washington insider and policymaker turned activist in frustration with the ineffectiveness of the political process. In his later years, he backed off from radical activism after that, too, failed to turn the public in support of environmental causes.[21]

---

19 Spiking trees is the act of inserting large metal spikes into large trees which, when struck by a chain saw, can cause the saw to buck and potentially injure the user. This method was used by some radical environmental activists to save forests by making them dangerous to harvest.

20 Edward Abby, *The Monkey Wrench Gang* (New York: Harper Perennial, 2006).

21 Dave Foreman, *Confessions of an Eco-Warrior* (New York: Harmony Books, 1991).

SUSTAINABILITY AND RESILIENCE

The work of Pinchot, Muir, Leopold, and others presaged the more recent global adoption of sustainability as an organizing framework for environmental policy which continues to gain momentum. The Native American tradition of planning for the seventh generation was an early and enduring articulation of the idea that we are not only providing for ourselves in the current generation, but should also be providing for those who come after us. The *Report of the World Commission on Environment: Our Common Future* is frequently referred to as the "Brundtland Report" after Norwegian Gro Harlem Brundtland, the chair of the commission. The 1987 report formally incorporated the concept of multigenerational environmental sustainability, and despite its shortcomings in scope, can be credited with being the benchmark for the gathering of global momentum on protecting more of Earth. Perhaps its greatest achievement is its most quoted sentence. The report defined sustainable development as "development that meets the needs of the present without compromising the ability of future generations to meet their own needs."

"Sustainable growth" seems an oxymoron, since all growth has limits. The earth's resources are finite. Even in the many cases where resources are renewable, many are not renewable over a time frame relevant to the human experience. For example, the old growth forests that once occupied most of North America would take hundreds of years to regenerate, thereby precluding them from being renewed for each human generation. Even our water resources, which we think of as renewable over months or years, in the case of many aquifers are actually renewable only over thousands or tens of thousands of years. When we deplete these aquifers in a matter of decades, for all intents and purposes they are no more renewable than oil and gas. Two good examples of this are the Ogallala Aquifer in the high plains region of the United States and the Nubian Sandstone Aquifer that lies under Chad, Libya, Sudan, and Egypt.

Sustainability is subject to the critique that it implies some ideal steady state of use and renewal that is achievable and desirable. Our understanding of Earth systems and ecological processes teaches us that at any given time, any ecosystem is in a state of transition, even if that transition is slow. There are intakes and outputs, losses and gains, births and deaths. The natural predisposition of systems to change and reorganize thus shows that sustainability must ultimately be something more than maintenance of a steady state.

The concept of resilience is slowly replacing sustainability as a goal in designing human-built environments as well as assessing the health of natural systems. Resilience is defined as the ability to adapt and recover in response to external stresses. In some cases, that recovery is to the original, pre-disturbed state. In others it is to an altered but still functioning state. Originally a concept from ecology and psychology, the idea of resilience of social systems and the related resilience of socio-ecological systems is now informing the environmental debate.[22] Resilience is a useful concept when we talk about the greatest threats to human society today: climate change, water shortages, and food shortages. The question is not whether these things will change ecosystems and human life. They undoubtedly will. The question may be more about whether any particular species (including humans) or ecosystem on the earth will be able to respond and adapt to these changes and survive long term.

THE ENVIRONMENT AND THE LAW

Our understanding of the environment is strongly tied to the ever-growing body of scientific knowledge of ecosystems and human–nature interactions. Translating this knowledge into laws that regulate human activity is critical to preventing large-scale, long-term environmental harms that ultimately could endanger our own existence. The role of law is to create the world we want to live in through the modification of human behavior. As such, environmental laws play a significant part in achieving that world.

The decade between 1970 and 1980 was "the environmental decade" in US legal history. During this time, many nascent federal US environmental laws were strengthened and new ones were created. Some of the most important among these are the modern Clean Water Act (1972); the modern Clean Air Act (1970); the Resource Conservation and Recovery Act (RCRA, 1976); the Federal Insecticide, Fungicide, and Rodenticide Act (FIFRA, 1972); the Toxic Substances Control Act (1976); and the

---

22 For example, M. Cotes and A. J. Nightingale, "Resilience Thinking Meets Social Theory: Situating Social Change in Socio-Ecological Systems," *Progress in Human Geography* 36, no. 4 (2012): 475–789.

Comprehensive Environmental Response, Compensation, and Liability Act (CERCLA, 1980), better known as the Superfund Act.[23]

CERCLA was unique in addressing past environmental damage because it provided for identification and cleanup of key sites of significant contamination. In other words, the US government agreed to pay for (through tax dollars and the federal budget) hazardous waste cleanup and remediation of land and water that had become toxic to life. The results of its implementation also surprised American lawmakers because the number of contaminated sites so far outnumbered what Congress had predicted, and the extent of the damage and cost of cleaning those sites was even more unexpected.

Environmental laws in the United States have their origin in the much older and more developed legal traditions of tort and nuisance. Tort law addresses intentional or negligent harms to people or property, and is a useful way of addressing some pollution claims. For example, if a person or company spilled chemicals and contaminated the neighbor's property, under tort law the owner of the contaminated property could sue the spiller and the spiller could be found liable for the harm to the neighbor's property. However, the plaintiff (the person bringing the lawsuit) had to prove that the defendant (the person being sued) had either acted intentionally or negligently in bringing about the harm. A small area of tort law held people liable for "abnormally dangerous activities"—those activities that, no matter how carefully conducted, had a high likelihood of causing damage to nearby people. The abnormally dangerous activities category included actions like using dynamite and crop dusting. However, for all other harms, the fairly high bar for proving intentional negligence, coupled with the cost and uncertainty of filing a private lawsuit, often discouraged would-be plaintiffs from seeking compensation through the courts.

Nuisance law creates a remedy—either in the form of action or money damages—for people who are denied the enjoyment of their own property due to some activity by another person. In the case of environmental nuisance, usually someone who owns or operates a neighboring or nearby property is preventing the plaintiff from enjoying his or her own property. Noise, vibrations, light, and smells can create nuisance and give rise to a

---

23 Many of today's environmental laws had earlier, weaker precursors. The typical trajectory of an environmental law runs from early versions that call for data collection and analysis, to stronger laws that provide causes of action for lawsuits and allow for private and public plaintiffs, and under some circumstances even encourage citizen suits by providing for awards of attorney's fees, thereby effectively deputizing citizen enforcers of environmental laws in areas where government enforcement might otherwise be difficult.

successful lawsuit under nuisance law. Environmental laws like the Clean Water Act and Clean Air Act created statutory causes of action (means by which a lawsuit can be brought) and in many cases—but not all—made traditional actions in nuisance unnecessary. In short, environmental laws lowered the hurdles for many plaintiffs who were bringing lawsuits for harms to the environment. But the common law claims of nuisance and tort are still used in environmental law where the statutory laws do not provide a cause of action.

The new environmental laws gave the government the right to fine or require certain parties responsible for environmental harms to pay administrative fines and, in some cases, to fix problems they caused as much as possible, including cleaning up spills. In addition, these laws clarified rights of neighboring landowners and vilified activities that pollute the environment, thereby showing a way forward that made it easier to bring private suits. Furthermore, the laws were testimony to the seriousness with which the federal government was addressing the pollution problem. After the federal laws were passed, many states passed their own versions of the Environmental Protection Act, some of which spelled out the responsibilities of various state agencies to protect the environment. Some federal environmental laws, such as the Clean Water Act and Clean Air Act, delegated most components of standard-setting and enforcement to the states, thereby encouraging states to develop their own environmental pollution prevention strategies.

While these laws were significant improvements, it is important to understand that they by no means forbid pollution of the environment. Instead the laws require permitting and reporting of pollution, and systematic efforts to reduce pollution. They are a mechanism to balance pollution with economically beneficial activities, and therefore critics frequently point out that they largely fail to substantially meet their stated goals. For example, section one of the Clean Water Act of 1970 states as the objective of the act, "to restore and maintain the chemical, physical, and biological integrity of the Nation's waters" and more specifically, that "the discharge of pollutants into the navigable waters be eliminated by 1985."[24] As a nation we are close to achieving neither of these. This may be an unfair critique though. Perhaps the real comparison should be between the water quality we have in the United States today and that which we would have had absent the Clean Water Act.

---

24   Clean Water Act section 101(a), (1972).

Our pollution laws tend to focus on point-source pollution: pipes and smokestacks. Non–point-source pollution comes from diffuse runoff from agricultural fields, storm water from city streets, or pollutants from lots of individual automobiles. Non–point-source pollution is more difficult to measure, inspect, and control, and therefore it is more difficult to regulate. However, non–point-source pollution makes up a significant part of water and air pollution, necessitating alternative mechanisms for regulation.

In devising better ways to prevent, mitigate, and repair pollution, it is important to remember that environmental law does not regulate the environment; it regulates human actions that impact the environment. As such, it is important to put serious thought into what motivates people to act and to devise incentives that encourage individuals and corporations to make decisions that promote the long-term health of the environment. Economics, sociology, and psychology all can contribute to our understanding of environmentalism.

THE IMPACT OF SOCIAL SCIENTISTS ON ENVIRONMENTALISM

Social scientists have influenced environmental thought through theory and practice. Marxist theories of class structure and struggle inform understandings of human–environmental interactions. In many cases, socioeconomic status affects the degree to which people have access to the benefits of the natural environment, or are vulnerable to environmental risks such as drought, flood, and other natural disasters.

In 1968, Dr. Paul Ehrlich published *The Population Bomb*, which built on theories from Thomas Malthus's 1798 "An Essay on the Principle of Population." Ehrlich predicted a mass crash in human population during the 1970s and 1980s due to an inability to feed the world's growing numbers. This did not come to pass; it has been avoided in part due to the advent of what is known as the green revolution in agriculture. The green revolution brought unprecedented increases in agricultural production worldwide through the application of chemical fertilizers and pesticides, which increased crop yields and decreased losses. However, the idea that the earth and its resources are not unlimited, and that human population and consumption will be constrained by resource limitations, continue to be key concepts in environmental sustainability scholarship and policy decisions today.

In 1969, Garret Hardin published *The Tragedy of the Commons*, an essay that attributed the deterioration of natural resources to the fact that they were a commons—owned by nobody, and therefore overused to exhaustion or extinction. Hardin's basic theory proposed that for a resource with "N" users, each additional unit any one user takes from the resource results in a full additional unit of benefit for that user. But the cost to that user is $1/N$, where N is the total number of users. As N reaches a very large number, each additional unit costs a user close to nothing, but gives that user a full 1 unit of benefit. Therefore, each individual has the motivation to take an additional unit. The overall result of rational decisions by each individual results in ecological catastrophe though when the resource is exhausted or cannot renew itself as fast as each user takes a unit. The essay remains widely quoted today, though it has been critiqued by Ostrom and others.

In 2009, Elinor Ostrom won the Nobel Prize in economic sciences for her empirical and theoretical work contributing to a better understanding of how common resources such as fisheries are managed.[25] She distinguished common pool resources such as fisheries—where a limited number of players share the resource—from those resources from which users cannot be excluded (e.g., air). Ostrom then explained the ways that common pool resources can be managed effectively, including through the use of institutions and agreements among users. This work challenged the idea that private ownership of resources was the only way to avoid Hardin's "Tragedy of the Commons."

In particular, Ostom's many years of research show that achieving lasting management of a common resource is possible when several characteristics are present. The resource should be available to a known set of users. People who do not qualify for that set of users should be excluded. The eligible users should be able to participate in rule making and decision-making about sustainable continued use of the resource. Effective penalties can and should be used for infractions of the rules that apply to all qualified users of the resource. Her writings, such as *Governing the Commons* (1990), showed through international examples from different cultures and a variety of shared resources how people can and will manage their resource in everyone's best interest.

---

25   See "Elinor Ostrom," *The Official Website of the Noble Prize*, http://www.nobelprize. org/nobel_prizes/economic-sciences/laureates/2009/ostrom-facts.html.

Most of this chapter focuses on Western, and more specifically European and North American environmentalism. However, environmental thinking and development of environmental consciousness has historical roots in Native American cultures, religious traditions of Asia (e.g., Confucian, Daoist, Hindu, and Shinto traditions), and the indigenous people around the globe.

For example, philosophy professor Dr. Eric Nelson describes the Dao as "the lived or performative enactment of the intrinsic value and life of the myriad things, of 'sky and earth' or the natural world."[26] As such, this tradition promotes valuing all things in the world for their own sake, separate of their economic or utilitarian value, setting the stage for a particular type of relationship with the natural environment. Other Chinese texts associate degradation of the tangible natural environment with injury to or degradation of the human soul.[27]

In modern China, the government has long been intolerant of political activists. However, the environmental movement enjoys a surprising amount of tolerance. Water and air pollution and looming water shortages threaten most large cities in the country; urban pollution spreads via air currents to places as far away as the western United States.

The Chinese government's almost welcoming treatment of nongovernmental organizations addressing environmental harms seems to stem from a realization that failure to address pollution and environmental quality could very easily impact the nation's economy and ultimately the legitimacy of the government itself.[28] In this way, the threats of a deteriorating environment are resulting in fundamental changes in the way the central government governs, at least in this area.

If environmental nongovernmental organizations have been tolerated and accepted in China, it is reasonable to assume they can spring up—and be effective—just about anywhere. In this era of international travel, Internet access, and instant communication, the environmental movement is global as well as local. Secular and religious groups alike are tackling problems of environmental degradation on an international scale. As they do so, they influence where and how awareness of the environment is engrained in our daily lives.

---

26   Eric S. Nelson, "Responding with Dao: Early Daoist Ethics and the Environment," *Philosophy East and West 59*, no. 3 (2009): 295.
27   See Nelson's discussion of the writings of Zhuangzi and Mengzi, ibid.
28   See C. Larson, "The Green Leap Forward," *Washington Monthly*, July/August 2007.

One such example is the work of Kenyan and Nobel Peace Prize winner Wangaari Mathai in raising awareness of the consequences of deforestation in Kenya, the disproportionate impact of environmental degradation on women, and the positive consequences of reforestation. Her daughter and others continue her work with the financial support of international charitable foundations.[29] Projects like the Alliance of Religions and Conservation (ARC), draw on multiple religious traditions to join together to address environmental concerns. The ARC traces its beginnings to the mid-1980s and includes representatives of nine major world religions in a collaborative effort with such organizations as the World Bank to promote conservation of the environment and reduction of poverty. [30]

Development of US environmental laws gave rise to further development of environmental laws in other countries, many of which have since surpassed the United States in protection of the environment and human health. The advent of multinational and transnational corporations resulted in the need for laws that bridge national sovereignty to hold polluters accountable to not only their investors, but also to the countries where they mine and manufacture. Some of this has become accepted inside the idea of corporate social responsibility.

International environmental law attempts to do this. Operationally, it is distinct from domestic environmental law in that there is no international arbiter of most claims for damages due to pollution. Individual claims are heard by countries where the polluter is registered for business activity and in the countries where the pollution occurs. The pursuit of legal responsibility is dependent on countries' adherence to international treaty obligations. As such, the comparative political strength of the countries at issue and their mutual political relationship can impact the degree of political will of any court to enforce against a multinational corporation. In less developed countries, courts may be under considerable pressure not to enforce against multinational companies that bring investment dollars and international political leverage.

Pollution has become an international problem and the activities that cause it are increasingly international in scope. In response, protests against polluters have also become international. One example of this is the global response to the proliferation of horizontal drilling and hydraulic fracturing technology to harvest oil and gas. Many oil and gas companies

29 See "The Green Belt Movement," http://www.greenbeltmovement.org.
30 "Alliance of Religions and Conservation—History," *Alliance of Religions and Conservation*, http://www.arcworld.org/about.asp?pageID=2.

are international in scope, operating in more than one country and traded on international markets. The broad implementation of their technologies resulted in an international movement against some of their technologies and the known threats to the environment that intensive exploration for oil and gas entails.

Dubbed the "global frackdown," coordinated resistance erupted across Europe and North America, made possible by Internet access and almost instantaneous communication across national boundaries.[31] The internationalization of opposition to activities with international backing but still very local impacts is driving a new way of thinking about the environment. A problem that is simultaneously local and global requires both local and global solutions.

Activists like Maude Barlow and Vandana Shiva are key players in the internationalization of environmental conservation movements in the face of the increasing power of multinational corporations. Among other things, Barlow and Shiva have called into question the wisdom of widespread use of chemical fertilizers and pesticides, and of putting management of water—a resource without which people cannot survive—in the hands of corporations whose management is primarily beholden to shareholders and not to the recipients of the water. This is in marked contrast to a local public water utility. It is particularly problematic for water systems in the developing world where the shareholders are mainly people in the developed world, far away from the on-the-ground consequences of business decisions made by these corporations.[32]

CONCLUSION

The concept of the "environment" and the human relationship to it has changed over time. Changes in technology and the passage of time create an iterative process of increasing ability to dominate the non-human world we live in and the deeper realization of our dependence on that which we cannot fully understand. This in turn results in the evolution

---

31   See Benjamin E. Griffith, "The International Community's Response to Hydraulic Fracturing and a Case for International Oversight" in *Beyond the Fracking Wars: A Guide for Lawyers, Planners, Municipal Leaders and Citizens,* eds. E. Powers and B. Kinne, (Chicago: American Bar Association, 2013).
32   For further discussion, see Maude Barlow, *Blue Gold: The Fight to Stop the Corporate Theft of the World's Water* (New York: The New Press, 2005).

of ways of thinking about, talking or writing about, and advocating for the environment. The environment—that which surrounds us, feeds us, shelters us, and is capable of consuming us—creates in us the often contradictory impulses to revere, abuse, preserve, deplete, restore, study, and manipulate. The evolution of environmental thought is not so much a linear path as one of concentric circles that over time illustrate our constant human struggle to redefine—and to do it better this time—our relationship with the non-human natural world.

REFERENCES

Abby, Edward. 1975. *The Monkey Wrench Gang*. Philadelphia: Lippencott Williams and Wilkins. Reprinted by Harper Perennial, 2006.

The Aldo Leopold Foundation. "The Leopold Legacy." Available at http://www.aldoleopold.org/AldoLeopold/leopold_bio.shtml.

Alliance of Religions and Conservation, http://www.arcworld.org/about.asp?pageID=2.

Barlow, M. 2005. *Blue Gold: The Fight to Stop Corporate Theft of the World's Water*. New York: The New Press.

Clean Water Act, 42 USC 1251 et seq. (1972).

Cotes, M. and A. J. Nightingale. 2012. "Resilience Thinking Meets Social Theory: Situating Social Change in Socio-Ecological Systems." *Progress in Human Geography* 36(4): 475–489.

Emerson, R. W. 1836. "Nature." In *Emerson's Prose and Poetry*, edited by Saundra Morris and J. Porter. W W Norton & Co., 2001.

E. O. Wilson Foundation, eowilsonfoundation.org.

Foreman, Dave. 1991. *Confessions of an Eco-Warrior*. New York: Harmony Books.

The Green Belt Movement, http://www.greenbeltmovement.org.

Griffith, Benjamin E. 2013. "The International Community's Response to Hydraulic Fracturing and a Case for International Oversight." In *Beyond the Fracking Wars: A Guide for Lawyers, Planners, Municipal Leaders and Citizens*, edited by E. Powers and B. Kinne. Chicago: American Bar Association.

Larson, C. 2007. "The Green Leap Forward." *Washington Monthly* July/August. Available at http://www.washingtonmonthly.com/features/2007/0707.Larson.html.

Leopold, A. 1933. "The Conservation Ethic." *Journal of Forestry* 31(6): 634–643.

Leopold, A. 1933. *Game Management*. New York: Charles Scribner's Sons. Renewed by Ella B. Leopold, 1961; foreward copyright, Board of Regents at the University of Wisconsin, 1986.

Nelson, Eric. S. 2009. "Responding with Dao: Early Daoist Ethics and the Environment." *Philosophy East and West* 59(3): 294–316 at 295.

Pinchot, Gifford. 1947. *Breaking New Ground*. Estate of Gifford Pinchot. Reprinted by Washington, DC: Island Press, 1998.

The Sierra Club. "The John Muir Exhibit." Available at http://vault.sierraclub.org/john_muir_exhibit/about/.

The Official Website of the Nobel Prize. "Elinor Ostrom." Available at http://www.nobelprize.org/nobel_prizes/economic-sciences/laureates/2009/ostrom-facts.html.

US Forest Service. "Historical Information: Conservation." Available at http://www.fs.fed.us/gt/locallinks/historical-info/gifford/conservation.shtml.

US National Park Service. "Invasive Species: What Are They and Why Are They a Problem?" Available at http://www.nature.nps.gov/biology/invasivespecies/.

The Wilderness Society. "National Wilderness Preservation System." Available at http://wilderness.org/article/national-wilderness-preservation-system.

CHALLENGES FOR GLOBAL SUSTAINABILITY TODAY

SECTION 2

Chapter 2

ENERGY: CHANGING THE RULES WITH EFFICIENCY AND RENEWABLES

BY DARRIN MAGEE AND BETH KINNE

"What if we could make energy do our work without working our undoing?"
—Amory Lovins, *Reinventing Fire*[1]

DOWN THE DRAIN

Picture for a moment a cup of your favorite coffee or tea. Imagine that it is at just the right temperature, served in a nice cup as you sit in your favorite chair after a restful night's sleep. You take your first few sips, draining about one-third of the cup.

Now imagine dumping the rest of your coffee down the sink, then preparing a second cup of exactly the same beverage. Now dump that one, too.

I have just described a very inefficient and wasteful process. Why would anyone waste two-thirds of a perfectly good product only to then repeat the process? As we shall see in this chapter, inefficiency pervades the way we extract, convert, and utilize energy—from taking fossil fuels out of the ground and refining them, to lighting our homes and workplaces, and moving ourselves and our goods by land, sea, and air. The inefficiency of some processes

---

1 We are exceedingly grateful to Amory Lovins and other colleagues at Rocky Mountain Institute for the inspiration their book *Reinventing Fire* (Lovins and Rocky Mountain Institute, 2011) and the institute's ongoing work has provided for this chapter. To learn more, see www.rmi.org/reinventingfire.

is simply a fact of physics and cannot be avoided. But what we can do is avoid, or at least minimize our use of, those processes that are most inefficient and environmentally degrading. First among these is converting fossil fuels to electricity in thermal power plants where some two-thirds of the energy is simply dumped—like the beverage above—down the drain.

ENERGY BASICS

Energy has many forms and many uses, and even though in common parlance we may hear talk of energy "production" and "consumption," it is vital to recall one fundamental fact: energy—the same as matter—is neither created nor destroyed. Thus it makes more sense to think of energy transactions, all of which, whether at the cellular or the global scale, consist of transformations of energy from one form to another. A complex orchestra of cells in our bodies transforms the energy stored in the food and drink we consume into forms useful for the myriad processes necessary to keep us alive, a process called respiration. A petrochemical refinery might be understood as an industrial analog to those cells, as it separates and transforms the mix of hydrocarbon chains in crude oil into the products such as gasoline, diesel, lubricants, and plastics precursors that fuel and undergird modern industrial societies.

In each and every one of those transformations, however, some energy is degraded into less useful forms, most commonly into heat. We frequently speak of this as "energy lost" or "energy wasted," but in reality, that energy is simply—and irreversibly—transformed into less useful forms, in which its ability to do work is reduced. This concept is crucial to understanding the important role efficiency *must* play if human society is to transition to a more sustainable model.

Energy at its most basic is the capacity to do work, and in a physical sense is frequently understood as simply equivalent to work. Since this is not a textbook on the quantum mechanisms at the subatomic scale that give rise to the energetic outcomes we observe at larger scales, it is perhaps most useful to think of energy first as the fuels in which it is stored. Energy that is used as it exists in nature, without transformation or conversion into another form, is called primary energy.[2] Examples include fossil fuels such as coal, natural

---

2   The US Energy Information Administration maintains a very useful primer on energy basics called "Energy Explained: Your Guide to Understanding Energy," available at http://www.eia.gov/energyexplained/index.cfm.

gas, and petroleum, all of which are fuels that may be combusted[3] to provide heat, which can then be used to do work (as in a blacksmith's shop or steam engine). These primary energy sources may also be transformed into other forms as final or delivered energy, the most common of which is electricity. As we shall see below, the transformation of thermal energy into electricity is one of the most significant sources of wasteful energy transformation.

It is important to note that primary energy does not refer exclusively to fossil or nuclear fuels; hydroelectricity is also considered primary energy, since it derives directly from the potential energy of water falling downward and spinning turbines and generators.

You may recall from high school science classes a distinction between kinetic energy and potential energy. Kinetic energy is the energy of motion (e.g., the energy of a moving train); a body of a certain mass, traveling at a certain velocity, possesses a kinetic energy that is proportional both to the mass of the object m and to the square of its velocity v, related by the following equation:

$$E_k = \frac{1}{2}mv^2$$

Here, m represents the mass of the object, and v its velocity. We can see, then, that tripling the velocity would yield a nine-fold increase in the energy of the object, whereas tripling the mass would only yield a tripling of the energy. In addition to the energy of motion, it is also important to understand the energy of motion that has not yet happened, otherwise known as potential energy (e.g., the energy of a ball held above the ground but not dropped). For the purposes of this chapter, we are most concerned with understanding gravitational potential energy, or the potential energy contained in a mass held a certain height above the ground. This concept is crucial to understanding hydropower, a form of electricity production entirely dependent on the potential energy of water falling over a distance. The gravitational potential energy U of a given mass m suspended at height h above the ground is given simply as the product of m, h, and g, the gravitational constant[4] as follows:

$$U_g = mgh$$

---

3   Combustion indicates burning of a fuel in the presence of oxygen.
4   The gravitational constant represents the acceleration due to gravity. In metric units, $g = 9.81\ m/s^2$.

As noted above, understanding how to use energy in a more sustainable fashion requires an understanding of efficiency. At its simplest, efficiency is a measure of how the outputs of a process compare to the inputs. When using this term in an energy context, it is usually understood as the ratio of energy (or work) output to energy (or work) input, as follows:

$$E = \frac{energy\ out}{energy\ in} \times 100$$

ENERGY UNITS

Energy can be measured in a variety of units, all of which are related via conversion factors. Joules are most common in scientific uses, but others include watt-hours, British Thermal Units, and calories. And while temperature is certainly related to energy, the two concepts are not equivalent. The latter is simply a measure of the average kinetic energy of a substance.

Since the units in the numerator and denominator are the same, the ratio is expressed as a percentage (hence multiplication by 100). Thus a simple machine that takes in 100 units of energy and does 50 units of work would be 50% efficient. We can assume in such a case that the remaining 50 units of energy that did not do useful work were "wasted," that is, converted to low-energy heat through friction and similar processes. Later in this chapter, we will learn just how vital a role efficiency plays in contemporary discussions of where we get our energy.

One concept related to, and often confused with energy, is power. In everyday conversation the terms are often used interchangeably, but there is an important distinction between the two. Understanding that distinction enables us to participate in a fuller and more informed fashion in educated discussions about different future energy (and climate) scenarios. Ignoring it makes us more likely to be dismissed by those who insist on keeping our energy production standards exactly as they are.

We learned above that energy represents the capacity to do work. Power, on the other hand, may be thought of as energy at the ready, and represents the ability of a machine—as simple as a lever or as complex as a nuclear reactor—to deliver a certain output of useful energy over a certain time period. In that regard, power is a *rate* of energy (or work), expressed in units of energy over time. The standard unit for power is the Watt (W), defined as one Joule per second. Multiples of Watt based on thousands are commonly used: a kilowatt (kW) equals 1,000 W; a megawatt (MW) equals 1,000 kW; a gigawatt (GW) equals 1,000 MW;

and so forth. A second common but less standardized and widely used unit is horsepower (hp).[5]

The distinction between energy and power is confusing for many, but consider the following clarifying examples. A gasoline-powered lawn-mower might have a 2hp engine, but when that engine is not running, it is doing no work. Thus the 2hp rating is a measure of power only, and we only obtain an energy (work) output when the engine runs for a certain time. Similarly, Brazil's 14-GW Itaipu hydroelectric dam, one of the largest hydroelectric facilities in the world, would produce no energy at all if the Paraná River ran dry or no water were allowed through the turbines. We will see below how and why not all power is equal, a vital concept for understanding future energy options, especially electricity.

As you have no doubt gathered by now, energy is a complex, multi-faceted topic impossible to cover comprehensively in one chapter. As we strive for a more sustainable existence on Earth, humans face complex challenges but also exciting opportunities about how we harvest, convert, and use energy. This chapter is designed to provide the reader with basic energy literacy with an eye to understanding some of those challenges and opportunities. We begin with an examination of electricity, then we move to briefer discussions of transportation, buildings, and industry.[6]

ELECTRICITY: TIME TO BREAK WITH CONVENTION

Electricity is best understood as an energy carrier. In its final form—that is, excited electrons itching to flow along a conductor and do work on the way—electricity is clean, flexible, storable,[7] and convenient. It is no surprise, then, that one of the highest-value uses of the stored thermal energy in fossil fuels and radioactive material comes when that thermal energy is transformed into electricity.

---

5   As the unit's name suggests, horsepower was originally a unit designed to express the work an average horse could do over a certain time period. Estimates of that figure, not surprisingly, varied widely.

6   The decision to cut the energy "pie" into the four slices of electricity, transportation, buildings, and industry was inspired by Rocky Mountain Institute's Reinventing Fire project. For a more technically detailed examination of these sectors, see Lovins, A. B., and Rocky Mountain Institute, *Reinventing Fire: Bold Business Solutions for the New Energy Era*, White River Junction, VT: Chelsea Green Pub (2011).

7   Electricity is storable in its direct current (DC) form only.

FIGURE 2.1: A tree fern, a plant little changed since the time of the dinosaurs.

Conventional energy systems powered by fossil fuels have been responsible for the release of millions of years of stored carbon into the atmosphere in a matter of decades. Put simply, energy from our sun was stored, through photosynthesis, by prehistoric plants like tree ferns (see Figure 2.1) millions of years ago. When those plants died, fell to the forest floor, and decomposed, the long hydrocarbon chains resulting from their youthful photosynthesis were compacted and stored in swamp muck. Over the millennia, that muck was compressed and transformed into the liquids (petroleum), solids (coal), and gas (methane) we have now come to know as fossil fuels. Burning those fuels releases the ancient solar energy stored in the hydrocarbons' bonds, simultaneously transforming the stored carbon into gaseous carbon dioxide, which contributes to the earth's greenhouse effect. The human ingenuity that engendered the Industrial Revolution, then, also engineered the release of several million years of solar energy over a short century-and-a-half.

Rather than begin this section with a detailed explanation of coal-fired power plants and petroleum refineries—those dinosaurs of our modern world's energy system—it is perhaps more fitting in a textbook on sustainability to begin instead with the good news about renewable, non-carbon energy sources that are rapidly overturning conventional energy sources—and conventional wisdom. In fact, after new generating capacity additions in renewable energy surpassed those of thermal energy for the second year in a row, Bloomberg New Energy Finance proclaimed that the "race for renewable energy has passed a turning point . . . and there's no going back."[8] These resources include headliners such as solar

---

8 See Tom Randall, "Fossil Fuels Just Lost the Race Against Renewables," http://www.bloomberg.com/news/articles/2015-04-14/fossil-fuels-just-lost-the-race-against-renewables.

photovoltaics and wind turbines, but also their lesser-known cousins such as tidal energy, geothermal energy, and biomass.

One energy source that is frequently overlooked, even seen more as an inconvenience than as an important resource in its own right, is the one we reviewed above as an equation: efficiency. As we shall see, the biggest energy payoffs from increasing efficiency come at the end of the line, where electricity arrives to do its final work (such as providing light, turning a motor, or heating a building), rather than at the power plant or the solar panel.

In the paragraphs that follow, we learn about currently affordable and available advances in efficiency, solar energy, wind energy, and hydropower. Then we step back from the promise of a future powered by renewable and low-carbon energy to consider the fossil-based energy that has revolutionized the world's economy in the past century-and-a-half, but which has also radically altered the chemistry of our atmosphere, the contours of our landscapes, and the integrity of our bodies and our planet.

Efficiency

Recall that efficiency measures how the outputs of a process compare to the inputs. We learned in the Energy Basics section above that the relationship can be expressed as the following ratio:

$$E = \frac{energy\ out}{energy\ in} \times 100$$

Calculating the actual efficiency of complex processes can be quite difficult. For instance, the overall efficiency of a waste-to-energy facility that uses municipal solid waste (MSW)[9] as a fuel source to produce electricity can be difficult to calculate due to the challenge of first obtaining an accurate estimation of the energy contained in the garbage. While the energy content of fuels like bituminous coal, natural gas, and crude oil can vary based on purity, that of garbage can vary much more widely based on the relative concentrations of items as diverse as plastics, food waste, scrap metal, old paint, and any of the myriad items that end up in our waste stream. If we do not have an accurate understanding of the energy content of the waste used as fuel, then we cannot know with any certainty how much of that energy escaped through the flue or the cooling water.

---

9   For more on waste-to-energy (WTE), see the chapter on garbage, "Waste Management: Rethinking Garbage in a Throwaway World."

With new problems come new solutions. The efficiency of a thermal power plant increases greatly if the "waste" heat (from cooling and exhaust) is used for such purposes as district heating[10] or industrial processes like cleaning. This fact is a key tenet of the field of industrial ecology, and well understood in some places. Sweden, for example, where winters can be quite chilly, gained international attention in recent years as it practically begged for garbage from neighboring countries in order to power its waste-to-energy incinerators. These were designed from the beginning as combined heat and power plants (CHP) and reached enviable efficiencies of 70% and higher.

The emphasis in this section is on electricity production, yet great inefficiencies exist in many of the other ways we use energy today. Two examples are illustrative: single-passenger automobiles, where the vast majority of fuel consumed goes to moving the vehicle rather than its passenger and contents; and single-family homes, where the heating and cooling efficiencies gained from shared walls in multiunit dwellings such as apartments or row houses are not available.

For much of the world, producing and delivering electricity to end users, whether to homes, hotels, cities, or factories, is a complicated endeavor in which a web of transmission and distribution lines (collectively called a grid) connects centralized power plants to end users. Power plants use the energy in sunlight, wind, or water, or that which is released when fuels such as coal or natural gas are combusted, to excite electrons to higher energy levels, producing a charge and forcing those electrons to move across the wires that make up the connective tissue of the grid. Yet at each step, from the initial conversion of the chemical energy in fuels or the potential energy in falling water, to the final delivery of electricity to a light bulb, motor, or other device, some energy is "lost", or, more accurately, transformed to less useful forms, principally heat. Recall that this process is known as degradation; every time we touch a laptop computer that is warm, or hear the hum of high-voltage power lines overhead, we are witnessing energy being degraded to a less useful form.

---

10 District heating refers to a system where steam or hot water from a central heat source (furnace or power plant) is used to heat surrounding buildings, eliminating the need for those buildings to have their own heat sources except perhaps as backups. Overall efficiency increases greatly if the heating energy is a by-product from a thermal power plant or waste-to-energy incinerator that would otherwise have been vented to the atmosphere or a water body.

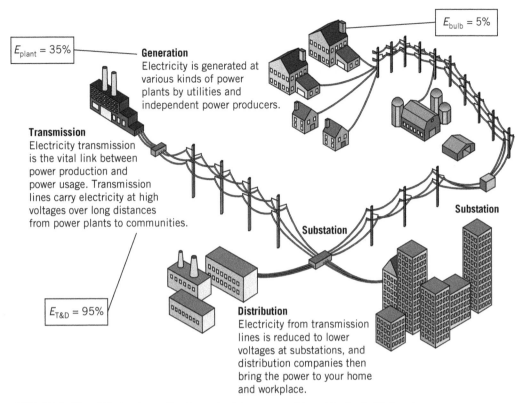

FIGURE 2.2: Simplified schematic of an electric power grid and typical efficiencies.
Adapted from U.S. Department of Energy.

From a sustainability perspective, the most important lesson in efficiency is that improving end-use efficiency has significant multiplier effects "up the line," all the way back to the point where the energy source was initially procured and through its various transformation and distribution steps. Figure 2.2 illustrates this concept with a simplified schematic of coal-fired electricity being delivered to a highly inefficient incandescent light bulb, which surprisingly has evolved relatively little (and certainly has not gained much in efficiency!) since its invention by Thomas Edison in the late 1800s. In the figure, the combined efficiency of the entire process from converting coal to electricity all the way to providing light (the end use) would be calculated by multiplying the efficiencies in their decimal forms:

$$E_{total} = E_{plant} * E_{T\&D} * E_{bulb} = 0.35 * 0.95 * 0.05 = 0.016$$

We see, then, that the total efficiency of converting the chemical energy embodied in coal to useful light can be dismally low, less than 2% in this case! Two equally important but more subtle lessons arise from this exercise. First, the combined efficiency of a multi-step process can be *no greater than the least efficient step*. Second, reducing energy demanded at the final step means that less energy is wasted *getting to that final step*. Thus when seeking to increase the efficiency of a process, it is vital to first reduce the energy demand at the end of the line (e.g., for powering a light bulb, turning a wheel, or pressurizing a liquid). The second priority, then, is to tackle the least efficient step, what energy experts often call the "low-hanging fruit." In this example, even if a revolutionary thermal power plant with efficiency of 95% (physically impossible[11]) were paired with the 95%-efficient transmission and distribution infrastructure, a 5%-efficient light at the end of the line would drag the efficiency of the entire process down to a shameful 4.5%. The same holds for automobiles, buildings, cities, factories, trains, and any other complex system.

The good news is that by doubling the efficiency of the light bulb in the above example to 10%, we not only double the efficiency of the entire process, but also cut the initial fuel input in half. Indeed, saving a single unit of energy at the end-use by making light bulbs, pumps, air conditioners, or any number of other devices more efficient, can translate into energy savings 10 to 100 times greater at the power plant.

Solar Energy

While solar energy seems in some ways to be a twenty-first-century story, humans have been harnessing the energy of our fusion-powered sun for centuries for things such as cooking or drying food, making bricks, and warming homes. Photosynthesizing plants beat humans to the solar energy prize eons before that, using light from the sun to rearrange simple atoms and molecules into much more complex structures—sugars and starches—that served as building blocks for the plants themselves, and energy-rich food sources for anything that consumed them. In fact, fossil fuels—our dirtiest energy resource—are simply the rotten,

---

11 The most common way of calculating the theoretical efficiency of a thermal power plant (or, in physics, any heat engine) is by calculating its Carnot efficiency, which is given as the difference of the hottest steam temperature in the plant minus the coldest cooling water, divided by the hottest temperature, then converted to a percentage. Thus a plant's efficiency is directly dependent on how hot the steam can get (a reflection of how much energy it stores) before it spins the turbine. That maximum temperature, in turn, is constrained by the simple physical realities of the materials used to construct the plant: when pressures and temperatures get too high, steam pipes made with currently available materials and technologies simply explode, rendering the plant useless.

compressed, and thermochemically altered residues of solar energy stored millions of years ago by prehistoric plants like the tree ferns discussed above.

This section briefly explains three technologies currently used to capture energy directly from the sun: solar thermal heating, solar thermal electricity, and solar photovoltaics. Solar thermal systems use the sun's energy to heat a medium such as water or salt, which is then used to do other work. Solar photovoltaic systems, on the other hand, use photons from the sun's light to kick-start

FIGURE 2.3 A rooftop-mounted solar hot water heater in China. The name roughly translates to "Beijing Sun Spring."

Copyright © 2010 by Popolon / Wikimedia Commons, (CC BY-SA 3.0) at https://commons.wikimedia.org/wiki/File:Taiyangneng_Beijing.jpg.

the flow of electrons through a semiconductor, creating a current that can be stored or used directly. All three technologies hold great potential for meeting humanity's energy needs in the future, while allowing us to keep all those millions of years of stored sunshine (and associated climate impacts) in the ground.

The most common use of solar thermal technology is simply to heat water, the simplest form of which is a black plastic bag warmed by the sun and used as a camping shower. The rooftop solar hot water heaters across much of China are a slightly more complex version of the same principle: the sun's warmth is absorbed by water passing through dark pipes, which then flows to showers or other facilities in the building below (see Figure 2.3).

In recent years, scientists and engineers have made significant advances in concentrated solar power (CSP) systems, where mirrors direct and concentrate the sun's rays on one place. The mirrors are usually controllable so they can track the sun and optimize collection of its energy. That focused energy superheats a working fluid such as water or salt, which is then used to produce electricity through a steam turbine in the same way that steam produced from coal combustion or nuclear reactions turns turbines. In some designs and locations, the energy stored in the superheated (salt) is enough to continue to generate electricity or provide warmth well after the sun has set. Spain moved early to implement large utility-scale CSP, and currently boasts 50 installations around the country.[12] In 2014,

12 See Concentrating Solar Power Projects" *US National Renewable Energy Laboratory,* http://www.nrel.gov/csp/solarpaces/by_country_detail.cfm/country=ES.

a public–private partnership in the United States completed the 392-MW Ivanpah CSP in the Mojave Desert of southern California, the largest CSP facility in the world.[13] By contrast, some of the largest hydropower stations in the world have 10 or more times that capacity.

Uzbekistan recently committed to develop homegrown solar energy expertise and add more renewable energies to its electricity mix, including the largest solar power plant in Central Asia at 100 MW of installed capacity.[14] The country boasts 320 days of sunshine per year, making it a prime location for large-scale solar power installations. A massive solar furnace, a futuristic leftover from the Soviet Era, uses mirrors to concentrate the sun's rays to temperatures hot enough to melt metal, and is a testament to the industrial potential some have seen in Uzbekistan's rich solar resources.

For many people, the term "solar energy" is more likely to conjure images of solar photovoltaic (PV) panels, which convert the sun's light directly into electricity. The sun's light is comprised of photons of different energy levels, which is reflected in their wavelength, ranging from the lower-energy infrared colors, through the visible spectrum, and to the higher-energy ultraviolet. Solar PV panels intercept a fraction of those photons, which then excite electrons contained in the crystalline silica of the panel, creating an electric current. Far more complex than solar thermal systems, solar PV panels demand innovations in materials chemistry, engineering, and power electronics in order to convert sunlight to electricity, and do so with efficiencies only in the 15–20% range.

Solar energy may also be categorized as passive solar or active solar. A greenhouse or sunroom is a perfect example of

FIGURE 2.4 Ivanpah CSP in southern California.
Source: National Renewable Energy Laboratories, available at http://energy.gov/articles/celebrating-completion-worlds-largest-concentrating-solar-power-plant.

---

13 See "Celebrating the Completion of the World's Largest Concentrating Solar Power Plant," *U.S. Department of Energy*, http://energy.gov/articles/celebrating-completion-worlds-largest-concentrating-solar-power-plant.

14 See "ADB to Help Uzbekistan Build Central Asia's First Solar Power Plant," *Asian Development Bank,* http://www.adb.org/news/adb-help-uzbekistan-build-central-asias-first-solar-power-plant.

a passive solar energy system, where the sun's light enters transparent or translucent walls or windows and warms the inside of the structure. Including a thermal mass, such a stone floor, masonry wall, or even a pond that can absorb and retain heat for a long time, can allow storage of the sun's energy even after sunset, as the mass slowly returns its stored warmth to the surrounding area. Active solar systems, on the other hand, are those that use the sun's energy to create electricity.

FIGURE 2.5 Parkent solar furnace.

Scientists working in the exciting field of artificial photosynthesis have sought for decades to better understand the solar energy-powered chemical processes that happen inside the leaves of green plants.[15] While we are not yet to the point of feeding ourselves via chlorophyll-coated crania, scientists and engineers have made huge steps in harnessing the free energy provided by the sun. Given the abundance of free solar energy that strikes the earth's surface every day, in every location, it makes sense to imagine solar energy playing a much greater role in the sustainable energy systems of the future. Despite the expense of solar PV at present, there are no fuel costs once the panels are in place, and when coupled with reasonable electricity storage mechanisms such as batteries or pumped hydropower, solar energy can continue to provide power after the sun has set. Equally important, the price per kilowatt of solar photovoltaics has dropped sharply in recent years, and is expected to continue to do so as the technology matures and the market expands.[16]

Wind Energy

Imagine a lightweight but strong cube-shaped box, one meter on a side, filled with air. Lifting that box would be no problem for most people;

---

15   Professor Devens Gust at Arizona State University is one of the pioneers of artificial photosynthesis work. See http://photoscience.la.asu.edu/photosyn/faculty/gust/index.htm. He is also a contributor to the broader field of biomimicry, popularized by Janine Benyus's book by the same title (Benyus, 1997). For more details, see the Biomimicry Institute's website at http://biomimicry.org.
16   See, for instance, the US Department of Energy's 2012 Report on solar photovoltaic pricing (Feldman et al., 2012).

GENERATORS AND MOTORS

Did you know that a generator is simply an electric motor running in reverse? When electricity is supplied to an electric motor, the electricity energizes electromagnets in the motor to push against other magnets, in the same way that two magnets of the same polarity will repel rather than attract each other. That repelling force makes the spindle of the motor spin. If we reverse that process and use steam, wind, or water to spin the spindle, we create a flow of electrons out of the motor, making it operate as a generator. As we discuss below, pumped-storage hydropower systems utilize reversible pump-turbines in precisely this way, at times to generate electricity via the push of water, at times to push water via the flow of electricity.

air at sea level has a mass of less than one gram per cubic meter. Now imagine that same box, this time filled with water. Lifting it in this case would be next to impossible without machinery, as water's mass is 1000 *kilograms* per cubic meter, or roughly a million times that of air. Recall that density refers to the measure of mass per volume, and the enormous difference in density between air and water explains the similarly large differences in the energy density of the two substances. That density difference also explains why it is more difficult to extract large amounts of energy from wind through wind turbines than it is to do so from water through hydropower, discussed below.

The wind energy sector has seen stunning growth worldwide in recent years. After an early heyday of experimentation in places like California, the industry slowed somewhat until advances in new materials in the 1990s, such as powerful but lightweight magnets made from rare earth minerals, led to a second boom. Countries with strong engineering sectors and rich wind resources such as Germany, Denmark, and the United States led the way, but soon ceded their first leading positions to China, which experienced a nearly 300-fold growth in wind turbine capacity from 1990 to 2010. Clearly, something was in the air.

The technology of wind power is relatively simple compared to the complex chemical processes needed to make solar photovoltaic panels or nuclear fuel rods. Long before the advent of modern wind turbines, of course, humans used wind power to turn grinding stones in grist mills and to pump water. Modern turbines, like their analogs operating in water, create electricity simply by using the kinetic energy of the fluid (air or water) to turn a turbine. The turbine, in turn, is connected to a generator, which creates electricity. Mass-produced wind turbines with power ratings

from 1 MW to 2.5 MW are fairly common today. Prototypes up to 7 MW and even higher are being tested for both land-based and offshore use.

In many parts of the world—Spain, Denmark, the Midwest United States, and China—one can find wind farms consisting of tens and even hundreds of wind turbines spread across large swaths of land (or ocean). Perhaps most famous is Denmark's Hornsrev facility, consisting of 80 turbines each rated at 2 MW, which set Denmark in a class by itself in terms of offshore wind capacity. As wind speeds near the ground are often lower and frequently deflected by objects such as trees and buildings, the largest wind turbines are built on masts that tower up to 100 meters or more above the ground.

In addition to variations in size, wind turbines can also vary in their axis of rotation (see Figure 2.6). Most common are horizontal-axis wind turbines (HAWTs), inspired by the slowly spinning windmills that have powered grain mills around the world for centuries. Less common, though perhaps more artistic in design, are vertical-axis wind turbines (VAWTs). Each design has its strengths and weaknesses.

The key advantage of HAWTs is their size or power rating: MW-scale turbines are already commonplace around the world. With that size, however, comes both a need for speed and space. Large horizontal-axis turbines usually only function in winds greater than a certain velocity (called "cut-in speed"), making them unsuitable for many locations where breezes prevail but strong winds are rare. They also need space, as one turbine can be negatively affected by turbulence in the wake of nearby turbines. In order to avoid such turbulence effects, turbine spacing is usually based on a multiple of individual rotor diameter. With rotor diameters in the 100-meter range for the largest turbines, it is easy to imagine how the footprint of a large windfarm can cover tens or even hundreds of square kilometers.

Unlike their horizontal-axis cousins, VAWTs can operate in much lower wind speeds. Since the power in a unit of blowing air, however, increases with the cube of the air's velocity, lower cut-in speeds do not necessarily translate into higher energy outputs from HAWTs. Moreover, VAWTs tend to be smaller (kW scale as opposed to MW scale). Their smaller footprint and lower cut-in speeds combine to make them more suitable for installation in urban areas, including on top of buildings.

Wind turbines are contemporary refinements of centuries-old technology that is relatively simple and robust. The chief challenge to wind power, as noted above, is the low energy density of air. Yet as with solar energy, there are no fuel costs for wind energy, and in some parts of the world with consistent strong winds, large-scale wind farms may play an important role, especially where space constraints are not a concern.

Hydropower

As with wind power, humans have long used falling water to turn wheels to do our work, most commonly in the form of grist mills for grinding grains into flour. Using water to spin turbines and generators is a much newer phenomenon, but hydropower is at the same time the most mature of all renewable, non-carbon energy sources. Experts estimate more than 40,000 large dams exist around the world, many of which have hydropower capabilities. Yet as anyone familiar with the story of Egypt's Aswan High Dam, China's Three Gorges Dam, or any number of other large dams knows, the social and ecological impacts of dams can be great, with as many as 1.3 million people displaced as a result of the Three Gorges Dam's 600-km-long reservoir.

Conventional hydropower systems convert the potential energy of water at higher elevation into electrical energy by capturing the energy

FIGURE 2.7 Hoover Dam in the western US (left) and a run-of-river hydropower station in Japan (right). Dams create hydraulic head (the difference in vertical elevation that translates into electrical energy) by separating a river into an upper portion (the reservoir) and a lower portion. Run-of-river facilities divert a portion of the river's flow far upstream via pipes, then send it down penstocks (shown in the image) to the turbines below.

of the falling water and using it to spin turbines connected to generators. Such systems can take one of two forms: run-of-river or impoundments. Run-of-river systems are generally smaller in terms of their power capacity. They involve taking a portion of a river's flow at a certain point, diverting it downstream via pipes or channels, and then dropping it back down to the river via pipes (called penstocks) and turbines. As the water flows down the penstocks and over the blades of the turbines, it imparts its kinetic energy to the blades, which then turn the generator to produce electricity. Impoundment-type hydropower systems involve dams that create artificial lakes, called reservoirs. These are more common, have larger power capacity, and tend to be more visually striking (as shown in Figure 2.7).

Pumped-storage hydropower systems function in essentially the same fashion as conventional systems, except that the turbine mechanism can be reversed and used to pump water from a lower reservoir to an upper reservoir. Thus at a time when electricity demands are high on the grid, a PSH operator can decide to release water from the upper reservoir almost instantaneously, providing power in time to avoid or at least minimize costly blackouts and brownouts (voltage dips) on the grid. Electricity pricing provides a major incentive to PSH operators, as power grid operators are usually willing to pay a premium for electricity supplies that help meet unexpected peaks in demand. Later, when electricity supply exceeds demand (such as during the night in most areas) and prices are cheaper, the pump-turbines are reversed and the upper reservoir (i.e., the water "battery") is recharged.

Hydroelectric dams provide carbon-free electricity[17] that is easy to dispatch and control, with many facilities able to go from zero output to full output in a matter of seconds or minutes to respond to grid needs, compared to much slower ramp rates for thermal power stations. Yet hydropower has its share of problems. Large dams and their reservoirs can displace thousands or even hundreds of thousands of people, forcing their resettlement into areas that might not always be welcoming to newcomers. In many rural communities, resettlement means disrupting social networks that are vital to community life and well-being. On transboundary rivers such as the Mekong, Nile, Danube, or Colorado (to name just a few), upstream dam projects can cause geopolitical tensions with downstream neighbors. Perhaps most important is that the geographies of benefits and costs are not equivalent: those living nearest the dam and reservoir suffer the bulk of the negative impacts, while those living farther away benefit from more stable and reliable electricity.

The non-human impacts of hydropower are also significant, as dams and reservoirs alter and fragment riparian and aquatic habitats. For instance, the salmon populations on the Columbia River, and its tributaries in the northwestern United States and southwestern Canada, have in all likelihood been irreparably harmed by the system of 29 large dams and dozens of smaller projects on the main river and its tributaries.[18] Dams not only present a tremendous obstacle for a fish swimming upstream to spawn or downstream to reach the sea; they also turn free-flowing rivers into lakes, which can confuse fish needing current to navigate. Even in places where migratory fish such as salmon are not part of the equation, dams decrease water quality, change water chemistry and temperature, and alter siltation patterns, thereby affecting habitat. Run-of-river dams, despite their lack of reservoirs, have their own set of environmental impacts, including diverting the entire flow of a river and leaving sections completely dry, or "de-watered." Obviously, such conditions are not ideal for aquatic life.

Some studies have demonstrated that reservoirs in warm areas that submerge large tracts of vegetated land are actually significant producers

---

17 Electrical output from hydroelectric dams is carbon-free as long as the emissions involved in constructing the dam are ignored.

18 For more on the Columbia River hydropower system, see the 2001 report, "The Columbia River System: The Inside Story," *Bonneville Power Administration,* http://www.bpa.gov/power/pg/columbia_river_inside_story.pdf.

of methane, a potent greenhouse gas some 20 times more effective at trapping heat near the earth's surface than carbon dioxide. The methane production occurs as a result of biomass (plant matter) trapped underwater and decomposing in anaerobic or low-oxygen conditions. Capturing that methane is virtually impossible, and underscores the importance of careful scientific research to truly understand the scale of the problem and get a truer assessment of the risk in terms of climate change.

Challenges of Renewable Electricity

In this section we have learned about the promise of four renewable energy sources that can help meet society's electricity needs: end-use efficiency, solar energy, wind energy, and hydropower.[19] End-use efficiency stands in a class all its own because of the compounding energy savings that result from demanding *less* electricity at the end of the power line. That reduced end-use demand, then, means less energy is converted to electricity in the first place (a highly wasteful process in thermal power plants), and less is lost to heat through the transmission and distribution networks. Solar, wind, and hydro all benefit from zero fuel costs, and while solar photovoltaic technologies have not yet reached full maturity, wind and hydro are already quite mature.

One of the greatest challenges to wind and solar power is their intermittency. Simply put, the sun does not always shine, and the wind does not always blow. Intermittency impacts two key characteristics of a power source: its capacity factor and its dispatchability. Since these terms are critical to understanding the power sector, including the conventional power sources discussed below, both bear explaining here.

Capacity factor is the ratio of the actual output of a generator compared to its maximum possible output. If a 1-MW wind turbine ran at 100% of its power rating for 100% of the time, its capacity factor would be 100%. Likewise, if the 18,200-MW Three Gorges Dam ran at 100% power for 100% of the time, it, too, would have a perfect capacity factor. Yet such conditions do not exist. Periods of slack wind, downtime due to service or repair, and even grid conditions all contribute to keeping wind turbine capacity factors in the 20% to 30% range worldwide, just as cloudy days (and nighttime!) lower the capacity factors of solar photovoltaic panels. In the case of hydropower, competing demands or alternative priorities

---

19   There are others, of course, such as tidal, geothermal, and hydrogen, but they play a very limited role at present and are omitted here due to space constraints.

for the river, such as irrigation, navigation, fisheries, or flood control, limit hydro's capacity factors to the 40% to 50% range worldwide.

Dispatchability is a second key characteristic of power sources for which there is high demand, and on which intermittency has a profound impact. Recall that one of hydropower's principal assets is the ease and speed with which a hydroelectric station can go from standstill to full power in a matter of minutes or even seconds. As you can imagine, owing to the unpredictability of the sunshine and wind, solar photovoltaics and wind turbines are simply not dispatchable—at least, not without batteries or other storage. That lack of dispatchability makes them ill-suited for meeting temporary spikes in demand on the power grid due to a power station that unexpectedly failed or an overuse of air conditioners on a particularly hot afternoon.

Conventional Electricity Production through Thermal Power Plants

Whereas capacity factors are often seen as a shortcoming of intermittent renewables and even hydropower, they tend to be much higher in thermal power plants, the more conventional means of producing electricity. Proponents of thermal power plants cite high capacity factors (often in the 80% to 90% range or higher) as a key indicator of thermal power's reliability and ability to produce base-load electricity on a 24/7 basis. As long as fuel is available, thermal power plants can theoretically run continually at full power. Not surprisingly, factors such as repair downtime, reduced grid demand, and simple mechanical and material stress mean that most are not operated full-throttle around the clock.

The concept behind thermal power plants is relatively simple, even though the engineering is complex. Coal, natural gas, petroleum, and even trash can all be used as fuels for thermal power plants. These fuels, when combusted in the presence of oxygen, release thermal energy, which produces superheated, energy-dense steam by heating water to very high temperatures and pressures. That superheated steam then spins a turbine connected to a generator, which produces electricity. As discussed in the "Energy Basics" section above, the efficiency of that process of converting thermal energy to electricity is constrained by the difference in maximum and minimum temperatures of the steam and cooling water, respectively. Even though efficiencies could theoretically reach 60% or higher, the realities of materials, metallurgy, engineering, and applied physics mean practical yield limits closer to 45%, with the vast majority of thermal plants falling in the 30% to 40% range.

Think for a minute about the planetary implications of the previous sentence. If a power plant burning coal, natural gas, or petroleum is only 35% efficient, that means that 65% of the energy contained in the fuel—all that stored solar energy from eons ago—is being dumped into the air

HYDROFRACKING—TECHNOLOGY WITH A BIG IMPACT

Hydraulic fracturing, or "hydrofracking," is the process of using water to create microscopic fractures in underground layers of rock. It is primarily used to harvest oil and gas that are trapped in layers of rock, and it has a secondary use for increasing productivity of water wells. Since the early 2000s, hydraulic fracturing techniques have been developed in combination with directional drilling—the ability to turn a drill bit once it is underground to create a precise, non-linear path for a well. Combining the two technologies allowed for exploration and harvesting of oil, natural gas, and other hydrocarbons previously inaccessible via traditional drilling methods. The resultant boom in domestic oil and gas production has resulted in significant changes in US energy use patterns and energy infrastructure development. It has also had significant environmental, social, health, and legal impacts.

Hydrofracking of natural gas and oil resources, sometimes called "unconventional oil and gas development" or simply "fracking," is more accurately described as high-volume, long-lateral, slick water hydraulic fracturing. In this process, the well is drilled, first vertically into the target shale layer, which lies at a depth of 2,000 to 10,000 feet or more. Then the well path turns and runs horizontally along the shale layer to maximize access to the target formation (that is, the shale layer where the hydrocarbons are trapped). After the well bore is stabilized with cement and lined with stainless steel pipe, a perforation gun is sent down into the piping to create holes in the pipe through which the fracking fluid will be forced in order to fracture the surrounding rock.

Large volumes of water mixed with chemicals (friction reducers and biocides) and sand are then injected at high pressures ranging up to over 10,000 pounds per square inch (psi) into the surrounding rock layer to create microscopic fractures about 1/100th the width of a human hair. The fractures allow molecules of gas or oil to escape from the rock formation where they are held. Key ingredients in the fracking fluid include surfactants to reduce friction (thus the term "slick water"), biocides to prevent bacterial growth, and microscopic silica beads or sand, which move into the microscopic fissures in the rock and prevent them from closing up again when the pressure of the fluid is released. Once released from the rock substrate, the gas molecules move toward the area of lowest pressure—the well bore—and up out of the well.

At this point the product of the well contains a variety of things, including the target methane, some water, and usually some other hydrocarbons. These things are separated and the methane is pressurized before being transported away from the well via pipeline. Some fraction of the water and other fracking chemicals return from the well when the pressure is released, along with compounds from the substrate such as salts and naturally occurring radioactive materials (also referred to as NORMS). This mix is called "flowback" or "produced water" and is stored either in open, lined pits or in closed containers, depending on state regulations. Some flowback water may be diluted with fresh water and used for another fracturing job nearby, but eventually it is trucked to a disposal site. The most common disposal method for produced water is deep well injection, usually into older, depleted oil and gas wells. Safe deep well injection requires specific geological conditions not universally available, which means development of alternative methods of disposal is desirable.

HYDROFRACKING OR HYDROFRACKING?

One phenomenon to notice when reading about hydrofracking, is that the term "hydrofracking" is used in different ways by different writers. The divergent use of the term results in statements from industry and environmentalists that seem to be in direct opposition to one another, and many readers might conclude that there is genuine disagreement among scientists as to the impact of hydraulic fracturing on the environment. However, when you look at how different people define the actual term "hydrofracking," you see that the disagreement is more about what this term encompasses than it is about real environmental impacts. From a technical perspective, "hydrofracking" is the discrete process by which water and other chemicals are inserted into a well at high pressure to fracture the surrounding rock formation. When most industry spokespeople speak of hydrofracking, they are using this narrow definition.

However, in order to complete this stage of well development, many other things have to happen, including piping or trucking in millions of gallons of water; mixing large quantities of chemicals into that water; and collecting and treating or disposing of the flowback or produced water after fracturing is complete. When most environmentalists and municipal leaders speak of the impacts of "hydrofracking," they are referring to *all* the activities required to allow the more narrow activity of fracturing of the rock by liquid under pressure to take place. Therefore, when industry lawyers or spokespeople say, "No water pollution has ever been documented as a cause of hydrofracking" they are correct because they are using a very narrow definition of hydrofracking. When environmentalists say, "Hydrofracking has caused many cases of water contamination and negative environmental and health impacts" they too are correct, because they are including the impacts of all the activities required to facilitate the capturing of hydrocarbons using hydraulic fracturing. If one is analyzing impacts of hydrofracking, the broader definition is the more logical one to use, because the discrete act of hydraulically fracturing rock to obtain oil and gas cannot occur absent the larger ensemble of activities.

THE GREENHOUSE GAS REDUCTION DEBATE

The annual production of natural gas from US shale gas (hydrofracked) wells has gone from a little over 250 billion cubic feet (roughly 7 billion m³) per year in 2007 to over 1 trillion cubic feet (roughly 28 billion m³) per year in 2015.[1] This large increase in domestic gas production has caused some thermal electric power plant managers to switch from coal to gas. As older coal-fueled plants have been closed, they have been replaced with natural gas–fueled plants in response to abundant natural gas at low prices. This change has resulted in lower greenhouse gas (GHG) emissions at the smokestack, as combustion of gas emits less CO_2 than combustion of

[1]   See "Natural Gas Gross Withdrawals and Production" tables published by the US Energy Information Administration at http://www.eia.gov/dnav/ng/ng_prod_sum_dcu_NUS_m.htm.

coal. However, research on so-called fugitive emissions of methane (CH_4) during the drilling of wells and compression, transport, and distribution of natural gas suggests that the total GHG contribution of natural gas may be just as significant as that of coal (Shindell et al. 2009). Technologies and implementation of regulations that reduce fugitive emissions have the potential to reduce the climate impacts of the natural gas boom.

From a regulatory standpoint, state and federal laws passed since the advent of hydraulic fracturing encourage methane recapture. Some states, such as Colorado,[2] Texas, and Wyoming require companies to implement "green completions" also known as "reduced emissions completions" in all or certain shale drilling regions. Green completion technology allows capture of methane that would otherwise escape during the connection of the well to the pipeline system.[3] At a certain price point, industry has the incentive to recapture methane because it becomes a salable product, so reducing the cost of capture will increase industry efforts to prevent fugitive methane emissions. Federal Air Regulations for the Oil and Gas Industry passed in 2012 apply to production, processing, transmission, and storage of natural gas and require emission reductions. However, they do not apply to the gas distribution mains and smaller lines at the user interface. In many instances the small user distribution lines are many decades old and deteriorating, releasing methane into the air in urban environs. Detection and repairs to these systems is also needed to reduce the greenhouse gas impacts of natural gas.

OTHER ENVIRONMENTAL IMPACTS OF HYDROFRACKING

Environmental impacts of hydrofracking vary depending on the location of the well. For example, water withdrawals for use in fracturing wells can have significant negative impacts if taken from small headwaters of streams or stressed aquifers, but impacts could be negligible where water is taken from large rivers, lakes, or aquifers with rapid recharge rates.[4]

2 See Colorado Oil and Gas Conservation Commission Rules, Section 800-3, available at http://cogcc.state.co.us.
3 See US EPA, Reduced Emissions Completions for Hydraulically Fractured Wells, Lessons Learned from Natural Gas STAR Partners (2011), available at http://www.epa.gov/gasstar/documents/reduced_emissions_completions.pdf.
4 The recharge rate of an aquifer is the rate at which new groundwater flows into the aquifer. If the withdrawal rate exceeds the recharge rate, the aquifer will likely be depleted.

Air emissions could have local or far-reaching impacts, depending on the characteristics of regional airflow and proximity to populated areas. Development of pad sites, roads, and pipelines in forested areas results in fragmentation, which impacts migratory songbirds, amphibians, and larger fauna that require large contiguous tracts of woods to thrive. Gas development sites in already more developed areas might have fewer deleterious ecological impacts.

Wastewater is a consistently difficult problem for drilling companies in all locations. Produced water is highly saline. The salinity combined with the chemical content, and in some cases radioactivity, make it unsuitable for processing by typical municipal wastewater treatment plants and it cannot be discharged untreated. Some industrial wastewater treatment plants may be able to handle produced water, but most is trucked to where it can be disposed of in deep injection wells, many of which are depleted oil and gas wells. In some states, produced water can be held in large open pits until it is removed for disposal. Pit liners can fail, causing contamination of soil and groundwater, and volatile compounds easily escape into the air. Produced water can also escape into the environment when valves, pipes, or other containment vessels leak, or when operators simply make mistakes.

Air emissions can occur during the process of completing a well and connecting it to a pipeline system. Leaks or modifications of pipeline networks, leaks at compressor stations, and leaks in the consumer distribution pipelines all create releases of methane. Methane is a more powerful greenhouse gas than carbon dioxide over a 100-year time frame, and therefore curtailing fugitive emissions of methane should be a high priority. Air emissions at the well site can have significant health impacts on workers, particularly if exposure is prolonged or repeated over time.

Other potential worker hazards include exposure to dust particles, prolonged exposure to noise, and contact with harmful chemicals. The chemicals used in hydraulic fracturing are often listed under their trade names only, since the chemical content is the proprietary property of the chemical manufacturer, protected as a trade secret. This means that if workers are exposed and become ill, burned, or otherwise incapacitated, emergency responders often have a difficult time determining how to treat the worker because they cannot find out what the worker contacted. In addition, there are documented instances of groundwater contamination near well sites, although the proprietary protection of identities of chemicals used in most drilling processes makes it difficult to definitively determine whether contamination resulted from surface spills, failure of flowback pit liners, faulty well cementing, or movement from the well bore in the target geological layer to aquifers along natural vertical fractures in the rock.[5] These hazards are real and numerous and suggest that stringent regulation of the industry is overdue.

PROMISING BRIDGE FUEL, OR A BRIDGE TOO DANGEROUS TO CROSS?

The expansion of natural gas development using hydraulic fracturing is changing the energy picture in the United States and around the world, as many countries are tapping into underground hydrocarbon resources that were previously inaccessible. Some suggest that natural gas can be an important, even vital "bridge fuel" to get us from dirty fossil fuels to cleaner renewables. The economic impacts of the rapid increase in available natural gas are significant, and the environmental and health impacts of hydrofracking are potentially many and not well understood. While it is difficult to say with confidence that this method of drilling for hydrocarbons is better or worse than any other (coal and offshore oil drilling have their own enduring legacies of environmental pollution and cost to human lives and welfare), there is significant room for improvement in the technology, regulation, and enforcement of hydrofracking and associated activities to minimize the negative impacts to people and the environment.

---

5   For research attempting to understand contamination pathways, see (Llewellyn et al. 2015).

and water, right now. How, any reasonable person should ask, could the planet *not* be warming?

Proponents of nuclear energy see the resistance to burning fossil fuels and the concern about global warming as their opportunity. They emphasize that nuclear is a "clean" and "cheap" way to provide the heat source for thermal power plants. Instead of combustion, nuclear reactors rely on fission reactions that split the nucleus of certain very heavy elements (most commonly Uranium, or ^{235}U) into smaller atoms. In doing so, large amounts of thermal energy are released, along with free electrons that can then bombard other uranium atoms and split them, creating a chain reaction. Proponents of nuclear power boast that it is emissions-free, since no combustion occurs.

It is worth noting that a single kilogram of ^{235}U contains approximately the same amount of energy as a 100-car train full of coal. In addition, nuclear power plants do enjoy relatively high capacity factors, some even in the 90% range. Yet they are still thermal plants, dumping two-thirds of the heat energy to the environment. We are all well aware of the destruction that nuclear plant disasters can bring (as they have already occurred at Three Mile Island, Chernobyl, and Fukushima) and of the much down-played, but perpetual problem of storing waste. Notwithstanding the fact that the cumulative waste of all nuclear power plants in the United States would fit on a single football field in a block a few meters high, that block of waste remains toxic and radioactive for millennia.

OTHER SECTORS: BUILDINGS, INDUSTRY, AND TRANSPORTATION

In this chapter, our energy discussion has focused almost exclusively on the power sector. In some ways this makes sense, as the vast majority of the world's electricity comes from coal-fired power plants in a process that is dismally inefficient, and which can only expect marginal improvements even with breakthroughs in plant design or materials. We have neglected three other major energy-using sectors of our society, namely buildings, industry, and transportation, each of which could easily inform its own chapter on sustainability. Fortunately, many of the lessons from the power sector, or from general best practices in energy management, apply to the other three sectors, so we share a few examples.

Earlier, we showed how changing a light bulb to a more efficient model enables us to reap the compounding efficiencies and avoid energy losses all the way back "up the line" to the power plant. The same logic applies to passenger and freight vehicles: if we reduce the energy needed for traction where the tires meet the pavement or the wheels meet the track (the end use), then we can reap the compound rewards resulting from not losing energy between the engine and the tires. In an average single-passenger automobile, less than 1% of the energy in the gasoline actually reaches the tires and moves the passenger; the rest is degraded to heat through friction with the air (drag), friction in the engine, friction between the tires and the pavement, and onboard electrical loads, among others. The greatest tool for reducing those compounding losses is to change the way we manufacture vehicles and make them much lighter, so that less energy is used to move the excessively heavy vehicle itself.

Industrial energy use, especially in developing countries whose manufacturing sectors drive economic growth, can be a significant portion of a country's (or region's) energy demands. Yet as with vehicles and light bulbs, focusing first on the end use can yield some surprising results in terms of energy (and money) saved. Since a factory consumes far more energy than a household light bulb, the onus to reduce final energy use is, well, on us. Installing new pumps, blowers, motors, and other major energy-hogging equipment is an important step, as is changing the very architecture of our factories to take advantage of renewable sources such as natural light, waste heat from other nearby factories, or rooftop solar energy. The field of industrial ecology explicitly explores such opportunities and the design principles behind them.

Finally, let us not forget buildings. Think about the sheer number and diversity of buildings in the world: from one-room stick and thatch huts in rural areas of developing countries to 100-story steel and glass skyscrapers that punctuate the skylines of major cities around the world. All are energy users to some extent, whether through a single cooking fire whose fuel is yak dung or fallen branches dutifully collected by a peasant farmer, or through the grid-connected technologies in the headquarters of a contemporary multinational corporation. The US Energy Information Administration estimates that residential and commercial buildings account for nearly half of all energy use in the country. Rocky Mountain Institute goes further, estimating that US buildings alone use more energy than entire countries, including major energy consumers such as Russia, Japan, Germany, Canada, and France.[20] Many existing buildings are ripe for radical retrofits that increase their efficiency, and higher standards for new construction residential energy efficiency are long overdue. Hyper-efficient windows, for instance, might have a higher initial purchase price

---

20 See graph on "US Buildings' Energy Use Relative to Total Energy Use of Major Energy Consuming Nations," *Rocky Mountain Institute*, http://www.rmi.org/RFGraph-US_building_energy_use.

compared to regular windows, but if they insulate so well that they allow for smaller or even elimination of costly heating, ventilation, and air conditioning (HVAC) equipment, those windows might be worth their weight in gold.

Energizing our Vision for a More Sustainable Future

At this point, it is perfectly acceptable to ask yourself, "Why did I read this chapter? What should I take away from all this?" Let us step back and try to answer that question.

You have no doubt understood by now that energy is a an extremely complex topic from a pure physical and natural science perspective, and that it only gets more complicated when we consider the economic, political, ethical, and historical aspects of energy access, use, and conservation. This chapter has hopefully given you an idea of the magnitude and extent of the challenges human society faces if we are to truly clean up our energy act and achieve a more sustainable existence on Earth. Our day-to-day decisions matter! Over the past century-and-a-half, humans have opted to use ancient energy from deep within the ground—fossil fuels—to light, warm, and power our society. Yet if we hope for a future that is bright rather than gray, we must choose a different path forward.

This chapter has also empowered you to think creatively and boldly about the specifics of overcoming those challenges and about what a cleaner, kinder, more sustainable energy scenario for the future might involve. You do not have to have an advanced degree in energy physics or economics to do some basic drawings or calculations to identify where wasteful processes could be made more efficient, and how much we can do to change the big energy picture for the better. Prosperity, development, and happiness are not well measured by lopsided indicators such as kilowatt-hours of electricity or barrels of oil consumed per capita. Doing so is like trying to gauge the health of a society by the size of health care expenditures, rather than the actual outcomes those expenditures produce. For energy, this means measuring for services delivered more than for power produced.

We have—*right now*—the technology and scientific know-how to produce clean energy affordably, and to deliver many of the services we desire from energy much more efficiently. The primary obstacles are entrenched interests who stand to profit from prolonging the status quo, and political leaders more intent on staying in political power than on truly leading the way to a brighter future. Fortunately, their days, like those of fossil fuels, are numbered.

Capacity factor: The ratio of the actual output of a generator compared to its maximum possible output.

Dispatchability: The ease and speed with which an electricity generator (thermal power plant, photovoltaic plant, wind turbine, hydroelectric dam, etc.) can be put into service to meet grid demand for electricity.

Efficiency: The ratio of energy (or work) output compared to energy (or work) input. For a power plant, this measures how well a particular plant converts energy from its primary form to electricity. For a light bulb, this measures how well the bulb converts electricity to light (the bulb's intended purpose) as opposed to waste heat.

End-use efficiency: Efficiency in energy services at the point where energy is finally delivered to do the desired work. For electricity, this means focusing on reducing the electricity wasted at the light bulb, for instance, rather than on energy wasted at the power plant.

Energy: The capacity to do work, defined most commonly as kinetic energy (energy resulting from movement) and potential energy (energy resulting from position).

Energy content: The amount of energy (chemical or nuclear energy) contained in a certain mass of material, which could potentially be released to do work.

Flowback (aka **produced water**): Water and other materials that flow forth from a hydrofracked well once the pressure on that well is released. Produced water contains a fraction of the original fracking fluid, as well as compounds such as salts and radioactive materials that were naturally present in the rock.

Fuels: Liquid, solid, or gaseous substances containing chemical or nuclear energy.

Grid: The collection of hardware and software that enables the generation, transmission, and distribution of electricity throughout a society. This includes physical assets such as power plants, power lines, substations, transformers, and

Grid: The collection of "hardware" and "software" that enables the generation, transmission, and distribution of electricity throughout a society. The "hardware" includes physical assets such as power plants, power lines, substations, transformers, along with "software" such as Information and Communication Technologies (ICT) that enable electricity users and producers to improve system reliability and efficiency.

Hydrofracking: Short for hydraulic fracturing, a process of using pressurized water to create microscopic fractures in underground layers of rock. The process is used primarily to facilitate extraction of hydrocarbons such as oil and natural gas.

Power: An amount of energy delivered over a unit of time. Alternately, an amount of work done over a certain time period, as energy is generally considered equivalent to work in a physical science context. Power can also be understood as a rate of energy production or use.

Power plant: A facility that supplies electricity to the grid. While traditionally this has referred to large-scale, centralized thermal power plants fueled by fossil fuels, nuclear material, or water (in the case of hydroelectric dams), the term is increasingly used also to signify renewable electricity sources such as wind and solar farms.

Primary energy: Energy resources in their original form, such as crude oil, coal, natural gas, water, sunshine, and wind, before these resources have been transformed into refined products such as gasoline, diesel, or electricity.

Turbine: One or more rotating fans on a shaft, designed to capture energy from an energy-bearing medium such as wind, steam, or water as it passes by the turbine. In most cases, turbines are connected to a generator to produce electricity.

REFERENCES

Benyus, Janine M. 1997. *Biomimicry: Innovation Inspired by Nature.* New York: Morrow.

Feldman, David, Galen Barbose, Robert Margolis, Ryan Wiser, Naïm Darghouth, and Alan Goodrich. 2012. "Photovoltaic (PV) Pricing Trends: Historical, Recent, and Near-Term Projections." *National Renewable Energy Laboratory and Lawrence Berkeley National Laboratory.* http://www.nrel.gov/docs/fy13osti/56776.pdf.

Llewellyn, Garth T., Frank Dorman, J. L. Westland, D. Yoxtheimer, Paul Grieve, Todd Sowers, E. Humston-Fulmer, and Susan L. Brantley. 2015. "Evaluating a Groundwater Supply Contamination Incident Attributed to Marcellus Shale Gas Development." *Proceedings of the National Academy of Sciences* 112(20): 6325–6330. doi: 10.1073/pnas.1420279112.

Lovins, Amory B. and Rocky Mountain Institute. 2011. *Reinventing Fire: Bold Business Solutions for the New Energy Era.* White River Junction, VT: Chelsea Green Publising.

Shindell, Drew T., Greg Faluvegi, Dorothy M. Koch, Gavin A. Schmidt, Nadine Unger, and Susanne E. Bauer. 2009. "Improved Attribution of Climate Forcing to Emissions." *Science* 326 (5953): 716–718. doi: 10.1126/science.1174760.

US Department of Energy. "Benefits of Using Mobile Transformers and Mobile Substations for Rapidly Restoring Electric Service: A Report to the United States Congress Pursuant to Section 1816 of the Energy Policy Act of 2005." Accessed 5 May. Available at http://energy.gov/sites/prod/files/oeprod/DocumentsandMedia/MTS_Report_to_Congress_FINAL_73106.pdf.

Chapter 3

HUMAN POPULATION EXPLOSION

BY ELISE BOWDITCH

INTRODUCTION

Our individual lives seem long, but compared to the 25,000 years of modern human existence, each life is short. Sustainability is about ensuring that actions in the present do not wipe out the options for future people. For much of human history, populations expanded and changed their immediate environments in a perceptible but slow fashion. Actions with no large or immediate consequences appeared reasonable and normal, even as their cumulative effects grew. The "cradle of civilization" in the Middle East gave way to desert and abandoned empires. Europe's forests disappeared into boats, houses, fireplaces. Some cultures proved sustainable over a long time span—most have not. New Guinean societies persisted for millennia, as did the Tikopia and the Pueblo (Diamond 2005). But where are the Cucuteni-Trypillians, the Nazca, Great Zimbabwe, or the Aksumite Empire? These people were not able to maintain their cultures under multiple pressures of environmental change and conflict, and most of us today do not know about them.

Today, we live in an age where we have tapped fossil fuels for cheap power. The industrial age brought large, noticeable, and unprecedented alterations to the world. Improved water systems and health care lengthened survival, agricultural yields tripled, and global communications, transportation, and finance systems came into being. With improved health and increased wealth, population exploded. Now, the world faces population increases and environmental threats unimaginable to our ancient ancestors and inconceivable to our grandparents and great-grandparents. Within one lifetime, population growth and its effects on the environment threaten the prospects for future generations.

TERMS

What is population? We can talk about the population of Norway in 1975, the population of left-handed African American women in Chicago in 1983, or the population of yaks in Tibet last year. In all cases, we mean a group or collection of similar organisms at a particular time and place. When we talk about global population, usually we mean now, and we qualify references to historical populations by referring to their time frame.

What affects population size? At the core is the population growth rate. The growth rate is the percent change in a population (often measured by country) over a period of (usually) one year. It summarizes the increase due to births and in-migration and the decrease due to death and out-migration. This formula of births and deaths and in- and out-migration is the balancing equation of population change. When births and in-migration outnumber deaths and out-migration, population grows. When death and out-migration outnumber births and in-migration, population declines.

There are two ways to discuss births. The birth rate is the number of babies born per 1,000 people per year. In 2014, it ranged from 46.12 in Niger to 6.72 in Monaco. The total fertility rate (TFR) is a more common measure. It represents the average number of children a woman would give birth to if she lived through her childbearing years, given the fertility rates at each age (young women being more fertile than older ones). Since it measures the expected number of children per woman, it is easier to envision. TFR ranges from 6.89 in Niger to 0.80 in Singapore.

Fertility is a key component of population growth, but changes in the death rate (number of deaths per 1,000 people per year) affect population, too. On a global average, the death rate fell from an annual 20 per 1,000 people in the 1950s to about 8 per 1,000 now. Just as the birth rate must account for differences in age, a more precise measure of mortality is the age-specific mortality rate. This indicates the number of deaths per 1,000 people per year in a given age group. Life expectancy is another measure of population and usually means *from now forward*. This takes into account the high child and infant mortality rates in parts of the world today and in most of history. For instance, a medieval peasant who survived to age 15 could expect to live another 35 to 40 years, but for the population as a whole, average life expectancy at birth was around 35 due to the high death rates for infants and children.

Understanding population change requires studying changes in age groups. Children and the elderly do not reproduce and die more frequently than the rest of the population. Age groups, or cohorts, are a group of people united over time. For instance, all freshmen entering college in the fall are a cohort, as are American children born during the Great Depression of the 1930s.

Demographers use two kinds of calculations to figure out how many people will exist in the future knowing a population's age structure: forecasts and projections. Forecasts are short-term projections with assumptions close to reality. They use past data to predict a future population. For instance, a demographer might be asked to forecast the Hispanic population of Miami in the next five years using current immigration rates from Central and South America, Hispanic births and deaths, and the number of Hispanics leaving Miami in the last five years. Projections are more formal, mathematical models that can be calculated backward or forward in time. A projection question could be something like "What would the population of India have been in 1990 *if* its birth rate had dropped by 50% after 1945?" or "What will the population of Mexico be in 2150 *if* its birth rate doubles?"

When births and in-migration cancel deaths and out-migration, the population is stationary and the total number does not change. This is a special case of a stable population. Stable populations have constant, age-specific fertility and death rates, and age-specific migration rates net to zero. The growth rate and each age group's share of the population remain the same. The population total itself may grow or shrink, but changes affect all age cohorts equally. A stable population is desirable from a demographic standpoint because stability makes projections and forecasts much easier.

Demographers also consider migration when examining a particular geographic location's population. When large numbers of people move out of or into an area, such as a country or region, the population changes. The ratios of different age groups of the population may change. Some areas may find they have a disproportionate number of elderly, while others scramble to create housing or schooling for the new arrivals. Where immigrant and native populations are young, they determine the future direction of population growth through momentum. Momentum refers to the ongoing births that a large cohort of youth will have because those are the prime years for bearing children. Populations with high numbers of young people will continue to grow, even if couples have fewer children than their parents did.

To take variation in age groups and sex into account, populations are often represented graphically by population pyramids. If, for instance, there are years with many (or few) births, that group of children will grow up and their fertility will differ from other cohorts and affect the population for decades. In the Great Depression, as in economic downturns more recently, couples delayed or decided against having children. So those born in that era had fewer peers; less families formed and less children were born in total for the following years, showing up as shrinkage in the pyramid.

Traditional population pyramids reflect the experience of much of human history. A wide base (many children) and narrow top (few elders) shows high birth rates coupled with high death rates. Reaching old age is rare. As an example, if you look at Uganda's population pyramid on the website "Population Pyramids of the World from 1950 to 2100" from 1950 on forward, it is always a pyramid. Compare that to Japan's more uniform graph of today, in a society with fewer children and more elders. The shift from pyramid to pillar indicates a change from high birth and high death rates characteristic of pre-industrialization to lower rates for both births and death in a post-industrial society.

THE DEMOGRAPHIC TRANSITION

Traditional agricultural societies need children to help the family survive, with high birth rates an advantage to offset high death rates. In industrialized societies, children become an expense rather than a source of income for the family. Low death rates accompany low birth rates. The demographic transition is the name for this trend toward fewer children and longer lives in industrialized countries.

Demographers divide the transition into four stages (see Figures 3.1a-d). Pre-transition societies, such as Uganda, have high births and deaths and a slow population growth rate. In Early Transition, mortality decreases but birth rates remain high, causing population growth and large cohorts of youth, as in Yemen. As mortality rates stabilize and fertility declines, countries enter the Transitional phase, exhibiting population pyramids that resemble temple roofs, such as Botswana. Urbanization, the rising cost of children, contraception, and women's education and participation in the labor market contribute to lower fertility rates. Once the total

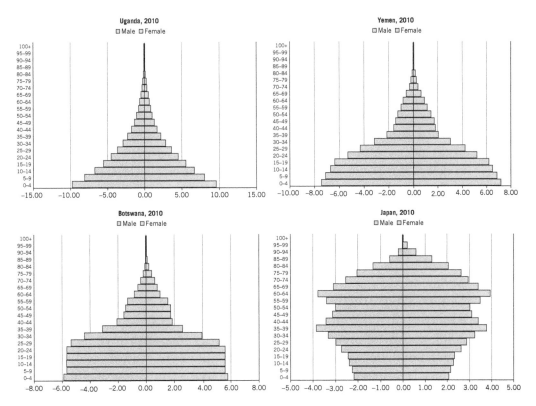

FIGURE 3.1A-D above. Population pyramids.
Source: United Nations.

fertility rate (TFR) falls below 70%, further decline occurs quickly. The last stage, post-Transition, exhibits low birth and death rates with a return to low growth rates, such as the United States, most European countries, and Japan. About half of all countries have a TFR below 2.1, which is the replacement level (the extra .1 allows for differences in the sex ratio at birth, infant death, and women's infertility). The shift in birth and survival rates caused the population pyramid to become a more uniform pillar.

CURRENT TRENDS

Predictions

The population growth rate rose from almost nothing in pre-industrial society to around 1.8% today. World population already passed the 7.2 billion mark in 2013. By 2100, UN and academic projections put population size at anywhere from 6.6–8.5 billion on the low end to

10.9–17 billion on the high end. Low estimates assume that Asia and Latin America drop below two births per woman and that the demographic shift begins in places like sub-Saharan Africa. The difference in high and low estimates is about half a child per woman. Of course, women do not have half-children, but a decision by two women to have one child more or less between them has profound effects for population growth in the next century. High estimates use current growth rates and factor in delayed or nonexistent demographic transitions in developing nations. High or low, these numbers represent an amount of people that dwarfs prior populations.

Megacities

Another trend is more people living in bigger cities. At the turn of the last century, about 10% of the world population lived in cities. Over the last hundred years, the number and size of urban areas expanded rapidly. In 2008, the world crossed the urban majority line, with over 50% of the population living in cities. That share continues to grow as smaller cities become larger and larger cities develop into megalopolises. In 1970, there were only two megacities, cities with 10 million or more people: New York and Tokyo. In 2011, about 61% of urbanites lived in cities of less than a million. By 2025, the urban population will shift to cities of more than one million, with increasing numbers of megacities (23 in 2011 to 37 by 2025) having 10 million residents or more. Most of these will be in Asia, with others in Latin America and Africa (World Urbanization Prospects 2012).

Variation

Countries have their own unique pyramids, and population growth shows variation on every continent. Many developed nations will have stable populations or see a decrease. Brazil's projection shows almost zero growth, and the Russian Federation is expected to decline by about 29% from 143.6 to 101.9 million. However, developing nations and the poorest areas will experience the most increase—69%—since they have the largest shares of young people, highest momentum, and least access to birth control. African projections estimate a 306% population increase over the next century (Andreev, Kantorová, and Bongaarts 2013). Nigeria's population, for example, is expected to rise almost six-fold, from 160 to 914 million. That figure should give pause to anyone who says population size does not matter. A graphic representation may say it best (see Figure 3.2).

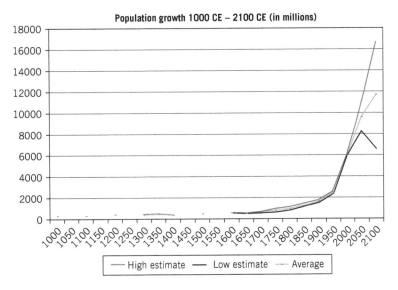

Population growth 1000 CE – 2100 CE (in millions)

FIGURE 3.2 Population growth from 1 CE to 2100 CE.
Source: United Nations.

Population Doubling Time

Even with declining birthrates in much of the world, population will continue to grow in the near and mid-term future. Population doubling, which used to take millennia or centuries, now occurs within 68 years—a life span. The next doubling will take less than that, and the one after even less. This change in the pace of doubling has grave consequence for Earth's ability to supply the systems and resources necessary for survival. In spite of the demographic transition, the world population carries a great deal of momentum. Even if everyone limited childbearing to replacement level, *total* world population will continue to rise for some time.

DO POPULATION SIZE AND GROWTH MATTER?

In 1968, Paul and Anne Ehrlich published *The Population Bomb*, in which they proposed that the earth could only support a finite number of people and that overpopulation was a threat to continued civilization. They hoped to bring population growth to the attention of environmentalists, but the book sparked outrage and criticism from both the Right and the Left.

Marxists felt it went against Engel's optimism for mankind's power and that technology would solve any short-term problems. Many on the Left worried that population control could be used to promote eugenics or limiting births to the "right" kinds of people. Free-market advocates and the Right worried that it would promote government involvement in areas they felt were not appropriate. Social conservatives who opposed abortion or contraception did not want sex and reproduction as part of any public debate or government effort. Studies that exposed how population distribution, not quantity, was an underlying cause of poverty and hunger argued that talking about overpopulation was blaming the wrong entity.

At the same time that messengers of the overpopulation threat came under fire, demographers demonstrated that birth rates around the world were declining in countries that moved toward modernization and industrialization. These arguments against worrying about population growth dominated the latter part of the twentieth century. Overpopulation was not an issue in the forefront of environmental movements or governmental policy. Family planning services that made contraception available to couples were debated under other banners, not as a global tactic for population reduction. Meanwhile, the total number of people on Earth kept and keeps on growing. Almost 50 years after *The Population Bomb*, it is time to pay attention to the earth's ability to support everyone.

Carrying Capacity

In any ecology, the concept of carrying capacity denotes the number of individual units that can be supported over time. For instance, an island may have populations of prey and predators (wolves and deer, for example) whose numbers vary with favorable or harsh weather conditions but remain in some balance overall so that neither species starves. Taking the wolves away starts a cycle of rapid deer population growth to the point where the deer browse all the plants, and the population collapses as most starve to death. This is an oversimplified model, but the idea that a particular resource base can only support so many beings over time forms the basis for thinking about Earth's carrying capacity for humans.

In 1798, Malthus proposed that because population increases geometrically and food production grows arithmetically, society would always run up against limits. Disease and starvation would follow unless people voluntarily limited their family size, and we would be forced to live within Earth's carrying capacity. He did not consider the ways that people would find to increase yields and production, however, nor could he anticipate modern contraceptives. While Malthus was concerned initially with food for all, today's Neo-Malthusians are concerned that the massive rise in population will not be sustainable for food or water, fossil fuel demand, or arable land.

Notions of limits run contrary to belief in the power of human capital. In the 1960s, Boserup, a Danish economist, argued that humans form a well-spring of ingenuity. Under population pressure, she argued, people will adapt their agricultural practices in favor of higher density production to meet the increased demand for food, and innovative technologies will support the need. Those who are confident that technology and innovation will answer a growing population's needs believe our ability to use existing materials in new ways, in combination with the free market as the means, will bring about sustainable development.

Malthus and Boserup illustrate the range of opinions about whether population size matters for human standards of living and for the ecological health of the planet. These differences in perspective will continue to influence policy and urban planning in the future.

AGGLOMERATION AND INNOVATION

Those who argue against a "carrying capacity" for humans point out that humans have always enabled denser populations with technology throughout history. Initial forays into farming, for instance, occurred when land for hunting and gathering was occupied. Hunter-gatherers live closer together as their population grows. There is good evidence that agglomeration—the tendency of people to group together rather than spread out evenly over the landscape—fosters ongoing creative solutions to problems of food, energy, and water. Cities are often sources of innovations, from water purification systems to financial systems, from production facilities to distribution networks. Ideas spread quickly in denser habitats, and more people can learn and improve new inventions (Harvey 1981, Sassen 1991, Decker, Elliott, and Smith 2002, Amin and Thrift 2002). Under this framework, the increased urbanization of the world will continue to produce improvements for human living. Although the benefits are far from evenly distributed, the last century saw vastly improved literacy, longer life spans, much lower infant and child mortality, and ongoing efforts to ameliorate the pollution from the early industrial era.

Yet longer lives and lower infant mortality contribute to population growth. Most people who experience these benefits do not want a return to high birth and high death rates, but the idea that population can continue to grow exponentially without any consequences is contradicted by history. Two examples below discuss this, one from the past and one possibility for the future.

Cautionary Places

Easter Island is the "poster place" for environmental collapse and is a metaphor for planet Earth and its human population. People settled Easter Island sometime around 400 C.E. Population grew slowly until 1100 and doubled over the next two centuries, at which point the forests declined and possibly disappeared around 1400. A population of 10,000 by the late 1680s abruptly dropped to 2,000 over the next century. Soil erosion, loss of farmland, loss of trees to build canoes for fishing, rats (which arrived by boats with the humans), and human decimation of bird-nesting colonies all contributed to the precipitous population drop (Cohen 1995, Diamond 2005). The Easter Islanders overshot their carrying capacity, a process that is not limited to Pacific islands or prior centuries. Right now, in Nigeria, demographers predict rapid population growth in a place where people already strain the resources available in the country.

Watching Nigeria

Nigeria's population has tripled since the 1960s and is expected to triple again by 2100, according to the U.N.'s World Population Prospects 2012 Revision. Even as Nigeria tries to anticipate how to handle this projected growth the country experiences problems brought about by population size. Erosion, mining, overgrazing, and bushfires destroy the forests, while drought and desertification slowly erode available farmland into marginal land. In the 1990s, grain harvests were 15% less than required, and Nigeria averted famine in 2005 only with international aid (Cleland et al. 2006). Farmland loss spurs rural-to-urban migration, with Lagos now on the list of growing megacities.

Lagos is hardly ready for the in-migration, as urban health care, shelter, and basic waste-disposal services are in short supply. Trash and garbage are dumped in open-air sites that breed pathogens and facilitate disease outbreaks, such as cholera. Rural people in outlying areas lack access to water and fuel distribution and turn to the forest for food and firewood.

The World Health Organization reports that 40% of children five years old or under in Nigeria suffer from stunting due to malnutrition. This creates short-term risks of child vulnerability to death from infectious diseases and long-term risks of impaired cognitive development, which has serious implications for productivity in the future. Child mortality is about one in four, and maternal mortality is also high (8 in 1,000). Yet in one survey, Nigerians with at least four surviving offspring wanted up to eight or more children. Couples participating in the survey did not plan to use contraceptives in the future although most men and women were aware of them (Cleland et al. 2006).

Contraception is known, but it has been hard to implement successfully over the long term. Ibrahim Babaginda's military government tried enforced family planning in the 1990s, which met with wide resistance. Speaking at a family planning summit in London in 2012, then Minister of State for Health, Dr. Muhammed Pate, expressed commitment to raising contraceptive use to 36% by 2018. Effective family planning is deterred by religious leaders, who downplay family planning and encourage false beliefs such as contraceptives making women promiscuous or causing cancer.

What will happen in Nigeria? In some projections, Nigeria will surpass the United States in population size by the end of the century, with over 900 million by 2100 in a country that is roughly the size of Arizona, New Mexico, and Nevada combined. This seems inconceivable without something occurring to curb that growth. Whether it will be out-migration, more rapid adoption of birth control, some ecological disaster, or a combination of these or other possible events, we do not know. But we can see that Nigeria's situation acts as a caution for the rest of the world.

Fair Warning

Nigeria's situation is an extreme, and, unlike Easter Island, the country is not completely surrounded by water—it borders several other nations. But, like Easter Island, its population projections appear to fit at least two criteria that give us fair warning for environmental and social collapse. There was (and now is) rapid population growth that increases resource use and waste production. There were (and are) limited resources available and limits to waste-processing capacity. Leaders then (and now) delayed responses to impending crises, failing to address potential overshoot. We do not know directly the political or social responses that preceded the collapse on Easter Island and can only guess at famine or warfare, but current and near-term generations will bear witness to whatever events unfold in Nigeria.

In spite of places past and present that demonstrate how important population impact is, common objections sideline population growth as a problem in its own right. One popular idea is that the earth is very big and that there is plenty of room.

WRONG IDEAS ABOUT POPULATION GROWTH

The Question of Land

Since more than half the world's population now lives in cities, some people assume that more land will be "left over" for agriculture and other natural resources, arguing that there is plenty of acreage based on density measures. If, theoretically, the world's population could fit into the state of Texas with 1,040 square feet each (based on 7.2 billion people today put on 268,820 square miles for Texas), that measure overlooks how much land outside of immediate living area is necessary to support one person. We do not just occupy our own space—each of us needs "other" land apart from shared resources such as stores or libraries. We each need an allocation of farmland for food, roads to travel, mines for metals, watersheds for our bathing water, and so on.

Hunter-gatherers, in very hospitable climates with a variety of plants and game animals, need about two to three square miles *per person*. Even primitive farming increases the number of people per square mile 50- to 80-fold. Industrialization and urbanization allow us to live in a world with over seven billion people. However, those 1,040 square feet per person in Texas will shrink to 688 square feet at 10.9 billion and 452 square feet if the population reaches 16.6 billion (the high U.N. prediction). Earth's population is not going to squeeze into Texas. If we were to envision an environmentally balanced planet with adequate wetlands to filter pollutants, watersheds to provide enough water, and corridors of wilderness to support biodiversity, then the required square miles per person could be more than the current ratio of people to land. With 7.2 billion people on 24,642,757 square miles of habitable land (not glaciers, mountains, or deserts), each person has .003 square miles, or 95,417 square feet, at his or her disposal. That is about 2.2 acres per person *for everything*: food, water, fuel, waste recycling, and air. Put another way, that is about 292 people per square mile—an area that must provide *all* the necessary items for life. That square footage will only get smaller as population grows. But another idea is that the demographic shift means population will not grow.

Demographic Transition II

In Europe, the demographic transition began in the late 1700s and took until the late twentieth century. In much of the developing world, it began in the mid-1960s or later and took mere decades. In Western Europe, once the shift started, people never returned to their pre-shift fertility rates. Yet the proportion of youth in the world, and their momentum, means that *numbers* of people will increase even as birth rates fall. World population projections are based on the demographic transition starting in places where it has yet to occur, which may or may not be realistic. Each country has its own trajectory—some start and the birth rate plummets, while others have less dramatic drops in births. Since many nations have yet to begin the transition, if they experience the transition as many others have before them, there will be a period of continued rapid population growth as the nation enters the early transition phase with its high births and low deaths.

For a long time, demographers believed that once stage 4 in the demographic transition occurred, fertility levels would continue to hover at or below replacement. However, there are circumstances where fertility rates increase even after the transition. Countries with higher Human Development Index scores are associated with higher fertility, perhaps because wealth and stability support parents' desires and ability to invest in slightly more children. At the other end of the scale, when large-scale suffering recreates the conditions of pre-transition, fertility again rises. Botswana and other countries have high mortality due to AIDS/HIV, famine, and chronic conflict. In the face of instability and insecurity, people have more children to ensure some of their offspring survive, as they did in pre-modern times.

This raises the next belief about overpopulation, which is that natural processes or limits will take care of "extra" population.

Natural Limits?

One Malthusian approach is thinking that war, famine, and disease will kill off extra population. Massive deaths occurred in the past from the Black Death in the Middle Ages, the American Indians' exposure to smallpox and other European diseases, the Justinian Plague of late Roman times and a plague outbreak in China in the late nineteenth and early twentieth centuries. Yet as terrible as these were, they did not appreciably limit or slow *world* population growth. As devastating as HIV/AIDS is, especially in Africa, the actual annual death toll is equal to just 10 days' births in developing nations (Bongaarts 2003).

Even though entire societies may be decimated through genocide, war does not cause large declines in *total* world population. If the deaths from World War II are estimated at a low of 40 million and a high of 80 million, then those deaths represented only 1.7–3.5% of the world population in 1940. Putting aside the physical and emotional damage to people and the structural and environmental damage that war, famine, or plague bring, it is obvious that any ideas about letting "natural limits" take care of overpopulation are mistaken.

But Development Will Take Care of Population Growth!

Most economists today do not consider population growth a factor in development. Demographers ask whether economic growth by itself will hasten a nation's demographic transition. The relation between population size and wealth is tricky. High-density countries may be rich (like Japan) or not (like Bangladesh). Low-density countries may have few poor people (like Kazakhstan) or many (like Suriname).

A number of economists, such as Simon Kuznets and Julian Simon, argue that large populations increase human capital, with improved economies creating smaller families. In this approach, investment belongs in sectors that will move toward industrialization and service industries. Free trade will stimulate economic growth, which in turn will alleviate poverty. Under this philosophy, any discussion of population size and growth distracts from the main goal of getting national economies on the track of the industrialized West.

It seems negligent at best not to ask the corollary question: does deliberately limiting fertility speed up economic growth? In the 1970s, analysts at places like the United Nations and the National Academy of Sciences felt that slowing population growth would improve economic growth by reducing demand on resources and infrastructure. They thought that large families inhibit economic growth since resources of time, money, and people are devoted to caretaking and women find it difficult to participate in the workforce. Studies show that more young children at home do inhibit growth since they cost the family more to raise, and women enter the workforce later, if at all. A large elderly population also needs health care and support.

A better question asks about the relation of the economy to the working-age population. As the number of employable adults increases, the opportunities for economic growth do, too. If society cannot make the necessary investment in health and education, then fewer children get educated, reducing human capital in a country. Failing to take advantage of possible workers costs society. Unemployment, rising crime rates, worsening child health (the next generation of workers), and elderly poverty are some side effects of insufficient investment.

It's Not People, It's the System

This leads to another argument about economics and population size: that it is not the numbers of people who need resources that is the problem, but unequal control, access, and distribution of those resources. For instance, the amount of grain available per capita is enough to stem malnutrition and hunger worldwide, but in recent years, a substantial amount of that total is used for biofuel production and cattle feed or rots in granaries in one part of the world while people in other parts go hungry.

There is merit in this argument. The rising inequality between nations and populations within nations has everything to do with control over money, production, jobs, housing, education—the list goes on and on. However accurate this description is, it ignores questions of scale and solvability. Even if equitable distribution were achieved, a solution could not guarantee that supply meets future demand. Since distribution *is* unfair, having more people in need does nothing to hasten everyone getting a fair share.

Most of these arguments avoid looking at family planning. Yet the complex relations between population size and poverty mean that some discussion of family planning is overdue.

WHAT ABOUT FAMILY PLANNING?

In hunter-gatherer societies, the need to move around precluded large numbers of small children. Long breastfeeding times to inhibit ovulation, cultural customs concerning the timing and frequency of sex, adoption, abandonment, and infanticide were all tactics to limit fertility. In some traditional, sedentary, agricultural economies, big families were economically necessary, and fertility was encouraged, not restricted.

Contemporary people share a link to the past in that planning optimal family size is influenced by the society they live in. What we have that previous generations did not is modern contraceptives. Availability of contraceptives leads into discussions about sexuality, sexual customs, possibly abortion. These are controversial topics in many societies. For instance, the Catholic Church has long opposed any form of birth control, save abstinence or the "rhythm" method. In many places, the thought that women have the right to control their own childbearing, their own bodies, is treated as a "sensitive, delicate, controversial subject" (Campbell 2012). Restrictions on sexuality are considerably looser in post-industrialized, modern economies with access to inexpensive, reliable birth control. Women in these societies have a great deal of control over the timing and spacing of their children. Control over family size is linked to women's participation in the workforce. Besides contraception availability, a key enabler of fertility decline and overall economic growth is women's education.

Family Planning and Women's Education

As rates of female education rise, the fertility rate drops. Increased economic growth that emancipates women and educates all segments of society lowers fertility rates, as happened over and over again in developed countries. This occurred because industrial society puts pressure on traditional families. It creates educational and occupational hurdles to starting childbearing. Higher education for women increases their participation in the workforce and delays the age of marriage and the age of having the first child. A shift to consumerism creates a need for dual incomes, and couples decide against children in favor of other things, or they delay childbearing until they feel they have the right conditions to support a family. Industrial societies also have accessible contraceptives so that unwanted pregnancies are far fewer in number than in places that lack access. In contrast, places with high proportions of women with little to no education will likely continue to have high fertility rates.

KAP-Gap

In developing countries, the discrepancy between what couples say they want for family size and their actual number of children is called the "KAP-gap," or the gap between knowledge of, attitudes toward, and practice using contraceptives. Although economists do not like the idea that market forces leave needs unmet, and demographers argue that unwanted pregnancy is not a big contributor to population growth, high numbers of unintended or unwanted pregnancies indicate that there are unmet needs in contraception. To understand why this gap still exists today, we go back to the early 1990s.

From Cairo to the Millennium Development Goals

At the International Conference on Population and Development (ICPD) in Cairo in 1994, the participating countries created a Program of Action for women's reproductive and sexual health. Asian governments used KAP-gap to justify targets and quotas, incentive payments, disincentive policies, and condoned community pressure, including coercion, to stem rising populations as a way of creating economic growth. Human rights and women's health organizations objected to these tactics but missed the ramifications. They overlooked the way that unwanted pregnancy and unwanted children might also be an attack on women's health, by indirectly assuming that everyone wants many children. As a result, interest in state-sponsored family planning efforts has fallen since the mid-1990s. Six years later, when nations assembled to create the Millennium Development Goals, reproductive health and family planning were not included on the list.

One reason for the continued drop in family planning policy support is the United States. The largest donor nation for family planning efforts worldwide has, since 1984, dropped funding for any foreign nongovernmental organizations that were in any way associated with abortion, legal or illegal, even if they used their own funds for those activities. This is also known as the Mexico City policy or the "global gag rule."

EXAMPLES OF GOVERNMENT'S ROLE IN
FAMILY PLANNING

The Gag Rule

The gag rule was in effect off and on from 1984, reflecting the United States' political ups and downs. The rule was enacted under President Reagan, rescinded by President Clinton, then reinstated in 2001 under President G. W. Bush and withdrawn again in 2009 by President Obama. When in effect, the rule closed domestic clinics, especially in the poorest neighborhoods. This eliminated reproductive and general health care for those who needed it most under the guise of opposing abortion. It may have aided population growth since lack of reproductive health care is one cause of higher fertility. Losing an infant (especially the first-born) increases the likelihood of having another child soon and of less space between subsequent pregnancies.

The irony is that in places where contraceptives and family planning are in short supply, abortion (legal or illegal) becomes the de facto form of birth control. In countries like Romania and Russia, abortion has been known as a main form of birth control for decades. That the United States stopped shipping contraceptive supplies during times when the rule was in effect, did not reduce the incidence of pregnancy termination. Impeding the flow of contraceptives simply delayed the transition from abortion to pregnancy prevention.

Government Intervention Works Both Ways

The United States is not the only government that helps or hinders people in their desire for family planning. Comparing Pakistan, Bangladesh, and China illustrates the roles that governments can play in lowering population size.

Both Pakistan and Bangladesh had the same fertility rates and desired family size when Bangladesh achieved its independence in 1971. Bangladesh prioritized family planning, while Pakistan had poor family planning services, hampered by internal politics. By 1990, twice as many couples in Bangladesh used contraceptives as in Pakistan, while Pakistan's population went from 5 million fewer than Bangladesh to projections of 62 million larger by 2050 (Cleland et al. 2006).

China

Another example of governmental population control exists in China's one-child policy, which was enacted in 1979. Prior to then, a voluntary policy called "late, long, few" stressed a later start for childbearing, longer times between children, and fewer children overall. Under that policy, China's birthrate dropped from 5.9 to 2.9. In the late 1970s, China enacted a "one-child" policy, limiting family size for urban and government workers. Rural and some ethnic minorities were allowed an extra child under some circumstances. Women used contraceptives, sterilization, and abortion to avoid or terminate pregnancies. Steep fines, loss of jobs, and other consequences enforced the rules. While this policy achieved the desired result by reducing China's population growth, it left the country with some new demographic problems.

The Chinese, like many other Asian countries, favor boys over girls. Now China, like Thailand, has a high ratio of men to women, enough that some 40 million Chinese men will not be able to marry a Chinese spouse. Limiting families also created the "4:2:1" problem: two spouses with four aging parents and one child to care for, often simultaneously.

The government has recently eased the original policy somewhat; but now, even with more options, half of all couples decide against a second child, citing the expense. Chinese culture is becoming oriented toward small families, with an estimated fertility rate of 1.55 in 2014 according to the CIA World Factbook. Even with less than perfect reporting of births in China, that number represents a substantial drop in fertility.

Family Planning—Criticisms and Responses

Some critics of family planning say that it is not effective in spite of the evidence from Bangladesh, where a fall in the number of children per woman (over six to three) accompanied the rise in contraceptive use from <10% to over 50%. Iran shows a similar pattern. Through a network of village health centers, the government provided contraceptives, and fertility declined from over six births per woman historically to two in the 1980s. These are just two examples of many places where family planning services assisted in bringing down a national birth rate.

Another objection to state-sponsored family planning is its expense. Yet family planning services are on the same level as other health efforts, such as short-course chemotherapy for tuberculosis, or condom distribution to prevent HIV/AIDS. Low-cost methods of birth control coupled with maternal and infant health care make services highly cost-effective.

A final objection is that family planning is coercive. This is rooted in the initial experience of Asian family planning, with the one-child policy of China and coercive tactics in other countries that are no longer considered necessary, and maybe never were. Voluntary programs worked well in many countries, as revealed by many community studies and surveys. For instance, Thailand dropped from 6.4 to 2 children per woman, and Korea from 5.6 to 2.2 (Bongaarts 2003).

It is also worth considering that *lack* of contraceptives is a subtle form of coercion—the 137 million women worldwide who are estimated to want family planning but cannot obtain it are at high risk of unwanted pregnancies. Many women want to raise fewer, healthier, and more educated children but are restricted by lack of contraceptives and will bear more children than they want. Since the inability to obtain contraceptives often overlaps with poverty and poor education, these women are also at higher risk for complications and infant and maternal mortality.

If family planning is cost-effective, desired, and helpful, future efforts to stem population growth will need to promote these services as part of general national development efforts. Family planning and economic development work together to produce drops in fertility to replacement levels. Even so, attempts to limit population growth are opposed by free market ideology-based institutions that claim we will invent our way out of any problems posed by high population.

WON'T TECHNOLOGY AND INNOVATION SAVE THE DAY?

One way that humans differ from other species is that we are able to use tools and fashion technologies from raw materials with great sophistication. Crows and apes use sticks, gulls use rocks, and dolphins fish with bubbles, but humans continuously adapt materials that were not considered resources prior to the need and skill to use them. Our ability to increase food production (agriculture and agribusiness), find substitutes for natural resources in short supply (oil), and engineer reuse through recycling is the basis of optimism for those who believe that we will find solutions to scarcity as it arises. They point to the ways that technology has ameliorated problems of population growth, from agriculture's beginnings to improved fishing and plastics substituting for many natural but scarce materials. Under this scenario, they argue that Earth has no physical carrying capacity, that carrying capacity is only a conceptual limit in our thinking.

It is true that technology can help solve some of the problems it creates. Advances in air conditioning removed Freon from general use, stopping damage to the ozone layer. Increased gas mileage in cars with better emissions technologies reduced the carbon output for individual vehicles. Yet the hole in the ozone layer still exists and carbon emissions continue.

Technological solutions can also perpetuate the underlying problem. More efficiency often means more use rather than less, so industries that contribute to environmental damage continue to grow. Better gas mileage did not translate into less driving or fewer cars, and the electric power needed for air conditioning has not decreased.

Just as economic power is not distributed evenly, neither are technology's benefits. Developed nations enjoy high levels of health care, material goods, education, and interconnectedness due in part to easy and cheap technology. In general, citizens of France, for example, have better access to televisions, computers, and sneakers than citizens of Zambia. But food is often the main criteria for measuring technology's benefits.

The Green Revolution that created high crop yields depends on high levels of synthetic fertilizers and irrigation. Increased food production helped feed rising populations, but large-scale firms and industrial agriculture require a lot of arable land. Their takeover of fertile lands displaced subsistence farmers and locked others in debt cycles due to the cost of fertilizers and machinery. Control over seeds, methods, and land is concentrated in smaller numbers of farmers, and a small number of companies (such as Cargill, Archer Daniels Midland, ConAgra, and Monsanto) thereby exercise global control on industrial farming products. At the national level, countries that used to be barely food self-sufficient no longer are, as more land comes into cultivation for export crops and small farmers are driven off (see the following chapter on food production in Africa). Malnutrition in the poorest segments of global society is a common result.

This brings up a last objection to blithely assuming technology will solve all resource issues. There are actual, physical limits on some resources, and substitutions may be expensive or nonexistent. In the American Southwest, water-intensive agriculture and rapid, high population growth increased the demand for water in the Colorado River Basin (an area containing Arizona and sections of Colorado, California, Nevada, Utah, New

Mexico, and Wyoming). To fill that demand, states pumped groundwater with no clear coordination or oversight across the region. Recent satellite studies show the basin lost 17 trillion gallons between 2004 and 2014. It takes thousands of years to replenish groundwater, and no one has any idea how much water is left. Now that the situation is dire, some states are planning some form of groundwater management, grey water reuse, and irrigation efficiency reform. However, these efforts will not replace groundwater. There is a very good chance that the 30 million people and the 4 million acres under cultivation will not be sustainable in any way they have been accustomed to.

BUT WE HAVE ALWAYS ALTERED OUR ENVIRONMENT!

This is a common complaint for those who are skeptical about sustainability and potential problems of overpopulation. Yes, humans have always altered their landscapes. Native Americans burned woodlands to create more open spaces and promote greater deer populations. Farmers in Southeast Asia created terraced fields on mountainsides to grow rice. In the northeast United States and later in the Midwest, settlers cut trees at astonishing rates to feed the demand for houses and railroads, industry and glass. Most landscapes have been meddled with, overcut, overrun, polluted, altered, and reshaped from complexity to simplicity by human beings for millennia.

Question of Scale

One major difference between now and then is that the scale and scope of our effects on the environment are regional or often global rather than local. The ecological footprint of pre-modern societies was constrained by their transportation methods and limited contact with other parts of the globe. Romans did not know about the Mayans, who, in turn, did not know about the Chinese, nor did they exchange goods, diseases, or information. Their ecological footprints did not overlap. Since footprints overlap when certain people and societies consume oversized shares of water and other resources, people will compete for ecological resources.

Megacities magnify the problems that affect cities in general. Aside from the well-known issue of air quality, the ecological footprint of dense megacities puts a strain on their regions and affects more than their local environments. For instance, piped water infrastructure is scarce in many developing cities and their corresponding urban peripheries, so waste and sewage are not treated before returning to nature. Thus, megacities pull in more natural resources and expel more waste and contaminants to the surrounding environment.

Large urban agglomerations affect their own weather due to different heat absorption from the surrounding countryside. Megacities are as prone to hazards as smaller urban areas, but their population density puts more people at risk during hurricanes, floods, and the ensuing breakdowns in supply networks. When Pompeii was buried in ash from Vesuvius' eruption it was tragic, but the scale was small. When flooding strikes coastal cities in India, the larger scale affects millions of people simultaneously.

Question of Scope

Even assuming that we could put political, social, and technological adaptations in place that would continue to feed, house, and warm or cool the upcoming generations, there are other problems associated with human population size that are less amenable to clever inventions. As human populations expand, we take away living space for other animal species large and small, which begin to decline, become endangered, and die off. This pattern is not new, but it, too, is exponential in magnitude.

The records of extinction on islands such as Hawaii and Madagascar demonstrate that expanding human populations in limited areas hunt other species to extinction. We are presently seeing a die-off that rivals previous natural massive extinctions known from the fossil record. Our rapidly growing human populations ramp up the rate of extinction and fragmenting of ecosystems. Worse, measures of extinction only count species we know, a tiny portion of all organisms in the world. Our bias toward vertebrate land mammals means that we know little about microbes, insects, amphibians, and reptiles whose presence may be more important to any given ecology.

What overall biodiversity losses mean for humans is unknown, but the consequences of losing large land animals is known to promote increase in rodent populations, certain undesirable insects and then common disease vectors. Aside from ethical questions (do we have the right to kill off everything else?) or aesthetic ones (do we really want an ocean that is full of jellyfish and plastic debris?), the practical consequences of fragmented and out-of-balance natural systems are not fully understood and likely to threaten human health.

This foray into examples regarding the scale and scope of our changes to the environment links to concerns about increased population growth. More people mean more disruption to existing ecosystems and more pressure on natural systems. The wide range of any area's ecological footprint and the interaction of ecological systems means that increased population will disrupt entire webs of interlocking processes, and we do not yet understand the possible consequences.

Even if we had a stationary population tomorrow, with births equal to deaths, we face severe environmental challenges. We do not feed everyone now—if we make huge breakthroughs in crop yields or protein supplies tomorrow, we could not guarantee that food would be equitably distributed, as it is not now. Lack of access to fresh, safe water in developing countries is a major health concern. Rivers that used to run to the sea, such as the Yellow River in China or the Ganges in India, run dry for part of the year. The demand for energy continues to grow, and like food, access is uneven. While entire Appalachian mountaintops in the eastern United States disappear for coal mining, and people in Chinese cities breathe intense air pollution from burning coal, other populations (as in Haiti and parts of Nigeria) turn to the forest for fuel, decimating their woodlands. Human activity currently touches every place on the globe.

And if food, water, energy, and waste crises are not enough, the changes expected in the global climate due to CO_2 accumulations will bring increased challenges. Greater storm activity, sea level rise, continued loss of biodiversity, increased woodland fires, and glacial melt will affect societies around the world throughout the next century. None of these challenges are going to be helped by dreaming about technological fixes or regulating emissions. The real problem that needs global attention is human population growth. Humans have always altered their environment, but not at an exponential rate—until now.

What to Do?

The question is then what kind of attention should be brought to bear on population growth. Joel Cohen, a demographer, outlines positive steps in his many articles and books. He categorizes our possible responses as (a) creating a bigger pie, (b) using fewer forks, and (c) treating each other with better manners (Cohen 1995, 2005). These are not mutually exclusive; indeed, they must each be implemented to avoid the hazards of overpopulation.

By "bigger pie," Cohen is talking about continuing to generate economic growth so that more societies experience increased standards of living and start or continue the demographic tradition. "Fewer forks" supports family planning efforts toward limiting population growth, and "better manners" indicates that we need to pay special attention to social justice and find a different or better way to raise living standards without mimicking the West's destructive processes. These three must occur simultaneously to achieve a slowdown in human population growth.

THE CONUNDRUM

The social justice aspect of sustainability regarding population growth is critical, though it leaves us with a conundrum regarding our relation to resources and the environment. Industrialization *has* improved life for many—longer lives, less maternal and child mortality, better nutrition—and industrialization also contributed to the fertility decline in developed and many developing nations. Yet the very processes that did this for some of the earth's population also created environmental conditions that are threatening everyone's well-being, not just in industrialized nations. The growth model provided by the West's experience under capitalistic growth is not sustainable, nor are our current ecosystems anything like their original states.

High economic growth accompanies high environmental costs in the developed world. The northern developed countries consume disproportionate amounts of energy per person and have the largest ecological footprint of any region. Raising living standards lowers family size but, under the existing models of growth, increases the ecological footprint. The pattern of industrialization by developed countries has been the template for others—China especially—but if everyone in these emerging countries lives as Western citizens do, the environmental impacts will be staggering. Using the ecological footprint method, we would need five more Earths to support everyone living in the style of the United States (and not everyone in the United States lives at the same level; there are big wealth discrepancies here as elsewhere). The question about how many people can or should live on Earth is bounded by parameters of quality of life and consumption. Earth could likely support more people living on $15 per day than people living in wealthy, gated communities, but will those lives be healthy, productive, and satisfying? Estimates of

Earth's carrying capacity range from two billion to a wildly extravagant one hundred billion (Cohen 1995). Caveats concern how much food is consumed and what level of material wealth is expected. Social justice and "better manners" posit that we must find a different or better way to raise living standards without mimicking the West's destructive processes.

LOOKING TOWARD THE FUTURE

There may yet be demographic surprises in the next 50 years, but for the moment, humanity will continue adding many more people every day—219,000 a day, by one estimate (Lester Brown 2012), many of them poor. Technology will provide us with some temporary solutions, but not everywhere, not for everyone, not for every problem. Both Neo-Malthusians and those who believe in unlimited growth will be incorrect about some part of their predictions. Family planning efforts will increase in some areas, and larger numbers of women will become educated. Other places will resist contraception and continue to have more children than can be raised well with respect to health and education. At some point, the damage to Earth's varied ecosystems brought about by unfettered population growth will be so blatant, and the human suffering caused so severe, that we will have to pay attention to population size.

Population graphs that show patterns for animal population growth and decline in finite-resource settings can be instructive. Depending on the species and situation, population may stabilize as an S-Curve, show boom-and-bust cycles, or peak and then cycle near that peak (see Figure 3.3). Optimists see human population future in the first and third styles, and Neo-Malthusians fear the second.

The question we must grapple with is *how* we want to live, and at what cost. We may continue to kick the can of difficult decisions down the road, all the while continuing to add millions of new people

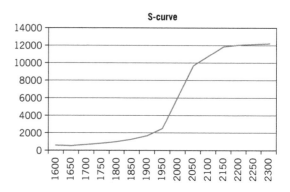

but creating a future with severely comprised ecologies and continued economic inequality.

Nations could work together to bring more people on Earth to a higher standard of living by encouraging smaller families through reproductive health and planning. Or, we could continue with the status quo, assuming that there is ample room and time for economic and population growth. If we do that, we gamble that environmental changes will not pass some unknown tipping points in the planet's ability to support life. We gamble that the environmental challenges of the near future will be mild, not severe. We gamble that we will avoid massive human suffering and death. These gambles point to the final question: do we want to find out the hard way?

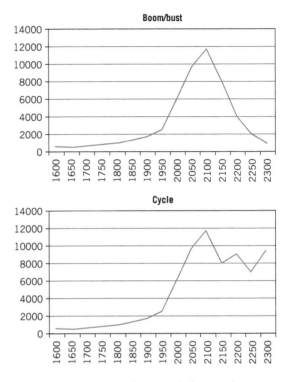

FIGURE 3.3 Future possible population graphs.
Source: United Nations.

For this chapter, the definitions are contained within the text when the word first appears in bold.

REFERENCES

Adetitun, D. O., and G. P. Oyeyiola. 2011. "Environment Health Hazard Assessment of Municipal Wastes in Ilorin Metropolis." *International Research Journal of Microbiology (IRJM)* 2(7): 220–225.

Akanbi, Festus, and Malachy Agbo. 2011. "Nigeria's Growing Population, a 'Time Bomb,' Warn Analysts." *THISDAY Live.*

Amin, Ash, and Nigel Thrift. 2002. "Chapter 2: Propinquity and Flow in the City." In *Cities: Reimagining the Urban*, 31–50. Cambridge, Oxford, Malden, MA: Polity Press in Association with Blackwell Publishers, LTD.

Andreev, Kirill, Vladimíra Kantorová, and John Bongaarts. 2013. "Demographic Components of Future Population Growth." New York: United Nations Department of Economic and Social Affairs, Population Division, Technical Paper No. 2013/3.

Ankomah, Augustine, Jennifer Anyanti, and Muyiwa Oladosu. 2011. "Myths, Misinformation, and Communication about Family Planning and Contraceptive Use in Nigeria." *Open Access Journal of Contraception* 2: 95–105. doi: http://dx.doi.org/10.2147/OAJC.S20921.

Bloom, David E., David Canning, and Günther Fink. 2011. "Implications of Population Aging for Economic Growth. *Harvard School of Public Health, Program On The Global Demography Of Aging.*

Bongaarts, John. 2003. "Completing the Fertility Transition in the Developing World: The Role of Educational Differences and Fertility Preferences." *Population Studies* 57(3): 321–336.

Brown, Lester. 2012. *Full Planet, Empty Plates.* New York: W. W. Norton & Company.

Caldwell, John C., and Thomas Schindlmayr. 2003. "Explanations of the Fertility Crisis in Modern Societies: A Search for Commonalities." *Population Studies* 57(3): 241–263.

Campbell, Martha. 2012. "Why the Silence on Population?" In *Life On the Brink: Environmentalists Confront Overpopulation*, edited by Philip Cafaro and Eileen Crist, 41–55. Athens, GA: University of Georgia Press.

Casterline, John B., and Steven W. Sinding. 2000. "Unmet Need for Family Planning in Developing Countries and Implications for Population Policy." *Policy Research Division Working Papers* 135.

Cleland, John, Stan Berstein, Alex Ezeh, Anibal Faundes, Anna Glasier, and Jolene Innis. 2006. "Family Planning: The Unfinished Agenda." *The Lancet* 368(9549): 1810–1827. doi: 10.1016/S0140-6736(06)69480-4.

Coale, Ansley. 1973. "The Demographic Transition." *Proceedings of the International Population Conference, Liège.*

Cohen, Joel E. 1995. *How Many People Can the Earth Support?* New York London: W. W. Norton & Company.

Cohen, Joel E. 2005. "Human Population Grows Up." *Scientific American* (September): 48–55. Accessed 30 July 2014. Available at http://www.rockefeller.edu/labheads/cohenje/PDFs/324CohenHumanPpnGrowsUpSci Am2005.pdf.

Cohen, Mark Nathan. 1977. *The Food Crisis in Prehistory: Overpopulation and the Origins of Agriculture.* New Haven and London: Yale University Press.

Cohen, Susan A. 2003. "Global Gag Rule Revisited: HIV/AIDS Initiative Out, Family Planning Still In." *The Guttmacher Report on Public Policy* 6(4).

Decker, Ethan H., Scott Elliott, and Felisa A. Smith. 2002. "Megacities and the Environment." *The Scientific World Journal* 2: 374–386. doi: 10.1100/tsw.2002.103.

Demeny, Paul. 2003. "Population Policy Dilemmas in Europe at the Dawn of the Twenty-First Century." *Population and Development Review* 29: 1–28.

Diamond, Jared. 2005. *Collapse: How Societies Choose to Fail or Succeed.* New York: Viking Press.

Ehrlich, Paul R. 1968. *The Population Bomb.* New York: Sierra Club/Ballantine Books.

Ellis, Erlie C. 2013. "Overpopulation Is Not the Problem." *New York Times*, September 13, Opinion. http://www.nytimes.com/2013/09/14/opinion/overpopulation-is-not-the-problem.html?_r=1&.

Gillespie, Duff G. 2004. "Whatever Happened to Family Planning and, for That Matter, Reproductive Health." *International Family Planning Perspectives* 30(1).

Grimm, Nancy B., Stanley H. Faeth, Nancy E. Golubiewski, Charles L. Redman, Jianguo Wu, Xuemei Bai, and John M. Briggs. 2008. "Global Change and the Ecology of Cities." *Science* 319: 756–760. doi: 10.1126/science.1150195.

Hamilton, Marcus J., Bruce T. Milne, Robert S. Walker, and James H. Brown. 2007. "Nonlinear Scaling of Space Use in Human Hunter–Gatherers." *Proceedings of the National Academy of Sciences of the United State of America* 104 (11): 4765–4769. doi: 10.1073/pnas.0611197104.

Harvey, David. 1981. "The Urban Process Under Capitalism." In *Urbanization and Urban Planning in Capitalist Societies*, edited by Michael Dear and Allen J. Scott, 91–122. London: Methuen.

Hesketh, Therese, Li Lu, and Zhu Wei Xing. 2005. "The Effect of China's One-Child Family Policy after 25 Years." *New England Journal of Medicine* 353(11): 1171–1176.

Huesemann, Michael H., and Joyce A. Huesemann. 2008. "Will Progress in Science and Technology Avert or Accelerate Global Collapse? A Critical Analysis and Policy Recommendations." *Environment, Development and Sustainability* 10: 787–825. doi: 10.1007/s10668-007-9085-4.

Klare, Michael T. 2014. "Why We Could Still Be Worried About Running Out of Oil." *Mother Jones Magazine*, January 9.

Kolankiewicz, Leon. 2012. "Overpopulation versus Biodiversity: How a Plethora of People Produces a Paucity of Wildlife." In *Life On the Brink: Environmentalists Confront Overpopulation*, edited by Philip Cafaro and Eileen Crist, 72–121. Athens, GA: University of Georgia Press.

Krass, Frauke. 2003. "Megacities As Global Risk Areas." *Petermanns Geographische Mitteilungen* 147: 1–15.

Levin, Dan. 2014. "Many in China Can Now Have a Second Child, But Say No." *New York Times*, February 25. http://www .nytimes.com/2014/02/26/world/asia/many-couples-in-china-will-pass-on-a-new-chance-for-a-second-child.html?_r=1.

Malakoff, David. 2011. "Are More People Necessarily a Problem?" *Science* 333: 544–546.

Mather, Mark. 2012. "Fact Sheet: The Decline in U.S. Fertility." *Population Reference Bureau.*

Myrskylä, Mikko, Hans-Peter Kohler, and Francesco C. Billari. 2009. "Advances in Development Reverse Fertility Declines." *Nature* 460: 741–743. doi: 10.1038/nature08230.

Obi, Pual. 2011. "Family Planning, Birth Control and the Raging Controversy." *THISDAY Live.*

Omo-Aghoja, L. O., V. W. Omo-Aghoja, C. O. Aghoja, F. E. Okonofua, O. Aghedo, C. Umueri, R. Otayohwo, P. Feyi-Waboso, E. A. Onowhakpor, and K. A. Inikori. 2009. "Factors Associated with the Knowledge, Practice and Perceptions of Contraception in Rural Southern Nigeria." *Ghana Medical Journal* 43(3): 115–121.

Oorimoogunje, O. O. I., S. A. Adegboyega, O. O. Banjo, and O. A. Funmilayo. 2011. "Population Growth: Implications for Environmental Sustainability." *Ife PsychologIA* 19(1).

Park, Chai Bin, Seung Hyun Han, and Minja Kim Choe. 1979. "The Effect of Infant Death on Subsequent Fertility in Korea and the Role of Family Planning." *American Journal of Public Health* 69(6): 557–565.

Preston, Samuel, Patrick Heuveline, and Guillot Michel. 2001. *Demography*. Oxford, U.K., Malden MA: Blackwell Publishing.

Roberts, Callum. 2007. *The Unnatural History of the Sea*. Washington, DC: Shearwater Books.

Rosset, Peter, Joseph Collins, and Frances Moore Lappé. 2000. "Do We Need New Technology to End Hunger?" *Tikkun Magazine*. Accessed 1 October 2014. Available at http://www.twnside.org.sg/title/twr118c.htm.

Samsel, Anthony, and Stephanie Seneff. 2013. "Glyphosate's Suppression of Cytochrome P450 Enzymes and Amino Acid Biosynthesis by the Gut Microbiome: Pathways to Modern Diseases." *Entropy* 15(4): 1416–1463. doi: 10.3390/e15041416.

Sassen, Saskia. 1991. *The Global City: New York, London, Tokyo*. Princeton: Princeton University Press.

Singh, Susheela, and Jacqueline E. Darroch. 2012. "Adding It Up: Costs and Benefits of Contraceptive Services—Estimates for 2012." New York: Guttmacher Institute and United Nations Population Fund (UNFPA).

Taylor, Jerry. 2002. "Sustainable Development: A Dubious Solution in Search of a Problem." *Policy Analysis* 449.

Turner, B. L. II, and Marina Fischer-Kowalski. 2010. "Ester Boserup: An Interdisciplinary Visionary Relevant for Sustainability." *Proceedings of the National Academy of Sciences of the United State of America* 107(51): 21963–21965. doi: 10.1073/pnas.1013972108.

United Nations, Department of Economic and Social Affairs: Population Division. 2012. "World Urbanization Prospects: The 2011 Revision Highlights."

United Nations, Department of Economic and Social Affairs, Population Division. 2013. "World Population Prospects: The 2012 Revision."

Wackernagel, Mathis, Larry Onisto, Patricia Bello, Alejandro Callejas Linares, Ina Susana López Falán, Jesus Mendez García, Ana Isabel Suárez Guerrero, and Ma. Guadalupe Suárez Guerrero. 1999. "National Natural Capital Accounting with the Ecological Footprint Concept." *Ecological Economics* 29: 375–390.

Wahlberg, Katarina. 2008. "Green Revolution versus Sustainable Agriculture." *Global Policy Forum*. Accesssed 28 September 2014. Available at https://

www.globalpolicy.org/component/content/article/217-hunger/46156-causes-and-strategies-on-world-hunger.html.

Young, Hillary S., Rodolfo Dirzo, and Katharina Dittmar. 2014. "Declines in Large Wildlife Increase Landscape-Level Prevalence of Rodent-Borne Disease in Africa." *Proceeding of the National Academy of Science* 111(19): 7036–7041. doi: 10.1073/pnas.1404958111.

Zelizer, Viviana A. Rotman. 1985. *Pricing the Priceless Child: The Changing Social Value of Children*. New York: Basic Books.

Chapter 4

FOOD SECURITY AND SUSTAINABLE FOOD PRODUCTION IN AFRICA

BY FRANKLIN C. GRAHAM IV

INTRODUCTION

From 1999 to 2001, I served as a Peace Corps volunteer in the West African country of Mauritania. I lived in the Adrar Region, a place where food production is limited ecologically to nomadic herding and the cultivation of dates, millet, peas, and melons at the oases for roughly three months per year. This northern region of Mauritania is heavily dependent on food imports from other parts of Mauritania, neighboring West African countries, and overseas. Curious about other food-producing regions, I took a trip, visiting other countries in Africa at the end of my Peace Corps service.

One of the countries I visited was Guinea. I was impressed with the biodiversity, the farmland, and the healthy appearance of domesticated animals. I met other Peace Corps volunteers working in Guinea and commented to them about the limitations of food production in northern Mauritania. I praised what I saw of local food production in Guinea, but the volunteers were quick to inform me Guinea is not the utopia that I initially observed. One volunteer, in particular, put my observations in a new context. She commented, "You served in a country where there is not enough food and life is difficult because people have no choice but to buy expensive, imported foods. We serve in a country where despite the abundance of food, healthy foods at a low cost, people don't eat

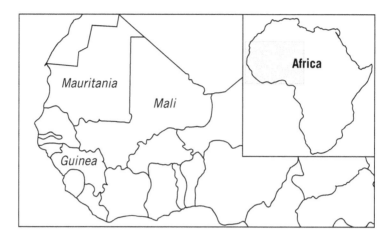

FIGURE 4.1 Location of field sites in Western Africa.

them. They prefer instead, if they can afford it, to buy imported or processed foods from Dakar, Abidjan, or overseas. Can you understand our frustrations in trying to improve life here?"

Africa is a diverse continent of various climates and peoples. It is the home of the Sahara, the largest and hottest desert on the planet. Still, this is not the dominant climate type. There are humid and dense forests known as jungles, carrying great biodiversity, present near and along the equator. The coast of North Africa and the country of South Africa are known for their Mediterranean climates, producing many fruits and vegetables for both local consumption and export. But the landscape that typifies Africa are the savannas, the grasslands where drought is periodic and Africans compete with other Africans as well as foreigners for the control, decision-making, and use of land in food production. Guinea, with the exception of its coast, is primarily savanna. Even Mauritania, known as a Saharan nation, produces food along its southern and eastern margins where savanna is present.

Africa is a complex continent of peoples and environments, but there are commonalities that we can draw upon in order to understand the evolution and changing dynamics of the crops that are planted in the fields and the food reaching African dinner tables. What is happening today in Mauritania, Guinea, other African countries, and on other continents is a growing dependency on foods produced by international corporations.

The purpose for this chapter is to introduce issues that many Africans face, yet the issues are not unique to Africa. They are also challenges for food producers and consumers in other world regions, including the industrialized world. The role of agribusiness in food production is growing in Africa, but so too are the phenomena of urbanization and land-grabbing. These interconnected issues shape local decisions in Africa about crop choice and food markets, as they do in Asia, Europe, and North and South America. Out of all these continents, however, Africa continues to have the largest numbers of small-scale farmers (generally referred to as peasants), and these peasants contribute significantly to food security and nutrition for everyone (Figure 5.2). Peasants today are under great pressures they did not have in the past: competition with both foreign corporations competing for consumer markets and the population losses as young people move to the cities seeking off-farm employment.

Mauritania, at least its northern region, was always dependent on food importation. The region does not have the climate to produce the sufficient amount of grains and produce needed for its population. Guinea as a whole, however, has the capacity to feed its population and export surplus food to neighboring countries. Yet peasants here are struggling, as the growing urban populations around them prefer either to buy foods from overseas (essentially European, North American, and Asian) or processed foods coming from African cities like Lagos, Nairobi, and Casablanca, which are often owned by multinational enterprises. These types of foods are generally inferior in quality and certainly not as beneficial to good health as foods produced locally.

This unfolding conversion underscores the importance of finding the sustainable path for agriculture and food production in Africa. The goal is to determine the ideal combination of small-scale and large-scale farming along with the role imported foods have to ensure food security for the continent. Some, mostly outsiders, question the ability of small-scale farmers to feed everyone in Africa, especially when African countries are the fastest-growing in terms of human population. Yet large-scale agriculture is not without its critics as well, who point out the very real occurrence of socioeconomic displacement and disenfranchisement of the poor, as well as the ecological consequences of disturbing biodiversity, using pesticides, and growing mono crops. Imported foods are also controversial in that they reduce diversity in the African diet, are not as nutritious as locally produced foods, and are increasing in price with the spikes in transportation costs. These common traps of modern food production are as real in Africa as they are in other food-producing countries around the world.

The expansion of food imports and processed foods in Africa benefits a minority of African food producers and their contemporaries on other continents, but most Africans are marginalized in the process. Peasants, commonly identified as female, poor, and responsible for feeding the children in the household, are most often impacted in this trend. The household economies have been destabilized further by changes in nutrition. For instance, Africa had its share of disasters in adapting foreign foods that appeared advantageous to farmers or consumers but instead caused malnutrition in their own right. In addition, urban African consumers are vulnerable to price increases for imported and processed foods. Prices for imports are increasing with the rise in energy prices since the global recession of 2008. Secondary costs of higher petroleum prices include the cost of petroleum-based fertilizers, the operation of food industries, and the food's packaging. These are passed on to the African consumers of packaged food products.

Finally, the promotion of imported and processed foods in Africa raises a larger concern. In the reality of globalized trade today, other forces are at play influencing what people eat in Africa. Some of these are quite different from the transformations taking place elsewhere. Europe and North America and to a lesser extent Asia are experiencing growing demands among consumers that food be produced locally. Discerning consumers seek out foods that are not produced by an agribusiness but are organic and come directly from the farmers. Should this trend continue along with energy prices remaining high, this may reduce food exports from European, North American, and Asian countries and also push multinational agricultural corporations to shift their products and marketing to Africa.

In fact, a visit to the official websites of Monsanto, Cargill, and Syngenta (to name a few of the dominant agribusinesses) confirms their growing commitment in Africa. In the long run, with Africa receiving food imports and processed foods outcompeting locally produced foods, and with African farmers and their families displaced from their land and moving into the towns, the continent is losing both a livelihood and its means of maintaining food security. These conditions create greater food insecurity for African consumers in the cities and peasants in the countryside.

A MIXED PAST OF LOCAL AND TRADED FOODS IN AFRICA

Africa, although integrated with Europe and Asia long before the Common Era (CE), is a mystery for many non-Africans today. In its past, it rested on the fringe of Eurasia to the north and east, where the physical barrier of the Saharan Desert and the known dangers of tropical diseases kept many non-Africans out. Today, in terms of material wealth, it is the poorest continent in the world. Although its aggregate population is relatively small compared to other continents, it has the highest population growth rate and the lowest rates of life expectancy. African countries have among the highest infant and child mortality rates on the global indices. Since food is crucial to child development, nutrition, and overall health of populations, the changes that occurred over time in the foods grown in Africa and adopted from other lands are important to understand when addressing these disturbing demographics.

Trade in the Old World

Collectively, Africa, Asia, and Europe are described as the Old World as they were exchanging people, animals, foods, technologies, and diseases long before 1500 CE. From what is known in the anthropological record, the continent of Africa was never isolated in its food production from the rest of the Old World. Africans, starting as early as the second millennium Before Common Era (BCE), received from the European Mediterranean and Levant wheat, barley, grapes, olives, dates, peas, figs, lentils, eggplant, cherries, cucumbers, and citrus fruits. Local farmers in northern Africa adopted many of these. Bananas and taro arrived first on the East African coast and were easily adapted to the tropical environment. Asian varieties of rice likely reached both northern and eastern Africa first and spread to other parts of Africa later. In special cases, some food exchange occurred without human traders. Some foods washed ashore, where they either germinated naturally or were collected and cultivated by people. The coconut, coming from Southeast Asia, likely arrived to the East African coast by way of ocean currents. Although contested, it is believed that the gourd was carried from Africa by ocean currents to South America or vice versa.

The promotion and acceptance of all these foods, however, depended on various conditions. Plant species either adapted well or were obstructed by the local environment. For example, coconuts and bananas fared well in humid environments but wheat and barley did not. Farming technologies also factored into the adoption of new foods. Groundwater and irrigation made date and citrus cultivation possible in dry land areas like the Sahara and its periphery. Storage was also an important factor. Peas and lentils could be dried and stored easily; eggplant and cucumbers had to be consumed shortly after harvest. Preparation also weighted the decisions communities took in adopting foods. The Mediterranean climate of

North Africa certainly contributed to the popularity of olives and grapes, but so too did the ability to convert grapes to wine and olives to olive oil (both of which simultaneously served as a means of storage). Finally, the cultural preferences of local regions weighted on which seeds were sown in their plots and which foods were sold in markets.

Africans traded their local sorghum, teff, other local millets, okra, and watermelons to the north and east with success. African millets easily grew in Eurasian climates that were too dry or too hot for crops like rice and wheat. Some African foods were not traded beyond local markets. There were three main reasons for this: rapid spoilage placing limits on transport, the methods of production, or cultural choice. African yams are one example of a crop that could not survive the difficult conditions on trade routes bringing foods to the Eurasian landmass. Palm oil and kola nuts are examples of products holding great significance to African diets but were of little use to Europeans and Asians, at least not until the late nineteenth century. Rice production in Africa, too, was limited to perennial water sources. In the other direction, some foods from the Eurasian landmass never reached African food markets due to impracticality of transporting perishables, such as spinach, or lack of interest, such as oats.

Trade in domesticated animals was robust: the camel, cow, horse, sheep, and goat came from Eurasia; the donkey was exported from Abyssinia. Debates exist as to whether the pig and fowl came originally through the Levant or East Africa. But here, as with foodstuffs, the adoption and expanded use of domestic animals were dependent on cultural acceptance and ecological opportunism. The camel, able to adapt to water-scarce areas, facilitated caravans on trade routes across the Saharan Desert and eastern Africa to expand trade with North Africa and, through ports, the more distant markets of Europe and Asia. Cattle promoted self-sufficiency as a source of recurring dairy products and meat for a household. This became a livelihood for many pastoralists in west, east, and southern Africa.

Meat and dairy from the cattle were consumed and traded with farming groups for grains and produce. Pigs did not become a major staple livestock as cattle, goats, and camel had. Part of this was due to their susceptibility to tropical diseases. Cultural restrictions placed by the Eastern Orthodox Church and Islam for abstaining from pork further limited pig husbandry. Thus, both early Africans and the environment dictated the changing nature of food production in Africa over the centuries. Over time, Africans diversified and adapted new foods into their diets through the importation of foods, animals, and agricultural technologies or innovations from Europe, Asia, and other African regions.

Trade with the New World

The age of exploration brought greater opportunities and foods to Africa and other continents in the following centuries. Despite the tropical diseases that prevented non-Africans from traveling into Africa's interior, Asians and Europeans developed maritime routes that established trading harbors along the African coastline. Asian merchants brought coffee, a native plant, from Abyssinia to Arabia. Southwest Asia produced and consumed the beverage for centuries to come. Later, in the twentieth century, coffee changed the livelihoods of farmers inhabiting arable land in montane climates, as global demand placed pressure on them to grow this mono crop.

The age of exploration also ushered in the Colombian Exchange, where African food producers and consumers diversified their crops and diets further after contact with the Americas by 1500 CE. North and South America, known as the New World were now connected through international shipping to the Old World. Corn, coming from the Americas, was a food that at first had minimal acceptance when planted at port colonies but did impact African livelihoods and diets over time. Despite its high consumption of water, corn yielded more food than African millets or rice, and when dried, it could be stored for years. Europeans grew this grain to feed both their sailors and their cargo; that is, humans they transported for the purpose of slavery. This was the era of the slave trade, and corn became the staple that facilitated the extent of the African diaspora over the long term. On the other end of the slave trade, the production of sugar cane in the Caribbean was made possible by the newly arriving slave labor. Sugar cane, a crop that originated in Eurasia, has little nutritional value, yet demand increased in the age of exploration, and the crop grew easily in tropical climates. Sugar plantations were established on tropical islands in both the Old and New World with European enterprises profiting from the use of African slave labor.

Trade Brought New Crops and Changed the Diet

Despite what consequences New and Old World foods had on African communities, the addition of the landmasses in the Americas to these international trade networks revolutionized African diets by bringing new foods first to the coastal communities and then to the peoples living in the interior. The slave trade did bring civil disorder to many African communities, but it also brought new foods: corn, potatoes, cassava (manioc), sunflowers, peanuts, sweet potatoes, varieties of beans, squash, pumpkins, tomatoes, peppers, avocados, guavas, and pineapples. Some foods were quickly adopted and their seeds carefully sown into African fields; others took longer, sometimes decades, if not centuries. For instance, the planting of potatoes was limited to European ports and settlements in southern Africa up until the nineteenth century. Only then were potatoes adopted by Africans inhabiting temperate-to-highland environments. Sweet potatoes reached popularity more easily and grew well in warm climates. The sweet potato was so popular it displaced the nutritionally superior indigenous yam.

The introduction of manioc from South America is an interesting case in the shaping of the African diet. Like the sweet potato, its introduction further contributed to the decline in yam production. It was a locust-resistant crop, grew well in poor soils, and was ideal for lowland tropical environments. These attributes convinced many African farmers to plant manioc. Unlike yams and sweet potatoes, however, manioc has poor nutritional value—at least under the known preparation methods in historical times. African communities that relied on manioc as a staple crop became vulnerable to malnutrition in the centuries that followed.

Despite its nutritional deficiency, manioc, like the other staple crops, maize and potatoes, contributed to increases in population growth. Historians have found that despite the depopulation resulting from the slave trade to the Americas, there was little impact to the total population of Africa. The population continued to grow.

The larger picture for this phenomenon is that human populations everywhere produced more and more food throughout the centuries by selecting foods that yielded greater harvests. Anthropological-archaeological evidence shows that humans at certain points in history had great diversity in their diets, including some foods no longer consumed today. Over the centuries, many forms of innovation, from seed selection to harvesting tools, allowed human populations to produce more food. More food is perhaps the single most important factor that contributes to the growth of populations in both past and present. In 1800, the world's population reached one billion; in 1930, it was at two billion; by 1990, it was five billion; and at present, it is counted at just over seven billion. By 2050, it is estimated the world's population will likely be around nine billion.

Modern Times Bring Loss of Nutrition and Diversity in the Diet

Those isolated observations made over a decade ago in Guinea and Mauritania are data points in the much larger story of what is happening to local food production and consumption worldwide. As the planet grows more crowded and food production becomes more streamlined into the hands of fewer and fewer producers, major shifts are taking place. The diversity of everyone's diet is diminished, and the reliance on imported or processed foods puts control over the foods we eat into the hands of agribusiness and not in the hands of small-scale farmers.

The ethical question is the same in Africa as it is in other countries: what does this transformation mean for the overall health of populations? Nutritionists argue that for people to consume only a select number of foods, particularly limiting oneself to eating just staples like maize, wheat, and rice, is neither beneficial to child development nor the overall quality of adult health. Our ancestors lived with greater food insecurity brought on by insects, drought, and other natural disasters, but on average, they ate foods of higher nutritional value and had more diversity in their diet than we do today.

Still, for Africa, the Colombian Exchange was a time when foods circulated through or were adopted into non-African diets. For example, bananas have their origins in Asia, but the word for the fruit is African. Easily digestible starch crops, such as taro, originated in Southeast Asia and spread in importance to tropical Africa millennia ago, and during the Colombian Exchange, taro was brought to the tables of families in South America. Also, foods that were confined to localities in the New World were introduced to other regions of the New World through African slave groups. Peanuts, rich in nutrients and high in protein, originate in South America. They did not arrive in the southern states of the United States until slaves introduced them, planting them in their new environment.

The 1500s to the 1800s was, however, an age where African stewardship over the crops grown and foods arriving at their markets was gradually slipping out of their control and into the hands of foreigners. As markets expanded, Europeans and, to some extent, Asians oversaw the trade and transportation at African ports; Africans were losing authority to those from other continents. It took centuries and was never a complete conquest, yet foreigners eventually began dictating not only the terms of trade at the ports they occupied, but also influencing, if not commanding, what farmers grew in neighboring areas. This would have profound consequences on the picture of African agriculture and markets once Europeans improved their medicines and technologies, allowing them to expand their jurisdiction into the interior of Africa.

The transformation of African lives during the period of the Colonial Exchange cannot be understated. From the abolition of the slave trade in the mid-nineteenth century to the large agriculture projects undertaken after World War II, Africans witnessed profound changes in their societies, agriculture, economies, and diets. First, Europeans imposed their choice of crops in African fields and what was sold in African markets. African populations continued increasing during the colonial era, and able-bodied workers, important to colonial administrations for the clearing of land, the building of infrastructure, and for military or civil service, were greatly needed. Corn, rice, and potato production in Africa expanded and increased, while imported grain (producing surpluses since the 1700s) also reached African markets to feed the growing populations.

Second, in terms of making their colonies profitable or useful to the metropole, the colonial powers pushed the production of mono crops for export on African farmers. The experiences during such agriculture transformations varied from an imposition on African farmers, to forced labor, to outright violence committed in the requisition of these products. Peanuts were one such product. They were grown in West and East African colonies, but not for local consumption. They were refined into lubricants for factories in Europe and later in the colonial period for cooking oils. Another product, rubber, was collected from trees or raised in plantations in Anglophone colonies in West Africa and the Congo Free State. European and Asian settlers, with the assistance of African labor in East African highlands, grew tea or coffee. Cotton was requisitioned by colonial officials in West, Central, and North Africa. Cocoa beans were originally a Mesoamerican crop, but West Africans began clearing land to cultivate the cocoa bean as an export commodity. Today, West African countries are responsible for 70% of the world's supply of cocoa beans.

Third, European preferences began to influence African diets. Colonial officials imported their tastes for coffee, tea, bread, and other foods made from wheat to the colonies they served in, and these new foods influenced African preferences. The importation of global wheat surpluses introduced the production of bread and other baked goods in sub-Saharan African colonies. Tea became a standard beverage in North and West Africa; coffee became a popular drink throughout sub-Saharan Africa. The cultivation of cocoa and coffee beans, crops that were limited in nutritional value in addition to being produced for the benefit of foreigners, diverted water, land, and labor away from local food production.

African agriculture was thus under pressure from the technologies and projects implemented by colonial officials as much as by the European tastes that began to permeate African communities. Dams were built, motor pumps were used to exploit reserves of groundwater, arable land was requisitioned to grow mono crops, and local African communities were disenfranchised as a consequence. How these foods and practices were efficacious or, more importantly, beneficial to African communities was not asked. They were part of a colonial system whose purpose was to extract natural resources from its colonies first and improve the well-being of African populations a distant second.

FOREIGN INFLUENCE EXPANDS IN AFRICA'S FOOD PRODUCTION

In the 1950s, 1960s, and 1970s, the work of African independence movements and anti-colonial sentiment among younger generations of Europeans led to the decolonization of Africa. Many African leaders continued the same socioeconomic path of growing mono crops or exporting natural resources, but in doing so, they made deals with international corporations, some of which worked in partnership with the former colonial power. This was problematic, as once a commodity (such as rubber, cotton, tin, bauxite, coffee, chocolate, or tea) dropped in price on the international market, so too did the needed funds to feed African populations. A few African leaders, recognizing the volatility of the international market, made efforts to dismantle the previous colonial socioeconomic systems but fell prey to corruption, mismanagement, or resistance from key administrators within various levels of government. In some cases, African communities became prone to food crises and, in extreme cases, famine. Media coverage of these disasters inspired the international community to act, but these actions sometimes had unintentional consequences and other times had ulterior motives attached to them.

The 1950s–1970s was the height of the cold war era. Food assistance coming from the USA, Western Europe, or from the Soviet Bloc arrived or was withheld based on political and economic allegiance. Furthermore, either through siding with a cold war power or attracting a nongovernmental organization (NGOs), when food aid did arrive to African markets, its timing affected local food production by offsetting local food prices. Instead of helping, this food aid set off a new set of debilitating effects on local food production. The drop in food prices had the negative consequence of farmers shifting instead to subsistence or abandoning farming altogether. Many fled to the cities for better work opportunities.

This led to the further consequence that African governments sought food assistance once again from outside. The post–World War II food aid to Africa programs thus set in motion forces that broke down local food production and created dependency relationships between African governments and foreign assistance.

The concept of dependency has different meanings to different audiences, but in African food production, it is a loss of self-sufficiency and reliance on foreign food producers to meet food demand. The country of Mali, a neighbor of Mauritania and Guinea to the east, is a good example of this. Before 1960, Mali was self-sufficient in its food production; in fact, it exported grain to neighboring countries. The 1960s were the era of independence for many African nations, and Mali was no exception. Mali's new political elite, both ambitious and revolutionary, promoted industry and engineering, diverting resources and attention away from small-scale agriculture. This restructuring lead to the problems of both mismanagement and corruption by some unscrupulous individuals, bankrupting Mali's economy and turning it from a food exporter to a food importer. When drought hit during 1968–1974, food aid from overseas only further drove Mali into a relationship of dependency with food producers from the outside.

A Downward Spiral of Dependency

Even in years of food security, Africa experienced the dumping of surplus foods on its markets coming from other continents. At this point, it no longer became about food being available at the market or the quality or variety of foodstuffs. Instead, finance and economics further distorted supply and demand relationships. Europe and North America had surplus staples readily available for export because farmers were paid with subsidies to produce more, while their markets were protected by high tariffs placed on food imports. This was a turning point for Africa, where imports started to outsell local farmer's crops at the African marketplace.

It was more than just the price of food when Africans went to markets to shop for themselves and their families. Upon returning to their villages, they witnessed how local productivity could not compete with imports. Like the Asian and South American peasant, most African farmers did not have the needed cash flow to pay for the hybrid seeds, fertilizers, pesticides, and machines to achieve the economies of scale that could compete with large farm operations well-established in Asia and South America. African farmers, like their contemporaries on these two continents, had to compete alongside the food surpluses coming from countries like India, Thailand, the Philippines, and Indonesia. These were made possible through the Green Revolution.

The person credited with starting the Green Revolution, Norman Borlaug (1914–2009), was both a humanitarian and a biologist. Among the scientists concerned about the exponentially growing human population, especially the high growth rates in developing nations like Mexico, Pakistan, and India, Borlaug worked on developing wheat hybrids in the 1940s to improve food security. His achievements were then emulated by other scientists working on hybrids for rice and maize. Together with the farming implements supplied by the Ford and Rockefeller Foundations, the Green Revolution took off with large agricultural operations in South America and Asia.

Food aid and foods produced through the Green Revolution were promoted and disseminated as entirely benevolent crops to feed the world. But in practice, the arrival of the Green Revolution constricted African states through restrictive new trade regulations, sometimes imposed on them by their former colonizer or a cold war power, other times by international lending institutions, such as the World Bank or International Monetary Fund (IMF). It was common practice for these outside organizations to encourage African governments to maintain the production of mono crops or practice mineral exploitation, leaving the governments dependent on price fluctuations on global markets.

RURAL AND URBAN DISPARITY

Outside actors are not the only forces undermining local food production. Africa is, as a whole, the most rural of all continents in the world, but this is changing. The disinterest in agriculture by many national governments and the newer African generation has made rural-to-urban flight, or urbanization, much more common. The growth of African urban centers predates colonial times, but under European rule, various educational and employment opportunities as well as essential services were centralized in towns and cities. In the countryside is where the burdens of colonial programs were felt most acutely. Farmers were forced to plant cash crops to meet their government's taxation demands. Another less common but more permanent threat was the displacement of peasants by mining operations seizing their customary lands through eminent domain.

The disparity between rural and urban life did not change during decolonization either. African families that had the means to move to the towns or cities found greater opportunities there. The gains to be made by someone living in the capital or larger towns and working as a mechanic, carpenter, retail worker, clerk, custodian, or security worker were greater than those living in the countryside as a small-scale farmer, herder, or fisherman. Yet the greatest catalysts increasing rural flight were the famines and civil wars. These caused high food vulnerability and insecurity in the countryside, while people in the urban areas had access to greater security and aid organizations, such as international NGOs providing food aid during these crises. As African families moved into the urban centers, they found opportunities for themselves and their children, and as greater risk persisted in the countryside, living in the towns became the only viable choice.

In the 1990s, with the African peasantry diminishing, African development took a turn in favor of rural people (at least on paper), as many national leaders and international agencies wrote laws and developed institutions for decentralization. This is a complex term, having various and different meanings to the parties involved, but in general, this policy was designed to transfer the decision-making powers and revenues needed for development away from the capital and to local, commonly rural, African communities. It was a program encouraged in order to end the civil strife and grievances that were voiced since the end of colonialism up through the 1980s. The difficulty was that these new laws and institutions at times came into conflict with other laws or government agencies already in place, or the revenues needed for developing rural communities were simply not available due to the commitments African states had with lenders such as the World Bank, the IMF, or other international banks based in Europe or North America. These conflicting interests and the resulting inaction maintained the disparity between rural people and urbanites, and the future of African decentralization remains unsure at best.

DEEPER CHALLENGES TO PROMOTING LOCAL FOOD PRODUCTION IN AFRICA

African demographics show three consistent trends. First, the total population is growing the fastest compared to other continents; second, the majority of the population is young; and third, these younger generations are motivated to leave the countryside for the towns or cities. These trends are also seen in other developing nations like China, Turkey, India, and Brazil. For Africa, young people are migrating for both cultural and personal reasons, and Mauritania is a good example. Slavery is still a chronic problem there. Slave owners could easily manage their slaves when they were tending the fields or livestock in the countryside. Young captives who manage to visit the cities and towns, however, today find informal social networks that assist them in finding opportunities with schools or vocational apprenticeships. Slavery is eroding as urban migration breaks the dependency captives have with their masters in rural areas.

Social Pressures and Change

In almost all African countries, married women who live in urban environments have greater educational opportunities, more opportunities for generating income, and better chances of establishing a network of friends. These are important sources of female empowerment because the women have more money to pool together during personal or household crises compared to married women dependent on their spouses who live in the countryside.

Even among families where young adults wish to remain with their families and assist on the farms or the pastures, there is pressure to migrate to the cities and towns. If they remained, there is an extra mouth to feed, yet if they leave to start earning an income at a job in a town center, it is more income for the family while younger siblings tend to the crops and herds.

Social and familial pressures that push young people to abandon the countryside are compounded by the forces pulling them to the towns and cities. Media shapes the perception of life in the city simply in the way young people are depicted. Irrespective of whether it is an international or African production, the movies, television, and ads on the Internet and in magazines that young people view convey a concise message: young people in urban environments always succeed in their studies or at their work; the countryside is a place to either vacation or retire. It will come as no surprise that when young people are depicted in these urban settings leading a good life or on a pathway to success, there is a Nestlé instant coffee, a Magnum ice cream bar, or a Coca-Cola in their hands. These images, no matter how superficial they may appear, have significant influence over young people's choices and the rural-to-urban migration trends.

Africa after Independence

The preceding example, where African youth are influenced by corporate products like Coca-Cola, is an example of a phenomenon many call globalization. Definitions for this term are numerous and contested, but if one applied this term to food, it could be defined as the exchange and adoption of new varieties of comestibles into local food production and consumption. If this is the case, then globalization occurred in Africa as early as the long-distance trade networks between Africa, Asia, and Europe. The type of globalization that existed centuries ago, however, is much different than the picture of agricultural production and consumption occurring today.

In the past, Africans localized which foreign foods made it to African markets. They were, in essence, the producers and the gatekeepers of the foods reaching their domestic markets. This local management shifted over time with the increasing domination of Europeans in the African marketplaces as their colonial interests took hold. Although Europeans withdrew or lost their political power to African elites by the latter half of the twentieth century, the colonial agricultural institutions they created left a legacy of dependency toward foreign governments and corporations. African states could not dismantle the monocropping infrastructure or the exploitation of raw materials without creating great economic or social turmoil. They remembered well the effects of drought or civil disorder in generating food insecurity and the immediate, desperate need for food assistance from Europe and North America. Even in times of stability and good harvests, commodity prices were rarely stable. Drops in a commodity's price forced African governments to borrow more from the World Bank and International Monetary Fund. Their debts rose to keep their economies afloat.

Africans today still produce food, but it is difficult to call them masters of their own destiny when foreign powers and corporations place their food aid and products on African markets while international lending organizations impose austerity measures that essentially bankrupt government services responsible for assisting local food producers.

Roots of Dependency

The roots of this dependency date back to colonial times. From the 1880s to the present day, foreign corporations gained momentum in either controlling or dominating African food production and food markets. For instance, Unilever partnered with the Belgian Congo and Anglo and French colonies along the West African coast in collecting palm oil at the start of the twentieth century. They now sell brands of tea, ice cream, and other comestibles throughout all of Africa. Coca-Cola derives the caffeine in its soft drinks from the kola nut found in West Africa and markets its soft drinks throughout Africa. Its main competitor, PepsiCo, entered the African marketplace later in the 1970s. Others, such as Kraft Foods and Nestlé, promote various processed foods like powdered milk, instant coffee, candies, ice cream, and cookies. These were once exclusively imported from afar. More recently, however, the expensive overseas imports are sold next to processed foods coming from manufacturers in the large African cities like Johannesburg, Accra, and Cairo.

The New Foreign Power

Other multinationals have made their gains in the African agricultural sector. Monsanto and Syngenta, although weakly established in Africa because of the high cost of their products, are gaining ground in supplying seeds, fertilizers, and pesticides to large-scale farm operations, which have the means to afford such inputs. Cargill stimulated the rise of cocoa bean production in West Africa after World War II, and it is now a large player in the production of cocoa and sugar cane in West Africa, as well as having a large stake in the global production of chocolate. These corporations influence what is grown in the African soil and have gained a foothold of power that creates an ongoing form of dependency for African farmers.

In an effort to diversify their economies, generate more revenue, build infrastructure, and promote job opportunities in the countryside, African governments started in the past 15 years to lease out large tracts of land to agribusinesses based in the Americas, Europe, and Asia. On paper, this appears as a win-win for everyone. It allows countries that are farmland-scarce, such as South Korea or Saudi Arabia, to grow and import foods for their populations while generating for African states needed revenue and labor opportunities in rural areas. With the increased presence of agribusiness, African states receive needed roads, ports, irrigation, schools, and hospitals. In practice, however, this recent development is controversial. It is widely referred to now as land grabbing. Local farmers are very often evicted from prime agricultural land. They become landless sharecroppers, wage laborers for these large-scale agricultural projects, or migrants seeking other employment in the urban areas. At the same time, water, fertilizer, and other agricultural inputs are monopolized by the export-oriented agribusinesses.

Ethiopia has already leased out 1.7 million hectares of its 2.7 million hectares of arable land to 8,420 foreign investors. Mozambique is currently witnessing the fastest rate of land grabs, as almost half its arable land is allotted to foreign interests, even ones like Brazil, which previously experienced land grabs itself. The African laborers hired by these companies generally work long hours under severe conditions and are paid poorly. What looked like a good idea at the outset is creating new forms of injustice. Whether these injustices will persist or be renegotiated in the future depends on the actions of the various institutions and stakeholders (African government, agribusinesses, and African communities) involved.

Agribusiness and the Environmental Cost

The agricultural inputs used by agribusinesses and on large-scale African farms are another major concern. Insecticides, pesticides, herbicides, and fungicides that are either banned or highly regulated in Europe and North America are exported and used on African croplands. They remain unregulated. DDT (Dichlorodiphenyltrichloroethane), methyl bromide, lindane, organophosphates, and paraquat (to name a few) are shipped to Africa to increase yields and used liberally and in hazardous ways at large-scale agricultural operations. These increases in yields are, as so often, only short-term. In Africa, as elsewhere, insect pests, weeds, and fungi often develop resistance to the chemicals used in eradicating them. Meanwhile, health consequences from using unregulated chemicals that are banned abroad impact African workers directly. Moreover, local water sources are contaminated, neighboring wildlife becomes threatened, and the broader African communities that are exposed to these chemicals in the air, soil, or water develop acute health problems over the long term.

Social Choice and Its Influence on Demand

The previous discussion showed the complexities African agriculture has faced in recent times. Current issues include concerns about younger generations leaving their villages for the urban centers, the interventions and influence of foreign agribusinesses, environmental degradation, and health consequences for people. These are only some of the challenges, however. The consumption side at the marketplace is also problematic. Consumers can support or break down local food production norms, as was happening in Guinea back in 2001. By their food choices, African consumers inadvertently affect the health of everyone in the community. By exercising a preference for purchasing imported and factory-processed foods over locally grown ones, shoppers squeeze out the small-scale African farmer. Aggressive marketing of these processed foods by corporations with big advertising budgets show success in African markets as they have in European or North American ones.

The most notable example of a corporation's marketing power is Nestlé and its efforts to promote its powdered milk products (such as its infant formula) in the 1970s. At the height of famines and civil war throughout many parts of Africa, Nestlé distributed infant formula to hospitals and famine relief organizations and sold such products on the African market, advertising its milk formulas as a good alternative to breast milk. Africans began using such products, but the consequences, like the adoption of manioc during the Colombian Exchange, meant disaster.

First, many African communities did not have access to potable water, and the mixing of the formula to feed their babies exposed infants to cholera and other waterborne diseases. Even when water sources were clean, parents on a limited income commonly diluted the formulas in order to economize the formula, with the devastating long-term consequence of causing malnutrition in their babies. It became known that instant formulas also lacked certain nutrients and antibodies needed for child development. But these health concerns did not pressure Nestlé to scale down its advertising.

Progress through Global Interaction

Globalization has contributed to a variety of destabilizers for Africa: the loss of agricultural land and stewardship of African land to foreigners, the dependency of selling monocrops or natural resources on volatile global markets, the importation or increase of processed foods into African diets, and, not least of all, chronic environmental and human health issues for Africans.

Globalization has also brought to the African continent the tools to fight these injustices. During the colonial era, much skullduggery was committed by colonial empires in Africa with little or no concern for reaction by the metropole or larger international community. This changed, however, with the influx of international organizations and technological advancements in communications starting in the post-colonial era. Despite what short-comings international NGOs had in bringing food aid and development to Africa, they have since refined their policies to include Africans and the social and ecological challenges Africans face into the dialogue. Today, there are local African NGOs and advocacy groups demanding the restoration of land stewardship to African communities.

Media coverage of the dependency and debt plaguing many African states, caused not by African ineptitude, but by international corpora-tions and lending institutions, has compelled movement toward greater transparency and equity in business dealings and in African governments. Through the use of cell phones and Internet, African communities have new tools to expose environmental injustices and health issues and gain supportive allies anywhere in the world. These are small steps, but these are advancements in the implementation of human rights, fair trade poli-cies, and international law. Significantly, they facilitate Africans regaining their voice in development.

FIGURE 4.2 A view of Sikasso market.

CONCLUSION

Somewhere in the long span of history, the stewardship of what is produced in African croplands and what is served at the African table became a power play for others. The interlopers (colonial authorities, government leaders, multinational corporations, international lending institutions, and NGOs), at various times and more callously than not, imposed alien foods, difficult quotas, and unfavorable terms of trade on the African peasantry. Add to these difficulties drought, the volatility of a commodity's price on the global market, civil wars, and the dumping of foods from overseas on African markets, all of which pushed African farmers to marginality. Despite the trend of African urbanization, however, the African peasantry did not vanish.

Peasants are still a major part of Africa's food production and are fighting for the restoration of their voice in agricultural development throughout all of Africa. These actors are not deeply entrenched in opposing camps though, nor is the contest a winner-take-all. In fact, African farmers would like better representation in their governments, a greater say in development, access to credit from lending institutions, be they national or international, and affordable farming inputs if they are to be supplied by international corporations.

There are choices African farmers make in their fields and customers make in the local markets that are not beneficial to the farmers in the long run and need redressing. Dependency on monocrops and a commodity's price on the global market are two factors contributing to livelihood instability. What is missing is a critical review of what peasants choose to grow. Some African farmers diversify their plots, raising grains, vegetables, fruits, and, when possible, a commodity like cotton, coffee, or rubber. But there are those who raise only one food or commodity crop and lack either the incentive or desire to grow others. A more in-depth look at what is grown and reaches markets would also reveal that some foods are chosen by farmers for easy maintenance and high yield (as was the case with manioc). This trend can homogenize food, break down diversity in the African diet, and cause greater health risks to Africans as a whole. This is where outside actors, NGOs, central governments, and international organizations can play a role in researching and promoting practical innovations in African cropland management and market food diversity, especially nutritious African foods (like yams). So far, for the most part, they have only promoted Western food crops.

On the consumer end, imported and processed foods have a role in African diets, particularly in food-insecure areas and during food crises. They are nonperishable, can be shelved for months, are convenient to the consumer, and in emergency responses provide relief to people who are vulnerable to illness or famine. It is also a benefit to the Africans employed in the food-processing plants found in cities such as Abidjan, Nairobi, Johannesburg, and Cairo and the farmers who supply the food processors. But these are a small minority compared to African peasants who must compete with aggressive marketing that undermines the confidence of the consumer in local foods (as was happening in Guinea). Instead, public media for Africans should create awareness that these foods are often not as nutritious as local foods. Thus, Africans do not need to choose one extreme or the other, but they do need greater representation (and control) in ensuring both local food production and the selection of imported, processed foods are complementary, improving and not undermining the other. It means food security for Guinea, for Mauritania, and for Africa as a whole.

GLOSSARY

Abyssinia: A historical nomenclature commonly used to describe the African empire that encompassed the Ethiopian highlands and Eritrea.

Agribusiness: A term combining the words "agriculture" and "business," it is commonly used for international agriculture corporations that produce and supply seeds, agrochemicals, farm machinery, food processing, marketing, and/or retail sales.

Colombian Exchange: The historical period after 1500 CE when populations, animals, plants, diseases, technologies, and ideas were exchanged between the *New World* (Western Hemisphere) and the *Old World* (Eastern Hemisphere).

Colonial Exchange: For Africa, this is the historical period after 1884 CE when Europeans began promoting the planting of mono crops and African diets were influenced by European tastes.

Decentralization: A contested term, but one that involves the transfer of powers, resources, functions, or people away from a central authority to peripheral areas.

Dependency: An economic relationship between a financially poorer country and economically more powerful nations.

Diaspora: A mass exodus of people from their homeland, commonly of an involuntary nature, such as the Atlantic slave trade, or a widely dispersed group outside its original homeland, such as Jews from Eastern Europe.

Ecological opportunism: When a particular environment has the conditions (climate, soil, minimal amount of competitors) necessary for a plant or animal to adapt and reproduce within that given environment.

Eurasia: The continents of Asia and Europe.

Food security: The ability for a population to secure food availability and accessibility over a foreseeable amount of time.

Globalization: A term with various interpretations; for the purposes of this chapter, it is the exchange of seeds, fruits, vegetables, etc. across continents and their influence on local diet and farming practices. Or, the influence of global economic positioning by outside interests as related to agriculture in Africa.

Green Revolution: A historical period, concentrated in the 1960s, when efforts were made to improve and increase global agricultural output, particularly in the developing world, through the use of modern science for improving yields, especially in staple grains like wheat and rice.

International lending institutions: A term commonly designated to the World Bank and International Monetary Fund; although it also refers to banks established by international organizations (European Union, North American Free Trade Agreement), these actors play a significant role in African development.

Land grabbing: A phenomenon that continues to spread in Africa where richer nations which are land poor or have large populations acquire large tracts of land in Africa to grow food for direct export back to their home countries.

Levant: A region known as the modern states of Syria, Lebanon, Israel, Palestine, and Jordan, these countries were a gateway for the *Trans-Eurasian Exchange*.

Metropole: The center of an empire.

Mesoamerica: A historical term used for the civilizations that existed before European contact from central Mexico to northern Costa Rica.

Mono crops: Also known as cash crops or export crops, these are agricultural crops that are not for subsistence, but instead for some type of return or profit. The term mono refers to the unitary emphasis on planting one crop at a time, which carries inherently higher risk and reward for the farmer.

Montane climate: Mountains, highlands, or high-elevation environment.

Multinational corporations: Also known as MNCs, multinational enterprises or international corporations, these are businesses that are headquartered in one country but operate in many other countries.

New World: The Western Hemisphere (North, Central, and South Americas).

Nomadic herding: A livelihood based on mobility where individuals or families herd livestock (typically sheep, goats, cattle) to take advantage of seasonal vegetation and water sources across a certain territory.

Old World: The Eastern Hemisphere (Africa, Asia, Europe, and Oceania).

Small-scale farmer: Also referred to as peasants, this is a livelihood where people depend on an area of land and favorable weather to produce subsistence or marketable crops.

Soviet Bloc: Also known as the Eastern or Communist Bloc, this was the confederation of communist states in eastern and central Europe, especially in the post–World War II era, until the fall of the Berlin Wall in 1989.

SUGGESTIONS FOR FURTHER READING

Blakie, P. et al. 1994. *At Risk: Natural Hazards, People's Vulnerability and Disasters*. London: Routledge.

Bond, P. 2006. *Looting Africa: The Economics of Exploitation*. London: Zed Books.

Bourne, Jr., Joel K. July 2014. "The Next Breadbasket." *National Geographic* 226(1): 46–71.

Bryceson, D., C. Kay, and J. Mooij, eds. 2000. *Disappearing Peasantries? Rural Labour in Africa, Asia and Latin America*. London: Intermediate Technology Publications.

Crosby, A. W. J. 2003. *The Colombian Exchange: Biological and Cultural Consequences of 1492*. Westport, CT: Praeger.

Daño, E. C. 2007. *Unmasking in the New Green Revolution in Africa: Motives, Players and Dynamics*. Penang: Third World Network.

Devereux, S., B. Vaitla, and S. Haunstein-Swan. 2008. *Seasons of Hunger: Fighting Cycles of Quiet Starvation among the Worlds Rural Poor*. London: Pluto Press.

Heiser, Jr., C. B. 2007. *Seed to Civilization: The Story of Food*. New Delhi: Indo American Books.

Jackson, W., W. Berry, and B. Colman. 1984. *Meeting the Expectation of the Land: Essays in Sustainable Agriculture and Stewardship*. San Francisco: North Point Press.

Lawrence, G., K. Lyons, and T. Washington, eds. 2010. *Food Security, Nutrition and Sustainability*. London: Earthscan.

Magdoff, F., J. Bellamy-Foster, and F. Buttel. 2000. *Hungry for Profit: The Agribusiness Threat to Farmers, Food and the Environment*. New York: Monthly Review Press.

McCann, J. 2005. *Maize and Grace: A History of Maize in Africa*. Cambridge, MA: Harvard University Press.

Mittal, A. and M. Moore. 2009. *Voices from Africa: African Farmers and Environmentalists Speak Out Against a New Green Revolution in Africa*. Oakland, CA: The Oakland Institute.

Patel, R. 2007. *Stuffed and Starved: Markets, Power, and the Hidden Battle for the World's Food System*. London: Portobello.

Polyani, K. 1944. *The Great Transformation*. Boston: Beacon Press.

Sauer, C. O. 2011. *Agricultural Origins and Dispersals: The Domestication of Animals and Foodstuffs*. Charleston, SC: Nabu Press.

Sen, A. K. 1981. *Poverty and Famines: An Essay on Entitlement and Deprivation*. New York: Oxford University Press.

Shiva, V. 1992. *The Violence of the Green Revolution: Third World Agriculture, Ecology and Politics*. New York: Zed Books.

Van der Veen, M., ed. 1999. *The Exploitation of Plant Resources in Ancient Africa*. New York: Kluwer Academic/Plenum.

Vandermeer, J. 2009. *The Ecology of Agroecosystems*. Sudbury, MA: Jones and Bartlett.

Zohary, D. and M. Hopf. 2000. *Domestication of Plants in the Old World*. Oxford: Clarendon Press.

Chapter 5

GLOBAL CLIMATE CHANGE AND ANDEAN REGIONAL IMPACTS

BY CARMEN CAPRILES

INTRODUCTION

Planet Earth has been through many extreme temperature fluctuations in the eons of geological time, yet this is the first time that climate is changing due to human activity, and scientists have good evidence to prove both the causes and the effects.

The scientific evidence of the last decades has confirmed that global warming is a fact and is the main cause of climate change around the world. While this is not the first time that our planet has suffered extreme changes in temperature, it is the first time that the balance has been altered by human activities and it has occurred in a relatively small range of time when compared to other extreme climatic eras.

Although climate variability is a natural phenomenon that we can study through meteorology and many other scientific disciplines, climate change involves man-made activities and recognizes no boundaries. For this reason it is considered a global problem. It is becoming a political issue which requires us to understand the science behind it, the social and economic situation related to the causes and the effects, and the urgent need to act in order to avoid a bigger crisis.

Climate change is arguably the biggest challenge that humanity has faced until now; therefore, it is important to take the problem into account and realize that the solutions require global effort and strong political will. There is a need to learn more about the problem to realize how our daily decisions at every scale of society can help improve this situation. If we multiply our efforts in a positive way, we will create healthy communities that can take action at the local level and scale up to the global level.

This chapter explains the basic concepts for climate change and its precursors; we will try to understand the anticipated global consequences by looking at the Andean Region and how global warming is putting life-giving water resources at risk. We will examine how people are already being impacted—both by the lack of water in some places and by an excess of water in others.

By providing the basic concepts related to climate change, we hope to help you understand the complexity of the interrelated effects to the atmosphere, hydrological cycle, and biosphere, and to appreciate, or perhaps join, the effort for international measures that can help reduce the impacts. We hope that each reader will be encouraged to examine this subject in meaningful ways and to identify how it relates to their everyday life.

WEATHER AND CLIMATE

The Atmosphere

The atmosphere is a mixture of gases and other non-gaseous elements like dust and other suspended particles called aerosols. This mixture goes around the planet and covers the earth. The atmosphere is very important for life; the gases it contains include the oxygen that we breathe and the water vapor transformed into humidity that prevents dehydration. Since almost all living things are made up of mostly water, life on Earth needs humidity in the air.

The estimated proportion of gases found in our atmosphere is

- Nitrogen = 78%
- Oxygen = 20%
- Argon = 0.93%
- Other gases known as greenhouse gases = 0.93%
  - ◊ Carbon Dioxide = 0.04%
  - ◊ Hydrogen, neon, cryptonym, helium, xenon, and ozone in tiny percentages.

The atmosphere's composition is fairly constant from the ground to a height of 100 kilometers. This is due to the continuous turbulence that maintains a more uniform mixture of gases; this turbulence is produced by the air currents.

The gases that surround the earth also protect it from the powerful radiation during the day and at night prevent an excessive loss of heat and energy. Without the atmosphere above us, temperature at day would heat up to 95° C and at night it would plummet to 180 ° C below zero, making the planet unsuitable for life as we know it. Instead, we benefit from a global average surface temperature of 15° C, which is very comfortable for us, and many other forms of life.

The Weather

The weather is the product of the daily interaction of regional or local atmospheric elements that generate changes in temperature, rainfall (rain, snow, hail, etc.), humidity (the amount of water vapor that exists in the air), wind, and cloud cover (solar radiation) at the local level. Thanks to the winds, the gases that make up the atmosphere circulate around the planet. The weather conditions can vary from one day to another and from one place to another, while the weather behaves consistently and predictably over considerable periods of time.

The weather is different from the climate. The climate, for example, will determine what kind of plants and animals live in a specific location, and especially what kind of crops and food production one can have. In contrast, the weather will determine if it is going to be a good year for the crops or not. This is especially noticeable in places where there are no irrigation measures, such as high mountain areas. If the year is too dry, farmers may lose most of the production, but they can keep on planting the same crop because the climate is the same and the next year could bring more rain again.

The Climate

The climate is a set of all atmospheric phenomena and weather conditions such as temperature variation, the rate of precipitation or rain, the

Some of our ancestors—the sages and wise elders of the community as well as farmers and gardeners—have information about the kind of weather that is coming and how to predict the weather. Thanks to continuous observation of certain signs over the ages that help us know what to expect, most of the agricultural harvests over the years have depended very much on the knowledge of weather and its patterns

Some of the indicators most commonly used in the field are the starry sky and clouds, and the behavior of some birds and frogs. Even the stones and the moon are used to predict whether it will rain or we will have a good harvest.

intensity, frequency, and wind direction, etc. that are repeated over a long period of time: periods of several years, centuries, or millennia. It refers to the state of atmospheric conditions that influence a given area based on the flow of energy from the sun.

The climate is determined by the geographical position, altitude (height above sea level), the types of winds, and the distance from the equator and the sea; these factors will also determine the type of plants and animals that are able to live in a specific area.

GREENHOUSE EFFECT

The greenhouse effect is a process where the atmosphere absorbs energy by a curtain of gases that retain the solar radiation. During the day, the sun warms the surface of the earth, generating heat. Much of it escapes into space at night, but some is retained thanks to the gases found in the atmosphere that have the ability to absorb and emit radiation at specific wavelengths—as energy or as heat.

This system, where gases in the atmosphere act as a protective, transparent cover around the earth, lets the sunlight in and retains enough heat, which helps maintain a constant temperature at the surface of the planet. Without our atmosphere, the temperatures would be so extreme that most species could not survive. The greenhouse effect can be illustrated by the glass roof of a greenhouse that lets in light and retains heat, allowing plants to grow very well—if the greenhouse itself is well regulated.

Without greenhouse gases, the heat from the sun would bounce back immediately from the surface and would be lost in space. The greenhouse gases are important for regulating the temperature of the earth, but in higher concentrations they can increase the temperature to dangerous ranges for life on this planet. A greenhouse made of glass will become a graveyard for the plants inside if the glass panes and doors cannot be released to circulate air and humidity and the heat becomes trapped inside.

The Greenhouse Gases

The greenhouse gases have a very low atmospheric concentration (less than 1%), but are of fundamental importance in increasing the temperature of the air near the ground, stabilizing it at a range of values suitable for the existence of life on the planet. We can measure these concentrations as we

TABLE 5.1: Greenhouses Gases Found in the Earth's Atmosphere

The Most Abundant Naturally Occurring Greenhouse Gases	The Most Abundant Man-Made Greenhouse Gases
Water vapor (clouds)	Halogenated (HCFs or HCCs) or halocarbons
Carbon dioxide (CO_2)	Chlorofluorocarbons (CFCs)
Nitrous oxide (N_2O)	Sulfur hexafluoride (SF_6)
Methane (H_4C)	Hydrofluorocarbons (HFCs)
Ozone (O_3)	Perfluorocarbon (PFC)

do temperature and other invisible atmospheric elements. The presence of each greenhouse gas is measured by its concentrations in the atmosphere as ppm or parts per million, where 10,000 ppm = 1%.

As we see in Table 5.1, there are a number of naturally occurring gases, many of which are familiar to us, and there are a number that are man-made gases, usually of industrial origin.

The industrial gases are emitted from their specific sources of production which may be anywhere in the world, but they are distributed to the atmosphere that surrounds the entire Earth. The gases that do not have a naturally occurring source but come from a man-made source have a greater potential to become concentrated and thus heat the atmosphere. Some can absorb 300 times more heat than CO_2.

The Impact of Atmospheric Gases on Global Surface Temperature

After millions of years and thanks to the greenhouse effect, the average surface temperature of our planet has been stabilized at 15°C as we mentioned before. The actual range of temperature allows for the existence of liquid water, which is essential for life. Since we, as well as most other plants and animals, consist mostly of water, this is of great consequence. Obviously, hardly any living organism on Earth today would survive if planetary temperatures ranged from -180° C to 95° C daily.

But this is where the trouble starts. Our modern society is based on the paradigm of "unlimited growth and development" that depends on a high consumption of fossil fuels and an intensive use of resources. This modern paradigm and the lifestyles made possible by industrialization and global transportation are causing a rise in the concentration of man-made gases—especially CO_2—in the atmosphere. As a result, we have a high greenhouse gas concentration in the atmosphere; therefore, global average surface temperature is rising.

GLOBAL WARMING

As we mentioned previously, the greenhouse effect is a natural process by which the atmosphere regulates (through absorption, reflection, and radiation) the temperature of the planet, which makes it suitable for life. Global warming is caused by higher concentrations of emissions of greenhouse gases from human activities in excess of what the planet can regulate. These emissions slowly and continuously have been heating up the global average surface temperature.

Global warming is caused by an increase above an acceptable range in the concentration of greenhouse gases in the atmosphere. Scientists have identified a number of main causes worldwide. This increase is related to the substantial rise in fossil fuel energy consumption, especially since 1850. As you learned in chapter two, fossil fuels include coal, petroleum, and natural gas; these concentrated forms of carbon produce energy when burned in power plants or in combustion engines, such as in automobiles. As they burn, they release CO_2. Similarly, agricultural activity and livestock release methane, or CH_4. Industrial emissions from manufacturing contribute most of the other emissions.

By most accounts, around 85% of greenhouse gas emissions that contribute to global warming have being generated in historically wealthier countries whose economies depend on intensive energy use. Though we do not fully understand all the processes that occur within the earth and atmospheric system, and we are not totally sure how this will have an impact on the different life form systems on the planet, we do have enough data to reasonably conclude that humans are the reason why climate is changing currently and may continue to do so during our lifetimes.

There is something else we know with reasonable certainty. To counteract the effect of rising temperatures associated with increased concentrations of greenhouse gases, we need to lower the rate and quantity of industrial emissions into the atmosphere. In that sense it is important to establish some kind of control over man-made emissions as soon as possible to slow down global warming. We also want to replace some emissions-intensive technologies with those that do not emit greenhouse gases (carbon neutral) or those that emit less (low carbon). At the individual scale, this can mean replacing gas engines with electric powered vehicles; at the larger scale, this can mean solar power instead of coal-fired power plants.

When the greenhouse effect became well known and understood, scientists developed additional theories based on statistical models and simulations. These models predicted a future rise in temperatures around the planet

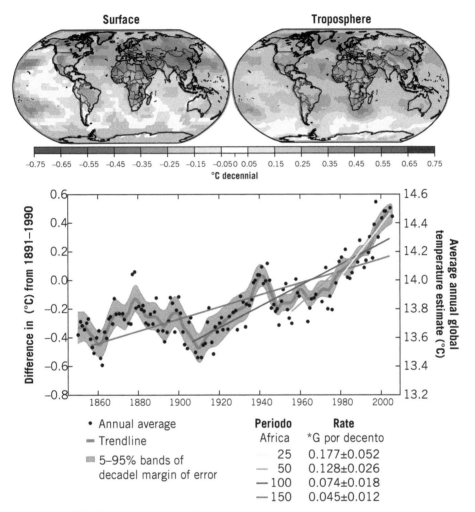

Surface   Troposphere

| | | | | | | | | | | | | | | | |
| -0.75 | -0.65 | -0.55 | -0.45 | -0.35 | -0.25 | -0.15 | -0.050 | 0.05 | 0.15 | 0.25 | 0.35 | 0.45 | 0.55 | 0.65 | 0.75 |

°C decennial

- Annual average
- Trendline
- 5–95% bands of decadel margin of error

Periodo Africa	Rate *G por decento
25	0.177±0.052
50	0.128±0.026
100	0.074±0.018
150	0.045±0.012

FIGURE 5.1 Global temperature trends.
Source: IPCC.

and gave the scientific community much to debate and reasons to create more sophisticated measurements of what is happening all over the earth. From here they developed models to predict, in an approximate matter, the impacts on different areas around the world. These models combined different kinds of data records. They take into account the influence of human activity and changes in temperatures measured on the surface of the earth, in the atmosphere, in the oceans, and at the poles in recent decades.

CLIMATE CHANGE

Climate change is what we call the most recent observed compilation of scientifically measured phenomena on Earth. While scientists have been able to trace periods of massive change in climate over tens of thousands of years, they now synthesize data from many different fields, from atmospheric sciences to dendrochronology, that show that climate change is happening more rapidly in our time, and that increased greenhouse gas emissions resulting from human activities are a primary suspect. The greenhouse gases which contribute to global warming are troublesome because an increase in temperature of even a few degrees Celsius has a direct impact on the different climates found all over the planet.

The earth regulates itself through a variety of cycles, some of which occur annually, others occur more intermittently. As the earth adjusts to steadily increasing temperatures, extreme weather conditions may occur. These can cause localized damage or profound changes to ecosystems. These alterations, such as alterations to the frequency and intensity of sporadic weather patterns like El Niño (also known as ENSO) in the Pacific Ocean, as well as short-term and longer-term changes in rainfall patterns locally, are considered to be indicators for climate change.

According to the 4th Assessment Report of the Intergovernmental Panel on Climate Change (IPCC),[1] the measures made on a 100-year linear trend (1906–2005) demonstrate a global average increase in temperature of 0.74° C. The IPCC report confirmed that temperature increase is widespread over the globe and is greater at higher northern latitudes.

Continental regions have warmed faster than the oceans. Temperature increase for the oceans has other future implications, discussed in chapter six. Currently the warming of the ocean is matched with something of greater immediate concern: a rising sea level. Global average sea level has risen since 1961 at an average rate of 1.8 mm/yr and since 1993 at 3.1mm/yr. It is a combination of factors, including thermal expansion and the melting of glaciers, ice caps, and polar ice sheets which contribute to this rise at the shorelines. A measurement of several millimeters may seem like nothing, but it has profound implications for low-lying countries and many islands.

---

1 Contribution of Working Group I to the Fourth Assessment Report of the Intergovernmental Panel on Climate Change, 2007, Solomon, S., D. Qin, M. Manning, Z. Chen, M. Marquis, K. B. Averyt, M. Tignor and H. L. Miller (eds.) Cambridge University Press, Cambridge, United Kingdom and New York, NY, USA. https://www.ipcc.ch/publications_and_data/ar4/wg1/en/tssts-3-1-1.html.

TABLE 5.2 Short- and Long-Term Effects of Climate Change

Short-Term Weather Effects	Long-Term Effects
More severe droughts	Rising temperatures
More floods	Disappearing glaciers
More hail	Transformed ecosystems
More widespread frost	Larger oceans
Stronger winds	Shrinking coastlines
More intense tornados	Thawed permafrost at high latitudes
More intense hurricanes and typhoons	Increased desertification

What to Expect

According to current expectations and scientific understanding, not all places will suffer the same alterations in climate-related events. Some places will have more obvious alterations than others. Over the long term, some of the expected impacts include changes in the frequency, intensity, and season of rains, winds, and snow cover. This does not necessarily predict a better snow season for alpine skiers. Rather, some places will get far more and some places will get less than they are receiving now. To talk about climate change is to talk about a global phenomenon that will continue to show a high degree of variability, that has different manifestations at local and regional scales, but that on average will, at the global scale, produce great changes to climates as we have known them.

Scientists are concerned about climate change because it means thinking about consequences - some potential, some unavoidable. Change is already appearing in different kinds of weather events from regular rainstorms to hurricanes. Recent years have demonstrated short-term variability outside of previously understood norms for the seasons, such as extremely cold winters in eastern North America, flash flooding events, or the size of hailstones. Should these continue, this will result in long-term effects, for example changes in vegetation. It is important to identify the short-term effects as indicators of what we can expect for long-term impacts, but we must remember that not all short-term effects will result in long-term effects.

Causes of Climate Change

The greatest and most disturbing contributor to climate change is CO_2, so it frames the discussion about how to mitigate climate change. Most scientists agree that climate change is a result of the increase of greenhouse gases and the consequent enhancement of the greenhouse effect. This is a by-product of human activities including the burning of fossil fuels and land-use change. These two activities significantly affect the concentrations of greenhouse gases that produce more heat in the atmosphere. Remember too that the increase in CO_2 is directly related to the increase in global temperature.

The data for 2010 shows that 90% of the CO_2 in the atmosphere comes from burning fossil fuels, 1% from the cement industry, and the other 9% from land-use change. The CO_2 produced has three main destinations: around 50% goes to the atmosphere, 26% is reabsorbed into land, and 24% ends up in the oceans.[2]

The mitigation discussion is also framed by the ranking of the most serious CO_2 emitting countries. Data for recent years shows that emerging economies—those considered as developing countries—are emitting more than those classified as developed countries. This is interesting for two reasons. First, we consider current emissions in order to quantify and rank the most serious atmospheric polluters. Second, we are interested in curbing future emissions with a sense of equity and fairness among countries, whether they are developed or developing. For example, China currently emits more than the United States[3] due to its rapid industrialization, increase in manufacturing, and overall development—but historically, China has contributed far less CO_2 emissions. This creates a big question for all countries to grapple with in global forums such as the UN General Assembly and during the COP talks: What is an equitable development path for countries that do not have a historical share in the problem but are ready to develop today?

This is a significant question because scientists concur that global average emissions need to stabilize and, in fact, decrease. Recent studies based on historic climate data have concluded that we need to lower CO_2 emissions to a concentration of approximately 350 parts per million (ppm) to stabilize the planet's average global surface temperature and to slow down the changes happening at the poles.[4] The challenge is that data shows a consistent upward trend. Atmospheric concentration of CO_2 shows an increase of 2 ppm per year during the last 10 years, as we can observe in Table 5.3, and it is 40% greater than preindustrial levels.[5]

---

2 Le Quéré et al. 2009, Nature Geoscience 2009, Canadell et al. 2007, PNAS 2010. http://co2now.org/.

3 The Guardian, "World Carbon Dioxide Emissions Data by Country: China Speeds Ahead of the Rest," http://www.theguardian.com/news/datablog/2011/jan/31/world-carbon-dioxide-emissions-country-data-co2.

4 Hansen, J. 2009. *Storms of my Grandchildren.*

5 Annual CO_2 Data from the National Ocean and Atmosphere Administration, USA (NOAA): NOAA-ESRL Fund. Available at http://co2now.org/.

TABLE 5.3 Annual Average Concentrations of CO_2 from 1959 to 2014

Source: NOAA.

Year	Annual Average of CO_2/ppm	Notes
2014	401.88	April, first time the monthly average is over 400 ppm of CO_2 IPCC Fifth Assessment Report
2013	396.48	May, first time 400 ppm of CO_2 in the atmosphere is measured
2011	391.57	Action Durban Platform (UNFCCC)
2009	387.38	Copenhagen Accord (UNFCCC)
2007	383.77	Bali Action Plan (UNFCCC)
2001	371.02	IPCC Third Assessment Report
1997	363.71	Kyoto Protocol
1992	356.38	Earth Summit
1987	349.16	The last year when the annual CO_2 level was less than 350 ppm
1959	315.97	The first year with a full year of instrument data

The last two years have shown record-breaking averages for annual and monthly measurements of 400 ppm, thus we are currently 50 ppm above the calculated maximum safe emissions measurement.

The last year where the annual average CO_2 level in the atmosphere was less than 350 ppm was 1987.[6] In the same year, the Brundtland Report[7] (also known as *Our Common Future*) made the following statement about sustainable development: "Sustainable development has to ensure that it meets the needs of the present without compromising the ability of future generations to meet their own needs." As countries continue to fail to find agreement on real solutions to global warming, the ability of current and future generations to meet their own needs has already been compromised. Though the ppm measurements seem abstract to the average person, their precision and consistency should be a wakeup call for us to realize that a different approach is needed to protect life on Earth.

Quality of life has been measured as development status in comparison with other countries. Inequalities exist at every level, but our focus should continue to be raising equality without erasing habitability. Most developing countries have a very low emissions rate from burning fossil fuels, but these countries are accountable for burning their forests as a process of

---

6 CO_2 Data, Scripps Institution of Oceanography, CO_2 Program, http://co2now.org/current-co2/co2now/annual-co2.html.

7 *Report of the World Commission on Environment and Development: Our Common Future*, Chapter 2, http://www.undocuments.net/ocf-02.htm.

land-use change. The burning of forests in tropical lowlands, and especially in the Amazon, not only produces large amounts of carbon dioxide and methane but also produces carbon soot or black carbon. These air pollutants are compounded by the burning of biomass and swidden agriculture.

Fossil Fuels

Burning as a human activity on land is a wily culprit, from the simplest farmer burning off his crop residues to the most sophisticated industrial power plants. Burning any organic material or the combustion of fuels such as diesel or gasoline releases carbon that reacts with free oxygen and forms CO_2. Burning fossil fuels are a primary focus for industrialized nations, especially in the northern hemisphere, because emissions from easily identifiable point sources, such as coal or cars, have been steadily increasing in the second half of the twentieth century.

As countries develop, they build more power plants and factories, add more automobiles, and thus produce more emissions into the atmosphere. The rub of course is that the emissions from one country are shared by the atmosphere over all countries. Thus the impact on the cycling of gases is shared by all as well. As developing countries want to take part in the higher standard of living associated with more automobiles and electricity-intensive goods and services, the need for them to produce more energy grows with it. China's development in the last 20 years is a perfect example of this. The way to produce energy in the twentieth century was to rely on petroleum, coal, and natural gas. Our hunger for more energy was satisfied by burning these fossil fuels, and China, as but one example, did exactly that as it developed.

In recent years, during the beginning of the twenty-first century, we have scientific understanding, if not political agreement, on a few points with regard to fossil fuels. First, we have reached peak oil, which means that the global supply will continue to dwindle, necessitating the search for a fuel source after petroleum becomes unviable. Second, burning fossil fuels releases CO_2, which we now understand has negative consequences that we must begin to curtail to protect our atmosphere. Third, many advantages could be gained by replacing burning as a human activity with other forms of energy production. This includes the renewable energy sources and production in chapter four. Last but not least, the responsibility to lead on the mitigation of climate change lies with the developed countries.

Land-use Change—Deforestation

Land-use change is the process of deforestation taking place at a large scale in the rainforest belts of the tropics. The most commercially valuable trees (many of them hundreds of years old) are cut first for the global wood market; second the trees with limited commercial value are sold as firewood, for charcoal and local use. The remaining vegetation is burned away to the roots to prepare the land for crops. Often this means cash crops grown in monocultures and plantations. These include soybeans, corn, sugarcane, and oil palms. Alternatively, the land is converted to pasture to raise cattle for beef production.

The discussion about the value of crops to sustain people is left to other chapters in this volume. For the purpose of this chapter on climate change, we focus on the value of the forests left standing. Their value can be measured both quantitatively and qualitatively.

The Value of a Tropical Forest

Tropical forests are widely known to have the highest concentrations of plants and animal species. Public awareness about the value of tropical plants in medicine and the loss of tree frogs (a symbol for the loss of biodiversity) has been growing since the 1992 Earth Summit in Rio de Janeiro. But there is deeper significance to the presence and preservation of the world's remaining forests.

Trees are irreplaceable components for regulating Earth's biogeochemical cycles. Carbon in nature is present in solid form in living organisms including both plants and animals. It is nontoxic and nonreactive, but it forms compounds easily. When carbon is released into the atmosphere through respiration (in animals), carbon dioxide is formed, and photosynthesis (in plants) transforms that carbon dioxide back into oxygen. In other words, carbon dioxide is absorbed from the atmosphere.

The cycling of oxygen and carbon dioxide in the atmosphere is not only essential for our respiration, but we now understand that the existence of forests helps mitigate carbon dioxide emissions. Scientists have coined a term for the nutrient cycling that trees perform. Forests are valued quantitatively in climate change science as carbon sinks. By absorbing CO_2 from the atmosphere, forests, and every tree left standing, are an asset in the race to slow down global warming and lower the ppm counts discussed above.

Another way science quantifies forest value is in carbon sequestration. This refers to the storage of carbon, which forests do through the presence of trees, but also through the soils and decaying organic matter on the forest floor. When countries such as Malaysia, Indonesia, and Brazil cut down their swaths of forest, it impacts the global atmospheric benefits that carbon sequestration would continue to provide to everyone.

So far we have seen examples of a forest's extrinsic value. There is also an argument to be made for leaving forests intact because they have intrinsic value. Tropical rainforests are considered the most diverse ecosystems on Earth. But with a high rate of deforestation, habitat loss compounded by global warming means that between 50 to 85% of the existing species on Earth will be gone forever by the end of this century. Deforestation affects entire categories of taxonomy including primates, amphibians, ferns, and reptiles. It destabilizes ecosystems when a species disappears forever, but intrinsic value gives us an additional insight. There is value in the existence of each species of animal and plant in the forest, and also in the existence of forest people.

Forests are home to about 1.6 billon people worldwide. Many of those who rely on forests belong to tribes and communities of indigenous people. They have understood the intrinsic value of the forests they belong to since they first settled in them. Though dispersed without contact to each other, they share some attributes. They have preserved their own languages and their ways of living in the forests. They take only what they need, by knowing what animals to hunt, what fishes to fish, and which plants are good for eating or for healing. Much of their knowledge has not been documented, so if the forest each tribe lives in disappears, they lose their homes and their way of life. Global culture is impoverished when we lose the last remaining forest people.

When tropical forests are only valued extrinsically for short-term logging interests, many of the indigenous people of the forest are not going to survive the rapacious hunger for resources. Recognizing the intrinsic value of these people, of tropical biodiversity, and of the forest's contribution to carbon sequestration is an important message for Western society to absorb.

Other Greenhouse Gases

Methane

Methane is a greenhouse gas that is a cause for increasing concern in the climate change discussion. This concern arises because methane occurs both naturally and from certain human activities, and because methane traps solar radiation more efficiently than carbon dioxide, thus contributing to faster global warming. On the timescale of 100 years, methane has the capacity to heat the atmosphere 23 times more than CO_2.

Natural sources of methane include anaerobic bacterial decomposition in wetlands and rice paddies. Current concern over methane from food production centers on livestock, particularly the increase in cattle for beef production. The main contributors to global methane emissions from livestock are cows, specifically their digestive process as ruminants and subsequent releasing of gas. Other ruminants such as camels, sheep, and goats also produce methane, so livestock numbers and concentrations influence global methane emissions.

Fossil fuel extraction releases methane as a natural by-product of natural gas extraction. Methane is released at all stages of natural gas handling, from below ground to distribution and transportation above ground.

Large-scale waste management through landfilling also produces significant quantities of methane. Methane builds up inside the landfill through bacterial decomposition and is released through vent pipes inserted through the landfill caps.

The most remote methane repository is permafrost. Methane is stored (with carbon dioxide) as buried carbon originating from decaying organic matter from long ago, and it is frozen in place. As permafrost has begun to thaw with global warming in the Arctic regions, the potential for methane to be released at a large scale becomes a subject for ongoing scientific study. There is so much carbon stored in permafrost that it is measured in gigatons (one gigaton =one billion tons).

Natural and man-made methane emissions contribute significantly to global warming but are manageable and controllable at several sources. Two methane sources here are key: methane is produced as a by-product in natural gas extraction and landfills which can potentially be converted into energy—see the waste and energy chapters in this volume. This could initiate a series of long-term benefits, from greenhouse gas emissions reduction to energy production to mitigating climate change.

IMPACTS OF CLIMATE CHANGE

The biggest concern is how much the earth will warm in the foreseeable future and what effect this will have for all life on the planet. Three life support systems that will be altered by the imbalance caused by climatic changes are water, food security, and energy supply. These concern us on many levels and at every scale, so for this chapter, we introduce them as a helpful framework.

Water

The greatest impact to water resources has been ongoing for some decades already and has dramatic consequences. This is the gradual but accelerating melting of the glaciers and ice sheets. By some estimates, the melting of polar ice sheets can no longer be stopped. This means that at some point in the not-too-distant future, the Arctic will be ice free. This is a boon to global shipping, but we are not totally sure what acceleration effect this will have on global warming. The melting is leading to sea level rise.

Worst of all, this will result in an energy imbalance due to cold and freshwater mixing up with salty and warmer seawater. This reaction is already manifesting in a wide range of climatic phenomena like stronger hurricanes and typhoons for coastal areas. Temperature alterations contribute to acidification of the oceans, as discussed in the next chapter, and lead to irreplaceable biodiversity losses.

Therefore we must understand that an increase of temperature will have a direct impact on the cycling of water on Earth. More evaporation or melting ice sheets than we have already seen will change rainfall patterns in some places and cause droughts in others. The potential for a positive feedback loop feeding itself is high. This is why addressing the root causes of global warming is so important if we want to avoid the further unfolding of the anticipated effects we call climate change.

Food

Climate change threatens to reduce agricultural production due to higher average temperatures and shortfalls in water for irrigation and livestock. For Andean countries, the increase of frost and drought and the rapidly melting glaciers, which are the main water source, further compound the risks for agricultural production. Without glaciers, the rainfall could alter the Amazon basin ecosystem, which would then eventually run the risk of becoming desertified. Also, pest populations and disease vectors will increase because of the changes to the ecosystem. All of this will be reflected in new risks for local people if this kind of disruption affects all the rural livelihoods of the populations in the region.

The productive soil and water systems are beginning to deteriorate. Such seemingly small changes pose a huge challenge though, particularly to those relying most on native flora and natural resources for their survival. In the Andean regions, this applies especially to women using natural resources for household needs. It is critical to build resilience to these shifting patterns in available natural resources locally, and to mitigate the causes of climate change globally.

Energy

Dependence on energy from petroleum when it is past its peak is unsustainable. Petroleum energy will become more expensive as less and less of it is efficiently retrievable. Like any other commodity, petroleum is subject to supply and demand. Demand may continue to increase, but if supply does not, rising prices will collapse the demand.

The connection of energy to climate change is such that preparing a transition to renewable resources is not only important to lower greenhouse gas emissions, but shifting to solar, wind, water, and other emerging energy sources will shift the demand away from dwindling supplies and environmentally polluting petroleum.

CLIMATE CHANGE AS AN INTERNATIONAL AGENDA

The United Nations exists as a forum where representatives from all nations or member states can be heard and participate in the highest level international discussions. During the Earth Summit in Rio de Janeiro in 1992, officially known as the United Nations Conference on Environment and Development (UNCED), three key issues were identified as major challenges for sustainable development: climate change, desertification, and loss of biodiversity. Three conventions were written, the United Nations Framework Convention on Climate Change (UNFCCC), the Convention to Combat Desertification (UNCCD), and the Convention on Biological Diversity (CBD) to stop environmental degradation that leads to habitat destruction and species losses.

Conventions can be understood as documents that establish an issue as globally significant, and which, under the auspices of the United Nations, support the creation of the agenda and processes to address the issue from the global to the most local scales. The following section discusses the processes that stem from and connect to the UNFCCC.

UNFCCC (UNITED NATIONS FRAMEWORK CONVENTION ON CLIMATE CHANGE)

The UNFCCC United Nations Framework Convention on Climate Change is an international agreement that came into force in 1995 whose purpose is to achieve the stabilization of greenhouse gas concentrations in the atmosphere at a level that would prevent dangerous interference with the earth's naturally occurring climate system—and in sufficient time to allow ecosystems to adapt naturally to climate change.

COP (CONFERENCE OF THE PARTIES)

COP stands for Conference of the Parties, which are annual meetings that have taken place annually since 1995. It is also the highest decision-making body of the signatories of the UNFCCC and includes the 194 countries of the United Nations as well as 9 constituencies representing civil society. The COP has the mandate to assess the advancement of progress on climate change as well as to monitor and evaluate the mechanisms designed to stabilize concentrations of greenhouse gases in the atmosphere. This is seen as progress on implementing the specifics of the Kyoto Protocol.

IPCC (INTERGOVERNMENTAL PANEL ON CLIMATE CHANGE)

IPCC stands for Intergovernmental Panel on Climate Change; this panel is made up of scientists from around the world. Within the UNFCCC framework member scientists collect, analyze, and evaluate scientific research reports and data with respect to climate change. The scientists do not conduct their own research, but they write reports about the impacts and signs of climate change and publish the results as IPCC Assessment Reports. The most recent report is the 5th Report, published in 2014.

The IPCC is the most important international body in charge of centralizing and disseminating facts about the scientific basis of climate change. The assessment reports they prepare include recommendations which serve as policy tools for governments to negotiate internationally and for the development of domestic policies related to climate change.

The Fifth Assessment Report of the Intergovernmental Panel on Climate Change stated with certitude that our global climate system is warming and that it is mainly due to emissions of greenhouse gases from human activities, thus confirming that humans are responsible for over 95% of actual climate change.

The IPCC reports, and other studies, document how global warming will affect, and is already affecting, the basic elements of life for millions of people worldwide. The reports make recommendations on preventing

THE KYOTO PROTOCOL

The world came closest to a climate agreement in 1997 with the Kyoto Protocol. Its aim is to reduce emissions of gases that cause global warming.

ANTHROPOGENIC GREENHOUSE GASES:
- Carbon dioxide (CO_2)
- Methane gas (CH_4)
- Nitrous oxide (N_2O)

INCLUDING THREE FLUORINATED INDUSTRIAL GASES:
- Hydrofluorocarbons (HFCs)
- Perfluorocarbons (PFC)
- Sulfur hexafluoride (SF_6)

The Kyoto Protocol, adopted in 1997 and in force until 2012, was the only binding treaty as an outcome of the climate negotiations of the UNFCCC. It divided countries into Annex I (those with historical responsibility for producing greenhouse gas emissions) and Non-Annex I (developing countries and emerging economies that did not have much historical responsibility).

The United States of America, one of the biggest emitters and with a large share of the historical emissions debt, signed, but never ratified, the Kyoto Protocol. This step took a lot of strength out of the protocol. The following long-term results have been very weak relative to the years of effort in negotiating a binding agreement among member states. The lack of political will during the Bush administration that led to the United States pulling away from ratification, spilled over into a change in political will especially of emerging countries. These non-Annex I countries advocated for their "right to develop" along the same industrial development path that created the historical greenhouse gas emissions.

An extension of the Kyoto Protocol was proposed as the Doha Amendment in 2012, to be in effect from 2012 until 2020, but it was not ratified by a majority of member states. Therefore emissions reductions are currently set by voluntary commitments by individual countries.

As this book goes to press, COP21 is meeting in Paris. This Conference of the Parties is the first significant hope for binding agreements since talks broke down at COP15 in Copenhagen in 2009. COP21 is fueled by significant optimism that the urgency of reaching agreement over limits in CO2 emissions, and the importance of mitigating impacts such as sea level rise as soon as possible will transcend disagreement. The community of international observers considers this summit as potentially influential as the Kyoto Protocol was from 1997 onward.

further damage to the earth's biogeochemical cycles, and also technical recommendations on how to support resilience among certain populations. This framework proposes that the countries most vulnerable to climate change impacts must adapt to new climatic conditions gradually.

OTHER INTERNATIONAL TREATIES AND PRINCIPLES

Human Rights and Climate Change

Until this point, we have looked at atmospheric and earth science data that tells us that large-scale changes are afoot for planet Earth and how human activity has been a significant cause of these changes. Human beings will experience these impacts when sea levels and global average temperature rises. We are not only the agents of global change but participants and even victims of climate change.

Is there a conceptual and legal framework within which human rights and their relationship to climate change are discussed, analyzed, and addressed? There is. This framework has been adopted by governments, UN agencies, intergovernmental and nongovernmental human rights organizations, and environmental advocates, as well as by academics, to guide national and international policies on climate change under the United Nations Framework United Nations Convention on Climate Change (UNFCCC)[8] and the fundamental instrument of international human rights.

The analysis of human rights and climate change focuses on the expected consequences to humans associated with global environmental phenomena, including rising sea levels, desertification, rising temperatures, extreme weather events, and changes in precipitation. It also has a future orientation when it looks at adaptation and mitigation measures taken by governments in response to those phenomena. The results of this analysis may involve human or legal protections related to rights.

The Human Rights Council of the United Nations recognized this in its resolution 7/23, "Human Rights and Climate Change" (March 28, 2008),[9] expressing concern that climate change "poses an immediate and far-reaching threat for people and communities around the world" and asks the Office of the High Commissioner to prepare a study on the relationship between climate change and human rights.

The effects related to the projected climate change threaten the effective enjoyment of a range of human rights, including the right to safe and adequate water, food, effective healthcare, and adequate housing. In that sense, the perspective of human rights shows that climate change is set to hit the poorest countries and communities. The case has also been made that infringement of human rights with respect to climate change disproportionately affects women.

International human rights standards are therefore a useful guide for action to combat climate change. The fundamental moral and legal obligations to protect and promote the full enjoyment of the rights enshrined in the Universal Declaration of Human Rights and the treaty's core of universal human rights connect with a moral imperative to address climate change.

---

8   United Nations Framework Convention on Climate Change, http:// unfccc.int/.
9   Action by the Human Rights Council-United Nations Office of the High Commissioner on Human Rights OHCHR, http://www2.ohchr.org/english/issues/climatechange/.

PRINCIPLE OF COMMON BUT DIFFERENTIATED RESPONSIBILITY (CBDR)

At the first Earth Summit in 1992, the concept of Common But Differentiated Responsibilities (CBDR) appeared as Principle 7 of the Rio Declaration. The declaration states:

> *In view of the different contributions to global environmental degradation, States have common but differentiated responsibilities. The developed countries acknowledge the responsibility that they bear in the international pursuit of sustainable development in view of the pressures their societies place on the global environment and of the technologies and financial resources they command.*

Similar language exists in the Framework Convention on Climate Change; parties should act to protect the climate system "*on the basis of equality and in accordance with their common but differentiated responsibilities and respective capabilities.*"

The principle holds that although all countries are responsible for the development of global society, each has a different set of capabilities that they can contribute to this goal.

The Stockholm Declaration from 1972,[10] the first environmental declaration, set the stage by putting on record that policymakers must consider, "*the applicability of standards which are valid for the most advanced countries but which may be inappropriate and of unwarranted social cost for the developing countries.*"

CBDR sets the context for shared responsibility. All countries contribute to the problem but in different ways, and the realities and contexts of environmental protection are also different. Developed countries that achieved their status based on the systematic burning of coal and fossil fuels have a responsibility to developing countries which must face the consequences of development far away while finding solutions to local problems. A widely known example is the Maldives, which are threatened with loss of their islands due to sea level rise, yet they did not contribute to the global warming that melted the ice sheets leading to the rise in sea level.

---

10   Declaration of the United Nations Conference on the Human Environment, http://www.unep.org/Documents.Multilingual/Default.asp?documentid=97&articleid=1503.

This does not justify a "right to an extractive development" by certain emerging economies—resulting in the same errors of the past. Rather, it must be seen as a challenge to achieve sustainable development based on equality, equity, and renewable energy—which would reduce the gaps and, in turn, have multiple benefits for the entire population.

INTERNATIONAL RESPONSES TO CLIMATE CHANGE

As a result of the international negotiations between countries, two basic measures have been identified to help address climate change: adaptation and mitigation. These in turn rely on technology transfer, capacity building, and finance mechanisms to gain momentum and become effective.

Mitigation

Mitigation is perhaps the most significant but also the most challenging undertaking. Mitigation refers to the interventions we need to make as people, industries, and society to reduce the effects of problematic activities. This includes, for example, reducing the air pollution as a whole, or carbon dioxide and methane emissions in particular. Mitigation is intended to reduce the major contributing factors of climate change. The global goal is to analyze the sources of greenhouse gas emissions and eliminate them entirely or offset them, for example by finding carbon sinks that can be used to trade off emissions.

The most effective way to mitigate climate change on the whole is to bring down the ppm of greenhouse gases in the atmosphere. We can do this very strategically by reducing the dependence on and consumption of fossil fuels such as coal, and petroleum in particular. We can start using renewable energy sources, which are cleaner to produce and which do not contribute to global warming. Solar and wind emit few greenhouse gases to the atmosphere or to do it in smaller quantities than the conventional fuels we use today.

If we remember that the global belt of forests and the vast oceans are responsible for absorbing a great part of the carbon dioxide (CO_2) and providing us with the oxygen to survive, then their long-term conservation should be a global concern to all of us. There are only a few people who benefit from the resources near the forests and in the short term. Many of these are indigenous, poor, and not well connected to markets. But there is a multiplier effect of well-managed forests and it accrues for everyone. Countries must avoid deforestation and afforestation and promote reforestation as a national priority.

Similarly, the benefits of the carbon, oxygen, and hydrological cycles are generally not evident to the hundreds of millions who live in the cities. They benefit from the power plants that keep their buildings warm in winter and cool in summer. They benefit from gasoline- and diesel-burning transportation. They do not miss the forest directly, as they have never seen it. They do not perceive the changes in the atmosphere as the greenhouse gas concentrations are rising. But healthy forests and oceans benefit everyone equally, now and into the future.

Those who profit from cutting down the tropical rainforests do not take into account the needs of future generations, that is why stronger conservation and restoration policies can help ensure in the long term that future generations can have access to these resources. It is everyone's responsibility in small and large ways to care for the planet for the future generations. Mitigation actions can be taken by a person, a family, a community, or a country.

Adaptation

Adaptation is the most prevalent future-oriented concept about the effects of climate change. Adaptation is how people apply strategies for being prepared to meet anticipated survival needs and ensure their ongoing quality of life. It will be necessary to have policies and a regulatory framework at national and local levels to address climate change as a factor in different planning processes and to identify vulnerabilities and allocate resources.

Adaptation has two aspects at the individual scale. It is seen as the ability of a person or a community to adjust to climate change, climate variations, and extreme events. Adaptation depends on the ability to avoid and reduce damage to personal property (such as flooding events), seize opportunities, and face the consequences (such as with agricultural planting).

Adapting is also understood as preparing our communities and how we work as productive systems. This might mean planning for changes to houses, schools, and clinics, especially because of the weather events and temperature variability we have begun to feel and those we can expect in the future such as droughts, floods, hail, and seasonal changes, among many others. To adapt we must know what our vulnerabilities are and work to reduce them.

Capacity Building

Capacity building has many applications in human development. In dealing with climate change, people everywhere, including the least educated, have to understand the potential for future harm in their communities and learn to prepare for it at different levels. Capacity building is based on raising awareness, understanding the problem, sharing experiences, identifying solutions, and putting those solutions into practice. In most cases it will involve a lot of experimentation in order to be ready for what could come. Therefore we can say it is a trial-and-error process, because only when we see what works and what does not can we find the best ways to prepare for different impacts that may strike a specific community.

Capacity building has to be done at different levels. At the individual level, there has to be appropriate education and information so that everyone will be aware of the potential climate change impacts in their region. At the systemic level, regions need to implement policies that are supportive of adaptation and resilience in their own region and across regions.

Finance Mechanisms

Finance mechanisms refer to various financial instruments to support efforts to address the problem. These funds must reflect certain criteria to help take adaptation and mitigation actions by supporting technology transfer and capacity building. Hence, the funding should be

- Appropriate—in the sense that it should be directed by the principle that the "polluter pays" and not loans or voluntary contributions;
- Equitable—referring to the principle of common but differentiated responsibility, taking into account each respective capability;
- New and additional—meaning it will not be considered as official development assistance;
- Suitable—referring to the needs of developing countries and the amount of funds required; and
- Predictable—considering that flows should be guaranteed long-term funding.

Moreover, the structure should reflect its interconnectivity with other areas of development policy. International negotiations on climate change have agreed to create a financial mechanism for compliance. The purpose would be to help developing countries meet the challenge of climate change without incurring new hardships or setbacks. It can be understood that finance mechanisms are intended to help level the playing field for poor and developing countries and for rich countries to share in the accountability.

CASE STUDY: CLIMATE CHANGE IN THE ANDEAN REGION

The Andean region is infrequently discussed in the global news about climate change, but this is disproportionate to the impacts that are already happening ecologically, socially, and economically. The Small Island States, as one geographical grouping, is recognizing the need to work together in addressing their common concerns about rising sea levels and the loss of habitability of all or part of their territories.

Though my country is Bolivia, I would like to draw attention to the whole Andean region as having similar concerns. These concerns exist in alpine or high-altitude areas as much as lowland and they arise from the dissolution of the glaciers.

CHARACTERISTICS OF THE ANDEAN REGION

The Andean region is made up of basically four countries: Bolivia, Colombia, Ecuador, and Peru, linked together by the Andes mountain range. The countries of the Andean region have economic, social, and ecological similarities. This region is characterized by rich biodiversity, not only in the Amazonian forest but also differentiated by ecological zones at the different altitudes from the mountains to sea level. The region has been classified as a conservation hot spot because of its rich biodiversity (CI 2001).

The Andean region
- holds 25% of biodiversity in the world;
- is the center of origin for 35% of global food production;
- represents only 3% of the total surface of the planet; and
- is home to almost 10% of the available fresh water in the world.

The Andean region is also home to a number of native (indigenous) people whose ethnic and cultural diversity is rich and unique. But most of them are currently threatened by the impacts that have already been registered due to climate change.

	Units	Bolivia	Colombia	Ecuador	Perú	Region
Total area	1000 Km^2	1.099	1.142	272	1.285	3.798
	% Region	28.9	30.1	7.2	33.8	100%

Altitude ranges	0–6.746 (meters above sea level M.A.S.L)	Bolivia	252 – 6.542	
		Colombia	0 – 5.750	
		Ecuador	0 – 6.267	
		Perú	0 – 6.748	
Biomass	Humid broadleaf forest tropical and subtropical			
	Dry broadleaf forests tropical and subtropical			
	Grasslands, swannas and shrublands tropical and subtropical			
	Grassland and shrublands dry			
	Deserts and scrub serum			
	Mangroves			
	Tropical glaciers			
Precipitation ranges	31 – 9.000 (mm/year)	Bolivia	200 – 5.000	
		Colombia	300 – 9.000	
		Ecuador	125.5 – 6.000	
		Perú	31 – 3.838	

Source: Main indicators of the Andean Region 1996–2007 (SGCA, 2008c), (UNEP and SGCA, 2003) (WWF)

FIGURE 5.2 Climate attributes for the Andean region.

The Andean region covers about 3.8 million square kilometers, with a large variety of ecosystems and climate zones due to a complicated topography. Figure 5.2 shows how the Andes mountain range forms a sort of backbone, while the maritime influences of the Pacific Ocean are felt to the west, from the Caribbean Sea to the north, and the Atlantic Ocean to the east. Within the territory there is a combination of influences on the climate.

WATER RESOURCES IN THE ANDEAN REGION

Nearly 10% of the fresh water on the planet is stored in the Andean region (CAN Becerra 2009). It is considered the second largest reservoir of fresh water on the planet. Most of this fresh water is in the form of glaciers, thus frozen at high altitudes.

Among the main sources of fresh water in the Andes are rivers, lakes, wells, and continuous natural streams and tropical glaciers, where the

TABLE 5.4 Availability of Water in the Andean Countries

Country	Total Renewable Km³/year	Total Renewable m³/capital/year	Rank 180 Countries
Bolivia	623	74.7	16
Perú	1913	74.5	17
Ecuador	2132	50.6	24
Colombia	432	34.2	33

regional distribution of the water is 71% in Peru, 20% in Bolivia, 4% in Ecuador, and 4% in Colombia. Distribution appears dissimilar, but when we compare the countries for the reserves stored in glaciers (above), and the surface water availability in Table 5.4, we see that all four countries are water rich. The underside of the story is that this abundance is fed by an accelerated decline or melting of the glaciers since the 1970s. Table 5.4 shows that all the Andean countries are among the 35 countries with an abundance of water resources according to the ranking of the World Water Association.[11]

CONTRIBUTION TO GLOBAL WARMING

The Andean countries emit very low levels of greenhouse gases into the atmosphere from burning fossil fuels. Table 5.5 below shows a comparison among the Andean countries and in comparison to the historically greatest emitter, the United States of America, (before China took the top spot in recent years).

TABLE 5.5: Emissions of CO_2 by Andean Countries in $MtCO_2$

Rank	Country	$MtCO_2$	Population
42	Colombia	88	48,321,000
50	Peru	65	30,375,000
72	Ecuador	36	15,737,000
85	Bolivia	18	10,671,000
	Total for four countries:	207	105,104,000
2	Comparison country: USA	5233	320,050,710

---

11 WWP (2003) WWDR1, "Water for People, Water for Life," UNESCO, http://www.unesco.org/new/en/natural-sciences/environment/water/wwap/wwdr/wwdr1-2003/.

Since this region emits very low concentrations of greenhouse gases into the atmosphere in relation to developed countries, we could expect a lower regional impact of climate change indicators, but actually, this region is expected to suffer more intensely.

The Andean region is threatened by global warming as it impacts the glacial cover and accelerates melting. Due to a number of regional features, ranging from its complex geography to the distribution of the population and income variability, the Andean region is disproportionally vulnerable to the effects of climate change.

IMPACTS OF CLIMATE CHANGE

Until recently, a significant part of the world's freshwater has been found in solid state in glaciers and ice sheets around the world.

The increase in global temperature has already led to losses on several Andean summits. For example, the glacier Chacaltaya, located at 5,200 meters above sea level near the city of La Paz in Bolivia, officially disappeared in 2009. As the average surface temperature increases, these glaciers are melting at a rate that does not allow the regions to collect the glacial meltwater in order to restore it to the ecosystem. This fact has a big impact on the people who depend on water from melting snow and ice for their domestic supply and, in many cases, their power supply.

In the Andean highlands, agriculture is one of the most important activities and is based on irrigation by gravity. Irrigation takes a great deal of time mainly due to the fact that harnessing irrigation waters from melting glaciers is both tedious and harsh. Nevertheless, global warming is putting at risk the long-term availability of this resource; no glaciers on the summits means no water flowing downhill for irrigation and no water for other uses.

This water shortage situation also threatens a large number of urban centers in the region, including capital cities such as La Paz and Quito and big towns such as El Alto. Action based on precautionary measures to protect what is left of this precious resource is now needed urgently. People will begin to suffer hardship, and the local economy will be threatened if there is no water to power it.

Impact on Women

The changes in water flow patterns, loss of soil fertility, and destabilized socioeconomic factors are contributing to male migration to other urban centers in search of a better life. Women are left behind with increased responsibilities in the communities.

The feminization of rural areas brings its own concentration of hardship. In places where solar radiation is among the highest in the world, women must learn to cope with less water for domestic and productive activities, and more pest infestations on their crops and health effects to themselves. At the same time, they have less access to any kind of financial resources and struggle harder to produce sufficient food for their communities on increasingly infertile lands.

If the increase in global atmospheric temperatures continues, the loss of glacial water as a life supporting resource may become irreversible. If that were the case, the poorest populations of the Andean region will be the most affected, due to their ecological and economic vulnerability and low degree of resilience.

Legal Framework

The countries of the Andean region have known deficiencies in the regulatory, legal, and political systems with respect to water resources and climate change. This is even more the case in relation to rural and urban employment where the required legislation for both private and public sectors takes time to form. Social movements are the most common way for Andean nations to agitate for change in employment security and to respond to the known vulnerabilities in water supply. Rural and urban populations both rely heavily on continuous and safe provision of water.

Despite some cross regional disagreements, the overall aim is to ensure sustained access to water resources under conditions of climate change. Urgency has been a catalyst for the writing of guidelines and establishing policies for efficient and equitable access to water resources in the region.

But a new concern is growing; studies have shown that black carbon particles—soot from deforestation in the Amazon—accumulate once they reach the glaciers of the Andes, making the snow a darker color, which leads to more heat absorption. As a consequence, the Andean glaciers are melting even faster. It can be said that the burning of the forest therefore has an impact on the melting of the glaciers that in most cases is not taken into account. In order to keep the complex climate system of the Andes stable, strong measures should therefore be taken to stop deforestation and promote reforestation.

Regulatory Framework

According to IPCC Technical Paper VI entitled *Water and Climate Change*,[12] "So far, water resources issues have not been adequately addressed in climate change analyses and climate policy formulations. Likewise, in most cases, climate change problems have not been adequately dealt with in water resources analyses, management, and policy formulation. According to many experts, water and its availability and quality will be the main pressures on, and issues for, societies and the environment under climate change; hence it is necessary to improve our understanding of the problems involved."

CONCLUSION

From the case study we can draw a few important conclusions. First, it is important to understand that climate change is already affecting and will affect the entire Andean region. This forces people in the region at every level of society, from the highest legislators to the simplest peasants, to be prepared to face climate change and to take steps to reduce, mitigate, or stop its negative impacts. Second, climate change has a gender dimension, which is mainly due to a lack of education and lack of economic alternatives for women in rural areas. This leads to growing inequalities among men and women. Additionally, the women in rural communities are left to deal with climate change alone. Third, the Andean region is seeing a number of adverse effects on the livelihoods of different employment sectors of the society which will likely get worse as time goes by. It is in this sense, to avoid deeper social and economic crises, that the region urgently needs to create a regional strategy that will prevent or reduce these societal effects. With respect to the melting of the high altitude glaciers, the ongoing effects will be water scarcity in some places and floods in others. Nevertheless, some strategies like building small dams as well as building

---

12 Bates, B. C., Z. W. Kundzewicz, S. Wu, and J. P. Palutikof, eds., 2008, "Climate Change and Water," Technical Paper of the Intergovernmental Panel on Climate Change, IPCC Secretariat, Geneva, 210 pp. http://ipcc.ch/pdf/technical-papers/climate-change-water-en.pdf.

water reservoirs can be adaptive strategies for the region and serve as case studies for successful climate change adaptation.

Since the Andean region is one of the main reservoirs of high altitude fresh water for the planet, it is advantageous to have a strategic plan that all countries participate in. Considering that the region is already seriously threatened, there is no time to waste waiting for further evidence.

GLOSSARY

For this chapter, the definitions are contained within the text when the word first appears in bold.

RECOMMENDED WEBSITES:

http://www.universetoday.com/
http://www.globalcarbonproject.org/
http://www.globalcarbonatlas.org/?q=en/emissions
http://www.elnino.noaa.gov/
http://CO2now.org/
http://www.epa.gov/climatechange/
http://climate.nasa.gov/
http://keelingcurve.ucsd.edu/
http://www.climatechange2013.org/
http://350.org/about/science/

REFERENCES

Annual CO_2 Data from the National Ocean and Atmosphere Administration, USA. NOAA-ESRL Fund. Available at http://co2now.org/.

Bates, B. C., Z. W. Kundzewicz, S. Wu, and J. P. Palutikof, (eds.). 2008. "Climate Change and Water." Technical Paper of the Intergovernmental Panel on Climate Change, IPCC Secretariat, Geneva, pp 210. http://ipcc.ch/pdf/technical-papers/climate-change-water-en.pdf

CO_2 Data. Scripps Institution of Oceanography: CO_2 Program. http://co2now.org/current-co2/co2now/annual-co2.html.

Hansen, J. 2009. *Storms of my Grandchildren*. New York: Bloomsbury Publishing.

Report of the World Commission on Environment and Development. "*Our Common Future*, Chapter 2: Towards Sustainable Development." http://www.un-documents.net/ocf-02.htm.

Rogers, S., and L. Evans. 2011. "World Carbon Dioxide Emissions Data by Country: China Speeds Ahead of the Rest." *The Guardian*. http://www.theguardian.com/news/datablog/2011/jan/31/world-carbon-dioxide-emissions-country-data-co2.

Solomon, S., D. Qin, M. Manning, Z. Chen, M. Marquis, K. B. Averyt, M. Tignor, and H. L. Miller (eds.). 2007. "Contribution of Working Group I to the Fourth Assessment Report of the Intergovernmental Panel on Climate Change." Cambridge, UK and New York: Cambridge University Press. https://www.ipcc.ch/publications_and_data/ar4/wg1/en/tssts-3-1-1.html.

United Nations Framework Convention on Climate Change. http://unfccc.int/.

United Nations Office of the High Commissioner on Human Rights. "Human Rights and Climate Change." http://www2.ohchr.org/english/issues/climatechange/.

United Nations Environment Programme. "Declaration of the United Nations Conference on the Human Environment." http://www.unep.org/Documents.Multilingual/Default.asp?documentid=97&articleid=1503.

World Water Assessment Programme. 2003. "WWDR1: 'Water for People, Water for Life.'" http://www.unesco.org/new/en/natural-sciences/environment/water/wwap/wwdr/wwdr1-2003/.

Chapter 6

OUR COMMON GOOD: THE OCEANS

BY ELISE BOWDITCH

INTRODUCTION

Imagine you are at a party, and there is a plate of delectable shrimp. You pick one up, dip it in sauce, and proceed to eat. It is so delicious! Like the ocean it came from, that scrumptious shrimp has depths you do not imagine. It probably comes from a shrimp farm overseas. Before it got to your plate, the shrimp was grown with antibiotics and pesticides on an Asian shrimp farm. Before freezing, it was treated for shipment with sodium tripolyphosphate to reduce shrinkage when cooked. Figuratively, as you chew, you may be chewing up the mangrove swamps that are ruined in the making of shrimp farms. If it is wild-caught shrimp, the ghosts of sea turtles, terns, and other marine wildlife killed and discarded as bycatch in the maw of the shrimp trawler still haunt your mouthful.

That simple, delicious shrimp is delivered to our markets on a long chain of production that endangers the ongoing health of our oceans. This chapter reveals why we must include oceans in any sustainability discussion and each section in turn examines one of various expanding threats to ocean health. Later sections consider the remedies that could reduce or eliminate many of these threats.

The explosive expansion in popularity of shrimp consumption in the last several decades has unseen connections and relations that span the globe. In a similar way, the complexities of what goes on underneath the smooth surface of the sea have immediate and important implications for human sustainability.

The Sea is Rich with Life

Our attitude towards the ocean is a paradox. We often think of it as an ever-renewing cornucopia, able to produce vast quantities of fish and other edibles. Shakespeare's phrase "endless bounty of the sea" still appears in modern discussions of food resources. Earlier generations assumed that the quantity of fish found near the shore simply continued out into the deeper ocean. We realize now that the fecundity of plant and animal life that has continuously filled boats from wooden dinghies to steel-hulled behemoths since early human history is limited to the coastal waters and continental shelves. These extend out only around 200–300 miles from shore. The deep ocean does contain sea life but not at the same density as humans have been accustomed to filling their nets with. Areas with shallow waters allow sunshine to penetrate deeper and thus support plants and animals. Since the continental shelves are limited, how we use them is an important issue for sustainable fishing and other marine industries. Yet the attitude that the sea is inexhaustible persists, not only for what we take out of it but what we allow to go into the water.

The Sea Swallows our Wastes

We treat the ocean as a bottomless sink, capable of absorbing and transmuting human waste. Plastics, toxic chemicals, garbage, sewage, carbon dioxide, dead bodies, industrial waste—people believe the sea will somehow "take care of them." When past generations discharged industrial waste chemicals into rivers, they assumed that the waste would be washed far out to sea. It is not. Traces of toxic chemicals are much more concentrated near long-time industrial centers, where they originate. For instance, the Hudson River divides New York from New England in the Northeast United States. The sediment in 200 of its 315 miles still contains toxic levels of the 1.3 billion pounds of polychlorinated biphenyls (PCBs) discharged into the river before 1977. These and other toxins slowly make their way into the already polluted New York/New Jersey Bight (the waters near those states), a place once called the "Ocean Dumping

Capital of the World" (CleanOceanZone.org 2015). Although the United States banned PCBs after studies showed that they cause cancer, reproductive disorders, and developmental disorders, this knowledge came too late to protect the Hudson and keep it clean. Finding out what industrial by-products do to marine life has been even slower in coming.

Our Knowledge only Scratches the Surface

We have only begun, in the last 30 to 40 years, to be able to explore, document, and research what is happening beneath the waves. Submarines, scuba gear, and advances in understanding ecological interactions allow scientists to track fish migrations, measure seafloor health, and test seawater composition. What this new attention reveals is that, like every other natural system on Earth, we are changing ocean ecologies at an accelerated rate, similar to the way we have changed terrestrial biomes. These changes contrast with lived experience, and historical accounts and evidence. Considering the size of the ocean, this is human impact on a huge scale, since 77% of the surface of the earth is ocean. Sustainability is as key a concept for the marine world as it is for the land-based world.

Proposals to stem terrestrial sustainability quandaries—such as reducing CO_2 levels in the atmosphere—set timelines that reach decades into the future. Meanwhile, a four-year study out of Dalhousie University contends that if fishing continues at its present rates, there will be *global* fisheries disasters by 2050 (Worm et al. 2006). Marine policy researchers, such as the Global Ocean Commission (GOC) or the International Programme on the State of the Ocean (IPSO), both housed in Sommerville College at Oxford University, call for changes within the *next five years* to turn around declining ocean health (Figueres, Manuel, and Miliband 2014; Rogers and Laffoley 2013). Their warnings indicate that failing to meet sustainability goals that affect the ocean will have profound implications for human life, since our survival is intimately bound with that of the sea.

WE DEPEND ON THE SEA

Life Itself

Humans would not be here without ocean water. Precambrian production of oxygen (via algae) made life on land possible; therefore, without oceans there would be no terrestrial life: no animals, no humans. Phytoplankton in the ocean, like other plants, take in carbon dioxide and release oxygen—about 50% of our supply comes from phytoplankton. If we interfere with oxygen production, we will ultimately harm our ability to survive. To live, we must breathe. We also require fresh water to live, and that, too, depends on the ocean.

The immense surface of the ocean provides 86% of evaporation to the hydrological cycle on Earth, according to the US National Aeronautics and Space Administration (NASA). It is a major factor in creating the storms that bring fresh water to all landmasses through rain and snow. What is available to us as fresh water is a small fraction of what is in the salty oceans, which contain 97% of Earth's water. Without oceans, we could not drink any beverage, water our fields and gardens, or live longer than a few days. Another basic survival factor for humans is living in climates that support other life. The ocean's water temperatures and currents help regulate global climate.

For example, the Gulf Stream in the Atlantic Ocean brings warm water and a moderate climate to the northeastern United States and western Europe. This rain-fed climate supports types of agriculture not possible at the same latitudes in other places, like Labrador in northern Canada. The El Niño-Southern Oscillation (ENSO) cycle in the Pacific, near the equator, affects weather as far away as Canada. ENSO brings either warmer or colder temperatures, wetter or drier conditions depending on the point in the cycle. And, as warm water moves away from the equator towards the poles, it modulates sea ice. Without ocean currents and the global movement of seawater throughout the oceans, habitable areas would be much smaller.

Even if we had no economic relation to the sea, our need for healthy phytoplankton to produce oxygen to breathe, the hydrological cycle that provides fresh water, and the various climates that sustain us mean that ocean health is vital for humanity. However, beyond depending on the oceans for life itself, we *are* economically entwined with the oceans.

Economic Dependence

Out of the 7 billion people on Earth, about 350 million of them work in jobs directly related to with the ocean (Rogers and Laffoley 2013). About 3 billion, or nine times as many, are indirectly related. These jobs are in recreation (like snorkeling, whale-watching tours, or hotels that promote a beach vacation), mining (salt, jade, metals), oil, shipbuilding, and the host of services and goods that supply those industries. Among other items, the ocean provides kelp (used as an emulsifying agent for food and in pharmaceutical products), red algae (for carrageenan, used in toothpaste and peanut butter), sponges, and shark cartilage for cancer medications. The ocean is also the world's largest highway, transporting roughly three-quarters of the vast quantities of goods that flow between countries.

The Daily Catch

Most importantly, ocean fish and shellfish feed us. About a sixth of the animal protein we eat comes from the sea. For a billion or so people in coastal regions and island nations, seafood is the main source of protein. People eat many species of fish, but also sea turtles, anemones, jellyfish, octopus, squid, clams, scallops, seabirds, seals, whales, and crustaceans like crab, lobster—and shrimp.

But will oceans continue to be a source of seafood? Unsustainable fishing practices endanger wild fish populations and have deep historical roots wherever fish have been a commercial product. By the first century AD, Roman fleets had to travel further to find fish, and the herring fishery in the strait between Denmark and Sweden disappeared in the sixteenth century (Pitcher and Lam 2015). Freshwater species in Europe were thinned by the late Middle Ages, leading to increased marine fishing. The East Coast of North America once teemed with cod, Atlantic sturgeon, alewives, and shad. They were fished out during colonial times. Today, many popular commercial fish species have already disappeared, or are endangered. With sophisticated fishing equipment, more people are getting better at catching fewer fish, and expanding their operations to hunt species that were never considered edible before.

OVERFISHING

Catching More Than our Share

At first glance, we define overfishing as taking out more than can be replaced through natural reproduction. Looking deeper, we discover that overfishing is more than just netting a few too many fish. The desire for more fish and the industrialization of fishing methods has side effects that also reduce fish populations to unsustainable levels. Trawling, where giant nets scrape the floor of the continental shelves, destroys habitats and kills many other species in the process. Corals and sea plants, which provide safe harbor to juveniles, do not regrow easily or quickly once damaged.

Fishing targets a few desirable types of fish, but the nets catch everything that enters them. Up to 80% of the catch in the net may get thrown back out over the side of the fishing vessel, as reported through observer programs, logbooks, and reported catch figures (Davies et al. 2009, 2011). This is bycatch. Bycatch varies by type of fishery and netting, with the highest figures for shrimp trawlers everywhere. Not only fish, but sea turtles, sea lions, seals, dolphins, and sea birds are swept up into the nets. Injured and traumatized, fish and crustacean death rates range from 100% on down, with averages for particular types hovering around 40% (Alverson et al. 1994). The threat of overfishing finite marine resources has been pointed out since the 1990s by the Food and Agriculture Organization of the United Nations (FAO). Today the FAO warns that 70% of the world's fisheries are either overfished or fully exploited. This means catching fish at the maximum limit that (we hope) is sustainable.

We are reaching these limits for a number of reasons. Increased efficiency in fishing gear, giant factory ships that process catches at sea, consumer demand, rising prices, politics, the ability to fish year round and globally are all factors that contribute to ongoing overfishing. The recognition of this problem led to attempts to define a "maximum sustainable yield" (MSY). The MSY is the most number of *one species* of fish that can be taken without jeopardizing our ability to fish that species in the future. It is based on the theory that fish (like cows or grains) are a renewable resource. But we routinely overstep or miscalculate that limit, since measuring fish populations is far more challenging than land animals. Fish travel, their populations fluctuate naturally, and observing them in nature is difficult. MSY implies that we have precise scientific knowledge and measurements, when in reality it is an educated guess. To make that educated estimate, scientists rely on many models and techniques, using the size of the catch as the starting point. The size of the catch, however, has its own problems.

Measurements and Sizes Change with the Fish Populations

A familiar cultural image to many, sport fishermen can be eager to capture a photo opportunity with their largest catch of the day, but that 'large' has been shrinking for decades. More specifically, measurements of today's fish populations are using shifting baselines as the starting point of their estimates. The fish scientist David Pauly coined the term shifting baselines to describe how succeeding generations take stock sizes at the start of their careers as normal, even as the long-term numbers dwindle (Pauly et al. 1998). Someone measuring halibut on George's Bank, lying off the coast of Massachusetts in the United States, in the late 1950s would find catches below 100 million tons. Measuring again in the 1960s and 1970s, that person would find average catches in the 100's of million tons. The conclusion that halibut were recovering might lead to increasing the catch limits. What the numbers would not tell you is that from the 1800s until trawling was introduced in the early 1900s, halibut catches routinely exceeded 300 million tons per year, often exceeding 500 million tons and occasionally surging beyond 750 million tons (Col and Legault 2009). Estimates based on fishing in the modern era must take historic populations into account if they are going to restore fish populations to something approaching their original state. Even allowing for evidence from historic catch figures, scientists must also try to estimate catches that are not weighed because they are not reported.

Illegal Fishing

On average, 20% of the fishing done in the ocean is illegal, unreported, and unregulated (IUU). Many regulations that govern catch content and size are easily sidestepped. Ship registrations are one such loophole. Ships from one country can purchase the right to fly the flag of certain other nations (Panama, for instance, which allows that ship to fish as if it were a Panamanian ship). The flag allows the ship into waters it would otherwise not have legal access to. Or, the flag may allow a ship to exceed quotas that apply to its original country, but not the country whose flag it flies. These "flags of convenience" allow fishers to bypass laws they would otherwise have to follow regarding the catch they already carry on board. Transfers mid-ocean from one frozen seafood locker to another, ports where the laws are skirted or ignored, and general lack of governance on the high seas means that illegal fishing continues to decimate certain fish populations.

Most nations have signed on to international agreements such as the Convention on Fishing and Conservation of Living Resources of the High Seas, or the United Nations Convention on the Law of the Sea (UNCLOS). Because these Conventions were years in drafting, they are increasingly outdated with regards to the rapid increase in our understanding of marine ecosystems. They also recognize that no global entity is empowered to enforce rules on the high seas. In spite of good intentions, the high seas remain a tragedy of the commons. IUU fishing exacerbates legal overfishing, and both contribute to declining commercial fish populations.

Consequences to Everyone

When people catch fish until their stocks dwindle to 10% or less of their average size, this is called a collapse. That 10% represents the barest minimum for species survival. Early cod fishers in Newfoundland made jokes about walking across the fish between boats because they were so thick, yet the cod fishery collapsed in the 1990s and the fish population has yet to recover. The human population that depended on fishing has also not recovered their livelihood.

The economics of fishing being what they are, there is tremendous interest in catching the largest specimen, but this has biological consequences. The FAO estimates that the largest examples of tuna and swordfish no longer exist, the baseline has shifted in length, weight, and age of the largest fish caught. For some species, this impacts reproduction capacity. More and more fish are caught before full maturity, when they are large enough to spawn at their healthiest and most reproductive stage. For example, we see this in the Sheephead fish that lives on the California and Mexico Pacific coast. They start life as female and the largest turn male when old enough to reproduce, forming harems of females. Recreational fishing and commercial fishing both prize the largest specimens of Sheephead. Where recreational and commercial fishing for them is heavy, as at Catalina Island in Baja California, Mexico, they mature earlier and die younger and smaller than normal. In places where people only practice artisanal fishing (like Bahia Tortuga in Baja California), many more Sheephead mature to reach their optimal size (Hamilton S. L. et al. 2007).

Another fish that depends on size for breeding is the Slimehead from New Zealand. It is a deep-sea fish "discovered" after coastal waters were fished out, and the Slimehead was renamed Orange Roughy for better marketing. It was a popular fish in the 1980s because it tasted good and cooked easily. Slimeheads grow slowly, and have been shown to live over 100 years in the wild. It reproduces late, taking 25–30 years to reach spawning age. It took just 13 years for the Roughy to be almost wiped out in New Zealand. As people removed the larger fish from the total population, those left were too young to reproduce (Bartle 2003).

This example is a tragic tale of people in various locations repeating the same mistake over and over again. It illustrates that supplies of fish are not unlimited. It shows that counting numbers of a fish species population is not enough to determine abundance, but that reproductive capacity, that is female and male counts, youth, and age of the fish population must be carefully monitored over time.

The Orange Roughy was overfished in New Zealand (1970 boom to 1979 bust), Australia (1989 boom to 1991 bust), Northeast Atlantic seamounts (1991 to 1994), and Madagascar (1999 boom to 2001 decline). Fishers today still find "hot spots" of Orange Roughy, so it may appear on a menu or in a store display, but this amounts to an illusion. To understand the extent of the fishing crisis in the ocean, we want to see more of the reality that is true for many species than the cod and the Orange Roughy. The pattern of "boom" as a new population is discovered has been followed by the bust. Clearly, this kind of fishing on a population that is slow-growing and slow-maturing is not sustainable, and it is time to regulate fisheries differently and find a way to govern the oceans.

There is other trouble for the oceans besides insufficient regulation. As one species declines, the fishing industry often believes that it will always find another, or that technology advances will allow for exploitation of deeper, more remote fishing grounds. As species at the top of the food web become more difficult to catch, fishers catch other species to fill their ships. This is what marine scientist Pauly calls "fishing down the food web." As we reduce the stocks of large fish, like cod, tuna, snapper, or swordfish, fishers turn to smaller fish such as herring, squid, or mackerel. As these get fished out, sardines, anchovies, shrimp, and shellfish begin to make up the catch.

Layers in the Ocean Biosphere

Intertwined with turning to species lower down the food chain is the idea of trophic levels. A trophic level is the position a species occupies in the food chain. On land, plants feed rabbits that in turn feed wolves. In the sea, phytoplankton feed zooplankton that feed invertebrates such as starfish. Invertebrates feed fish, which may feed larger fish, on up to sea mammals. In any marine ecology, plants and animals live in a hierarchy of trophic levels. When we take out one species, it affects the others.

For instance, undersea kelp "forests" do more than give us emulsifiers. They provide mating grounds and nurseries for a variety of fish. They support invertebrate populations. Birds and mammals (including whales) use kelp forests for shelter and hunting grounds. The kelp forests protect all marine life during storms. Kelp are a keystone species, the entire ecosystem depends on their existence. Without kelp, the seabed is rock and sand.

Many kelp forests are endangered because people did not understand their role as a keystone species. By removing top predators, we removed the animals that ate the sea urchins that ate kelp. The collapse of the cod industry in Newfoundland and Maine did more than reduce the available fish in the supermarket, it allowed urchin populations to soar. In the Pacific Northwest, sea otters ate urchins, but the fur trade of the 1800s and 1900s decimated the sea otter populations. Without the cod and otters to keep their numbers down, sea urchins multiplied and kelp forests disappeared, creating urchin barrens. With increasing protection for sea otters in the Pacific, their numbers are returning, and with them, some of the forests. These are two simplified examples of processes that occur globally in marine environments.

A more complex interaction involves the role of sharks. The big shark species have been fished out on the East Coast of the United States. Smaller sharks, rays, and skates have increased. These fish prey upon scallops, Quahog clams, and oysters, to the extent that the North Carolina scallop fishery had to close. Thus, the elimination of the top marine predators changed the ecosystem and directly affected the livelihoods and food supplies on land.

Trophic cascades are not just about food for humans, they are a way of describing overall ecosystem health. The Tiger sharks in Shark Bay, Australia, are essential to that community's structure. They prey upon dugongs and sea turtles. Although dugongs and sea turtles are appealing animals that require protection from humans, when these herbivores eat sea grass, they uproot and remove the entire plant. In concentrated numbers, these animals can quickly denude the sea floor since sea grass is their preferred food. Sharks keep these grazers moving around, altering their locations and eating less tasty plants for fear of being easy targets for the sharks. Since sea grass supports a host of other marine animals, the overall ecosystem benefits by having a Tiger shark as top predator. Although a trophic cascade is one dynamic that can occur in a food chain in an ecosystem, and animals at each trophic level play important roles in maintaining that ecosystem.

Socio-Ecological Systems

Discussions of overfishing often center on one particular species, but the consequences of overfishing ripple through entire ecosystems, affecting all organisms within that system, including humans. Our long relation with the sea means that we are part of many socio-ecological systems (SES).

We interact with complex marine ecologies, often in ways that fail to recognize how integrated these systems are.

The Black Sea was once a productive marine environment, with dolphin, bonito, bluefish, and horse mackerel living in clear, well-oxygenated water. The advent of industrialized fishing in the 1950s and 1960s removed these top predators. The dolphin fishery closed in 1966. As larger fish and dolphin populations collapsed, fishers turned to smaller species. This in turn meant that phytoplankton increased since the small fish ate phytoplankton. As in many other parts of the world, runoff from agriculture and pollution contributed nitrogen, leading to eutrophication in some parts of the Black Sea. Eutrophication is the removal of oxygen from water; it leads to fish die-offs. The loss of oxygen, combined with overfishing and fishing down the food web, resulted in a positive feedback loop. The once teeming clear waters became murky, the biotic environment less diverse, and the ecosystem too compromised to resist invasion by nonnative algae species.

Today, the Black Sea is in recovery, although still far from being a completely healthy ecosystem. The dissolution of the Soviet Union in the 1990s meant less intensive agriculture and reduced runoff. The United Nations sponsored ecosystem recovery projects, and the nations that border the Black Sea agreed to control pollution and overfishing.

AQUACULTURE

The examples above illustrate that all too often, fish and marine ecologies are the losers in SES interactions with humans. If overfishing wild species is endangering marine ecosystems, then one answer that people turn to is aquaculture. The reasoning is that by breeding fish in captivity (as we do pigs, chickens, and cows) we will lessen our impact on wild stock. Fish farming holds the promise of having a managed food supply, providing much-needed protein to growing populations, and supplying new jobs.

Unfortunately, aquaculture has impacts and consequences for both marine life and us. Many, if not most, fish are carnivorous. Most of the marine food chain rests upon fish eating other fish. If you raise carnivorous fish, such as salmon, in captivity, you must feed them protein, so their food comes from other, smaller, wild-caught fish. This risks overfishing the small fish that are food to many marine species. The answer might appear to be raising vegetarian fish, such as tilapia or carp, but they share the problem of waste with carnivorous fish farms.

Pollution from aquaculture is an ongoing problem. Confining large numbers of animals into small spaces means that waste concentrates as well. While the problems of waste management from beef, chicken, and pork operations is more widely known, aquaculture also generates waste disposal and contamination issues.

There are subtler forms of contamination: for example, farmed fish are more prone to parasites; therefore, they need antibiotics to prevent infestations. Diseases can spread rapidly in farmed shrimp and fish, even to the extent of wiping out a particular aquafarm very quickly. Early Mortality Syndrome (EMS) first appeared in Chinese shrimp farms in 2009 and spread to Thailand and Malaysia, cutting their production in half. Antibiotics are available to fight disease, but parasites and the antibiotics themselves can leak out into the surrounding area.

Scotland once had large runs of wild salmon, with a tourist industry centered around wild salmon fishing. When salmon farms began springing up in the 1970s and 1980s, they were virtually unregulated. Sea lice and pollution escaped into the nearby seas, affecting wild populations. Today, there are heated debates over the role of salmon farming in the decline of wild Scottish salmon. A major study between 1996 and 2008 found that juvenile salmon without protection against lice suffered 39% mortality, much higher than ones given a protective spray (McKenna 2014, 2010). Clover (2006) writes about returning to Scotland to fish for salmon in the 1990s to find a moribund sports fishing industry compared to 20 years earlier. Scientists and environmentalists blame fish farms for the decline in salmon numbers. The industry counters that young salmon have high mortality rates anyway, and that sea lice infest salmon in the wild. Today, many websites advertise lodging for sports fishermen near Scottish rivers, promoting their access to rivers that host salmon and sea trout. Yet when the Scottish government released figures for 2014 rod catches of salmon, they were the lowest numbers since 1952. This situation reflects the complexities of trying to manage aquaculture—trying to balance the competing interests of creating jobs through fish farms with preserving recreational industries, while these two interests bump against species preservation.

Aquaculture is a multibillion dollar industry worldwide. It is often promoted as an answer to feeding and employing people. It has been shown to do just that, proving economically suitable for inland and coastal operations of catfish, tilapia, shrimp, carp, even tuna. However, the environmental considerations are more complex. As the Scottish salmon story above shows, the consequences of ecological imbalance, mismanagement, and human error in this industry can be devastating as well as costly. The damage occurs locally, while global companies command the production and the aquaculture outputs are valued commodities in global food trade. The following section reviews how aquaculture is not a neutral activity in coastal waters, but affects water quality.

Consequences

In the Asian tropics, in order to build shrimp farms, people destroy mangrove swamps. These swamps serve a number of ecological purposes. They protect against erosion, and their watery roots provide safe havens for juvenile reef fish. They filter pollution and create habitats for a variety of birds and marine animals. An especially important role is that they buffer the effects of cyclones and tsunamis by reducing wind speed and absorbing storm surges. One record storm, the Bhola Cyclone of 1970, killed more than 300,000 people in northeast India and what is now Bangladesh. As part of efforts to prevent that scale of death again, 3900 square miles of the mangrove swamps along the coast were declared a park in 1985. A study in Sri Lanka after the 2004 tsunami indicated that villages near mangrove swamps suffered far less damage than those where the swamps were removed.

In contrast, the 2008 cyclone Nargis killed over 22,000 in Burma, where mangrove swamps have been converted to fish and shrimp farms. Aquaculture, then, does more harm than reducing the diversity of wild fish. By removing mangrove swamps, people also destroy a natural system that keeps them safe from storms. The inability to contain disease and pollution threaten nearby ecosystems wherever aquaculture is practiced. That pollution joins other types of waste that also affect the sea.

In India, shrimp farms increased as Early Mortality Syndrome wasted away the shrimp, and with them the local businesses in Thailand, Malaysia, and China. Now, the salt from shrimp ponds contaminates groundwater in India too, and the generated waste kills local fish stocks. The salted groundwater is so prevalent that it seeps up and dissolves the bricks of homes from below. The villages are fighting protracted legal battles to make shrimp farming less damaging, but the salt incursion into the nearby environment continues. Contaminated drinking water and crumbling houses are hazardous by-products of aquaculture; sometimes the modern construction that aquaculture brings with it endangers life itself.

POLLUTION

The above section discussed our collective failure to recognize wishful thinking regarding how much we can take from the sea before we ruin the very systems that create the fish we eat, the kelp we harvest, or the coastal ecologies that filter and buffer us from harm. Just as we have treated ocean life as a bottomless grocery bag, we paradoxically assume it is an infinite garbage can. We act as if the ocean can recycle anything. This is partially because putting waste under the surface takes it out of sight, unlike trash dumps on land that are plain for all to see. But the problem is the same: concentrated piles of nonbiodegradable waste are proliferating, and throwing it "away" remains an illusion induced by language. Increasing knowledge about the underwater world is forcing us to reexamine our assumptions about waste in the modern world.

With the Industrial Revolution, and the rise of consumer culture, the quantity of what becomes garbage has expanded exponentially. Mass production of throwaway objects and cheap goods means the waste stream is larger than ever. Since many human populations concentrate around water, their trash works its way down and out to the sea. But the ocean as final destination for waste means that entire ecosystems—if not the entire ocean as a super-ecosystem—are under threat from anthropogenic changes. One of the biggest and most far-reaching of these changes is humanity's effect on the climate.

Global Warming

Acidification

One global threat to the ocean is climate change—the increasing amount of CO_2 and methane put into the atmosphere by burning fossil fuels. The ocean has absorbed much of the human-produced CO_2 over the last century, but at a cost of ocean acidification. As the ocean pH falls, the increased acidity reduces calcium carbonate mineral concentrations. This, in turn, makes it more difficult for organisms that need calcification. Shellfish (like oyster, scallops, and clams), sea urchins, and corals cannot obtain enough calcium carbonate to make strong, healthy shells. Just as important, calcareous plankton, like pterapods or foraminifera, form thinner or malformed shells at lower pH levels. Since salmon and other juvenile fish feed on these tiny creatures, ocean acidification may ultimately affect fish communities. The US National Oceanic and Atmospheric Association

(NOAA) says that surface water pH acidity increased by about 30% since the beginning of the Industrial Revolution. If our atmosphere increased its nitrogen by 30%, we would feel the ill effects, as animals in the ocean are experiencing now. While some (a few) species may adapt quickly to these changes, many will not be able to survive big changes in pH. This will lead to loss of diversity among sea organisms, which is as critical for ocean ecosystems and biotic communities as it is on land. Just as on land, complicated interactions threaten ecosystems that we rely upon for own health.

Warmer Waters

Coral reefs depend on calcium carbonate, too, and they also survive within a narrow temperature band. When the water gets too warm, they expel their algae. This is called coral bleaching, since the algae give them their color and coral turns white without it. Reefs may recover, but they are more susceptible to disease and stress after a bleaching event. Global warming's twin hammers of warmer and more acidic waters affect corals worldwide, with estimates ranging from 10–20% already dying or dead. When reefs die, the animals that depended on them for shelter also die. In turn, disappearing coral reefs mean the disappearing of coastline protection, tourism, and recreation. Estimates of the value of reefs worldwide range from US$30 billion (World Meteorological Organization) to US$375 billion (US National Oceanic and Atmospheric Administration). The death of a coral reef may seem like a small, localized loss, but it causes reverberations to the environment and the economy.

Other Consequences

Global warming has other insidious side effects: sea levels rise, there are ice-free channels in the Arctic year round, surface water temperatures increase, and there are warmer waters at deeper depths. Melting ice caps and glaciers may infuse polar regions with fresh water, which will in turn affect the availability of phytoplankton and zooplankton that live within certain salinity and pH levels. All these changes are occurring very rapidly, geologically speaking. Many species will not have time to adapt, as they have throughout the slow pendulum of ice ages.

Scientists tracking the effects of global warming on the ocean are working in the present using the past to try and extrapolate to the future. We do not really know the extent of the consequences with any scientific precision. Observations and measurements over time guide the research. Global warming's terrestrial threats such as desertification and deforestation show up in satellite images, and so do the ever-shrinking ice caps and glaciers. Satellite images also show sediment and runoff at the mouths of rivers and the annual "dead zones" that proliferate wherever rivers drain industrial agricultural regions. They show us the global frequency of eutrophication.

Eutrophication

Though the oxygen content of seawater varies according to temperature and salinity, most sea life depends on oxygen content of 7–8 mg/L. Water holds less oxygen than air, and seawater holds less oxygen than fresh water. Differences in oxygen content between the different temperature layers in the sea are not quickly balanced. Small changes in seawater's oxygen content have large impacts on marine life.

Every summer, coastal regions that lie downriver from large human populations experience increased influx of nitrogen-heavy fertilizer from agribusiness and lawns, organic waste from industrial animal farms and human sewage, and storm water runoff. Nitrogen and phosphorous prompt rapid algae growth. The algae use up the available oxygen in the top layer of the sea, die, and fall to the floor, where microbes decompose them and use up oxygen in the lower levels. When the oxygen is very low (less than 2 mg/Liter), this condition is called anoxia, and if oxygen disappears, hypoxia. Lack of oxygen kills masses of fish and other marine life, hence the term "dead zones." Although dead zones can occur naturally, their size and frequency have increased since the beginning of industrialization.

Most dead zones concentrate at the mouths of rivers where industrial agriculture is practiced, such as Europe; the eastern and southern United States; the Black Sea that takes in runoff from Russian farms; and, in Asia, portions of the Sea of Japan and the East and South China Seas. However, satellite evidence shows that the East Coast of South America, the West Coast of Africa, in fact, almost every continent has some dead zones, by some estimates several hundred dead zones exist today. One might even say there are different ways to measure the biggest and the worst. In 2005, the Baltic Sea, lying between Scandinavia and Northern Europe, became the location of the world's largest dead zone (determined by measuring the bottom of the sea). The Gulf of Mexico is the most widely known thanks to its being at the mouth of the Mississippi river and the location of the

BP oil spill. Some dead zones are continuous, while others are seasonal according to how algal blooms occur.

The effects of deoxygenation affect all life forms from the smallest to the largest. Fish can avoid going into a deoxygenated zone, or migrate out if it occurs slowly enough. But rapid deoxygenation stuns many fish, and marine organisms like shellfish, worms, or lobsters cannot escape. Eutrophication that occurs for interior seas, such as the Mediterranean or the Baltic, has disproportionately more serious effects compared to areas with more inflow and outflow. Once oxygenation is compromised, it is difficult to avoid feedback loops that further deteriorate the integrity of the local marine ecosystem and its capacity to provide healthy sources of fish and seafood.

Oil and Gas

The trouble with marine pollution is that some are visible forms, such as algal blooms and oil spills, but far greater dangers may lurk below the surface. Oil spills have this characteristic—we are rightly concerned with viscous oil slicks when they pollute the water surface, covering pelicans and other seabirds, otters, and seals in black ooze. There is often a rapid die-off of birds and mammals that suffer and cannot be saved in time. Even with the concerted efforts of volunteers and experts to clean up the beaches, oil spills leave long-lasting collateral damage. Once the oil is submerged or dispersed, the characteristics of the oil and its effects on the environment are less well understood, though vessels at sea have been spilling oil for a hundred years or more.

In earlier times, ocean-going ships were wind or oar powered. Then came the steam engine and the diesel engine. Many oil spills have occurred over the years as ships large and small foundered and sank. With the expansion of gas and oil production, offshore drilling adds new risks and fouls the environment more frequently than we may realize.

Hurricanes Katrina and Rita caused 125 spills, causing 685,000 gallons of oil to be released into the Gulf of Mexico. The biggest oil spill in history occurred in April 2010, at the British Petroleum Deepwater Horizon rig, 66 miles off the coast of Louisiana. A concrete cap meant to contain the well failed after the failure of several safety protocols meant to prevent a spill in the first place. The continuous leakage went on for months. Approximately 4.9 million barrels of oil (206 million gallons) escaped into the water. In spite of expensive cleanup efforts, the Gulf will experience the consequences of the spill for decades, and the fisheries and livelihoods that crumpled in the weeks following the spill may never return to their pre-spill scale. The long-term negative effects from the Exxon Valdez spill (1989, 11 to 38 million gallons) and the Torrey Canyon spill (1967, 35 to 39 million gallons) show how much slower recovery is than the initial devastation from the oil spill. The healthy schools of dolphins and sea turtles that swam in the warm waters of the Gulf before the accident continue to die in record numbers. The tidewaters have not recovered either, as the marshes, which can withstand the brunt of the hurricanes that pass through, do not easily handle the blobs of oil that wash in.

The Deepwater Horizon oil spill was the most dramatic recent evidence of the dangers that marine life faces from offshore drilling. There are other hazards associated with this form of extraction, including the waste muds that contain toxic metals like mercury, cadmium, and lead. The US National Resources Defense Council notes that each well brings up water filled with benzene, arsenic, lead, toluene, and varying amounts of radioactive pollutants—all of which find their way into the local habitat.

The sheer number of offshore rigs (nearly 3,000) increases the odds of accidents and spills. In order to at least be environmentally neutral, complex human-made systems like oil rigs need to operate at near perfection, taking all possible hazards into account—a state that is not attainable. In the push for fast returns on the expense of setting up an oil rig, the risk of poor inspections and the human tendency to err mean spills will continue to add to the existent pollution, further threatening life in the Gulf of Mexico.

Plastic

Most plastics are created from petroleum products. A steady stream of bottles, bags, and all types of plastic paraphernalia washes up on beaches worldwide, or floats around for years. Ecologist Mark Browne found that the microfibers of polyester that come off our clothes when we wash them constitutes the majority of microplastics on beaches around the world. When the Discovery Channel filmed a faux-reality show (*Naked and Afraid*) about surviving on an island, two villages there spent a week removing plastic trash to make it look as pristine as viewers expected. The star of the show returned at a later time, only to find the beach full of trash again. This prompted uncommon action by a television personality—raising environmental awareness about plastic in the oceans.

All this trash, like pollutants, is not evenly spread across the sea. Ocean currents and winds concentrate trash in gyres. A sailor, Captain Moore, discovered the first and largest in the northern Pacific. He founded Algalita, a nonprofit dedicated to researching and educating the public about plastic garbage and its dangers to ocean life. Recently, a new gyre was discovered, making six known "patches" of trash in the world's oceans. The gyres float, mostly just below the surface, rotate with the ocean currents, and contain any combination of plastic material, of all shapes and sizes. More disturbing is how much of it is microplastics, known as nurdles. These are pieces of plastic less than 1mm in diameter. Although plastic doesn't biodegrade (i.e., break down into its constituent parts) like organic matter does, it does break apart into smaller and smaller pieces. Or, like micro-beads in face and body washes, it starts and stays small.

The nurdles are worrisome because as plastic breaks down, it resembles food and gets eaten. Fish eat the floating plastics, and shore birds eat the plastics washed up on shorelines. Fish and other animals often judge food by size and shape, not taste or feel. Marine animals that ingest too many (or toxic) plastics starve. Naturalists who track albatrosses and other marine birds routinely find large amounts of plastic debris in the stomachs of dead birds. Eating plastics also harms marine life by concentrating pollutants. Nurdles attract and absorb pollutants such as PCBs to anywhere from 100,000 to 1,000,000 times the levels found in the surrounding water. Therefore, not only are marine animals eating things that are not food, they are eating things with the potential for extreme toxic biomagnification. Every organism that eats another ingests the toxins in its body, passing them up the food chain in increasing concentrations.

Derelict Fishing Gear

One final subcategory of trash is the nets that are lost or thrown away by fishing vessels. Depending on how old they are, they can be up to 50 kilometers long. Although current law limits them to two kilometers, that rule was put into place in the late 1980s and 1990s in the United States, then worldwide by United Nations agreements. Regardless of how wide they are, the ones made of plastic do not decay; they become "ghost nets." Drifting through the ocean, they snag wildlife until they are too heavy to stay afloat. They sink, the animals are eaten or decompose, and the nets rise again to repeat the cycle. Through this process, countless birds, seals, dolphins, even whales are lost to derelict fishing gear every year. They are macro-plastic pollution.

All these plastics in the ocean are visible, even if you have to look closely and under the surface to find much of them. Other forms of pollution are far less easy to notice.

Persistent Organic Pollutants

Not naturally occurring, the Persistent Organic Pollutants (POPs) are potent chemicals which quickly became popular for the problems they solved, but which are now regulated or banned because it has been proven that they are harmful to life. Their long-term correlation to disease is a subject for further scientific study, but their short-term effects are well-known. Particularly worrisome is their bioaccumulation in fatty tissues—in animals as well as humans.

"Organic" is a chemistry term that refers to the use of carbon in making chemical compounds. Especially in the last century, the growth of the chemical industry in response to industrial needs produced a number of synthetic compounds. Favored post war uses of organic compounds included agriculture, such as for pesticides and insecticides (for instance DDT, Aldrin, Chlordane, and Toxaphene), and industrial uses such as additives and flame retardants (polychlorinated biphenyls or PCBs are among these) Dioxin was an unintended byproduct of chemical experimentation but went into widespread use in the mid twentieth century.

We have known about the effects that POPS create when they accumulate in terrestrial systems since the 1960s. However, POPs were difficult to detect in the marine environment until new chemical and analysis techniques enabled scientists to measure their dispersal. They are (or were) used in many common items such as carpeting and outdoor clothing, personal care products, and plastics. Everyday use of these objects releases their molecules, which show up in food, breast milk, our own and animal fatty tissues, Arctic ice, soil, and, of course, oceans and marine life. Once in the environment, wind and water disperse them, and microorganisms ingest them.

In the ocean, POPs (and other hazardous substances) accumulate in organisms through biomagnification. Salmon, tuna, swordfish, dolphins, seals, and other large predatory marine animals can accumulate POPs to levels that endanger their own health and the health of those who eat them. In Alaska, the Native American Inuit population relies on large, fish-eating animals such as seals and whales for food, which also happen to be animals with an excess of fatty tissue. Due to their customary diet, Inuit carry seven times the amount of POPs in their tissues than other North Americans. Their food supply, and their health, can be considered compromised because of chemicals produced and utilized many thousands of miles away. Since scientific testing has shown that POPs damage the nervous, immune, and hormonal systems, this is no longer surprising. POPs are known to cause birth defects and cancer in humans and animals alike. Rachel Carson's classic work *Silent Spring* was the first of many books that alerted us to the dangers of using powerful chemicals on our agricultural fields, and of the disruptions to the cycles of life.

POPs resist being broken down through natural processes, which means they remain in the environment for decades, if not centuries. Many countries recognized the unacceptable dangers of using POPs and banned or reduced their manufacture during the last 40 years, and the 2001 Stockholm Convention regulates their use. However, some developed countries still produce these chemicals, even if they are banned in their home country, and sell them for use in developing countries. DDT, for example, is still used against mosquitoes in areas with high malaria risk. India was known to apply DDT in agricultural fields for many years after it was banned in the United States. Since they do not break down readily, they are absorbed by organisms or become runoff. This means that POPs have been concentrating in the ocean, and will continue to do so. This is but one of several human-produced pressures upon the marine environment.

Other Pollution

Another form of pollution is noise, which interferes with animals' abilities to hear, navigate, or reproduce. Water is a better sound conductor than air, so engine sounds from ships and military sonar have a bigger impact underwater. The tools used for seismic drilling blast repeatedly for days or months, disturbing marine mammals. Schools of whales and dolphins have been known to beach themselves to escape the noise. The problem is especially acute where offshore drilling is dense, like the North Sea in Europe or the Gulf of Mexico (International Fund for Animal Welfare 2015).

Just as noise affects wildlife, light does too. Many species are biologically cued to eat, breed, or rest by the level of available light. When oil rigs, coastal development, cruise ships, and trawlers fool animals, they become disoriented or out of sync with their natural survival instincts and reproductive patterns. Two recent studies illustrate how this can threaten an entire species. A study in Wales found that filter feeders avoided places with nighttime lights, while sea worms and barnacles, which cause havoc underwater when they proliferate, were drawn to them (Lewis 2015). Sea turtles, which hatch from their eggs at the same time, biorhythmically head towards the light of dawn to reach the ocean. Hotel and other man-made lights in Florida confused them by simulating early morning light. The turtles did not reach the sea and were dying in species-threatening numbers. To save the turtles, responsible businesses changed their beach lighting to LED lights with wavelengths invisible to turtles (Platt 2014).

LED lights for sea turtle hatchlings is a solution that indicates we could find many more ways to hold a less damaging role in the human–ocean socio-ecological system. Even though some scientists disagree with the alarm bells rung by IPSO and the Global Ocean Commission, this is no time to be complacent. The oceans are in trouble, and we have the awareness now that the oceans are alive. We must pay attention now to avoid calamity in the future. Unless we take steps today, soon, to shift our assumptions and behavior towards the sea, the ocean will harbor more pollution and be choked with more plastics. If we do not change our habits regarding fishing and waste disposal, Pauly's prediction of a jellyfish-filled sea could come to pass. This at the same time that our continued population growth will mean more demand for fish, and aquaculture is seen as a sustainable business that will provide quality protein to the growing human population.

STEPS TOWARDS HOPE AND RENEWAL

Some governments and a growing number of caring citizens are taking action to ameliorate some of the worst impacts we have on sea life. The ocean is still very big, and possibly more resilient than we know for sure, if given a chance at balancing itself. Our increasing global connectivity across communications platforms means we can make demands of big industry and slow governments to protect the oceans in ways we could not achieve before.

Ecologists, environmentalists, and scientists call for reform in how we conduct our land-based relationship with nature in part because we are a part of it every day. Air pollution, trash piles, invasive species, drought—these and many more ill results of our actions on land are obvious. Damage to the seas is much less visible. Most people do not know the underside of the ocean. A day at the beach, a cruise, or a fishing trip will not reveal the ecologies and interdependencies that play out beyond the beach sand, or underneath the boat. Yet, given the breadth of the ocean, and the many ways that our lives intertwine with marine communities, we can start approaching them with the same respect increasingly given to environmental protection on land.

Marine Parks

One action increasingly popular with governments around the world is creating marine reserves and protected areas. Protected areas may or may not allow fishing, but marine reserves prohibit all fishing and development. When fish stocks are allowed to mature, and the sea bottom is allowed to stay intact, many species rebound. This has other benefits. An area in Leigh, New Zealand, that was protected for research has turned into a prime destination for snorkelers, divers, and tourists because of the size and density of its marine life.

France, the United States, the United Kingdom, and Australia have all set aside some millions of acres in the sea as marine parks. These areas are still less than 1% of the ocean, though the idea is at least gaining traction in places where the people depend on the sea. Ecuador, nations in the Caribbean, Fiji, and other South Pacific nations have agreed to protect and preserve some of their waters. As the numbers of places where fish can breed and thrive undisturbed increase, at least some of their populations may rebound.

Still, we cannot rely on efforts to increase "wild" marine areas to make up for the lack of sustainable fishery management. Nor will marine preserves mitigate the waste stream that flows into the sea.

Reducing Pollution

Most people who study or care about marine ecologies agree that reducing CO_2 emissions and thereby reducing acidification is critical for ocean health. The ocean's capacity to absorb CO_2 will reach a saturation point, which may be beyond what calciferous organisms can survive. Reducing pollution of all kinds, especially plastics, will be an important step for preserving species and biodiversity, though the problem of the gyres remains. In spite of optimistic proposals, most environmentalists see the gyres as too large to clean up, thus solutions must begin on land where plastic originates. Other ways to reduce pollution include strict and binding environmental standards for oil and gas industries, and tighter regulations on cruise ships and shipping barges. These tactics can reduce what is going into the sea. A larger question for the human diet is how to reform fishing, how to achieve long-term sustainable ways to obtain fish without destroying habitats and fishing grounds.

Let Fish Stocks Recover

One radical suggestion is simply to stop fishing for a time, to place a moratorium on commercial fishing for 5, 10, or 20 years. The times vary, but the idea is that if we let marine species breed and feed other species that would then breed, we would obtain a more accurate picture of what normal stocks look like. We could then more closely approximate accurate maximum sustainable yield estimates when the ban is lifted in the future. This is, however, unlikely to come to pass, in part because of the resistance of the legal fishing industry and their lobbying clout.

Another proposed solution calls for an end to overfishing. This solution has many approaches. Various governments and agreements have changed netting sizes, put warning sounds on some fishing gear (to deter whales and dolphins), and attempted to control the size of the catch for certain species (like tuna). Tighter regulations about what can be caught, lower legal catch limits, and ending subsidies for fishers would weed out many in the industry, reducing the overall numbers of industrial fishing fleets worldwide.

A full ban on trawling would quickly improve fishery stocks, because the damage it causes to the ocean floor, where juvenile fish congregate, would stop. Many countries, including Australia, Brazil, Canada, Malaysia, and, to some extent, China and the United States have created no-trawl zones. Hong Kong, Palau, Indonesia, and Belize are among a growing list of countries which have banned trawling. Putting time and place restrictions on trawling is a step towards allowing the seabed to recover from legal fishing, although the problem of IUU fishing remains.

Need for Governance—But Where?

The trouble with overfishing and pollution is that they occur in the oceans, and the oceans are a commons. Elinor Ostrom, the Nobel Prize–winning economist, found the key features for successfully managing a commons, which can be summarized as effective communications among members, enforcement through trustworthy guardians, keeping nonmembers out, and agreeing upon ways to resolve differences. All of these criteria speak to the need for more governance of the oceans governance.

Countries have Exclusive Economic Zones (EEZ) and laws to govern individual national economic interests that apply 200–300 miles out from shore. Unfortunately, these legal boundaries do not overlay with the migratory life cycles of many marine species or the health of underwater ecosystems that span those borders. Even pollution is not contained by the waters "belonging" to one country or by the country that produced it.

Outside the EEZs, governance for the open ocean exists on paper, yet has little effect. The United Nations spent years negotiating a Convention on the Law of the Sea (UNCLOS) that it finalized in 1982 and which went into effect in 1994. It is both legally and technologically dated and should be renewed. It spells out rules about most marine uses such as fishing, mining, and shipping. Most countries have ratified it, but there is no over-arching authority to enforce it. Everyone relies on everyone else to monitor and enforce its provisions. Even though the Convention contained language that countries can control their own coastal zones, it recognized that the high seas are outside that control. A further problem with the Convention is that it was written when there was still little scientific knowledge about SES interactions with the marine world and does not encompass what we now know about marine ecologies.

Another United Nations document, the Brundtland Report, calls for strengthening countries' abilities to enforce their own laws, for better fishery management, and for reducing waste. It recognizes that much of the return to health for marine ecosystems will depend on cooperation among people on land. After all, the high seas are an enormous area to think about governing. As you shall read in the next chapter, global governance is not only helpful but necessary for sustaining the health of the commons we all share, from the air to the oceans.

Cooperation

Putting the known recovery steps into place requires taking regional approaches to many problems, with cooperation among different countries. People must recognize that the marine world has its own set of requirements for healthy and diverse ecosystems, and respect those differences. Coming late to the research table, scientists know too little about the possible cumulative effects of the increasing numbers and volume of human stressors on ocean ecologies. We can only model, speculate, measure, observe, and extrapolate what the near future will bring. Will the ocean become warmer, more acidic, and trashy? Can we rein in our impulses to fish the last fish or keep dumping with an out-of-sight-out-of-mind mentality? Can we rethink or reform shrimp farming so that coastal regions are preserved? What we can do, today, is to support those who move in that direction, and ask them to make governing the commons a reality.

This governance requires cooperation between all nations, and all nations need a say so that the costs and benefits of changes to our ways of treating the ocean are equitable. Reducing fishing by limiting quotas and ending gas subsidies, for instance, means finding other, comparable work for people to accomplish. Reducing agricultural runoff so that dead zones are fewer and last less time means negotiating with agribusiness and fertilizer manufacturers. Being stringent about plastic disposal, or sharply curtailing plastic production, means finding substitutes for materials, and alternative employment for the many who are employed in making plastics. Phasing out or banning offshore drilling implies finding alternative energy sources, and alternative jobs.

This sounds like an enormous task, and it is. The alternative is to wait and find out how overfished and polluted the oceans become before the consequences hurt people around the globe through losing an important food source, poisoning their bodies, and destroying the ecosystems that support us. It will take a united effort, but there is nothing beyond the sea that we can turn to for food, air, and water. We are bound to the large but limited oceans for our lives, and it is time to embrace that concept. We must, to paraphrase the Brundtland report, recognize our fundamental unity with the sea, a "unity from which we cannot escape."

GLOSSARY

Bioaccumulation: When an organism takes in food that contains toxins, those toxins accumulate and become part of the tissues of the organism. This can occur with pesticides, radioactive elements, and many other chemical compounds. The ingested toxin may kill the organism rapidly or over a prolonged period of time.

Biodegrade: To break down into natural compounds through being eaten by microorganisms. Natural substances such as wood, flesh, cotton, or leather can biodegrade, plastics do not.

Biomagnification: Also known as bioamplification or biological magnification. The increased concentration of toxins in animal tissues as it travels up the food chain. Bigger organisms eat smaller ones, ingesting whatever toxins exist in their prey. Since large organisms must eat many smaller ones to survive, the toxin accumulates in their tissues, to be taken up again when an animal at a higher trophic level eats the ones in the lower level.

Bycatch: The marine animals that are caught in the process of fishing for commercially desired species. Dolphin was an infamous bycatch of tuna, until fishing practices changed. The "Dolphin Safe" label is a result of awareness and fishing practice changes. Bycatch is any commercially unviable fishing catch. It is usually discarded overboard, and has low survival rates.

Collapse: A fishery collapse means there are not enough fish left to make it worth the effort to catch them. Typically, a collapse occurs when fish populations decline to 10% of their former school size, yet shifting baselines may indicate that we do not actually know what a healthy population size is for a species.

Coral bleaching: Coral contain algae in their tissues that give them their color. If the water gets too warm, they expel the algae and lose their coloration, appearing white. Increasing ocean temperatures are increasing the occurrences of coral bleaching. Coral may or may not recover their algae after a bleaching event.

Exclusive Economic Zones (EEZ): The United Nations Convention on the Law of the Sea prescribes the areas of coastal water and seabed within a specified distance from the coast as being exclusive to that country's control. This means that a country has exclusive rights to fish, drill, explore, conserve, or use the resources within that boundary.

Eutrophication: The process of deoxygenation in a body of water that occurs when too many nutrients in a short time span causes dense algae and other plant growth, depleting the available oxygen and killing off oxygen-dependent organisms in the water.

Fishing down the food web: When large, commercially desirable species are overfished, and their fisheries collapse, fishers turn to the next size down and overfish those species, then turn to the next size down, and so forth. Fishing down a food web has consequences for the entire ecosystem, since large predatory fish play an important role in overall ecosystem health.

Fully exploited: A resource that is fully exploited is being harvested at its maximum sustainable rate; there is no room for expansion. For fishing, this means that the catch taken is at the limit of what the population can sustain before becoming unable to reproduce in enough numbers to replace itself.

IUU fishing: Illegal, unreported, and undocumented fishing. Taking fish through illegal methods (like dynamiting), exceeding quotas or bycatch limits, and selling in undocumented markets are examples of IUU fishing. These actions violate fish management and conservation efforts established through international agreements. IUU fishing threatens all fish management efforts since the size of the catch can only be guessed at when countries try to establish accurate fishing quotas.

Keystone species: One species in an ecosystem that is critically important to the ecological balance of that system. Importance is not related to size or population, but to function. Removing a keystone species alters the ecosystem radically and quickly.

Marine protected area: A section of the ocean set aside and protected by law. Varying degrees of protection include limits on the types of fishing, fishing bans, and limits and regulations for recreational uses. Marine parks and protected areas attempt to give marine life a space for growth and recovery from overexploitation in other areas of the ocean.

Maximum sustainable yield: The maximum sustainable yield is the maximum amount of a resource that can be taken before the population falls below replacement capability. The MSY varies by year based on estimates of population size that are, in turn, based on the catch size of previous years.

Nurdles: Technically, a nurdle is a small plastic pellet that is the basis of plastic manufacturing. In practice, a nurdle is any small bit of plastic less than five millimeters in diameter. The microbits of plastic that threaten ocean life are often called nurdles.

Ocean acidification: The decline in the pH of ocean water brought about by the increase in CO_2 in the atmosphere. The ocean absorbs 30–40% of human-made CO_2, which in turn reduces the pH level, increasing the acidity.

Overfishing: Catching more fish than can be replaced by their natural reproduction, leading to their extinction or severe reduction in numbers, below replacement rate. Overfishing is inherently unsustainable.

SES (Socio-ecological system): The relation between humans and their surrounding ecologies. Viewing the world as an SES means including humans as part of nature, in a co-evolving and interdependent framework.

Shifting baselines: This refers to how change in systems, especially ecosystems, is measured and describes how slow shifts become the norm over time, leading to ignorance about what a healthy ecosystem looks like. For instance, your great-great-grandparents might have fished for species that no longer exist in your area, but you think that the current lack of fish is normal, even though they used to be quite numerous.

Trophic levels: The levels of a food chain in an ecosystem. For instance, sperm whales eat squid and fish; squid and fish eat mollusks and smaller fish; mollusks eat smaller fish, plants, and small crustaceans; and small fish and crustacean may eat microorganisms such as phytoplankton (plants) or zooplankton (animals). Each trophic level contains organisms that share similar functions and nutritional relationships.

REFERENCES

2000. "Contaminants in Alaska: Is America's Arctic At Risk?" In *Interagency Collaborative Paper*: US Department of the Interior; Alaska Native Science Commission; US Geological Survey; Alaska Native Tribal Health Consortium; US Environmental Protection Agency; US Fish and Wildlife Service; National Oceanic and Atmospheric Administration; Alaska Department of Environmental Conservation; University of Alaska Anchorage. http://www.akaction.org/Publications/POPs/Contaminants_in_Alaska.pdf

2010. "Sea Lice Killing 'Large Numbers' of Salmon." *BBC News*, November 7. http://www.bbc.com/news/uk-scotland-highlands-islands-20236291.

Alverson, D. L., M. H. Freeberg, J. G. Pope, and S. A. Murawski. 1994. "A Global Assessment of Fisheries Bycatch and Discards." FAO Fisheries Technical Paper. No. 339.

Bartle, Elinor (Summarized by). 2003. "Should We Eat the Orange Roughy?" Census of Marine Life. http://www.mar-eco.no/learning-zone/backgrounders/deepsea_life_forms/orange_roughy_story.

Brundtland, Gro Harlem (Chair). 1987. *Report of the World Commission on Environment and Development: Our Common Future*. United Nations. http://www.un-documents.net/our-common-future.pdf.

CleanOceanZone.org. 2015. "The New York/New Jersey Bight is a Little Sea in the Big Ocean." Available at https://cleanocean.wordpress.com/bight/.

Clover, Charles. 2006. *The End Of The Line*. New York, London: The New Press.

Col, Laurel A., and Christopher M. Legault. 2009. "The 2008 Assessment of Atlantic Halibut in the Gulf of Maine-Georges Bank Region." US Department of Commerce, Northeast Fisheries Science Center, Reference Document 09-08.

Daskalov, Georgi M. 2002. "Overfishing Drives a Trophic Cascade in the Black Sea " *Marine Ecology Progress Series* 225:53–63.

Davies, R. W. D., S. J. Cripps, A. Nickson, and G. Porter. 2009. "Defining and Estimating Global Marine Fisheries Gycatch." *Marine Policy* 33(4): 661–672.

Dell'Amore, Christine. 2014. "Gulf Oil Spill 'Not Over': Dolphins, Turtles Dying in Record Numbers." *National Geographic*, April 9.

Diaz, Robert J., and Rutger Rosenberg. 2008. "Spreading Dead Zones and Consequences for Marine Ecosystems." *Science* 15(August): 926–929.

FAO, Food and Agriculture Organization of the United Nations. 2014. "The State of World Fisheries and Aquaculture: Opportunities and Challenges."

Figueres, José María, Trevor Manuel, and David Miliband. 2014. "The Global Ocean: From Decline to Recovery: A Rescue Package for the Global Ocean." Global Ocean Commission.

Griffin, E., K. L. Miller, B. Freitas, and M. Hirshfield. 2008. *Predators as Prey: Why Healthy Oceans Need Sharks*. Washington, DC: Oceana

Hamilton, S.L,, J. E. Caselle, J. D. Standish, D. M. Schroeder, M. S. Love, J. A. Rosales-Casian, and O. Sosa-Nishizaki. 2007. "Size-Selective Harvesting Alters Life Histories of a Temperate Sex-Changing Fish." *Ecological Applications* 17(8): 2268–2280. doi: http://dx.doi.org/10.1890/06-1930.1.

International Fund for Animal Welfare. 2015. "Understanding the Sources of Ocean Noise Pollution." Available at http://www.ifaw.org/united-states/our-work/whales/understanding-sources-ocean-noise-pollution.

Karp, William A., Lisa L. Desfosse, and Samantha G. Brooke (eds.). 2011. "US National Bycatch Report." National Marine Fisheries Service.

Lewis, Danny. 2015. "Even Ocean Creatures Struggle with Light Pollution: Artificial Lights Are Disrupting the Lives of Underwater Animals." *Smithsonian.com*, April 30.

Mahr, Krista. 2011. "Hong Kong Sets High Bar with Trawling Ban." *Time*, June 10.

McIvor, Anna, Tom Spencer, Iris Möller, and Spalding Mark. 2012. "Storm Surge Reduction by Mangroves." *Natural Coastal Protection Series: Report 2.* Cambridge Coastal Research Unit Working Paper 41.

McKenna, Kevin. 2014. "Fish Farms Are Destroying Wild Scottish Salmon, Says Leading Environmentalist." *theguardian.com*, February 16. http://www.the-guardian.com/uk-news/2014/feb/16/fish-farms-wild-scottish-salmon.

Moore, Charles James. 2008. "Synthetic Polymers in the Marine Environment: A Rapidly Increasing, Long-Term Threat." *Environmental Research: The Plastic World* 108(2): 131–139. doi: 10.1016/j.envres.2008.07.025.

Narayan, Krishna. 2014. "How Thailand's Dying Shrimp Are Killing an Indian Village." *PBS.org*. Available at http://www.pbs.org/wgbh/nova/next/earth/shrimp-pokkali/.

Natural Resources Defense Council. "Lethal Sounds." Available at http://www.nrdc.org/wildlife/marine/sonar.asp.

Pauly, Daniel, Villy Christensen, Johanne Dalsgaard, Rainer Froese, and Torres Francisco, Jr. 1998. "Fishing Down Marine Food Webs." *Science* 279(5352): 860–863.

Pitcher, Tony J., and Mimi E. Lam. 2015. "Fish Commoditization and the Historical Origins of Catching Fish for Profit." *Maritime Studies* 14(2). doi: 10.1186/s40152-014-0014-5.

Platt, John R. 2014. "Sea Turtle Hatchlings Saved by LED Lights Funded by Deepwater Horizon Fines." *Scientific American*, May 1.

Rogers, Alex D., and Dan Laffoley. 2013. "Introduction to the Special Issue: The Global State of the Ocean; Interactions Between Stresses, Impacts and Some Potential Solutions. Synthesis Papers from the International Programme on the State of the Ocean 2011 and 2012 Workshops." *Marine Pollution Bulletin* 74(2): 491–494.

Volovik, Yegor. 2008. "Recovery Is on the Horizon for the Black Sea." International Commission for the Protection of the Danube River. http://www.icpdr.org/main/publications/recovery-horizon-black-sea.

Waage, Melissa, and Alison Chase. 2009. "Protecting Our Ocean and Coastal Economies: Avoid Unnecessary Risks from Offshore Drilling." *National Resources Defense Council*.

World Ocean Review. "Illegal Fishing." http://worldoceanreview.com/en/wor-2/fisheries/illegal-fishing/.

Worm, Boris, Edward B. Barbier, Nicola Beaumont, J. Emmett Duffy, Carl Folke, Benjamin S. Halpern, Jeremy B. C. Jackson, Heike K. Lotze, Fiorenza Micheli, Stephen R. Palumbi, Enric Sala, Kimberley A. Selkoe, John J. Stachowicz, and Reg Watson. 2006. "Impacts of Biodiversity Loss on Ocean Ecosystem Services." *Science* 314(5800): 787–790. doi: 10.1126/science.1132294.

Yee, Amy. 2013. "In Bangladesh, More Shelter From the Storms." *New York Times*, July 24, Opinion. http://news.bbc.co.uk/2/hi/science/nature/7385315.stm.

Chapter 7

THE POSSIBILITY OF GLOBAL GOVERNANCE

BY GASTON MESKENS

INTRODUCTION: THE NEED FOR A NEW UNDERSTANDING OF GLOBAL GOVERNANCE

Global governance is a concept that, on the one hand, vaguely denotes *"the multi-level collection of governance-related activities, rules, and mechanisms, formal and informal, public and private that exist in the world today"* (Karns and Mingst 2009) and that, on the other hand, is the subject of the deepest political disagreements of our contemporary times.

I will briefly sketch the meaning of global governance as it happens today and the actual landscape of critical views related to it. I juxtapose the conception of global governance as 'pragmatic accommodation' organized around the 'fact' of state sovereignty, and from there propose to consider the possibility of an ethical understanding of global governance that is initially not bothered with the issue of state sovereignty.

My idea is that there is a need for an engaged thinking and deliberation about global governance that is initially not worried with 'political complexity,' or thus with the question of whether world politics should be directed by nation-states or not. Alternatively, it could start from an assessment of the character of complexity of the various social problems and challenges we face, in order to enable an evaluation of what would be a fair way of making sense of that complexity in the first place. As an alternative to the various visions on (what I like to call) 'global governance as pragmatic accommodation,' I thus propose to take a step back in order to enable a blank page for making sense of the why and how of 'global governance as ethical commitment.'

Based on the insight that global governance essentially concerns a complex exercise of governing interlinked social, economic, industrial, and technological practices—of which the justification and assessment as such is complicated by various knowledge-related uncertainties and value pluralisms—I propose to understand the *ethics* of global governance as the concern with a 'fair dealing with complexity' in the *politics* of global governance. The motivation for this approach is in the fact that it would enable us to formulate a rationale on capacity building for fair and effective global governance that could essentially be grounded in a human rights perspective and that, at the same time, could provide a view on the nature of that needed political form of global governance, namely as a form of deliberative democracy.

This chapter has several parts. In the first, I consider a sketch of how global governance as 'pragmatic accommodation' is currently playing out. In the second, I will formulate a critique on that form of global governance by emphasizing an inherent contradiction in its rationale. Consequently, in part three, I propose an ethical understanding of global governance based on a specific characterization of complexity of our complex social problems, and suggest that reflexivity and intellectual solidarity would be the necessary public ethical attitudes to deal with that complexity in a fair way. This reasoning will be used to further elaborate on the meaning of 'global governance as ethical engagement' and on the consequences for the working of democracy, science, the market, and education. Finally, in conclusion, I will briefly reflect on the idea of capacity building for global governance as ethical engagement in relation to current understandings of human rights.

THE WHY AND HOW OF GLOBAL GOVERNANCE

Global Governance as a Newly Recognized Imperative

Global governance denotes a political activity, but theorists and practitioners have several answers to the questions of why some form of governance would be needed at the global level and in what sense it would actually differ from government. In a historical perspective, the need for global governance may be said to have been inspired by an awareness that the global community had to responsibly deal with a historically evolved situation, and that taking up this responsibility would require some form of cooperation between nation-states as the main political entities at the global level. The situation arose with the appearance of negative side effects to modern progress; industrialization, economic development, and new applications of science and technology not only brought forth practical comfort and well-being but also threats to that well-being in the shorter and longer term. The awareness was not only of a steady deterioration of our ecosystems and of a growing dependence of citizens and local communities on dominant global market powers, but also of the fact that modern progress apparently did not benefit every human being of that global community to the same extent.

In the third issue of the journal *Global Governance*, Finkelstein notes the dynamics of change in thinking about global governance when "the then UN Secretary-General Boutros Boutros-Ghali saw global governance as

> *a newly recognized imperative* [to democracy, taking into account the] *internationalization of problems of human rights and democracy, previously thought of as issues for states to deal with within their own boundaries.*
>
> (Finkelstein 1995)

The recognition of that imperative did not come in a flash of enlightenment, but slowly built up throughout the second half of the twentieth century. It is also known that the voices of concern were not primarily those of nation-states representatives, but rather those of nongovernmental critical groups and individuals.

An important 'act of consolidation' of the recognition of the need to take action was the agreement on an agenda for the twenty-first century during the United Nations Conference on Environment & Development in Rio de Janeiro in June 1992:

> *Humanity stands at a defining moment in history. We are confronted with a perpetuation of disparities between and within nations, a worsening of poverty, hunger, ill health, and illiteracy, and the continuing deterioration of the ecosystems*

on which we depend for our well-being. However, integration of environment and development concerns and greater attention to them will lead to the fulfillment of basic needs, improved living standards for all, better protected and managed ecosystems and a safer, more prosperous future. No nation can achieve this on its own; but together we can—in a global partnership for sustainable development.

(United Nations 1992, Agenda 21 Article 1.1.)

While global governance was thus originally seen as a way of joining forces in taking up responsibility to tackle emergent global disorder and crisis, it can now be understood as the way to regulate our global socioeconomic practices with the aim to improve their effectiveness and to anticipate and avoid disorder and crisis. In other words, in a future-oriented perspective, global governance is now generally perceived as a form of international politics that not only wants to resolve urgent matters but that, more systematically and sustainably, aims to pragmatically deal with a situational political complexity in function of a higher good: sustainable development.

A good account of that complexity is given by Weiss and Takur in their book *Global Governance and the UN*. Their reasoning advances on the following question:

How is the world governed even in the absence of a world government to produce norms, codes of conduct, and regulatory surveillance and compliance instruments? How are values allocated quasi-authoritatively for the world, and accepted as such, without a government to rule the world?

(Weiss and Thakur 2010, introduction–1)

The answer, according to the authors, lies in *global governance*. In their understanding, global governance is needed "*in normal periods of calm, stability, order, and predictability,*" and should also anticipate and deal with "*periodic bouts of market volatility, disorder, and crisis.*"

Global Governance Today is Really 'Pragmatic Accommodation'

So paraphrasing Agenda 21, we could say that we have come to a defining moment in history, as there is today a general consensus among political 'practitioners' (politicians, civil society representatives, activists, etc.) and academia that complex social problems such as climate change or extreme poverty now have global dimensions, and that, consequently, some form of governance at the global level is needed to tackle them. But while the meaning of *global* is rather unambiguous in its sense of encompassing everything and all in this world, what is then the meaning of *governance* as a political activity in the absence of a world government?

The Commission on Global Governance, an organization established in 1992 with the support of the then United Nations Secretary-General Boutros Boutros-Ghali, is credited with the standard definition of governance. In its report *Our Global Neighborhood*, published in 1995, the Commission wrote

> *Governance is the sum of the many ways individuals and institutions, public and private, manage their common affairs. It is a continuing process through which conflicting or diverse interests may be accommodated and co-operative action may be taken. It includes formal institutions and regimes empowered to enforce compliance, as well as informal arrangements that people and institutions either have agreed to or perceive to be in their interest.*
>
> (The Commission on Global Governance 1995)

The report of the Commission on Global Governance was one of four publications that appeared during the same time period and that are said to have been most influential in the emerging global governance discourse at that time, and especially on the debate on the role of the United Nations and on the issue of state sovereignty (Barnett 1997, 526). The other publications were Boutros Boutros-Ghali's own *Agenda for Peace* (Boutros-Ghali 1995b), the book *Cooperating for Peace* by Gareth Evans (Evans 1994), and the *Report of the Independent Working Group on the Future of the United Nations* (United Nations 1995).

While the definition of governance presented by the Commission on Global Governance might seem to be the most neutral (and vague) description of governance one can imagine, the report in which it appeared caused a stir among political theorists and practitioners. The reason was not necessarily the fact that it was original in its recognition that both the search for peace and security in a post–Second World War era *and* the emergent environmental threats and challenges of globalization brought on the need for a *"global civic ethic"* based on *"a set of core values that can unite people of all cultural, political, religious, or philosophical backgrounds.*"

What was controversial was that its view on governance could be understood as suggesting that, given the nature of the challenges ahead, the sovereignty and power of nation-states is not absolute (anymore). Although the report aimed to appease pro-state sovereignty voices by stressing that global governance "*does not imply world government or world federalism*," it was in fact criticized by those voices for promoting the reform of the United Nations with the aim to increase its power. Indeed, as Michael Barnett wrote about the report,

> *Our Global Neighborhood is less constrained by or committed to the idea of state sovereignty than is Evans, who is unapologetically statist, or Boutros-Ghali, who as secretary-general of an interstate organization is also committed to sovereignty. Indeed, the vision of global governance in Our Global Neighborhood situates states alongside international and regional organizations, nongovernmental and intergovernmental organizations, and other transnational actors.*
>
> (Barnett 1997, 532)

The vision on governance proposed and elaborated by the Commission on Global Governance describes best the global political situation of today: sovereign states are asked to cooperate with the aim to organize our global socioeconomic practices in a fair and effective way, and to tackle (and further prevent) disorder and crisis; while international and regional organizations, nongovernmental and intergovernmental organizations, and 'other' transnational actors are there to monitor, criticize, and/or facilitate that cooperation.[1] In practice, of course, cooperation on specific issues is not voluntary but determined by way of multilateral agreements that are the result of negotiation among those sovereign states.

Given that the global political situation is that of a historically evolved setting wherein nation-states 'accommodate' to cooperate in urgency although they were never meant to do so when they came into being, we could call this form of global governance a form of 'pragmatic accommodation.' But the fact that global governance happens this way today does

---

1   Intergovernmental organizations also regulate cooperation of their member states, but these regulations are of course agreed to by the member states of the organization itself, and not enforced from outside.

not mean that the discussion on the why and how of global governance is settled.

On the contrary, deep disagreements persist within academia and in civil society over what would be the desired global political and economic order and over how complex social problems should best be tackled at the global level. Despite these disagreements, we are able to sketch in a neutral way how 'global governance as pragmatic accommodation' is happening today. I will make that sketch here and return to the essential critical visions on the form of global governance thereafter.

Existing Assumptions within Global Governance Today

A good entry into how global governance is framed today is Karns and Mingst, *International Organizations: The Politics and Processes of Global Governance*. The authors characterize global governance as consisting of "the multilevel collection of governance-related activities, rules, and mechanisms, formal and informal, public and private" as they exist in the world today. Table 7.1 summarizes their framework.

In their book, Karns and Mingst observe that *"Post–Cold War liberalism and globalization have brought clear changes in who makes collective decisions over various parts of the international community and in the authority under which those decisions are made"* (Karns and Mingst 2009, 4). They further remark that *"Although states still exercise coercive power, global, regional, and transnational governance increasingly rests on new bases of authority,"* and they quote Adler and Bernstein in their analysis that *"the decoupling of coercive force and legitimate rule is the most striking*

TABLE 7.1 Aspects of Global Governance

International structures and mechanisms (formal and informal)	International Governmental Organizations: global, regional, other (governmental organizations) Non-Governmental Organizations (NGOs)
International rules and laws	Multilateral agreements; customary practices; judicial decisions
International norms or 'soft laws'	Regulatory standards
International regimes	Framework agreements; selected UN resolutions
Ad hoc groups, arrangements, and global conferences	
Private and hybrid public–private governance	

feature of contemporary global governance" (Adler, Emmanuel, and Steven Bernstein, "Knowledge in Power: The Epistemic Construction of Global Governance", in Barnett and Duvall 2005, 294–318).

Karns and Mingst recognize the United Nations, being an International Governmental Organization in itself, as "the centerpiece of global governance." It may not be a surprise that much of the global governance literature indeed focuses on the role and form of the United Nations as 'facilitator' of or 'mediator' in global governance, and it may not be a surprise that these voices do not always line up to praise the UN in taking up that role.

Reasons to have Global Governance

If global governance, as "the multilevel collection of governance-related activities, rules, and mechanisms, formal and informal, public and private" is still a somewhat elusive concept, then its topics of concern (and the motivation for its very existence) can be outlined in more concrete fashion. In their book, Karns and Mingst distinguish four topics, commonly agreed upon, that have global dimensions and consequently need to be tackled at the global level:

1. The search for peace and security
2. Protecting human rights
3. Promoting human development and economic well-being
4. Protecting the environment

Obviously these are also topics of concern for local policy and politics within the nation-states, and groups of states that cluster for specific reasons, such as the European Union (with its policy of regional cooperation and integration) or the G8 and the G20 (with their specific economic interests).

The essential reason why these topics of concern need to be tackled through global governance is the fact that they either need an intergovernmental organization that can take up a neutral mediating role in international affairs (as in the case of topics 1 and 2) or that has the authority to bring the collectivity of states together and to facilitate their negotiations (as in the case of 3 and 4).

In fact, states that are implicated in conflict or nuclear security issues or that are suspected of violations of human rights will never allow other states to interfere in their affairs but may eventually allow the United

Nations, as a neutral authority representing the whole world, to take up a mediating role. Combating climate change or ensuring fair global markets, on the other hand, are global problems that cannot be dealt with by way of eventual, voluntary national policies; they require an authority that motivates all states to come together to negotiate and take proper action.

It is in both senses of *mediator in* international politics and *facilitator of* international politics at the global level that the United Nations acquired authority since its conception after the Second World War, but the very existence of a network of states such as the G20 that organizes its own political economic affairs may be a sign that this authority is also relative. The United Nations currently publicizes its main tasks or activities as

- maintaining international peace and security,
- promoting sustainable development,
- protecting human rights,
- upholding international law, and
- delivering humanitarian aid.

If we compare these with the list of topics proposed by Karns and Mingst, we notice some interesting differences. First, the UN lists two extra topics not mentioned by Karns and Mingst (upholding international law and delivering humanitarian aid). Also, the UN does not aim to 'search' for peace and security but to 'maintain' it. More important, what is proposed by Karns and Mingst as separate topics, namely "promoting human development and economic well-being" on the one hand and "protecting the environment" on the other hand seems in the UN case to be combined under the topic of "promoting sustainable development."

This observation gives us an important insight into how the theory and practice of global governance evolved over time. All UN tasks except for the topic of sustainable development can be understood as preventing, controlling, or rehabilitating 'misbehavior' of nation-states. The topic of sustainable development, on the other hand, is a positive and forward-looking activity in which the UN wants to engage all those nation-states.

We could say that global governance started after the First and especially after the Second World War in an atmosphere of shock, disgust, and mistrust ('this should never happen again'). Since the wars, a global governance dynamic has emerged, driven by a positive mood and sincere motivation to really do something about enduring poverty and environmental degradation. Sustainable development is now seen as the all-encompassing normative rationale for global governance and, while they would never admit it in public, many of the protagonists of that formal dynamic hope that ensuring sustainable development will at the same time also make the other UN tasks superfluous.

Sustainable Development Goals

In 2015, the UN launched the 17 Sustainable Development Goals. In the words of the UN Secretary-General Ban Ki-moon, these goals comprise a set of concrete proposals that aim to set our global society on "the road to dignity by 2030," and this by "ending poverty, transforming all lives, and protecting the planet" (UN Secretary-General 2014). Goal 16 of that set aims to "promote peaceful and inclusive societies for sustainable development, provide access to justice for all and build effective, accountable and inclusive institutions at all levels."

Below, I will argue that there is an inherent contradiction in the happening of 'global governance as pragmatic accommodation' that hinders Goal 16 from ever coming true, and that, by this very fact, also endangers the fulfillment of all other goals. In order to situate my critique in the current spectrum of critical visions on the why and how of global governance, I will briefly sketch that spectrum in the next section.

The Political World Order

Deliberating the global dimension of societal problems like climate change, and possible understandings of global ethics and global justice with respect to the idea that global governance is needed, have now become an essential element of the global governance discourse. At the same time, there is the logic that normative visions on global governance need to take into account the reality of the political and economic order of today.

Despite the emergence of thousands of international institutions and nongovernmental and intergovernmental organizations, we do not need political theory to understand that nation-states are still the primary actors in any political dynamic at the transnational level. They not only take the political lead in negotiating global affairs, but the legitimacy and formal power of nongovernmental organizations, intergovernmental organizations, and international institutions depends on them. Secondly, there is the observation that, although globalization happens and is experienced in different ways (migration, growing possibilities of communication and transport, the global expansion of the market, intensified cultural interchange, etc.), an understanding of globalization is often politically conceptualized and expressed as the dynamics of a global economic order steered by the standard categories of actors (nation-states, private companies, international institutions).

Opposed to these 'realist' visions that see nation-states and the global market as the motor of global governance, are the many voices from civil society and academia that question the importance and even the relevance of state sovereignty as a central value in actual global governance processes and that advocate a reform to a pragmatic world order wherein strong international organizations take over part of the political power of nation-states. These voices often align with the views that think well-being in economic terms is not a strength but rather a typical ill of our contemporary society, and that arguing for well-being needs to start from ethical and spiritual thinking.

Global Governance as Pragmatic Accommodation: The Inherent Contradiction

One of the results of the 2012 United Nations Conference on Sustainable Development, as presented in the outcome document entitled "The Future We Want" (United Nations 2012), was a mandate for the UN to establish an open working group to develop a set of sustainable development goals for consideration and appropriate action by the General Assembly at its 68th session. The document further specified that the sustainable development goals should be coherent with and integrated into the United Nations development agenda beyond 2015. The work of the open working group, organized in 13 interactive sessions with participation of member states and civil society between March 2013 and July 2014, resulted in the document entitled "Open Working Group Proposal for the Sustainable Development Goals."[2]

Looking at the set of 17 Sustainable Development Goals, we can say that the intentions are good, but the striking thing is that there is not a single reflection in the goals about an eventual need for political reform to ensure fair and effective governance towards the realization of these goals. In other words, the assumption is that the Sustainable Development Goals can be reached without a need to reform the way we do politics on the global and national level today.

---

2   The Full report of the Open Working Group of the General Assembly on Sustainable Development Goals is issued as document A/68/970, available at http://undocs.org/A/68/970.

MOVING BEYOND PRAGMATIC ACCOMMODATION

Serious, critical political self-inquiry and consequent reform of political structures that posit nation-states as the highest form of leadership are needed. Many politicians, entrepreneurs, academics, and activists will state that the goals are clear, and that the only danger is in a lack of political will to realize them in practice. That overlooks the inherent contradiction in the way global politics is done today, and that contradiction is determined by four problematic ideologies that endanger global governance as such.

The first is the ideology that sees global governance as a pragmatic negotiation process between nation-states that, all in their own specific way, came into being through a process of independency and that, in this historically determined political setting, were never meant to cooperate with any urgency. As already introduced in the previous part, in this ideology of 'global governance as pragmatic accommodation,' nation-states privilege themselves (and each other) to still focus on preserving national integrity and on enabling strategic alliances in a global market despite the fact that they have to cooperate for a higher good.

This sense of privilege that comes with sovereignty drives the developed and developing nations equally, and all of them profit from the fact that, in this setting, they can only indirectly be held accountable for their local politics.

The second is the ideology of the competitive market and economic growth as drivers for prosperity and well-being. Any sort of regulation is seen as enabling competition and the playing of the game, but not as an instrument of democracy to a priori enforce the ethical boundary conditions and rules of that game.

The third is the ideology of democracy as conflict, or thus the ideology that sees democracy within the nation-state as a form of organized conflict between political parties that profile themselves towards the citizenry by way of strategic interpretations of the general interest and of consequent societal needs.

On a global level, the national position of a nation-state is consequently the position of the political party or coalition that 'won' the competition in the latest elections, which gives their national view on global issues an ad-hoc character in the context of global negotiations. Again this does not foster a broader question, let alone a realignment of ethical boundaries or political privilege.

Last but not least, there is the often overlooked ideology of scientific truth as a driver for political action. While the global challenges we face are typically marked by uncertainty due to incomplete and speculative knowledge, science is more and more coming under pressure to deliver evidence at the service of strategic positioning and competition in politics and the market.

Taking into account the practical manifestations of these ideologies, the contradiction in the way we do global politics today becomes clear: global governance as pragmatic accommodation pretends to aspire to global social and economic justice and environmental protection, although from the limited vision that one has to 'pragmatically accept' that we live in a world driven by the strategies of conflict, competition, and self-preservation.

If we take the Sustainable Development Goals seriously, then we have reasons to believe that global governance towards their realization is bound to fail if done through the same modes of conflict, competition, and self-preservation. The central argument I will develop to underpin this critique is that, while these modes do not obstruct the formulation of good intentions per se, it is their very existence and working that hinders any other fulfillment, as their internal logic is unable to deal with the complexity of our global social problems in a fair and effective way.

Thus, I propose an ethical understanding of global governance that does not hide itself behind the diplomacy of pragmatic accommodation in a world of conflict, competition, and self-preservation but that, alternatively, could start from an assessment of the character of complexity of the various social challenges we face, in order to enable an evaluation of what would be a fair way of making sense of that complexity in the first place. As an alternative to global governance as pragmatic accommodation, I thus propose to take a step back in order to enable a fresh start in making sense of the why and how of global governance.

My argument is that we cannot reach the Sustainable Development Goals or any other vision on global social and economic justice and environmental protection without a new vision on solidarity. That solidarity is not the pseudo-solidarity that would tolerate global governance as a pragmatic accommodation from out of the comfort zones constructed around existing strategic political and economic interests, but an intellectual solidarity that would allow new modes of decision-making and knowledge generation. These would have the potential to be fair and effective at the same time. In the following part, I will elaborate this vision in more detail.

The Idea of Complexity

It has now become trivial to say that we live in a complex world. Industrialization, technological advancement, population growth, and globalization have brought new challenges, and the global political agenda is now set by issues that burden both our natural environment and human well-being. Sketching what goes wrong in our world today, the picture does not look very bright: structural poverty; expanding industrialization and urbanization and consequent environmental degradation; spill of precious resources, water, food, and products; adverse manifestations of technological risk; economic exploitation; anticipated overpopulation; and derailed financial markets, all adding up to old and new forms of social, political, and religious oppression and conflict, make the world for many of us a hard place to live. The stakes are high and the need to take action is obvious.

What do we mean when we say that we live in a complex world? The need to tackle the problems listed above is clear, as is the picture of the world we want: we envision a world free from poverty and conflict and in which humans live in a healthy relation with their natural environment. Humans, whether in their private life or as citizens share interests that are self-evident in their practical necessity (food, water, and shelter) or in their universal desirability (happiness, well-being). In between the practical concern of survival and the universal desire for happiness and well-being, we find a variety of visions on how to organize our coexistence accordingly.

While happiness may have a rather relative character, the question of survival is a fairly absolute one. And many of the injustices in that respect seem to be rather absurd. As an example, today, about one in nine people on earth do not have enough food to lead a healthy, active life, but the Food and Agricultural Organization of the United Nations tells us that even today there is actually enough food to feed everyone adequately.[3] Is it only a matter of a proper distribution and reducing spills in production and consumption or is the problem more complex than that?

---

3   Source: The World Food Programme (http://www.wfp.org/)

Theoretical perspectives such as the World Systems Theory (see, among others (Wallerstein 2004)) or that of the Earth Systems Governance Project[4] may give the impression that the challenge we face is that of a proper organization of our society, in that sense more like a complex engineering problem.

There is indeed some logic in the claim that, in the interest of making sense of fair and effective global governance, it is important to first try to understand and assess 'the system' of the interlinked social practices and their relations with the natural and technological environment. The reasoning is that once we acquire this understanding, it would be possible to 'fix the system' and get the balance right. The problem however is that this 'earth-society system' is not a neutral given out there. It is not only subject to interpretation, it is also and essentially unimaginable, and this can be understood by taking a closer look at the character of the problems we face.

A Neutral but Imperative Characterization of Complexity

Whether we speak of clearly observable unacceptable situations (such as extreme poverty), perceived worrisome situations or evolutions (such as climate change or population growth), or practices or proposed policy measures with a potential controversial character (such as the use of genetically modified organisms or a tax on wealth), the idea is that we can characterize them all as complex social problems with the same set of characteristics. If science has a role to play in making sense of these problems, then it will typically face the fact that it has to deal with factual uncertainties and unknowns, which implies that its challenge in a socio-political context is not the production of credible proofs but rather the production of credible hypotheses. In addition to that, we know that our judgments on situations, evolutions, practices, and proposed policy measures as characterized above not only rely on available knowledge about them, but are first and foremost influenced by how we value them in relation to things we find important (nature, freedom, equality, protection).

Taking that into account, I want to propose a specific characterization of the complexity of complex social problems that, I believe, will support the insight that fair and effective global governance is initially not a matter of proper organization but essentially that of a fair dealing with its complexity. The complexity of a complex social problem such as climate change or that of providing affordable access to healthy food for all may in this sense be described with seven characteristics:

---

4   See http://www.earthsystemgovernance.org/

TABLE 7.2 Seven Characteristics of a Complex Social Problem

1. Diversified Impact	• Individuals and groups are affected by the problem in diverse ways (benefit versus adverse consequence, diverse degrees of benefits or adverse consequences). • The impact can be economic or related to physical or psychic health or individual or collective social well-being. • The character and degree of impact may evolve or vary in a contingent way in time. • The impact may also manifest later in time (with the possibility that it manifests after or during several generations).
2. Interdependence	• The problem is caused and/or influenced by multiple factors (social, economic, technical, natural) and relates itself to other problems. • Interdependence can change in time. • The context of concern becomes global.
3. Need to Integrate it in a Coherent Approach (Organizational Complexity)	• Due to the diversified impact and interdependence, problems need to be tackled together in a systematic, coherent, and holistic approach. This approach needs to take into account the following four additional complexities:
4. Relative Responsibilities	• Due to the diversified impact and interdependence and the organizational complexity, responsibility cannot be assigned to one specific actor. Responsibilities are relative in two ways: • Mutual: The possibility for one actor to take responsibility can depend on the responsibility of another actor. • Collective: Our collective responsibility is relative in the sense that it will need to be handed over to a next 'collective' (a new government, the next generations).
5. Knowledge Problem	• Analysis of the problem is complicated by uncertainty due to speculative, incomplete, or contradictory knowledge, and this as well with respect to the character and evolution of impact and interdependence as with respect to the effects of the coherent and holistic approach.

Characteristics 1, 2 and 3 show a factual complexity, and 5, 6 and 7 refer to a complexity of interpretation as a consequence of that factual complexity. Characteristic 4 (relative responsibilities) might be described as a combination of a factual complexity and a complexity of interpretation: the fact that a concerned actor does (not) act according to his responsibility may have practical consequences for other actors, also in terms of their own ability to act responsibly. On the other hand, the actor's motivation to act according

6. Evaluation Problem	• Evaluation of diversified impact, interdependence, and organizational complexity and of subsequent relative responsibilities is complicated due to • the knowledge problem; • the existence of different visions based on different specific values and general worldviews; • the existence of different interests of concerned actors; • the fact that it is therefore impossible to determine in consensus what would be the 'real' problem or the root of the problem; and • the fact that meta-values such as equality, freedom, and sustainability cannot be unambiguously translated into practical responsibilities or actions.
7. Authority Problem	• The authority of actors who evaluate and judge the problem and rationalize their interests and responsibilities related to it in a future-oriented perspective is relative, and this in two ways: • The 'individual' authority of concerned actors is relative in the sense that, due to the knowledge and evaluation problem, that authority cannot be demonstrated or enforced purely on the basis of knowledge or judgment. As a consequence, that authority needs to lean on external references (the mandate of the elected politician, the diplomas and experience of the scientific expert, the commercial success of the entrepreneur, the social status of the spiritual leader, the appeal to justice of the activist). • The 'collective' authority of concerned actors who operate within the traditional governing modes of politics, science, and the market is relative, as these governing modes cannot rely on an objective 'authority of method': the systems of representative democracy (through party politics and elections) and the market both lean on the principle of competition while science is faced with the fact that it needs to deal with future-oriented hypotheses. • Due to this, concerned actors have the opportunity to reject or question the relevance and credibility of the judgment of other actors and consequently to question the legitimacy of their authority.

to his responsibility is of course also dependent on his interpretation of the situation and of the arguments of others with respect to his responsibility.

Due to their factual complexity, complex social problems are social problems that create their own uncertainty and ambiguity relative to what is at stake and what is to be done. The complexity of interpretation may thus be understood as a complexity of making sense of the problem. As this complexity also includes 'the authority problem,' the complexity of interpretation of a complex social problem can be understood as a complexity that is experienced by all concerned actors together, and not only by each actor individually.

Returning to the example of the food problem, that complex social problem can now be described in terms of the seven characteristics listed above. More concretely, the characterization helps us to understand that the problem of providing affordable access to healthy food for all is more than an engineering problem. First of all, the problem affects people in dramatically unequal ways and is related to the complex problem of climate change and unsustainable agriculture.

In terms of the knowledge problem, it is difficult to assess how agricultural planning may directly benefit those in need, if only for the fact that phenomena such as extreme droughts, crop diseases, or plagues of insects are hard to predict and control. In addition, the contribution of genetically modified organism technology to make crops more resistant to diseases and plagues is controversial, and science is unable to mediate, as its hypotheses with respect to potential adverse human health effects cannot be convincingly proven (and this due to the long-term character and stochastic nature of these effects).

Another aspect of the evaluation problem is the fact that there are different visions about the role of markets and international trade agreements in providing affordable food for all. Then there is the observation that our habit of eating meat not only puts a serious burden on our environment, but that it is also counterproductive to solving the food problem. According to the United Nations Environment Programme, taking the energy value of the meat produced into consideration, the loss of calories by feeding the cereals to animals instead of using the cereals directly as human food represents the annual calorie need for more than 3.5 billion people (UNEP 2009, 27). And finally, besides fruit and vegetables, society is even in doubt over the question of what healthy food is anyway, and that issue obviously concerns everyone, not only the poor.

This chapter does not want to propose a manual, procedure, or instrument to solve complex social problems such as the food problem. Rather, the characterization of complexity is meant as an incentive and a basis for *ethical thinking*, as it opens the possibility to reflect on what it would imply to fairly deal with the complexity of those specific social problems and of the organization of our society in general. The possibility of doing so is in the fact that the characterization of complexity in the form of the seven proposed characteristics can be called a neutral characterization, in the sense that it does not specify wrongdoers and victims as such, which of course does not mean there cannot be any.

Representing the complexity as a complexity of interpretation enables us to describe the responsibility, in the face of that complexity, as a *joint responsibility* that is accommodating and not dividing. However, although nobody is blamed for reckless behavior, or of the evasion of responsibility, this characterization of complexity is in its way also imperative for all concerned. First of all, any reflection on what it would imply to deal with the complexity of the problem at stake fairly would, for those involved, imply the need to transcend the usual thinking in terms of their own interest. At the same time, due to the knowledge and evaluation problem, every concerned actor would need to acknowledge his specific 'authority problem' in making sense of the complexity of that problem. Indeed, looking again at the brief analysis of the complexity of the food problem, we must recognize that no political, scientific, economic, activist, or citizen voice would have authority in making sense of that problem and of eventual solutions.

Reflexivity and Intellectual Solidarity as Ethical Attitudes

Taking all this together, we could now say that the complexity of complex social problems implies a specific responsible attitude in face of that complexity for all concerned. That responsible attitude is *identical* for each of the concerned actors (being it the politician, the scientist, the entrepreneur, the activist, or the citizen) and can be described in a threefold way:

1. The preparedness to acknowledge the complexity of complex social problems and of the organization of our society as a whole;
2. The preparedness to acknowledge the imperative character of that complexity or thus to acknowledge the own-authority problem—in addition to the knowledge and evaluation problem—in making sense of that complexity;
3. Based on the acknowledgement of the own-authority problem, the preparedness to seek accommodation with other concerned actors, and this through specific advanced interaction methods in research and politics that would enable jointly making sense of that complexity.

The threefold preparedness suggested here can be considered a concession to the complexity as sketched above, and it may be clear that, with this understanding, we now enter the area of ethics. A simple but powerful first insight in that sense is the idea that if nobody has the authority to make sense of a specific problem and of consequent solutions, then concerned actors have nothing else than each other as equal references in deliberating that problem.

In his book *The Ethical Project*, the philosopher Philip Kitcher makes a similar reflection by saying "there are no ethical experts" and that, therefore, authority can only be the authority of the conversation among the concerned actors (Kitcher 2014). From the perspective of normative ethics, we can now (in a metaphorical way) interpret the idea of responsibility towards complexity as if that complexity puts an ethical demand on every concerned actor, in the sense of an appeal to adopt a reflexive attitude in face of that complexity. That reflexive attitude would not only concern the way each actor rationalizes the problem as such, but also the way he rationalizes his own interests, the interests of others, and the general interest in relation to that problem.

The responsible attitude considered here can thus be described as a reflexive attitude in face of complexity, and, as a concession towards that complexity, that attitude can now also be called an 'ethical attitude.' However, given that the responsibility as suggested above would also imply a mutual accommodation among concerned actors (politicians, scientists, entrepreneurs, activists, and citizens), one can understand that, in practice, this responsible attitude needs to be adopted *in public*, and that one needs advanced formal interaction methods to make that possible.

The joint preparedness for 'public reflexivity' of all concerned actors would enable a dialogue that, unavoidably, will also have a confrontational character, as every actor would need to be prepared to give account of his interests, beliefs, and uncertainties with respect to the problem at stake.

That joint preparedness can be described as a form of intellectual solidarity as—in arguing about observable unacceptable situations (such as extreme poverty), perceived worrisome situations or evolutions (such as climate change or population growth) or practices, or proposed policy measures with a potential controversial character (such as the use of genetically modified organisms or a tax on wealth)—concerned actors would need to be prepared to openly reflect towards each other and towards 'the outside world' about the way they not only rationalize the problem as such, but also their own interests, the interests of others, and the general interest in relation to that problem.

In this sense, intellectual solidarity is not some elite form of intellectual cooperation. It simply denotes our joint preparedness to accept the complexity of coexistence and the fact that no one has a privileged position to make sense of it. Intellectual solidarity is the joint preparedness to accept that we have no reference other than each other.

Applied Ethical Thinking

Moving now from normative ethical thinking to applied ethical thinking, the advanced formal interaction modes to enable reflexivity and intellectual solidarity as public ethical attitudes can be given a name and a practical meaning. Taking into account the knowledge problem and the evaluation problem as the central characteristics of the complexity of making sense of complex problems, reflexivity and intellectual solidarity as ethical attitudes naturally would need to inspire the method we use to generate knowledge about these problems and the method we use to negotiate and make decisions related to them accordingly.

The problem however is that, today, our methods of knowledge generation and decision-making are not inspired by reflexivity and intellectual solidarity as ethical attitudes. Instead, as I show below, the strategies of conflict, competition, and self-preservation not only undermine the possibility of intellectual solidarity among nation-states, but they also determine the working of the traditional governing modes of politics, science, and the market we inherited from modernity.

As a consequence, these governing modes are not able to grasp the complexity of complex social problems but rather stimulate strategic simplification of that complexity. Fair and effective global governance would not only require intellectual solidarity in international politics, but also an essential reform of the formal ways we make sense of the complexity of social organization and a new pragmatic vision on what the social responsibility of the market can mean in reality.

INTELLECTUAL SOLIDARITY AS ETHICAL COMMITMENT IN THE ORGANIZATION OF SOCIETY

In the previous section, I developed a vision on what it would imply, from an ethical perspective, to fairly deal with the complexity of our complex social problems. I argued that reflexivity and intellectual solidarity as ethical attitudes in face of that complexity would motivate advanced methods for knowledge generation and decision-making that would enable a fair dealing with that complexity. However, one could of course ask the question: In which ways would our traditional methods of democracy and science be unable to take up that role?

Why would the market system not be able to fairly deal with the complexity of social organization in its own way? In the following, I will briefly sketch how our traditional workings of politics, science, and the market are unable to fairly deal with the complexity of our global problems today. In conclusion, I will elaborate an understanding of reflexivity and intellectual solidarity as ethical attitudes in relation to the governing modes of democratic politics, science, and education on the one hand and in relation to the market on the other hand. I will also argue what the consequences would be for each of them.

The Triumvirate of Decision-making and Influence in Westernized Nation-states

In somewhat abstract terms, one could understand modern representative democracy (within the nation-state), science, and the market as the three formal governing methods to produce meaning for our modern society.

Representative democracy can be seen as the governance of our collective and personal interests, executed by an authority that received its mandate through elections in which different political-ideological parties competed. The policies initiated and executed by that authority can be seen as the produced meaning for society.

Science is the governance of knowledge generation, and its intended meaning consists of the fundamental and general knowledge at the benefit of society on the one hand and the applicable knowledge at the service of politics and the market on the other hand. The market, in its turn, can be understood as the governance of the production and consumption of products and services, and the functional and aesthetical benefits that come with these products and services can be considered as the intended meaning. All three of them are typical products of enlightenment and modernity, and we can say that their emergence and formation *in modernity* was, for each in its own specific way, the result of an emancipation process characterized *as modernity*.

As emancipation processes, all three of them have developed a system with their own 'internal logic' to produce their meaning for society, and the basic principles of those systems can be called essential accomplishments of the enlightenment and modernity: for politics, these are the principles of representative democracy, being the formal possibility to elect our political representatives, the formal possibility of negotiations among different and equally valuable political visions, and the formal possibility of a mandated authority and its opposition; for science, it concerns the necessity of independence and objectivity in the generation of knowledge meant to inspire and direct our coexistence and social organization; for the market, it concerns the possibility of innovation and of the variation and quality of products and services thanks to the freedom and competitiveness of that market.

However, because of their emergence through emancipation processes, one can understand that the actors in representative democracy, science, and the market were not concerned with their own 'problem of authority' in generating that meaning, in the sense that they saw no reason *to give account to society* with respect to their own working in producing that meaning. The simple idea was that the internal logic of their system—in the sense of their own *method of evaluation* with the production of their meaning—was *self-corrective* and that, in this way, their produced meaning was societally *relevant*, *credible*, and *justified* and therefore also authoritative.

The idea, however, is that, taking into account the characteristics of complexity of our contemporary complex social problems, that internal logic is bound to fail: the traditional internal logics of representative democracy, science, and the market are, each in their own way, no longer able to grasp the complexity of those problems and, as a result, they cannot be self-corrective. Therefore, the idea is that their governing methods are not able to generate relevant, credible, and justified meaning for society. For each of them, this idea can be made more explicit in the following way:

REPRESENTATIVE DEMOCRACY WITHIN THE NATION-STATE

The working of representative democracy inspired by the ideology of 'democracy as organized conflict' and, practiced through the system of elections and party politics, hinders a deliberate analysis of (the complexity of) complex social problems and is unable to represent the diversity of visions and interests in relation to those problems.

Analysis of complex problems is strategically prepared (to match party ideologies) and causes polarization. In addition, the system tends to stimulate populism and political self-protection and allows strategic interpretation of the possibility and necessity of public participation. In the case of complex problems that require deliberation on a global level, formal democracy remains restricted within the nation-state while nation-states profile themselves internationally according to the national political vision that happens to be in power that moment.

As interests of nation-states with respect to a specific complex problem that requires a global viewpoint as the context of concern do not essentially differ with respect to the nature of that problem, in global politics, the proclaimed central value of nation-state sovereignty tends to hinder rather than facilitate global governance of that problem.

SCIENCE

Science that aims to foster objectivity when dealing with complex social problems sees itself confronted with the necessity to work with future-oriented hypotheses that cannot be proven.

Given that situation, and taking into account an enduring spirit of positivism in the academy that now also tends to affect the social sciences, one can notice that political and commercial pressure on science to deliver usable evidence tends to stimulate tailor-made knowledge brokerage and scientific consultancy, expertise adapted to political preferences, political 'science shopping,' and thin interpretations of the 'knowledge economy.'

THE MARKET

A self-corrective and innovative free and competitive market is apparently not able to determine its own ethics, in the sense that its internal market logic is unable to
  - prevent conflicts of interest with politics;
  - deal with the justification of controversial products or services;
  - rule out labor exploitation ;
  - prevent environmental pollution;
  - justify the relevance of financial speculation ;
  - determine what would be a correct 'use' of animals; and
  - care for the needs of next generations.

In evaluating the working of politics, science, and the market, there is one criterion that is identical for all three of them and of which the legitimacy is supported by the critics as well as their subjects of critique: societal trust. Trust of citizens in politics, of laypersons in scientific expertise, and of consumers in the market, is seen by politicians, scientists, and entrepreneurs respectively as the ultimate criterion to evaluate their work.

While society perceives this criterion of trust as a way to judge whether those politicians, scientists, and entrepreneurs do not misuse the authority it delegates to them, those same politicians, scientists, and entrepreneurs are today still convinced that trust is automatically guaranteed by the so-called self-corrective internal logic of the systems wherein they function. Ironically, consistent critical analysis from academia and civil society, as well as the daily news feed about detached and populist politics, conflicts of interest among politics and the commercial sector, contradictory scientific advice on controversial risk-inherent technologies such as genetically modified food and nuclear energy, child labor and horrible working conditions in sweat-shops, unbridled financial speculation, indecent CEO bonuses, etc., could serve as support for the observation that politics, science, and the market are no longer able to generate trust based on their own internal logic.

In the interest of a fair dealing with the complexity of our complex social problems, concerned actors would need to be prepared to adopt reflexivity and intellectual solidarity as public ethical attitudes in the face of that complexity. In practice, this would require them to openly reflect towards each other and towards the outside world about the way they not only rationalize the problem as such, but also their own interests, the interests of others, and the general interest in relation to that problem. The previous considerations may support the argument that the traditional methods of representative democracy, science, and the market do not stimulate and enable reflexivity and intellectual solidarity as described above. Their internal logic is not self-corrective but self-protective, and this leads us to a conclusion.

By emphasizing the problem of authority and adding it as a third dimension to the complexity of interpretation (and thus to the classical knowledge–values problem), the idea of a fair dealing with complexity of complex social problems *informs in itself the need of critique* towards any rational attempt to make sense of that complexity. In other words, if there are no privileged positions to make sense of complexity or thus to rationalize complexity (no specific political-ideological positions, no specific scientific positions, no market logic), then a fair dealing with complexity would simply be a mutual making sense of complexity among all those concerned.

If the legitimacy of the basic principles of democracy, science, and the market remain unquestioned but the relevance, credibility, and justification of the meaning they produce at the service of society can no longer be tested by the internal logic of their method, then the only way to generate societal trust with the meaning they produce is by opening up these methods for the possibility of critique by society, and by ensuring the capacity of society to engage in that critique.

And from this point, the similarity between politics and science on the one hand and the market on the other hand disappears. While politics and science that open up their method towards society would become reflexive and thus more responsible forms of politics and science, a market cannot become reflexive, as it needs to follow its rigid logic of creating profit as return on investment. So for the market, the preparedness to open up its method can be understood as the preparedness to create transparency in its internal working and to accept that the rules of the game are set by politics and science in agreement with society.

The idea of reflexivity and intellectual solidarity as proposed ethical attitudes needed to fairly deal with the complexity of complex social problems, together with the critique that our traditional methods of representative democracy, science, and the market do not stimulate or enable that reflexivity and intellectual solidarity, provide us now with the necessary elements to sketch the idea of global governance as ethical commitment as opposed to the strategic form of global governance as pragmatic accommodation.

In the final section, I will sketch out that idea by suggesting a new science, democracy, and education for global governance. Then, in conclusion, I will suggest how the idea of global governance as ethical commitment can be related to a new perspective on human rights.

Trust by Method: A New Science, Democracy, and Education for Global Governance

A fair dealing with the complexity of social organization implies for all involved actors to be prepared to engage in intellectual confrontation with regard to the rationales they use to defend their interests. We may conclude from the previous considerations that intellectual confrontation in this sense needs to be organized in science as well as in democracy.

Since the challenge of science in making sense of complex social problems is no longer the production of credible proofs but the construction of credible hypotheses, reflexivity and intellectual solidarity as ethical attitudes for science underscore the need to engage in advanced methods that are self-critical and open to visions from outside of the traditional discipline of science. In other words, knowledge to advise policy would need to be generated in a transdisciplinary and inclusive way, or as a joint exercise of problem-solving with input from the natural and social sciences, philosophy, as well as from citizens. It may be clear that we do not need deep reform to make that new mode of science possible today.

An advanced method of political negotiation and decision-making inspired by the ethical attitudes of reflexivity and intellectual solidarity would be a form of deliberative democracy that sees deliberation as a collective self-critical reflection and learning process among citizens, political mandatories, scientists, entrepreneurs, and activists, rather than as a competition between conflicting views driven by self-interest. Political deliberation liberated from the confinement of political parties and nation-states and enriched with opinions from civil society and citizens and with well-considered and (self-) critical scientific advice would have the potential to be fair in the way it would enforce actors to give account of how they rationalize their interests from out of strategic positions, but also in that it would enable actors to do so from out of vulnerable positions.

It would be effective, too, as it would have the potential to generate societal trust based on its method instead of on promised outcomes. While the utopian picture sketched here would imply a total political reform on all levels, intellectual solidarity can already now open up old political methods for the betterment of society. On a local level as well as a global level, politicians could organize public participation and deliberation around concrete issues and engage in taking the outcome of that deliberation seriously. In addition, one could already now envision global governance as a 'cosmopolitan democracy,' a conception of democracy that, according to David Held, is based on the continuing significance of nation-states, although with *"a layer of governance (in the form of democratic institutions at regional and global levels) to constitute a limitation on national sovereignty"* (Held 2006).

Last but not least, there is the need for a new vision on education. It would be naïve to think that politicians, scientists, entrepreneurs, activists, and citizens will adopt the ethical attitudes of reflexivity and intellectual solidarity simply on request. Insight into the complexity of our complex social problems and an understanding of the ethical consequences for politics, science, and the market need to be stimulated and fostered in basic and higher education. Instead of educating young people to optimally function in the strategic political and economic orders of today, they should be given the possibility to develop as a cosmopolitan citizen with a (self-) critical mind and a sense for ethics in general and intellectual solidarity in particular.

In this text, I argued that we cannot reach the Sustainable Development
Goals or any other vision on global social and economic justice and environmental protection without a new vision for solidarity. That solidarity
is not the pseudo-solidarity that would tolerate global governance as a
pragmatic accommodation from the comfort zones constructed around
strategic political and economic interests, but neither would it be some
elite form of intellectual cooperation.

Intellectual solidarity simply denotes our joint preparedness to accept
the complexity of coexistence and the fact that no one has a privileged
position to make sense of it. That preparedness would be the prerequisite
to enable, foster, and use our human intellectual capital in this world, not
as a means for competition (there are no other creatures humanity should
compete with) but as a means for cooperation, in the interest of the self-
preservation of humanity as a whole and the respect for the dignity of
every one of its individual human beings.

In global governance, we must be solidary in the way we hold each
other accountable, but also in the way we give each other the right to be
responsible. Enabling this equal 'right to be responsible' for every human
is therefore the essential form of intellectual solidarity in global governance as ethical commitment.

REFERENCES

Barnett, Michael. 1997. "Bringing in the New World Order—Liberalism,
    Legitimacy, and the United Nations." *World Politics*, no. 49 (July): 526–551.
Barnett, Michael, and Raymond Duvall, eds. 2005. *Power in Global Governance.*
    Cambridge, UK ; New York: Cambridge University Press.
Beitz, Charles R. 2011. *The Idea of Human Rights.* 1st edition. Oxford: Oxford
    University Press.
Boutros-Ghali, Boutros. 1995a. "Democracy: A Newly Recognized Imperative."
    Global Governance 1 (1): 3–11.
———. 1995b. *Agenda for Peace 1995.* 2nd edition. New York: United Nations
    Pubns.
Evans, Gareth J. 1994. *Cooperating for Peace: The Global Agenda for the 1990s
    and Beyond.* St. Leonards, NSW, Australia: Allen & Unwin.
Finkelstein, Lawrence S. 1995."What is Global Governance?" *Global Governance,*
    no.1(3): 367–372.

Held, David. 2006. *Models of Democracy, 3rd Edition*. Stanford, CA: Stanford University Press.

Karns, Margaret P., and Karen A. Mingst. 2009. *International Organizations: The Politics and Processes of Global Governance*. 2nd edition. Boulder, CO: Lynne Rienner Publishers.

Kitcher, Philip. 2014. *The Ethical Project*. Cambridge, MA: Harvard University Press.

Lamb, Henry. 1996. "Our Global Neighborhood (Report of the Commission on Global Governance): A Summary Analysis." *Eco-Logic*, no. January/February. https://humanbeingsfirst.files.wordpress.com/2009/10/cacheof-pdf-our-global-neighborhood-from-sovereignty-net.pdf.

Malone, David M., ed. 2004. *The UN Security Council: From the Cold War to the 21st Century*. Boulder, CO: Lynne Rienner Pub.

Prantl, Jochen. 2006. *The UN Security Council and Informal Groups of States: Complementing or Competing for Governance?* Oxford University Press, USA.

Scheuerman, William E. 2011. *The Realist Case for Global Reform*. 1st edition. Cambridge: Polity.

The Commission on Global Governance. 1995. *Our Global Neighborhood: The Report of the Commission on Global Governance*. 1st edition. Oxford ; New York: Oxford University Press.

UNEP. 2009. *The Environmental Food Crisis*.

United Nations. 1992. "Agenda 21, United Nations Conference on Environment & Development Rio de Janerio, Brazil, 3 to 14 June 1992." https://sustainabledevelopment.un.org/content/documents/Agenda21.pdf.

———. 1995. *Report of the Independent Working Group on the Future of the United Nations. The United Nations in Its Second Half-Century*. Ford Foundation.

———. 2012. "Future We Want—Outcome Document: Sustainable Development Knowledge Platform." https://sustainabledevelopment.un.org/rio20/futurewewant.

UN Secretary-General. 2014. "The Road to Dignity by 2030: Ending Poverty, Transforming All Lives and Protecting the Planet (Synthesis Report of the Secretary-General on the Post-2015 Sustainable Development Agenda)." United Nations. http://www.un.org/ga/search/view_doc.asp?symbol=A/69/700&Lang=E.

Wallerstein, Immanuel. 2004. *World-Systems Analysis: An Introduction*. Durham: Duke University Press.

Weiss, Thomas G., and Ramesh Thakur. 2010. *Global Governance and the UN: An Unfinished Journey*. Indiana University Press.

PARADIGM SHIFTS FOR SUSTAINABILITY

SECTION 3

Chapter 8

EDUCATION FOR SUSTAINABILITY

BY ELISE BOWDITCH

INTRODUCTION

Finding answers to the challenges of environmental sustainability is a thorny process. Use less? Manage better? Create substitutes? Solutions depend on altering our ways of thinking. This is because sustainability is a wicked problem. The defining characteristic of wicked problems is that they do not have one ultimate resolution; there is no single true or false answer (Rittel and Webber 1973). They change over time. Facts and values are inextricably bound together because goals and strategies are judged by multiple standards. Those affected may hold varied and oppositional views and propose different solutions. If this sounds disheartening, consider that similar problems exist in developing software, raising children, creating laws, or other human activities that lack a golden standard.

When writing clean software code, parenting children, or arguing for particular policies, a key element of success is the ability to live with ambiguity while persevering toward possible multiple effective solutions over time. Education for sustainability (EfS) is a common path all nations can pursue to gain this ability. This education is more than creating awareness of today's wicked problems; it is teaching outlooks and skills that prepare people to address them.

The systemic and wicked problems we face include phenomena such as climate change, air pollution, ocean acidification, species die-offs, and environmental refugees. As we strive for sustainability, it makes sense to educate everyone to meet these challenges, since people everywhere experience the consequences of these environmental damages.

In this chapter, we explore how education in the twenty-first century needs to change. We are at a watershed. Current education standards are no longer adequate to meet sustainability's challenges. Some subjects are less valuable today, and other knowledge and skills are increasingly needed, but in short supply. A hundred years ago, young men studied Latin and young women learned sewing as part of a well-rounded education. Then manufacturing eliminated the necessity for a woman to sew the family's clothes. Business skills, modern languages, science, and technology became far more useful knowledge for both men and women. We are again at a juncture where we must reassess what is the best and most relevant education and what subjects no longer serve the future. As you shall see in this chapter, although some nations are ahead of the curve, in general, the connection between education and sustainability needs stronger connections around the world.

EDUCATION AND SUSTAINABILITY

But What Is Education for Sustainability?

Defining education for sustainability is the first step toward reorienting the school system and informal channels that educate people. EfS is education *about* sustainability as a necessary precursor to education *for* creating sustainable economies, ecologies, and societies. Learning is the first step; practicing that knowledge is the next. UNESCO talks about "education for sustainable development," but development is a subset of the larger question of sustainability. Education for *sustainability* entails systems thinking. Systems thinking recognizes that the whole is more than a collection of parts and requires keeping the larger picture in view. It takes different perspectives and interdependencies into account. It looks at long-term consequences and goals and considers the effects of changes over time. A systemic approach to problems yields better understanding of where the leverage points are that can lead to a desired outcome. In a world facing many wicked problems, EfS is a means to support the systems thinking that will identify those leverage points. EfS practices social sustainability when it asks people to change their behavior and take action while respecting cultural diversity, gender equality, and working for community health. Making progress toward a sustainable world requires restructuring our ways of thinking, and education is a path to those revisions.

Right now, EfS as a deliberate, official process has a short formal history. However, sustainability, and learning sustainable practices, has a long *in*formal history. People in some societies in all eras lived in ways that were sustainable. A few societies managed to survive for long periods of time but most cultures and civilizations in the past grew, flourished, and imploded in the course of human existence. In some instances, implosion occurred gradually because environmental change was slow. Early agricultural societies crumbled as centuries of irrigation caused soil salinization. In other cases, a small number of people with a large territory believed that spoiling places did not matter, as in the initial European settlement and expansion of agriculture in the United States. We are coming to the end of locating "new" places where careless resource use can be tolerated, and many of our "old" places show the effects of long-term environmental degradation. Still, even in past eras, some ancient Roman authors understood what good land husbandry was, some tribal peoples had practices to limit their effects on the environment, and some farmers had traditions that balanced human land and water use with the needs of their local ecology. In a sense, EfS seeks to inculcate what has often been this cautionary, minority outlook into the majority way of thinking. It is this intentional, reflective, and institutionally supported process that makes EfS a new approach to education.

BACKGROUND

The history of the twentieth century is typically taught as advances in well-being set against a backdrop of world wars and armed conflict. Improvements in crop yields, medicine, sanitation, transportation, and communication mean that many people are better fed, healthier, and longer-lived than ever before. But there are other, less popularized aspects of the flowering of the industrial age. The advances are not equally distributed among all populations, and they came with a cost. The twentieth century produced acid rain, endocrine disruptors, fallout, oceanic dead

zones, and a host of pollution-related ills. We also produce more garbage than we know what to do with; see waste management and oceans
chapters.

Initially, these harmful side effects were accepted as the price of growth,
but by the 1970s, their damages became visible enough that people
started to notice and care. Acid rain killing forests, DDT poisoning birds,
the Great London Smog, and fires in the Cuyahoga River in Ohio are a
few of many incidents that brought the environment to public attention.
This attention led to concentrated efforts to try to correct the damages.
International conferences and pressure for new laws were (and still are)
part of the effort to raise accountability and promote responsibility for
nations to repair and protect the environment. It was increasingly understood that we all share this planet and that although it is a difficult,
long-term process, delegates from each nation must sit down together and
negotiate fair terms.

These international processes are central to the progress made on recognizing the need for environmental protection. They are also key elements
of understanding that we need to stop some of our most noxious activities
from the last century and walk a new path to create sustainability.

The following section explores a few of the milestones in the international negotiations process as they relate to education. Other chapters
in this book explore more fully the international process as it relates to
governance, or how the global community can write international laws
and enforce compliance. Here, we focus on understanding how we benefit
today from the United Nations declarations of the last few decades and
what the best available knowledge is for creating a sustainable future.
That future is detailed in "The Future We Want," the document produced
at the Rio+20 conference on sustainability in 2012.

Writing Declarations to Promote Ideals

The U.N. produces many declarations in support of protecting the environment and creating a better world for people. These agreements often
introduce new vocabulary that signals a shift in global consciousness.
For instance, the Universal Declaration of Human Rights was achieved
in 1948. Before then, "human rights" was a vague concept with no legal
or moral binding. Today, we understand human rights as a fundamental
concept that applies worldwide to every human being. Whether our rights
are respected or abused, we know we have them. Organizations like
Human Rights Watch and Amnesty International monitor injustice and

serve victims of human rights abuses. This is similar to how sustainability developed as its own term. Just as people before us pushed to have human rights understood as a fundamental right, so too are people pushing today for the rights of the planet and our rights to live on a healthy Earth.

The Rio Conference in 1992 grappled with the question: what does sustainable development mean, and what are the guiding principles for the future? This initial effort has since spawned worthy initiatives and regional cooperation.

One of these is Agenda 21, a voluntary plan for implementing the principles embodied in the Rio Declaration on Sustainable Development. Agenda 21 outlines steps that the United Nations, governments, and other large organizations can take in support of sustainable development. The idea is that any nation can implement it on its own terms, so Agenda 21 is applied at a local, national, regional, or global scale. Agenda 21 specifically calls for sustainability education to raise public awareness of the interconnectedness of the environment and development activities.

As large as Rio and Rio+20 were, the United Nations as an institution is active on a much bigger scale than holding conferences and publishing declarations. There are cyclical campaigns that run on an annual and decadal timeline. We have just completed the United Nations' Decade of Education for Sustainable Development (DESD), which runs from 2005–2015. UNESCO, one of the United Nations' largest subunits, leads the campaign to increase EfS in all the member nations of the U.N. through awareness campaigns and releasing funds that support Education for Sustainable Development activities. Most nations recognize that education for sustainability is a central, critical element of creating a sustainable society.

Turning Declarations into Programs and Action Steps

In 1991, university presidents around the globe issued the Halifax Declaration in support of "commitment to the principle and practice of sustainable development." Over the last 20 years, other education-specific declarations followed, the product of conferences held in Europe. What the Swansea (1993), Copernicus Charter (1994), Universitas21 (1997), Lüneburg (2001), Graz (2005), and Bonn (2009) declarations have in common is a written commitment to sustainability.

It is not coincidental that all of these cities are in Europe. European countries historically led positive action for environmental protection, and they continue to lead on EfS. Today, more people and member countries want to achieve education-related goals. Declarations publicize a commitment to EfS and measurement reinforces it. For instance, the European Training Foundation initiated the Torino Process in 2010, creating a regular policy conference that publishes annual reports for member countries on their progress toward sustainable education goals. Progress means such tangible results as creating programs and encouraging research in sustainability, revising campus practices to align with sustainability goals, and promoting outreach to the community and other schools. In the United States, the Association for the Advancement of Sustainability in Higher Education (AASHE) invites institutions of higher education worldwide to join its efforts in tracking and promoting sustainability at the college and university level. The hope is that tackling education for sustainability from several angles will mean rapid and fundamental improvement in higher education.

How governments interpret EfS shows there are multiple ways to achieve solutions to wicked problems. Funding is an important way organizations invest in the search for answers. New Zealand's Ministry of Foreign Affairs underwrites the New Zealand Partnerships for International Development Fund, which focuses on sustainable economic development, including education. The United States government funds the National Science Foundation, which in turn supports research on a variety of sustainability topics. Large organizations, such as the MacArthur Foundation or The Branch Foundation's programs in Southeast Asia, partner with schools or nongovernmental organizations that have specific sustainability goals. Multinational companies, such as Dow Chemical, Pepsi-Cola, or Disney, offer grants in support of sustainability projects.

There is no official body, no international law that organizes this financing. Finding actual dollar amounts directly associated with EfS is difficult, as their cost is often subsumed under general education expenses. Still, funding comes through a variety of sources, and there are many initiatives underway toward achieving sustainability all around the world. Even if we do not hear about them or see them for ourselves, governments, non-profit organizations, and businesses invest hundreds of millions of dollars every year to promote sustainability and education.

Some Countries are Doing More

When a national government commits to achieving sustainability goals, that commitment leads to effective plans and strategies at various levels of government. Finland and Germany created boards and commissions to investigate the status of sustainability education in their respective countries. Then, following their published reports in the 1990s and early 2000s, they formulated plans to weave sustainability into education. In Germany, in 2005, the Federal Ministry adopted a National Plan of Action to implement sustainable development into education. Cooperation between ministries produced a Cross-Curricular Framework for Global Development Education. This program supports educators who create and revise curricula in elementary, secondary, and vocational education to include sustainability lessons, activities, and requirements.

In Finland, having completed studies and reports on sustainability in the 1990s, the government asked schools to create plans for implementing and monitoring EfS and to bring their policies and operations into agreement with EfS principles by 2010. The policies move beyond cultivating an interest in observing or passively appreciating nature by asking students to develop value systems and "become aware of the consequences of their own actions" (Loukola 2001). While Finland's EfS effort is largely concentrated in the natural sciences, it is connected with vocational education (including adult education), home economics, humanities, arts and crafts, and languages. Finland is already home to one of the world's most rigorous teacher training programs (Sahlberg 2010), with just 1 in 10 applicants accepted. Now, Finland is becoming a global leader and demonstrating how to act on sustainability and education ideals.

EFS EFFORTS

Public documents such as U.N. declarations, educational websites, and school policies give the appearance of a commitment to sustainability. The actual practice of EfS must be examined at a local level, where people live and their actions take root. Good intentions published as a tidy action plan on a website get tested in the real world since constraints on funding, time, and people impact successful implementation of what look like excellent objectives on paper.

Local, community-based efforts to create sustainable education are scattered across the globe. Communities develop their own principles for sustainable education that work in their local settings. This is often not an individual project but a result of collaboration between different stakeholders. These stakeholders can be regional or small-town government agencies, teachers, schools, and families. In the following section, we look at sample projects of how schools interpret education for sustainability.

Creating new solutions to existing problems at a single school can raise new awareness. Starting with one clear goal, such as fresh vegetables for the school cafeteria, can lead to any number of worthwhile projects. Establishing the school garden to provide organic food to students can prompt examining wasteful water use. That examination can lead in turn to capturing rainwater for the garden. Evaluating the impact of the cafeteria within the school can help the school administrators examine their energy footprint. That can lead to fueling the kitchen through biogas. One project can point to multiple ways of making the school successful at sustainability. That success turns a school into a place where students learn about sustainability by contributing to it.

This inherently expansive nature of sustainability projects, even at a small scale such as a single school, reinforces the idea that implementing EfS at its best requires a holistic and interdisciplinary approach (Hargreaves 2008). EfS is more than tacking on a module in a biology class. Ideally, it entails rethinking how schools are organized, how subjects are taught, and the relationship between educators and their surrounding community. EfS in the classroom aims to instill habits of inquiry, offer experiential learning, and treat what happens in the classroom as part of bigger whole. The classroom is one small system in the larger school. Using EfS, classroom and school together create new standards for education. The process often extends the school community beyond the building to the larger expanse of the neighborhood, area, and region.

Introducing EfS into Schools

Curriculum development is one of the initial steps when introducing EfS into schools. Following the United Nations' call for the Decade of Education for Sustainable Development, many countries created national or regional plans to incorporate EfS in the school system through reorienting existing curricula, developing new materials, and revising teacher training. Others had no specific EfS plans but were committed to social justice and education overall. A UNESCO survey in 2007 found that some form of EfS plans were present in places as disparate as Mexico, South Africa, Italy, and Vietnam (Tilbury, Janousek, and Elias 2007).

The survey results revealed that educators, administrators, government organizations, and parents believe EfS is valuable. They recognize EfS as a way for students at all levels to attain commonly desired educational goals such as student engagement, critical thinking, skill building, and a connection to the wider community. Four main strategies exist for introducing and teaching EfS in primary and secondary schools. Schools may choose to adopt one or all of them depending on financial and social circumstances. Sustainability as its own topic is the simplest since it involves adding to, but not reworking, existing materials. Project-based learning has the advantage of being engaging and time-limited. Using sustainability as a lens to redesign core subjects is another approach with an initial expenditure of time and money for revision. Schools that truly want to address EfS in a holistic manner do so at a school or district-wide scale. Administration-led programs educate teachers and students about the importance of EfS and build collaboration between teachers. This reduces the time it takes to develop new lesson plans and encourages educators to share and adapt innovative curricula and teaching methods.

Implementing EfS at the college or university level is different than in schools serving lower grades. Teachers have more freedom to design their courses. A simple way to bring EfS into the curricula is requiring one course in sustainability of all students, which some schools have added as a general education requirement. More strategic approaches recognize that post-secondary institutions compete with each other for students. One way to compete is by offering degrees that youth want. Universities and colleges are creating more sustainability programs in response to growing demand.

The AASHE website lists 419 schools with sustainability-focused baccalaureate degrees, most of them in the United States or Europe. Almost half of these degrees are in environmental studies and sciences. The next highest category is engineering, and about 10% are in sustainability studies as a field in itself. Sustainability has breached programs in urban studies, agriculture, business, and architecture, although it is not yet a significant part of international studies, education, public administration, or policy.

Examining the Self

Applying sustainability principles to education requires systems thinking, and this in turn prompts teachers and students to broaden the scope of their efforts. Students and teachers who are committed to EfS often scrutinize the closest institution—their own schools—and seek to raise the standards. What good does it do to design holistic, interdisciplinary, creative programs that incorporate sustainability concepts into all curricula if the cafeteria food is unhealthy, its workers ill-paid, and minimal recycling leads to mountains of waste piling up outside the school? Following efforts to bring sustainability into studies, schools have, whether by pressure from students or direction from the top, begun to address their own direct environmental impact. Every institution has an ecological footprint: the institution draws resources from and puts waste back into the world. The systems approach that is built into EfS encourages questioning that footprint.

Youth who learn about sustainability observe their immediate environment. When they see the inconsistency between what they study and where they study it, they want to act on the principles of sustainability. The elementary school students on the island of Eleuthera in the Bahamas serve as a simple example of this cascading effect. The students were tired of seeing Styrofoam trash on the roads, so they researched cornstarch alternatives. Their goal is convincing restaurants and hotels to replace Styrofoam with locally sourced, biodegradable products, and their efforts caused one local store to stock the Styrofoam substitutes.

In most schools, though, two common themes emerge with respect to sustainability principles. One theme includes agricultural projects such as school gardens, horticulture, and plantings for the school grounds. The other is improving how schools fulfill their energy requirements for heating, cooking, and cooling.

Gardens

While schools with gardens existed throughout history, the recent rediscovery of their advantages occurs as part of a growing appreciation for sustainability education that incorporates experiential learning. In many developed nations, only a tiny percent of the population is engaged in agriculture today, and school gardens are one way to reconnect youth with nature through food production.

Gardens provide a number of benefits, especially for children and youth in urban areas. Designing, building, and maintaining a garden provide hands-on learning that reinforces classroom lessons. Gardening is exercise, and discussions necessary about creating a successful garden promote cooperation and awareness. When gardens supply the school cafeteria, all children are able to eat a more nutritious diet, an important advantage in areas where healthy food is expensive or unavailable. In developing nations, school gardens are a significant support for students who are chronically malnourished. Community involvement, beginning with digging the initial plots, gives parents and other adults a stake in the garden's success. Even if the emphasis is on horticulture, not food, gardens provide hands-on connections between youth and nature.

Various organizations promote school gardens. The National Garden Club in the United States offers certification and a small monetary award for school projects that incorporate indigenous plants. The Slow Food organization's members created school gardens, starting in the United States and expanding to Europe, with "A Thousand Gardens" planned for Africa. In Australia, the government funded the Stephanie Alexander Kitchen Garden Program, which created gardens in 599 schools that involve children working the plots, eating around a common table, and learning about a variety of fresh, seasonal foods. In St. Petersburg, Florida, the Edible Peace Patch Project is a nonprofit that promotes sustainable local food systems through urban agriculture. They started their first school garden at Lakewood Elementary in 2008, added another in 2009, and plan more. Their vision includes building an urban farm to produce healthy local food for additional schools and even hospitals.

There are places where school provides children's only guaranteed meal of the day. In fact, government-sponsored free school lunch programs exist in most developed countries. The U.N.'s World Food Program feeds children in African, Asian, Latin American, and Middle Eastern schools but lacks the resources to reach every child in every school. In Bhutan, for instance, rural children often walk long distances to school, and some arrive hungry. School gardens are a way to feed them. Healthy students make better academic progress since hunger interferes with the ability to concentrate and learn. The "Vegetables Go to School" project of the AVRDC (World Vegetable Center) is a nine-year, three-phase effort to fight malnutrition worldwide through school gardens. They target six countries in Asia and Africa. Garden Africa facilitates school gardens as supplementary nutrition. In Brazil, INMED Partnerships for Children runs Garden Brazil, reaching over 95,000 students.

Other gardening projects emphasize horticulture. In a comprehensive school in Petrozavodsk, Russia, students learn vocational skills by operating greenhouses and maintaining the gardens that surround the school. The Homer Science and Student Life Center in California not only grows enough food for itself and for donating to local charities, it produces olive oil from a heritage stand of olive trees. Along with a garden that provides food for faculty and students, the Green School in Bali donates bamboo cuttings to local farmers and then purchases the stalks when they are grown. Since the school is constructed of bamboo, this provides a beneficial connection to the community and a continuous source of raw materials.

School gardens provide bountiful opportunities for learning about sustainability. They benefit students, but their impact goes beyond school walls as they engage the local community. Whether by feeding children who might not otherwise eat, introducing gardens into urban settings, or providing hands-on learning, school gardens are an exciting trend in education.

Energy

Schools, like any large building, have sizable energy demands for heating, ventilation, and transportation. Energy is often the largest line item on a school's budget, so investigating ways to reduce a school's energy footprint is another common way to bring sustainability principles into practice. Districts can choose renewable energy sources or build new construction using energy-efficient materials and design. These innovations reduce previously wasteful practices.

In the United States, schools can invest in renewable energy sources by taking advantage of the US Department of Energy's National Renewable Energy Laboratory (NREL) programs to promote alternative energy. Jeffco Public Schools in Colorado has 30 schools with solar panels, and the ongoing benefits are greater than just cost savings. Science students measure the energy generated and design their own real-world applications to store the solar energy, then find ways to use the energy produced for experiments in the classroom (Scanlon 2012).

The "Wind for Schools" program in Kansas started with turbines installed in two districts. Other states are starting to initiate wind power installations in their districts when that is the optimal source of renewable energy. In sunny Florida, a public–private partnership, SunSmart Schools, outfitted around 50 public schools with solar electric systems that can return excess energy to the local power grid and keep a continuous charge for banks of backup batteries. Since Florida is often in the path of major storms and hurricanes, these batteries will provide energy to storm shelters at these schools if needed.

Alternative energy in schools is not just wind turbines or solar panels, which make sense in some climates but not in others. Southern Maine Community College, located next to the Atlantic Ocean, adapted maritime engineering technologies to make an ocean-based geothermal system for heating and cooling its Lighthouse Building without fossil fuels (Beatty, Klinedinst, and Reinheimer 2013, Koenig 2011).

Natural disasters sometimes provide an opportunity to rebuild using sustainable principles. Schools destroyed or damaged by Hurricane Katrina in New Orleans, Louisiana, were rebuilt using energy-efficient cooling systems, proper insulation, and daylighting to reduce electricity use. After Greensburg, Kansas, was leveled by an EF5 tornado in 2007, the citizens chose to rebuild as a model sustainable community. All civic and commercial buildings, including the K-12 school, were constructed to be energy-efficient. The school has a wind generator, with windows and overhangs designed for best use of the sun in different seasons.

This movement toward using renewable energy in schools and designing with energy efficiency for new construction is gaining traction in an increasing number of countries. A few intriguing examples illustrate how lesser-developed countries can take the lead. The draw of being self-sufficient in energy and saving money motivated the administrators at Ostrog Elementary School in Croatia, where elementary schools are chronically underfunded. A combination of crowdsourced funding and seed money from a local regional council enabled the school to install new lighting and a solar panel system. Future fundraising monies will be spent to insulate the roof and switch from heating with oil to biomass. Ostrog hopes it can inspire the other 2,000 elementary schools in Croatia to save costs by switching to sustainable energy sources (Dorsey 2014).

In Kyrgyzstan, a new school in the city of Osh replaced an older, drafty structure built in an era of cheap fossil fuels. Since the country imports most of its oil, reducing the need for fossil fuel is a high priority. The school conformed to new building codes that required reducing energy consumption by 40% by 2020. Children now wash with solar-heated water, while energy-efficient doors, windows, and thermal insulation keep students and teachers warm. The design minimized the external surface to reduce heat loss, and skylights supplemented electric lighting. The school cut its energy use by 50% with this appropriate design (Kyrgyzstan: Energy-efficient school offers national lessons 2014).

In some climates, building self-sufficiency into the design for a new school eliminates the need for energy use altogether. The Panyaden School in Thailand did just this. Though located in tropical Southeast Asia, the school has no air-conditioning system (except in computer classrooms). Their rammed-earth wall construction controls variations in both temperature and humidity, making the interiors comfortable for learning.

The above examples show education for sustainability that occurs in the buildings where students and teachers come together. Their sustainability projects inspire others, but the main benefits accrue to the schools. In the next section, we look at how informal networks are motivated to practice the awareness and take action toward achieving EfS in their communities.

We often assume issues are so complex that youth need adults to direct them for change to take hold. This is not always the case, and youth leaders even coordinate other young people to act for sustainability. The Nigeria Youth Climate Coalition in Africa is the hub for a network of youth who work on sustainability issues. They establish clubs in school and colleges, hold and attend conferences, and train their members to teach others about reducing waste, conservation, and other topics. The Small Island Developing States (SIDS) Youth Network provides a forum for youth to strategize and act on their concerns about the effects of climate changes on their nations. Conferences and a website connect youth as far apart as the Atlantic, South China Sea, and the Mediterranean.

Model communities provide another route to sustainability education. Adults pledge to live sustainably without being attached to any particular school. By practicing the principles and educating their neighbors, members provide a living sustainability learning center. In Zimbabwe, Marianne Knuth founded the village of Kufunda (meaning "learning") a decade ago. Although small (about 30 people), each member is committed to studying and practicing some aspect of sustainable living. Organic farming, health, herbal remedies, renewable energy, ecological building, waste disposal, and more are learned theoretically and practiced daily. Other villages send visitors to Kufunda, where they learn sustainable practices to bring back to their home communities.

Kufunda does not stand alone. The Global Ecovillage Network (GEN) lists about 400 deliberately planned, ecologically sound communities worldwide. GEN is a hub for information sharing between the variety of these communities that exist in places as urban as Copenhagen or removed as Jeju Island in South Korea. Many ecovillages are small (under 100 people) and emphasize different aspects of ecologically sound living. Crystal Waters in Australia focuses on permaculture and calls itself a "living wildlife site," since people there coexist with native animals. Urban rejuvenation in the Los Angeles Ecovillage means residents continually evaluate ways to lower their environmental impacts. Artists and ecologists founded the small village of Huehuecoyotl in Mexico, while the many members of the Federation of Damanhur in Italy are spiritually oriented. Regardless of their differences, communities that practice ecologically sound living are also committed to reaching out and educating others to spread by example and word what they continually learn.

Sometimes, implementing EfS encounters a web of interlocking challenges. In low-income countries or in marginalized populations such as the homeless, immigrants, or refugees, immediate needs for food and shelter take priority over education. High illiteracy rates, especially among women, add to the difficulties of putting education systems in place. These needs are not met by building a new school that integrates renewable energy technologies.

Instead, consider how the United Nation's Millennium Development Goal of achieving universal primary education in all member states can be effectively paired with the ideals of social justice. Educating marginalized populations integrates them as members of their surrounding community. The process of including previously marginalized populations through education allows a community to create a better version of itself.

Loreto Day School in Sealdah, Kolkata, broke an old mold of social division in India. What started as a part-time effort to teach street children in one of the best local schools developed into an integral program for the school. Regular students tutor 50 to 70 street children a day, which builds empathy and academic skills for all the children. Some of the students receiving tutoring continue to higher grades with financial assistance from the school. This approach to reduce inequality of access to education in Sealdah models best practices in community service.

In keeping with social justice, the Seeds of Spring initiative in Brazil brings sustainability education to the schools of Osasco and educates youth about their rights (Favaro 2012). The initiative promotes students as agents of change, both in their school and community. Through "reading world" activities such as walks and interviews with local residents, students learn to incorporate critical observation and reflect on sustainability in their neighborhoods. They discover what is needed locally and how to ask for changes. Their efforts include improved playground access and reduced violence in and out of school, and they identified a big community concern with improved waste management. While particular projects may or may not appear obviously sustainable, Seeds of Spring develops students' skills for seeing what is needed and creating change. These abilities fit EfS's larger goal of promoting critical thinking and problem-solving.

Even more innovative initiatives bypass any missing traditional school education and train adults to be development assistance providers in their own communities. The Barefoot College in Tilonia, a small town in

Rajasthan, India, trains rural youth and adults, mostly women, as solar engineers. Their training empowers these people to bring electricity to their home villages. Founded in 1972 by visionary social activist Bunker Roy, students learn to make, install, use, and maintain solar solutions for water pumps, electricity, cooking, and desalinization. Roy's vision of rural self-sufficiency includes the campus, which runs on solar energy. The beauty of the program is that students learn about operating solar water pumps and lamps even if they are illiterate. For those who want education beyond this valuable job training, the college offers courses in reading, writing, and math skills to adults and children. Still, its main mission is bringing students in, training them, and sending them back with skills and tools so they can power their villages with solar energy. The college says it has trained students from several hundred rural Indian and African communities, lighting about 12,000 households.

India, with a largely rural and rapidly growing population of 1.3 billion, has many development needs. In recent years, innovative people have found ways to meet more of those needs. To understand them clearly and begin to address them appropriately, the Lok Bharati Institute in Gujarat, India, "adopts" nearby villages. Students and staff take a multipronged approach in the villages to improve soil and water conservation, expand solar electrification, organic farming, and animal husbandry, and mitigate health and sanitation concerns. As a step in earning their graduate degrees, students from the institute live with a family for up to six months to gain direct experience and understanding of the barriers to sustainability. Their experiences funnel back into the institute so people there can improve their efforts toward creating sustainable practices and help bridge differences between local residents and the institute.

Bali, Indonesia, is well known by tourists for its tropical climate and relaxed way of life. The Green School there ties itself to the local community through the bamboo-growing project, which entails ongoing collaboration and exchanging agricultural information. In this way, it maintains and enhances both social and ecological sustainability. These examples show how EfS is a two-way process where theory and practice combine for mutual learning.

Measuring Change

We have seen that any one school or community's vision and initiative can inspire people to create changes in their community. The process of developing these changes provides ongoing feedback about what is practical and successful, but how can people know if their work is achieving a greater good? How can they determine if their efforts are in keeping with others making similar changes? Furthermore, how can any of us know what sustainability efforts exist and whether they are making a difference in the turn toward sustainability and EfS? To answer these questions, governments and other organizations create ways to measure progress toward EfS using carefully chosen indicators and benchmarks. They often provide tools for creating ways to make progress, measure that progress, and offer recognition for success.

For instance, schools measure progress on any number of improvements. They can reduce their environmental footprints, use school gardens for fresh, healthy meals, or develop sustainability curricula. At the secondary level and above, schools can also institute "green" career paths, create departments that focus on sustainability, and offer degrees that demonstrate they value teaching and researching sustainability questions. At all levels, they can empower students to be active participants in the process.

In the United States, the Department of Education rewards elementary and secondary efforts through its Green Ribbon Schools environmental education program. Each year, all 50 states can nominate one to five schools for the honor of being a "Green Ribbon School." What does it take to win? In 2011, Watkins Elementary School in Jackson, Missouri, won by starting a recycling program that has since won other awards from the state. It created student gardens and added environmental learning activities such as trips to farms and agricultural museums to the curricula. Though not part of the Green Ribbon criteria, its performance on state assessments improved in the years after these efforts began.

The Green Ribbon program awards schools that make changes based on three main criteria: reduced environmental impact, improving student and staff health, and demonstrating effective environmental and sustainability education. How schools meet these criteria is up to them. In contrast, the Foundation for Environmental Education started the Eco-Schools program in the mid-1990s, a seven-step process for schools to change their habits and earn Eco-School's "Green Flag" designation. Building awareness of sustainability, assessing current needs, creating action plans, monitoring, curriculum development, and community outreach are broad terms that provide a framework for schools, but the problems chosen and the solutions vary depending on each school's situation. A critical piece is that students must be actively involved throughout the process. For instance, students at Edudelta, an agricultural college in the

Netherlands, developed a rainwater system for the toilets at the school and powered it with a windmill. Alongside primary school students, they operate a seasonal restaurant based on produce from their garden, and they are planning to create a bicycle taxi business for local transportation. In Slovenia, students at Zadobrova Primary School in Ljubljana Polje built a push scooter out of waste scooter parts to demonstrate recycling and reuse. Their design won the Toyota Fund's International Environment and Innovation Competition in the Sustainable Mobility category. More usual projects are gardens, outdoor learning, recycling, and reducing energy consumption. Each year, schools can apply for the award of the "Green Flag." Eco-Schools is the largest program for promoting sustainable schools in the world, with "Green Flag" schools in over 55 countries.

Colleges and universities also want to measure their progress toward sustainability. One major effort to track sustainability efforts in post-secondary institutions is AASHE, which started in 2005. AASHE's value is in providing a Sustainability Tracking, Assessment and Rating System™ (STARS) that allows organizations to measure their sustainability. While initially centered on higher education institutions in the United States, Canada, and Mexico, the program is open to any organization in the world. A small number of universities from the Global South and other areas, plus businesses and NGOs, have joined AASHE and use the STARS system to measure their sustainability and plan improvements.

Organizations like AASHE or Eco-Schools serve several functions. First, they offer road maps that schools (or other organizations) can use and adapt in their search for sustainability education, cost-cutting, or environmental responsibility. Second, by acting as hubs for information about what other schools are doing, they help people build a community where those who are committed to sustainable ideals can share their ideas and experiences. Finally, by offering awards, these organizations recognize and reward the changes in thinking and the hard work that results as schools embrace sustainability.

CHALLENGES TO IMPLEMENTING EFS

As we have seen in the sections above, people create exciting, engaging, and useful projects and programs when they get involved with EfS. Whether EfS starts as a deliberate effort to change a particular school's outlook and practice or is embedded within a larger mission, support for EfS is growing. The U.N.'s Decade for Education in Sustainable Development was a major push to make educational institutions, governments, and students aware of the possibilities and rewards of education for sustainability. Although the DESD winds down in 2015, its work is not finished. Challenges remain.

Many obstacles to expanding EfS overlap challenges for education in general. Nations are working to attain the Millennium Goal of universal elementary enrollment. There are still some 57 million children worldwide who were not in school as of 2011. Hard-to-reach rural populations, low secondary completion, and family poverty affect youth in all nations. In the developing world, child labor interferes with schooling. So does opposition to female education where women are constrained by law and custom, such as the Middle East and Pakistan. In addition to these general obstacles to education, EfS faces its own set of challenges due to its relative newness, sparseness, philosophic and practical resistance, and the need for financial investment.

Most EfS efforts date to the last decade, although a few, like Eco-Schools, started in the early or mid-1990s. Because it is still new (compared to institutions such as governments or most education systems), it is a sparse web on the education landscape. Eco-schools reached around 11 million students as of 2011, but those youth are about 1.5% of the world's 750 million students. The many schools and universities that sign declarations committing themselves to some form of sustainability are a minority within all the schools in any area. This puts EfS in the position of being "last hired, first fired." If EfS is not well established, then local or national economic crises that affect education funding will affect EfS, too. In higher education, cuts to research, decreased student grants, higher tuitions, and fewer faculty means all education quality deteriorates. These cuts make it more difficult to bring EfS into a school and endanger newly rooted programs.

At the primary and secondary levels, people opposed to changes in the "traditional" school model may resist EfS. In the United Kingdom, the education secretary tried to return to an older, "just the facts" model of education by removing references to sustainability for secondary exams and limiting its mention in curricula for the lower grades (Adams 2013, Portilla 2013). This attempt did not succeed since strong public outcry and teacher criticisms stopped the "reform." This story demonstrates that although EfS is new, it gathered enough support in the U.K. to resist efforts to eliminate it.

Even when EfS has widespread government support on paper, practical objections can stall its implementation. In New Zealand, the Ministry of Education published recommendations for EfS, but many schools have not (yet) widely adopted those suggestions. Educators objected to the extra effort to get EfS started and feared they were going to be told what to teach (Tulloch 2009, Curren 2009). This points to the importance of good support for educational professionals when introducing EfS to school. That support must address concerns from educators who are not proficient in environmental studies or do not believe that the environment is important. Otherwise, teachers and administration staff may wait to see if EfS is a passing fad. Their skepticism risks making EfS into a slogan rather than a program.

An argument against the fear that EfS will prescribe what teachers must teach is that EfS is educative by design. It requires exploring the problems and arguments surrounding sustainability, not determining exactly what those problems and arguments consist of. Learners are expected to develop their own critical approaches through practice, especially through focusing on local projects. Those who fear that EfS determines the exact subject matter or teaching method misunderstand its main goal. EfS is designed so that students can develop the necessary skills to meet the challenges of sustainability. These skills are not rigidly defined, just as critical thinking does not define the subject matter or outcome of that thinking.

Another objection to EfS is that it is inconsistent, as its many goals can conflict with each other in particular projects (Curren 2009). For instance, EfS may be easy to "sell" to local constituents in its ecological aspects, such as adding in environmental education to the science curricula. The more difficult goals of empowering students and fomenting change do not fit well with cultures or schools that emphasize memorization and obedience, such as those run by evangelical Christian or fundamentalist Islam communities (Berliner 1997, Dean 2005, Prokop 2003). Social justice may collide with environmental concerns. Panyaden School in Thailand feeds itself and provides its own energy, but as a private school, the tuition and fees easily equal ½ of the annual average salary in Thailand. The University of Minnesota's plans to build a showcase community demonstrating sustainable energy requires paving over prime farmland and constructing a gravel mine (both environmental issues; Belkin and Thurm 2012).

Criticisms that EfS is both prescriptive *and* inconsistent are at odds with each other. These objections overlook the process that new, major changes in thinking experience as they gather support. Developing new ways of doing things involves some incoherence and inconsistency in the beginning. For instance, early advocates for human rights argued about what rights were, who could hold them, and the best way to obtain them. Our general understanding of rights today comes after a century of ongoing attention and debate. EfS is in a similar position. No individual EfS effort can solve all pillars in all ways at all times. The definition of EfS stipulates that it be defined and implemented locally, that it be negotiated. If it had one blanket application, it would not be EfS. The politicians, educators, youth, and citizens who want to see EfS grow and succeed will continue to discuss and define what EfS means for their local communities, schools, and families. They will answer for themselves how EfS links to other themes in education and how to develop appropriate teaching materials and pedagogies. These ongoing discussions will not and should never resolve into one unified solution, as befits work on wicked problems.

Financial Investment

The greatest challenge to EfS is not its newness, sparseness, or internal inconsistencies, but that every sustainability effort needs a financial commitment. Retraining teachers takes time, and revising materials takes money. Transforming energy systems requires upfront costs. Even with governmental programs and support, money for EfS is a small slice of total education budgets. This is especially true for higher education, which runs on large institutional budgets and has many layers of income and expenses.

The fears and resistance to funding EfS play out within the general realm of scarcity, also known as poverty. Although nations with lower GDPs are not as capable of funding EfS as higher GDP countries, there are regional, family, and personal effects that make poverty a challenge to EfS at many scales.

Poverty's Challenges to EfS

The number one United Nations' Millennium Development Goal is eradicating extreme poverty and hunger. Goal number two is achieving universal primary education. There are reasons for these being the top two goals. Poverty and education are related: education helps fight poverty, and extreme poverty inhibits schooling. Lower education means a lower standard of living. Nations with the lowest incomes have the lowest school participation, while wealthier nations have higher enrollment and completion rates. Within countries, poor youth who do not or cannot finish secondary levels of school fare worse than those who can complete a post-secondary education.

Finland understood the importance of EfS and decided to make quality education a right for all children, building sustainability into their curricula. Still, Finland is small and wealthy, and gaps between the rich and poor exist within all nations. In developing countries, poor families lose critical income when child workers go to school, or they need youth to fetch water or herd animals. In developed countries, poor children often experience stress from living in violent neighborhoods, moving frequently, exposure to drugs, and disrupted family lives. In places with little state-sponsored schooling, such as Latin America, the private education available to the middle and upper classes is significantly better than the public education available to lower-income families. In the United States, a similar gap exists between the public schools in middle- and upper-class neighborhoods and poorer urban and rural communities. Lower teacher quality, crowded classrooms, outdated or inadequate material, and poor infrastructures are comparable among poor public schools in the United States and low-income nations.

All these factors inhibit adopting EfS, if only because the primary focus is on either establishing a school or maintaining the existing one rather than thinking about improvements. The first step toward building sustainable education is often improving the well-being of a population. Projects that improve a community's standard of living increase the odds of the children there getting a better education. For example, improved sanitation and installing nearby, reliable water supplies frees girls to attend school in areas where they are the family's water providers (Adams et al. 2009). Even better is including the youth in question as stakeholders. Approaches that respect youth and involve them in devising solutions can create educational opportunities without forcing undue hardship on families. Young workers in India insisted on having school in the evening so they could continue to contribute to their families through working (John 2003) yet still learn to read and write.

Regardless of their family income, EfS in primary and secondary education worldwide is one way of making sure that people are trained to think about sustainability. With EfS, youth can grow up accustomed to considering the larger systems that they live within. For instance, a case study in the Philippines incorporated youth into education for disaster risk reduction, with children feeling safer and being more aware of dangerous areas. The children took this information back to their homes and community (Venton and Venton 2012). As nations make progress on the first two Millennium Goals, higher literacy and better numeracy from increased primary education will feed into a demand for more secondary and post-secondary education. They will produce more engineers, scientists, medical staff, and businesspeople. Whether youth grow up in developed or developing nations, they will all make better decisions about the direction of their respective fields if they have an education that includes sustainability.

Youth who do not or cannot continue to finish a post-secondary education will still operate within social, economic, and governmental structures that are staffed by others with college degrees. These graduates, in particular, will occupy positions where they make policy decisions that affect their communities, the regions they live in, and even the world. Because of this, the challenges that EfS faces in higher education deserve a separate discussion.

Specific Challenges for EfS in Higher Education

Under an older Western model, education's benefits were understood as a public good. Educated citizens contributed through civic involvement in local governance and on parks commissions and boards of education. They started businesses, developed the arts, and generally improved society. This model depended on continuous government funding at a time when a smaller percent of youth enrolled in college (Altbach, Reisberg, and Rumbley 2009). EfS fits naturally into this schema of public support of the public good, but current societal values in the United States no longer uphold it.

The United States is still a leader, and often a model, for higher education. In the recent generation, a shift took place in how colleges and universities operate. Higher education in the United States became more of a private endeavor, with students and their families taking on higher portions of the cost, even as those costs increased. Depending on the measure, the price of a college education rose anywhere from 500–1,200% over the last 15 to 30 years (Jamrisko and Kolet 2012, Jamrisko and Kolet 2013, Carey 2012). The rise is fueled by a number of factors.

One reason for higher tuitions is that colleges in the United States used to rely on state and federal support. The decades-long push to dismantle government programs decreased tax revenues at federal, state, and local levels, and states made deep cuts to public health and education. While all sectors took hits, more states cut higher education funding than tampered with K–12 or health budgets (Oliff 2013). When students and families are paying more tuition, universities feel they must compete on amenities. Sport teams and their facilities and better dorms, gyms, and dining halls are but a few of the many construction projects undertaken in the last 10 to 15 years. Construction requires borrowing, and institutional debt at public four-year colleges doubled in the last decade. Another cause behind college's higher cost is that the number of administrative personnel ballooned. The newest president of the University of Minnesota found that there were 3½ students per employee—yet the number of teachers had not increased in the last dozen years (Belkin and Thurm 2012). A recent nationwide study found a 40% decline in the ratio of faculty and staff to administrators (Desrochers and Kirshstein 2014). Since faculty counts did not increase, that means that administrator positions did.

These developments affect research conducted at universities. The old model of funding, where universities distributed block grants as they saw fit, shifted to researchers competing for specific projects. Increased university ties to government and industry risk limiting the direction and scope and results of research. Industry likes to control the intellectual property rights for research it funded. The idea of generating knowledge as a public good thus comes into conflict with patents, licenses, and commercial results (Altbach, Reisberg, and Rumbley 2009). EfS, with its emphasis on sharing knowledge and interdisciplinary approaches, runs counter to knowledge production as a commercial endeavor.

The emphasis on amenities and administration costs in American colleges and universities mean that sustainability programs are in the mix of all educational programs competing for funding. Increasing class size and decreased hiring of tenure-track professors in favor of adjuncts undercuts the stability and authority needed for a creative EfS effort. With around 70% of teaching positions being adjuncts, this leads to an unequal and socially unjust hierarchy, the opposite of what EfS stands for. Budget tightening puts EfS in jeopardy through the relative newness of the subject and leads to a downward spiral of good faculty leaving for better opportunities, thus making the university even less competitive. The "solutions" to financial dilemmas threaten to push EfS efforts aside.

These responses to economic changes and demand are choices that university leaders make. They make these decisions operating within a larger sphere of government support. Universities around the globe experienced increased student admissions and rising tuitions in the past few decades and they too depend on government and donor funds in addition to tuition and other fees. The Global Financial Crisis of 2008 (GFC) provides a window into how different governments met the challenge of funding higher education, since the GFC affected the financial stability of many nations. Some countries, especially those with considerable existing debt, chose to cut their support for education as part of their general budget cuts. Most Eastern Europe nations took this approach, as did Iceland and Ireland. In other nations, the leaders believed that education was the key to short-term recovery and long-term economic health. South Korea, France, India, and Malaysia increased their spending for higher education. China used the crisis to restructure government support for low-income and rural students. The result? In 2012, many nations that cut higher education budgets had not recovered that money. Poland, Croatia, Spain, and Greece, for instance, had lower higher education support in 2012 than they did in 2008. Places that reinforced their commitment to higher education as a public good, such as France, Norway, and Hong Kong, maintained or increased that funding by 2012 (European Commission/EACEA/Eurydice 2013, Meek et al. 2012).

The United States was neither worst nor best in its response to the financial crisis. The USA's higher education financing system is state-dependent, and many states chose to cut their support. Although the federal government offered stimulus funding for education, those funds only partially replaced lost resources. Most money went to elementary and secondary rather than higher education. The effects of the GFC came on top of trends toward other budget cuts, increased tuition, new student fees, and reduced scholarships and grants (Altbach, Reisberg, and Rumbley 2009). As a result, middle-class and poorer students find it increasingly difficult to obtain a college education. This reduces the overall education level in society. It moves higher education in the USA along the path toward countries like Brazil or Indonesia, which have a long tradition of private, elite universities that do not recognize higher education as a *public* good or right. Worse, it encourages other nations to follow suit. The growing demand for private institutions in all countries contradicts sustainability's goals of social justice and educating everyone.

Bifurcation of Wealth

The increasing gap between private and public education creates a tension between wealth-generating processes for the few and the stated desire for more educated workforces and populations. This bifurcation in access to education is related to the concentration of wealth. The world is, overall, richer now than 30 years ago, but Credit Suisse reports indicate that almost half of the world's wealth is owned by about 1% of the population.

The goals and implementation of sustainability, with its social justice component, are at odds with the business interests of the wealthy. Wealth disparity means that control of who works on what problems is concentrated in fewer and richer hands. These hands do not necessarily recognize or care about sustainability. The oil and gas industry go to extreme measures to deny climate change, for instance, because acknowledging the role of increased carbon emissions jeopardizes their industries. In institutions that depend on unsustainable industry monies for support, EfS may find itself limited to environmental studies without the accompanying revision in pedagogy that a deep implementation requires. Recent changes, however, show a shift in priorities, as a number of institutions around the world are divesting themselves from fossil fuel assets. National church organizations, foundations, cities, Stanford University (in California), even the Rockefeller family are eliminating investments in gas and oil from their portfolios. In the United States and Europe, students are demanding that their schools divest. Fossil fuels are one obvious target, but similar pressure could be brought to bear on other unsustainable industries. The movement to divest, measured as concerned citizens taking action, indicates that sustainability is on many minds, and student involvement could mean that youth would welcome more EfS courses and degrees.

EFS IS HUMANITY'S NEXT PHILOSOPHICAL CHALLENGE

The ongoing wicked ecological problems, such as soil erosion, the demise of fisheries, or water shortages, find a common thread in the theme of maximizing short-term gains over long-term well-being. This human tendency goes back millennia. It is not tied to particular governments, economic systems, or religious philosophies; neither are the counter-examples of well-run local fisheries, proper plowing, or water conservation that existed in all eras. This demonstrates that sustainable livelihoods are not dependent upon particular institutions, but on people within those institutions being willing to think about how they live.

This is the major change EfS asks us to make: to prioritize the long-term over the short-term. This outlook runs counter to many current ways of thinking in business (with its end-of-quarter measures), in social issues that receive sound-bite solutions, and in conflicts that never end. In this aspect, EfS holds the seeds for a paradigm shift. It is not just education about social justice, environmental issues, or economic concerns—it is education *for taking a long-view systems approach* in understanding the interactions of society, economics, and the environment.

EfS requires new approaches to pedagogy. Cross-disciplinary studies and inquiry-based learning will have to overturn memorization and knowledge silos. Because of this, EfS is a wicked problem in itself. It requires cooperation from many stakeholders. Successful projects network and lobby for support up and down a community "ladder." For instance, the Peace Patch in Pinellas County partners with the schools, health department, Florida Department of Agriculture, and other agencies and institutions, public and private, in the Tampa Bay region. The SIDS Youth Network came about through collaboration between UNESCO, UNICEF, and other U.N. branches, regional agencies, and NGOs. These successes demonstrate how important top-down and bottom-up support is when implementing EfS. Local interest, activists, and forward-looking school leaders can raise awareness and bring EfS to life in classrooms, schools, and communities. EfS also needs institutional support with progressive governmental leadership and adequate funding to prepare the youth for the future.

The current generation faces challenges such as solid waste management or deforestation that are hugely different in scale and scope from similar problems in previous generations. We also face the new environmental problem of climate change and the host of consequences it brings. Yet we have unprecedented tools at our disposal. Worldwide communication makes it easier to disseminate the leaps in scientific knowledge gained in the last few decades. Computer speed and storage increase as their cost comes down so that we can store and make sense of vast amounts of data. We know more about Earth's systems than we did even 30 years ago and can apply systems thinking to understand these complex systems and their interactions.

Older models of education are no longer sufficient to prepare people for meeting wicked environmental problems, and those models must change. EfS is a means to include systems thinking and sustainability as everyday aspects of learning. One future for schools that respond to the need for more education about sustainability is that they attract more students and graduate more people with skills that meet real business, academic, and environmental needs. In that respect, having schools that teach with EfS scattered across many places and connected via the Internet can be an advantage. These schools may be a sparse web, but one local success story can breed another, one school can inspire nearby schools to emulate its attainments. As more schools at the elementary level adopt EfS principles, children (and their parents) will expect those principles to continue into secondary education and into higher learning. More and better schooling for everyone will normalize thinking about sustainability. Even successful partial implementations will mean that more youth will be aware of, and have skills for, addressing the wicked problems of sustainability. It will be a given to consider the bigger picture—and possible consequences of omission—over the long term when planning instead of the add-on it is now. Multiple, ongoing experiences will yield a solid body of best practices available to all schools. Through outreach to community and businesses, EfS efforts will move society toward planning for all aspects of sustainability: social, economic, and environmental. Thinking about the future and possible long-term consequences of decisions will be common and regular, while short-term-only thinking will be out of date. When that threshold is reached, more and more people in the world will have a better chance at living equitable and environmentally sustainable lives.

GLOSSARY

Agenda 21: A voluntary, non-binding action plan produced at the United Nations Conference on Environment and Development at the Rio Summit of 1992. The plan provides steps that local, regional, and national governments can put sustainable practices in place. The Agenda includes suggestions for poverty reduction, less pollution, and increased natural resource conservation. It also asked for financial commitments from developing countries to assist in this process.

Decade of Education for Sustainable Development: A 10-year program sponsored by the United Nations to promote Education for Sustainable Development worldwide. The Decade started in 2005 and ends in 2014, with UNESCO designated as the lead agency. The vision for the DESD included high-quality education for all in the knowledge, skill, and practice of sustainability.

Eco-Schools: Eco-Schools is an international program run under the Foundation for Environmental Education (FEE). It seeks to inspire, guide, and reward schools that empower students in sustainability education and projects. It offers the "Green Flag" award for schools that follow its outline for becoming more environmentally friendly.

Ecological footprint: A way of measuring the balance between what humans consume and the waste we produce versus what the environment can continue to produce and absorb. A large footprint indicates overconsumption and an excess of waste produced relative to what the environment can absorb per unit of measurement. A unit of measurement is usually per capita. In 2007, the global ecological footprint was estimated at 1.5 Earths; we would need another half an Earth to continue at our current consumption and waste production levels.

Education for sustainability: Education for sustainability focuses on developing students' knowledge and skills for creating a sustainable future. This process often entails revising curricula, changing pedagogy, and emphasizing holistic, inquiry-based learning. It emphasizes critical thinking and action to improve schools and their surrounding communities.

Global Ecovillage Network: An umbrella organization that collects and distributes information about the growing worldwide network of sustainable model communities.

Global Financial Crisis of 2008: The worst financial crisis since the Great Depression of the 1930s, it was brought about by the end of the US "housing bubble" of the late 1990s and early 2000s. Other contributing factors include deregulation of trading and the rise of "creative" trading practices, lack of adequate capital to back investments, and prioritizing short-term money flow over long-term wealth building. The consequences were huge: big drops in stock markets worldwide, higher and longer unemployment, and losses in the trillions of dollars.

Green Ribbon Schools: A United States Department of Education program that seeks to inspire schools, districts, and institutes of higher education to create sustainable practices. The program rewards schools that reduce environmental impact, improve students' and staff health, and implement environmental education.

Model communities: These are communities whose physical and social structures are carefully and deliberately planned from inception. They often have a mission of living in accordance with a set of beliefs (such as environmental balance or religious tenets) and a goal of being an example to the world of what is possible.

Public good: A public good is a service or item that any one person can use without reducing its amount or availability to others. Often government supported (or initiated), public goods are things like radio broadcasts, sewer systems, education, statistics, or data.

Rio Conference in 1992: The United Nations Conference on Environment and Development (UNCED) held in Rio de Janeiro, Brazil, in 1992. It is also called the Rio Summit or the Earth Summit. Over 170 governments and 2,400 representatives of nongovernmental organizations attended to construct international agreements for sustainability. The conference produced the Agenda 21 document. A similar conference in Rio, 20 years later, in 2012, is known as Rio+20.

Sparse web: This phrase is used in this chapter to indicate the incidence of schools with some form of sustainability education in place. There are many, but like knots in a net, they are thinly distributed.

Systems thinking: The process of analyzing the whole picture to understand how the various parts interact over time, what feedback processes keep the system in existence, and where the interdependencies are located. Systems thinking can be applied in any area of research.

The Future We Want: A document produced at Rio+20, the United Nations Conference on Environment and Development held in Rio de Janeiro, Brazil, in 2012, 20 years after the initial Rio Summit. The document outlines ways to build social, economic, and environmental sustainability. The 193 U.N. members that signed it also made voluntary financial commitments of over $500 billion to support its implementation.

Torino Process: The European Training Foundation initiated the Torino Process in 2010 as a way to measure the progress of vocational education and training, including incorporating sustainability. The Process uses a biannual, participatory, analytical review to obtain information about policies and best practices.

Wicked problem: A wicked problem is one that resists a final resolution, and each interim solution may address some aspects of the bigger situation but then beget other problems. Incomplete or contradictory information, multiple stakeholders, shifting requirements, and complex interdependencies among aspects of the issue are all hallmarks of wicked problems.

REFERENCES

Adams, John, Jamie Bartram, Yves Chartie, Therese Dooley, Hazel Jones, Kinoti Meme, Annemarieke Mooijman, Dinesh Shrestha, Jackie Sims, and Peter Van Maanen. 2009. "Water, Sanitation and Hygiene Standards for Schools in Low-Cost Settings." World Health Organization.

Adams, Richard. 2013. "'Tough and Rigorous' New National Curriculum Published." *The Guardian*, July 8. http://www.theguardian.com/education/2013/jul/08/new-national-curriculum-published.

Altbach, Philip G., Liz Reisberg, and Laura E. Rumbley. 2009. "Trends in Global Higher Education: Tracking an Academic Revolution." In *A Report Prepared for the UNESCO 2009 World Conference on Higher Education*: UNESCO.

Beatty, Scott, Robert Klinedinst, and David Reinheimer. 2013. "Harnessing Seawater: An Innovative Thermal Exchange HVAC System." Association for the Advancement of Sustainability in Higher Education. http://www.aashe.org/resources/case-studies/harnessing-seawater-innovative-thermal-exchange-hvac-system.

Belkin, Douglas, and Scott Thurm. 2012. "Deans List: Hiring Spree Fattens College Bureaucracy—and Tuition." *WSJ.com*, December 28.

Berliner, David C. 1997. "Educational Psychology Meets the Christian Right: Differing Views of Children, Schooling, Teaching, and Learning." *Teachers College Record* 98 (3): 381–416.

Carey, Kevin. 2012. "What's Driving College Costs Higher?" *National Public Radio (NPR)*. http://www.npr.org/2012/06/26/155766786/whats-driving-college-costs-higher.

Curren, Randall. 2009. "Education for Sustainable Development: A Philosophical Assessment." *Impact* 18: 1–68. doi: 10.1111/j.2048-416X.2009.tb00140.

Dean, Bernadette L. 2005. "Citizenship Education in Pakistani Schools: Problems and Possibilities." *International Journal of Citizenship and Teacher Education* 1(2): 35–55.

Desrochers, Donna M., and Rita Kirshstein. 2014. "Labor Intensive or Labor Expensive? Changing Staffing and Compensation Patterns in Higher

Education." In *Delta Cost Project*. Washington, DC: American Institutes for Research.

Diamond, Jared. 2005. *Collapse: How Societies Choose to Fail or Succeed*. New York: Viking Press.

Dorsey, Sherrell. 2014. "Croatian Elementary School Hopes to Become the First Energy Independent School in the World." *Inhabitots.com*. http://www.inhabitots.com/croatian-elementary-school-hopes-to-become-the-first-energy-independent-school-in-the-world/.

"Education and the Global Economic Crisis: Summary of Results of the Follow-Up Survey." 2010. Education International. http://download.ei-ie.org/Docs/WebDepot/05March10_Impactcrisisreport_followup_MDK.pdf.

European Commission/EACEA/Eurydice. 2013. "Funding of Education in Europe 2000–2012: The Impact of the Economic Crisis." Eurydice Report. Luxembourg.

Favaro, Fernanda. 2012. "Brazil: When Students Awake, the Whole World Changes." In *ESD Success Stories*. United Nations Educational, Scientific, and Cultural Organization (UNESCO).

Ginsberg, Benjamin. 2011. "Administrators Ate My Tuition." *Washington Monthly*.

Hargreaves, Lucy G. 2008. "The Whole-School Approach to Education for Sustainable Development: From Pilot Projects to Systemic Change." *Policy & Practice: A Development Education Review* 6 (Spring): 69–74.

"Higher Education For Sustainable Development: Final Report of International Action Research Project." 2007. Forum for the Future. Organisation for Economic Co-operation and Development (OECD). http://www.oecd.org/education/innovation-education/centreforeffectivelearningenvironments-cele/45575516.pdf.

Jamrisko, Michelle, and Ilan Kolet. 2012. "Cost of College Degree in U.S. Soars 12 Fold: Chart of the Day." *Bloomberg*, August 15. http://www.bloomberg.com/news/2012-08-15/cost-of-college-degree-in-u-s-soars-12-fold-chart-of-the-day.html.

Jamrisko, Michelle, and Ilan Kolet. 2013. "College Costs Surge 500% in U.S. Since 1985: Chart of the Day." *Bloomberg*, August 26. http://www.bloomberg.com/news/2013-08-26/college-costs-surge-500-in-u-s-since-1985-chart-of-the-day.html.

John, Mary. 2003. *Children's Rights and Power: Charging Up for a New Century*. London and New York: Jessica Kingsley Publishing.

Kamenetz, Anya. 2014. "$1 Trillion and Rising: A Plan for a $10K Degree." Third Way.

Koenig, Seth. 2011. "Southern Maine Community College Center an Example of 'Our Economic Future,' Pingree Says." *Bangor Daily News*, September 29. http://bangordailynews.com/2011/09/29/business/southern-maine-community-college-center-an-example-of-'our-economic-future'-pingree-says/.

Loukola, Marja-Leena. 2001. "Education for Sustainable Development in Schools." In *Education For Sustainable Development In Finland*, edited by Marja-Leena Loukola, Simo Isoaho and Kaisa Lindström. Finland: Ministry of Education.

Martin, Andrew. 2012. "Building a Showcase Campus, Using an I.O.U." *The New York Times*, December 13.

Meek, V. Lynn, Mary Leahy, Changjun Yue, Kai-Ming Cheng, Anatoly Oleksiyenko, Hak-Kwong Yip, Futao Huang, Jung-Mi Lee, Pilnam Yi, Morshidi Sirat, Rosni Bakar, Yen Siew Hwa, Philip Gunby, Nigel Healey, Jean C. Tayag, and Paitoon Sinlarat. 2012. "The Impact of Economic Crisis on Higher Education." Bangkok: UNESCO.

Montgomery, David R. 2007. *Dirt: The Erosion of Civilizations*. Berkely, LA; London: University of California Press.

Oliff, Phil, Vincent Palacios, Johnson Ingrid, and Michael Leachman. 2013. "Recent Deep State Higher Education Cuts May Harm Students and the Economy for Years to Come." Center on Budget and Policy Priorities. http://www.cbpp.org/cms/?fa=view&id=3927.

Portilla, Katherine. 2013. "Is Sustainability a Key Part of Education?" *theguardian.com*, June 17. http://www.theguardian.com/environment/blog/2013/jun/17/energy-efficiency-sustainability.

Prokop, Michaela. 2003. "Saudi Arabia: The Politics of Education." *International Affairs* 79(1): 77089.

Rittel, Horst W. J., and Melvin M. Webber. 1973. "Dilemmas in a General Theory of Planning." *Policy Sciences* 4: 155–169.

Sahlberg, Pasi. 2010. "The Secret to Finland's Success: Educating Teachers." Stanford Center for Opportunity Policy in Education. https://edpolicy.stanford.edu/sites/default/files/publications/secret-finland's-success-educating-teachers.pdf.

Scanlon, Bill. 2012. "Schools Raise the Roof on Solar Energy." *RenewableEnergyWorld.com*. http://www.renewableenergyworld.com/rea/news/article/2012/10/schools-raise-the-roof-on-solar-energy.

Skrbinjek, Vesna, and Dušan Lesjak. 2013. "Impact of the Financial and Economic Crisis on Public Expenditure on Higher/Tertiary Education in Europe and Slovenia." Management, Knowledge and Learning International Conference 2013, Zadar, Croatia, 19–21 June, 2013.

Tilbury, Daniella, Sonja Janousek, and Derek Elias. 2007. "Asia-Pacific Guidelines for the Development of National ESD." Edited by Caroline Haddad, Leanne Denby, and Jessica North. Bangkok: The Asia-Pacific Programme of Educational Innovation for Development.

Tulloch, Larry. 2009. "Education for Sustainability (EFS): Citizenship Education for Radical Resistance or Cultural Conformity?" *Teachers and Curriculum* 11: 7–11.

UNDP in Kyrgyzstan. "Kyrgyzstan: Energy-Efficient School Offers National Lessons." 2014. United Nations Development Programme. http://www.undp.org/content/undp/en/home/ourwork/environmentandenergy/successstories/kyrgyzstan--energy-efficient-school-offers-national-lessons/. Accessed September 30, 2014.

Venton, Courenay Cabot, and Paul Venton. 2012. "Disaster Risk Reduction and Education: Outcomes for Children as a Result of DRR Activities Supported by the EEPCT Programme." New York: United Nations Children's Fund.

Chapter 9

ECONOMIC SCHOOLS AND DIFFERENT PATHS TO DEVELOPMENT

BY FRANKLIN C. GRAHAM IV

INTRODUCTION

Kuma Baqqalaa is a 35-year-old migrant worker in Dubai, United Arab Emirates (UAE). He is from Addis Ababa, the capitol of Ethiopia, but his parents are from an Oromo village in the southwest part of the country. He came to Dubai in 2000 to raise money for both marrying and starting a family. He drives a truck for a construction company, although he jokes that he is in the "destruction" business because of the constant hauling away of debris to dump sites from homes razed to make high-rise apartment complexes. Although Kuma has lived and worked in Dubai for eight years, he does not plan to bring his future wife here, as both he and she are ineligible for citizenship. He knows this because he has made friends with people who were born and raised in Dubai, but because their heritage is Indian, Pakistani, or Bangladeshi, they are ineligible to become citizens.

Citizenship is limited to people who are Emirati, essentially Arab ancestry, and in regards to the economy, with the exception of small enterprises and manual labor, most businesses are owned and operated by Emirati entrepreneurs. There are some foreign investors, primarily from other Gulf countries, Eu-rope, North America, or East Asia. Kuma migrated to Dubai over a decade ago not to live permanently, but in order to make money both for remittances to his parents and to save money for his marriage. So far, he has succeeded in sending the equivalent of US$2,000 per year back to his parents in Ethiopia while clearing an average of US$1,000 savings each year for himself. As modest as US$14,000 in savings appears to people living in Western nations, it is enough to marry and start a family in Ethiopia. Still, from Kuma's perspective, it is not enough to sustain a family in the long term. Recognizing these limitations but longing for home, Kuma plans to leave the UAE in a year to two to return to Ethiopia, marry, and have children, but also start a business, which he believes will provide the financial security needed for his future family.

The inequalities that exist when Emirati are compared to Kuma and other migrant workers in the UAE also exist between countries. Historically, the UAE was a colonial backwater, dependent upon fishing and trade in pearls before the discovery of petroleum and natural gas in the 1950s. The growth and importance of the UAE in supplying oil and gas to the global energy market made the billions of dollars available to the government for spending on construction—the industry that brought Kuma and others like him to the UAE for work.

Yet, while Kuma initially came to the UAE unsure of how long he would stay, time and experience convinced him to return to Ethiopia. The UAE is a desert where temperatures can reach as high as 45°C (113°F). Where Kuma is from, the landscape is greener and the climate is milder, with temperatures rarely exceeding 25°C (77°F) throughout the year. Ethiopia is largely dependent upon agriculture and poorer when compared to the UAE, but this allows Kuma to take advantage of the strength of the Emirati Dirham in exchange for the Ethiopian Birr to live better, or at least gain better returns for his savings, once he is in Ethiopia.

People are, much like countries, part of the global economy, and Kuma is no exception to this. For the most part, the global economy is guided by capitalist principles. As a child in the 1980s, Kuma witnessed the devastation of both drought and civil strife that undermined the economy and society of Ethiopia. When he became an adult, life in Ethiopia was improving, but the opportunities available to him were few and far

FIGURE 9.1 Kuma in the United Arab Emirates.

between. Competition over what meager jobs existed in Ethiopia either inspired him or pushed him, as well as many other Ethiopians, to seek work elsewhere. He landed in Dubai at a time when laborers were needed in large numbers because construction was booming. Truck driving is just one of several high-demand professions for male immigrants. Despite the foreignness of this environment and the physical distance between him, his family, and his fiancée, Kuma is exchanging both his labor and time to acquire the means necessary for him to marry, start a family, and launch his own business in Addis Ababa. He is, in essence, one of the seven billion participants around the globe shaping the production, distribution, and consumption of natural resources, products, and services in the social interaction called economics.

Kuma's story, in terms of the events leading to his migration to Dubai 14 years ago, his current residence in Dubai, and his future plans, means different things for economists according to their schools of thought. Historically, the economic system that Kuma is a participant in, capitalism, competed with other forms of exchange both locally and globally. Today, the components of capitalism—free markets, monetary systems, wage labor, and few to no regulations on transactions—are the dominant terms of exchange, but this does not mean that other forms of social exchange and regulations are not coexisting along with capitalism. Individuals still barter amongst each other, nations protect home industries through subsidizing them or place high tariffs on imports, and environmental organizations, through media and litigation tools, influence countries or supra-regional organizations to lock up swaths of forests to preserve biodiversity and, although contested, possibly slow down the effects of global climate change. These acts are not for the sake of profit or through the actions of free markets self-regulating themselves. Individuals with a broader perspective are concerned that capitalism undermines social needs and degrades the environment.

Economists recognize that social injustices like the wealth gap and global disparities in health care, education, housing, potable water access, and food security are endemic. They acknowledge that the air quality in large cities is poor, the oceans are polluted, and that forests are cut down at a faster rate than they can rejuvenate. But after recognizing that the status quo cannot and should not be maintained, economists disagree on both the factors responsible for these social and environmental ills and what economic path, what some may call development, to take. The various actors contributing to this debate come from all walks of life. They are European farmers lobbying in Strasbourg, France, to protect their interests through advocating bans on external competitors or high tariffs on agricultural imports. They are the protestors who assemble at the World Trade Organization (WTO) to demand social and environmental justice. They are the professors and students at colleges debating and discussing economic theories and business practices. They are the tycoons who have made their fortunes and are now setting up charitable organizations to help with the eradication of tropical diseases in Africa, Asia, and Latin America. And they are the billionaires who use either their own or other people's money to influence legislation and voting at local and national levels to serve their own interests. Not everyone wields the same political, intellectual, or financial power in shaping the global economy, but we all contribute to it.

At the risk of essentializing the debate, four major camps of economists that are influential on shaping the present-day economic order will be discussed in this chapter: the Neo-Liberals, the Keynesians, the Neo-Marxists and the Radicals. Although all four camps are at work in the world today, not all of them have the same amount of influence. In fact, it is generally the Neo-Liberals and the Keynesian economists who shape the economic order (at least on a global scale). But that does not mean that the efforts of Neo-Marxist and Radical economists should be shelved or dismissed. Both have made important contributions in understanding the chronic problems affecting humankind and the environment in both the present day and with the foreseeable future.

NEOLIBERALISM: THE DOMINANT SCHOOL OF THOUGHT

Economists who support a purer practice of capitalism, a group known as Neo-Liberals, view Kuma's story as inspirational, where despite what difficulties he faced coming from a drought-prone, politically volatile country and the limitations imposed on him by Emirati immigration, he is working to fulfill his life goals of marriage, family, and launching a business in Ethiopia upon his return. For the Neo-Liberal economists, the absence of a capitalist economy in Ethiopia under the Derg, what was a Marxist-Leninist-led political movement from 1974 to 1991 creating a planned economy and prohibiting free-market practices, created the conditions for droughts to turn into famines and for famines to lead to civil disorder. These chronic problems pushed Kuma to leave Ethiopia as a young man and seek opportunity elsewhere. Hence, the UAE, well-linked to a global capitalist market since the discovery of oil in the 1950s, pulled Kuma into its territory as labor was in high demand.

At the same time, the UAE is guilty of enforcing regulations that hinder its own economic growth by stifling its growth in human capital. Its immigration policies bar Kuma and other immigrants from citizenship. It is likely that many who come to work in the UAE wish to return to their respective countries at some point, but the UAE does not provide any incentive for people to stay. Even when immigrants' children are born and raised in the UAE, they are ineligible for citizenship. Kuma is thus saving his money not only for his personal life plan, but also to become an entrepreneur in a new Ethiopia, the one that adopted capitalist practices in the 1990s.

Neoliberals would say Kuma is making a rational choice. They would further argue that what social and ecological ills This understanding ties into the argument Neo-Liberals make regarding the world today: what social and ecological ills exist in the world at present are the fault of the restrictions placed on free markets. To create a fair arena of business for all, where individuals have a chance to reach their full potential, free markets need to expand worldwide on all scales, and trade barriers in the market and restrictions on people's lives must be minimized, if not eliminated. Tariffs, customs, duties, sanctions, taxes, and bans, according to Neo-Liberals, are regulatory instruments that stifle economic growth. In a pure, free-market economy, they say, competition, innovation, and invention will usher in peace and stability to an otherwise volatile world.

Neoliberalism has its roots and is the grandchild in what is today called classical or liberal economics. During the age of exploration and European expansion, Adam Smith in *The Wealth of Nations* (1776) and David Ricardo in *On the Principals of Political Economy and Taxation* (1819) discussed the concept of comparative advantage, when, through competition in a free market, businesses produce goods or services that are lower cost and better quality. This may, and quite often does, push other competitors out of that particular industry. However, in a growing economy, those driven out can start or invent other goods or services. Despite the fact that capitalism was in its infant stage in the lifetimes of these writers, its popularity grew in the next 120 years, pushing out remnants of feudalism and competing with mercantilism in European colonies for global dominance.

Yet with the ascent of classical economics also came the critics of the economic system. The exploitation of African and Asian peoples by

European nations, the unethical business practices by US corporations in Latin America, the destruction and human cost of the First World War, and the stock market crash in 1929 culminated in governments leading the world economy to question following corporate-led development and other liberal practices—in both their economies and in a global market. From the 1930s to the 1970s, unregulated economic practices were removed from center stage and replaced with Keynesian economics (see below). The drive for economic liberalism, however, only remained dormant and would return by the late 1970s, resurrected under the term neoliberalism.

The economist leading the revival of liberal economics was Frederick Hayek. Hayek distrusted economic planning of any kind. Decades earlier, Hayek established the Mont Pelerin Society in 1947, a prestigious think tank devoted to promoting classical economics, as well as educating newer generations of economists at the University of Oxford and the University of Chicago, beginning in the 1930s. These foundations influenced the future political administrations and economic policies of Western politicians like Margaret Thatcher in the U.K. and Ronald Reagan in the USA and international lending organizations like the World Bank and International Monetary Fund. The concerns over inflation, unemployment, and the rise of world energy prices (Oil Crisis of 1973) on national and international scales already redirected policymakers back to free-market practices. By the time Thatcher and Reagan were leaving office, the policy of an unregulated free market was back on center stage for national governments and influencing trade relations in the global market.

By the late 1980s, technologies were also advancing and becoming vital components to the global economy: computers, the Internet, cell phones, satellites, and other wireless technologies. Their production stimulated new growth opportunities in the national economies of Western Europe and North America while creating rapid economic growth and restructuring the economies of East Asia. Because these innovations generated growth in the global economy, economists viewed technology as complementary to the health of developed nations where free markets were already in place and in the economic future for developing nations. The neoliberal doctrine was forged at this point: the promotion of free markets through corporate-led development, the claimed superiority of the private sector over the public sector, little to no market regulation (as the market will regulate itself), and the advancement of technologies. All were seen as crucial to eliminating civil unrest and disparity, overcoming vulnerability to natural hazards, and eliminating discriminatory cultural practices.

Today, neoliberalism remains the prevailing economic and market force for many national economies and in global finance. It is well represented and supported by individuals such as the Barclays family of the United Kingdom and Koch family of the United States. Institutional support is seen through international organizations like the World Bank, International Monetary Fund (IMF), and WTO, whose terms of doing business promote free-market reform.

Neoliberalism is not the sole economic practice in the world today, nor does it go unchallenged. In fact, critics like the French economist Thomas Piketty (1971–) point out the long-term consequence of Neo-Liberal practice in the acute and expanding disparities of wealth distribution. Critics like Piketty advocate greater action against such inequality through regulatory measures of taxing the wealthy. Neoliberalism's advocacy, however, by many large corporations and influential Western governments means it is often the terms of trade once a new product or service emerges on the common market. Even in times of crisis or debates over development, neoliberalism continues to be seen as a macro solution or engine of growth.

KEYNESIAN ECONOMISTS: THE REFORMERS OF CAPITALISM

Returning to Kuma's story, economists from other schools of thought are likely to interpret the circumstances differently. Keynesian economists are likely to agree with Neo-Liberals that overall capitalism is a sound economic practice throughout the world. They will dissent, however, in absolving capitalism entirely from blame regarding the constraints and challenges Kuma faces in achieving his goals. Keynesian economists, a particular kind of reformist economics, would argue that the rivalry that existed years ago between the Soviet-backed Derg in Ethiopia and the Western-backed neighboring Somali government squandered needed revenues for infrastructure, health care, and agriculture on wasteful military spending. This military buildup created the conditions where countries in the region were vulnerable once drought occurred. When drought became famine in Ethiopia, people grew disenchanted with the Derg government, violence ensued, and the economy collapsed. But as the Neo-Liberals argue, the Keynesians would say that the ruined economy and civil disorder certainly motivated Kuma and other men like him to leave Ethiopia for more secure, lucrative employment opportunities elsewhere.

Keynesian economists would also critique the effects of capitalism unchecked on the economy of the UAE. Despite the fact that Kuma is in housing construction, he jovially called it the "destruction business" because his days are occupied with cleaning up the wasteful planning, or lack thereof, by the Dubai housing industry. The city built one-story houses back in the 1960s and 1970s to accommodate housing to both citizens and the foreign workers coming for jobs to the UAE. Planning was forgone for expediency in meeting the housing demand. But as the number of immigrants increased in recent decades, so too did the demand for more housing. Because of this, neighborhoods where houses once stood are razed to build high-rise apartment buildings. There are other factors playing into this dynamic process, including the increasing value of property in Dubai and the increasing standard of living and expectations by incoming workers, but primarily these homes are destroyed to ensure housing for more people. However wasteful this is, migrant workers do not complain, as these demands create more employment for people working in the construction business.

Keynesian economists receive their name from John Maynard Keynes (1883–1946), a British citizen whose theories on economics influenced many national economies and international lending institutions from the end of World War II to the 1970s. Keynes believed overall in capitalism. For him, the free-market system ushered in progress and advancements for both advanced and emerging nations. Keynes was concerned, however, with the boom-and-bust cycles that occur during periods of growth and recession. From his perspective, the erratic behavior of free markets was not beneficial to the training, education, and employment of populations and to the health of a nation's economy as a whole.

Keynes was also a product of his time. He was a witness to the unethical business practices of corporations, the slaughter of colonized subjects by imperial armies, and the tragic events of World War I. His role as a financial representative to the treasury at the Versailles Peace Conference and his critique of the war reparations imposed on Germany forewarned of another future global conflict in his book, *The Economic Consequences of the Peace* (1919). Yet his true contribution, *The General Theory of Employment, Interest and Money* (1936), outlined an economic practice of a mixed economy, whereby free markets exist, but at the same time, the state, through fiscal intervention, planned and spent revenue to generate employment opportunities and stimulate the economy. The state has a role in economics, as capitalism in its pure form does not respond well in situations where underemployment and underinvestment occur. With the height of the Great Depression occurring the same year it was published, Keynes found a receptive audience to his theories among policymakers and economists willing to test out a mix of capitalism and planning.

Although there are other means to regulate volatility in a free-market system, Keynes' theories of state intervention into the economy are considered reformist because of the popularity in enacting them as an alternative to liberal economics after World War II. Western governments, lending institutions, and especially programs like the Marshall Plan rebuilt infrastructure and relaunched economies in Europe. Post-colonial states, with the assistance of lenders like the World Bank and IMF, enacted development schemes that emphasized mixed economies involving both free-market practice and Keynesian planning and spending. The two were not necessarily in conflict with each other. In fact, Europe was rebuilt, and the East Asian economies developed. As the global economy grew, more and more people were integrated into a monetary system, technologies and communication advanced, and even the mining of natural resources contributed to the expansion of a global market.

By the 1970s, however, national leaders and policymakers had new concerns. The direction national economies and the global market were taking—involving growth but also ballooning costs—resulted in a return to a purer practice of free markets that Hayek and his followers advocated. There was the expected tradeoff of inflation for job creation and development, something policymakers and economists tolerated as a symptom of Keynesian economics, but the unexpected turn of unemployment rising raised alarms. The spike in crude oil prices with the consolidation of the Organization of the Petroleum Exporting Countries may have had a hand in this economic downturn. Still, some economists viewed this as a serious flaw in Keynesian economics and called the phenomenon stagflation.

Furthermore, Hayek and other liberal economists called for the end of government interference with the economy and began their drive to bring back corporate-led development with minimal regulatory practices. Their message resonated well with political leaders like Ronald Reagan, Margaret Thatcher, Jacques Chirac, and their successors. While Keynesian economics lost favor with international lending institutions and Western nations, it continued to help drive the development of the Asian Tigers, the economies of Hong Kong, Singapore, South Korea, and Taiwan in the 1970s to 1980s. All of these countries used some form of state planning in education and the building of infrastructure to stimulate growth while participating in the deregulated global market through export-led growth. It was a serendipitous time to create such an economic pathway;

the personal computer rose in demand, and later innovations in communication like the Internet created new products and services that these same Asian economies supplied. Catering to consumer demand on other continents paid off at home, as these countries succeeded in generating wealth for their states and their citizens through the 1990s.

The recent global recession of 2008, generated in large part from the unregulated financial and real estate sectors, forced Western governments and international lending institutions to reevaluate the practice of allowing free markets to regulate themselves. To avoid greater economic downturn, the United States, Germany, the United Kingdom, and Spain all passed stimulus packages amounting to billions of dollars, based on Keynesian economics, to revive their economies. At the United Nations and even in the offices of the IMF, commonly viewed as a bastion of neoliberalism, economists proposed a coordinated international approach to revive the global economy through fiscal stimulus programs. Neo-Liberals may be the loudest and best-organized voice directing economies in the present day; however, Keynesian economists still gain receptive audiences among those influencing national and the international economy from time to time, certainly true when free markets enter their bust cycles, at the particular cost of human capital.

NEO-MARXISTS: BREAKING FROM CAPITALISM

For economists following, interpreting, and expanding the theories of Karl Heinrich Marx (1818–1883), Kuma's story is a tragedy, not one of inspiration, but instead exploitation. This school of thought looks at the underlying causes for the turmoil in Ethiopia, from the famines to the civil unrest, and the forces driving Kuma to Dubai, where only his labor has value. An economist viewing the world through the Marxist lens would start by suggesting that Ethiopia, before the Derg takeover in 1974, was primarily agrarian and, with the exception of a small gentry class producing some commodities for export, far from being an advanced capitalist economy, a needed phase before socialist transformation. The Derg takeover and tenure was turbulent not only because Ethiopia was not ready for the transformation to socialism, but because it was used like a pawn by Soviet powers to contain Western influence in East Africa. The Marxist utopia attempted by the Derg, at least on paper, was doomed to failure given the circumstances before and during their time in power. The consequence for Ethiopia, as well as many other states that attempted **communism** previously, was a dictatorship of the state where political elites entrenched themselves in the power structures and key sectors of the economy.

Kuma easily emigrated to the UAE because his labor was cheap and in high demand by the construction company employing him. Kuma from the perspective of Marxist economists, however, lives with the insecurity of being replaced by another immigrant worker who will do the same work for less money and work longer hours, an advantage employers can exploit when labor pools grow more accessible. Kuma may organize with others like him to defend his job security, his wages, benefits, and working conditions, but the laws of the UAE were written to favor Emirati citizens (the owners and most often the managers of the companies), not the workers (overwhelmingly immigrants). This situation makes Kuma dependent on the company he works for, both in terms of his wages and to maintain his residence status in the UAE.

Marxist economists would also critique the risks Kuma faces in his future goals. Should he return to Ethiopia with his earnings, he still faces the likelihood of rising costs of his wedding and, later, child care exceeding what he budgets for and the business he runs either failing or not providing the revenues needed for his family at some point. Even if Kuma succeeds in all three, there are many like him who do not. Marxists and other critics of capitalism, like Piketty, point to the disturbing statistics in the past 30 years showing that in both advanced and developing economies, the wealth of the world is becoming concentrated in the hands of a few. In Ethiopia's case, only the rich and those with close political connections to the national government have the security to take risks in new business enterprises. Such a disparity is created and intensified through the expansion of capital. Neo-Marxists say capital working in an unregulated market is ravenous, exploiting and draining the world of its resources. It creates disparities through the creation of classes and deepening the divide between rich and poor. In the end, as it continues unchecked and only for the benefit of few people, its unsustainable trajectory will create conflict — conflict that eventually pushes people to transform their society. Thus, once capitalism has advanced and exhausted itself, people will abandon free markets, private property, and the false belief of economies regulating themselves through the "invisible hand" for a system known as communism, where workers own the means of production. These are the tenets of Karl Marx.

Marx studied the disparities of wealth and class in the nineteenth century. He was more than an economist. He was also a news reporter, a historian, and a social revolutionary assessing the world political economy at a time when the Industrial Revolution and social and political upheaval were happening around him. His friendship with Friedrich Engels (1820–1895) shaped the direction of and contributions to these undertakings. Both explored the struggles between different classes in the long span of history: slave and master in the time of Antiquity, serf and lord in the age of Feudalism, and in their own age, the relation between worker and owner in a capitalist society. They argued that history was a series of struggles within these different systems, where classes came into conflict with each other in preserving their interests. When these conflicts grew too overwhelming, societies transformed into new systems of political-economic order. Marx and Engels also explored the relationship humans have with the material world, especially how forms of capital—money, debt and credit—influence these relationships. Marx concluded that humans become both detached and alienated from one another in the pursuit in capital. This is what creates the conflicts that lead to societal transformations.

Marx-Engels's theories influenced many who followed. Socialist and Communist parties emerged throughout Europe and North America during their lifetimes. In the twentieth century, revolutions took place in Russia, China, and Cuba. Several countries in Africa, Asia, and Europe adopted communist ideology into their political and economic programs. In what was certainly the origin of Neo-Marxism, these socialist and communist countries experimented with planned economies, where the governments controlled industries, trade, and the markets.

Among capitalist countries that were the ideological, political, and economic opponents of Marxist states, there were also periods of reform resembling socialist practice. For instance, Social Security and other social services created by New Deal politicians in the United States used government revenue to provide safety nets for the vulnerable and elderly starting in the mid-1930s.

Western European countries are participants and proponents of capitalism themselves, yet during the 1960s to 1970s, their governments ushered in comprehensive health care and education paid for through taxation and accessible to every European citizen. With the resurgence of neoliberalism by the 1980s, the US and Western European programs providing social safety nets came under scrutiny. These massive government programs are under threat of becoming privatized or even scrapped, but such actions come with the risk of losing political office; many people protect these services in how they cast their vote for political candidates.

The dissolution of the Soviet Union (1989–1991) generated great debate over whether Neo-Marxist economics was possible. Those studying the internal workings of former Soviet and communist states acknowledge that in practice, many states were not communist but dictatorships, a situation where cronyism, mismanagement of the economy, and a constituency that resisted the draconic measures imposed by the state led to their demise.

Another dynamic was the intermingling with the type of political-economic systems that existed before the socialist or communist takeover. Many of these societies, like Ethiopia, were agrarian, and efforts to compete with the more well-developed capitalist nations while somehow skipping capitalist development was simply not feasible. Today, China, Vietnam, Laos, North Korea, and Cuba are communist or socialist in name, but this is more political ideology than Marxist economic principles. Although some planning is still done for China, Vietnam, and Laos, these countries have adopted sweeping free-market reforms into their national economies.

The resurgence of free markets in the past 30 years has, however, allowed Neo-Marxists to attribute blame for the global injustices of racism, sexism, and exploitation of peoples and ecologies to capitalism. James O'Connor (1930–) has written on the cost of unregulated markets in contemporary times: the destruction of the physical environment. Forests are clear cut, habitats are disturbed, oceans are overfished, and mines and oil rigs contaminate the air, land, and water.

David Harvey (1935–) in several of his works has shown how capital flight ruined industrial areas in Western Europe and North America. Companies did this to take advantage of business relocation incentives in Latin America and Southeast Asia in addition to cheaper and unorganized labor pools. These destructive practices are the consequences of companies seeking profit margins, cutting out their competitors, reducing the costs of products and services to their customers, and even to improve the lives of wealthy people living elsewhere. Harvey, O'Connor, and other social scientists using Neo-Marxism as a critique show that capitalism is not a sustainable economic practice.

Despite their ability to connect the social and environmental injustices of the world with capitalism, Neo-Marxists are at the fringe, influencing some academics and a few policymakers but in the end marginal in terms of their clout and practice.

There are just a few exceptions to this generalization. Today, Europe's Mediterranean countries have very influential Communist parties with local politicians creating their own enclaves of socialism. One example is the township of Marinaleda, Spain, whose mayor, Juan Manuel Sánchez Gordillo, brought to his township one of the lowest unemployment rates in Spain and affordable housing for the region's residents.

Another example on a larger scale was the presidency of Hugo Chavez (1999–2013) of Venezuela. He nationalized their oil industry and initiated more social services for his country, although the economy remained a mix of planning and capitalist practices. Other countries like India, Brazil, and South Africa are also where Communist politicians and activism are shaping their economies. But these examples are small and show the challenge Neo-Marxists have in converting from critic to practitioner of economics at larger scales.

RADICAL ECONOMISTS: THE MOVE AWAY FROM DETERMINISM

The final school of thought is quite diverse and pulls together different ideas under the nebulous title Radical Economists. In order to present an alternative to capitalist and Neo-Marxist economics, this term is used to define the group that views the very nature of economics as fundamentally different from these other three schools.

For Radical Economists, Kuma's story is not awe-inspiring, nor daunting, nor destined for failure. An economist from this school will likely assign blame to both the non-capitalist and free-market forces for pushing Kuma out of Ethiopia as well as adding to the risk he faces in achieving his goals of marriage, family, and running an enterprise back in his home country. But at the same time, Kuma made his own conscious choice to leave his country; he was not pulled by an "invisible hand" into the labor market of Dubai. In addition, a true Radical Economist would abstain from predicting success or failure in Kuma's future. For them, Kuma and others like him are not pawns of economic forces that are either selected for success or destined for failure. Radical Economists believe in agency and the ability of people to shape not just their own lives, but of the society around them.

For Radical Economists, individuals, both separate and collectively, are the force shaping and changing the practice of economics. For instance, Kuma at present is part of a wage-labor, essentially capitalist, economy. This does not mean that all his economic interactions are exclusively capitalist. He does send remittances to his parents, income that is earned through his job but sent to his parents as both a gift and a social obligation to help his family. In the future, if he returns to Ethiopia, he will not necessarily need to base all his exchanges on money or credit; in fact, he is likely to have to barter, give gifts, and perform acts of reciprocity and other types of economic exchanges to achieve his life goals. Ethiopia, like some other African states, has subsistence and informal economies operating side-by-side with free markets. This plurality may frustrate advocates of either pro-capitalist or Neo-Marxist policies, but it is empowering for individuals like Kuma. This plurality allows them to maneuver in times of crisis and to trade their labor and resources within whichever arena provides them the greatest advancement—of their own interests.

The earliest work expressing such agency in economics and perhaps the one thread of thought that binds the various Radical Economists together is Karl Polanyi's *The Great Transformation* (1944). The earlier giants in economics, Smith, Ricardo, Hayek, Keynes, Marx, and Engels, either assumed or took the perspective of studying economics as a natural science guided by laws embedded in human nature. Karl Polanyi (1886–1964), however, questioned this traditional approach. He did not see economics as a natural science like biology, chemistry, or physics. Instead, he argued that economics is a social science, that the discipline is subjective, and that it is shaped and altered by the people who study and write about it. Economics affects everyone, including those who attempt to detach themselves from the study of it, and as a social scientist guilty of subjectivity, Polanyi expressed his own view of human nature, seeing people as more social and cooperative than individualistic and competitive.

Polanyi, however, is a good example of the complex thinking carried out by economists. They do not necessarily remain entrenched in one school of thought. Also included in the pages of *The Great Transformation*, Polanyi made a valuable contribution to Neo-Marxist theory. He developed the concept of a "double movement" in the global market system where neoliberal and reformist practices maintain their hold on the international system. Neo-Marxist and other alternative economic practices are marginalized or left at local scales. He judged that such a practice was not healthy for society or the longevity of the natural resources in the long term, ideas later developed by Thomas Piketty, David Harvey, and James

O'Connor. Still, he maintained his aversion to claiming capitalism would inevitably collapse. From Polanyi's perspective, the double movement between free markets and reform could be maintained indefinitely, even though its long duration is not healthy for society or nature as a whole.

Like Neo-Marxists, Radical Economists are more critics than practitioners. They pair well with the former in showing how Neo-liberal and Reformist economic schools are wrong in prescribing a path to global success, but unlike Neo-Marxists, they do not offer a clear alternative.

Part of this impotence comes from the reality that Radical Economists are not united in vision. Some lean toward the idea of local- or worker-based business models, very much the lifeblood of Neo-Marxists. Some side with anarchists on whether to create examples for others to follow or focus their efforts at undermining the dominant economic system of capitalism. Then there are others who advocate dualistic or plural economies worldwide. Informal (also known as black market), barter, gift, reciprocity, and subsistence economies are some examples of non-capitalist and non-Marxist economic approaches that still exist at local or limited regional scales but are constantly curbed if not rooted out by national and international law.

Radical Economists can agree that the social and environmental ills in the world today threaten the very existence of nature and society. Radical Economists took note when the World Bank in 2008 estimated that 1.3 billion people are living in absolute poverty, essentially a living standard deficient of sufficient food, potable water, shelter, health care, and education.

Deforestation in developing nations continues as capitalist interests cut trees for timber or clearcut a forest to expand agriculture. Oceans are neither respected nor protected, as they are used as dumpsites for industrial waste or sewage from metropolitan areas by some and overfished by others. In the Pacific Ocean, there is an island of floating plastic the size of Texas. The ice around the North Pole is now breaking up in the summer months, seen as a strategic advantage by shipping and energy companies to navigate and explore its waters. All of these ecological disasters continue to unfold, destabilizing the global climate and contaminating the water and food production zones that human and animal life depend on.

There is still divergence for Radical Economists on which approach to take since some Radical Economists do not believe in a macro solution, but everyone can agree that they want a break from the past rigid doctrines in economic theory.

CONCLUSION

Economics, whether it is a force driving people or an ideology sculpted by an elite drafting a set of laws and incentives, is a social relation, one in which each person interacts with others in society as well as with the man-made and physical environment. It is impossible for each person to meet all the other people in the world, visit each village, town, and city, including all uninhabited regions on Earth. It is important, however, for each of us to comprehend and appreciate the economic system we are a part of and contribute to, as our economic actions affect these unmet peoples and unseen landscapes. The impacts are not uniform, nor recognized or understood by all, but they are occurring. It is precisely because of the complexity of the many dynamics within this discipline that there is debate, conflict, and effort to influence whether the economy becomes either more competitive or cooperative.

Above are four outlined summaries of schools of thought to provide some background and explanation of theories that are, this very moment, discussed in the circles of economics. Economic theory underpins proposals at cabinet meetings for reviving a national economy or generating new markets for products of a multinational corporation. Theories influence the debates on parliamentary floors in adopting austerity measures or passing stimulus packages. Schools of economic thought penetrate the new articles of business brought up in union halls in order to protect workers' rights and benefits. They are the slogans and causes of activists or protestors at international conferences. It is crucial to understand that these four schools are permeable and that policymakers, influential businesspeople, scholars, and critics may move between them or adopt aspects of two or more.

Karl Polanyi was an academic who contributed both to Neo-Marxist and Radical Economics, but there are many more who switch or shift between schools of thought. For example, Bill Gates of Microsoft and George Soros, the man who broke the Bank of England, made millions as entrepreneurs in a free-market economy, but now their philanthropic activity resembles Reformist models of development.

Kuma Baqqalaa, who I have talked about all throughout this chapter, does not possess the same clout as an intellectual like Polanyi or millionaires like Gates or Soros, and like most people, he may not ever think about how he contributes to Ethiopian, Emirati, and the larger world economies, but his actions do affect the present and future direction of economic systems. It is a power that all individuals have.

Economics is about more than increases in production and growth, changes in output, or the better allocation of productive resources. In the past, these were the ideas generally thrown around in the rhetoric of theorists advocating a particular system of economics, but a consciousness is growing concerning the larger picture of economics and development. Economics is also a social relation where the interaction between individuals and groups is just as important as the goods and services exchanged. What is sacrificed, what is gained, and how this exchange allows a person to achieve basic human needs, if not also life goals like a career, marriage, and family, are shaping interactions we make. Also crucial is the way in which natural resources are extracted from the physical environment supplying these goods and services. Despite the changes and transformations our society has made in energy and technologies, we recognize that the world's resources are finite. They can be depleted, polluted, and destroyed to the point where biodiversity is compromised and we are flirting with our own destruction.

At present, social inequalities are rampant, and the destruction of the environment is occurring at a faster rate than its restoration. Almost all economists come to a consensus that change is needed to improve people's standard of living and at the same time sustain the environment. But not all agree what this change entails. Some argue for a purer, universal practice of one type of economics, some argue for some forms of regulation or liberalization, while a few propose duality, if not plurality, in economic practices.

Kuma was born into what was hailed as a Marxist economy. In reality, it was largely a subsistence economy growing vulnerable to population increase, climate change, and a lack of needed infrastructure. These factors destabilized his country, and as the violence intensified, it paralyzed the economy for several years even after the Derg was removed from power. Kuma migrated to a fast-growing, free-market economy, the UAE, but even there the economy was not completely free from regulation as controls were placed on migrant workers. This discrimination and his family ties compel Kuma to return to Ethiopia, where the economy has revived since the Derg era. Along with subsistence practices and other forms of exchange, there are sectors of the Ethiopian economy that are based on free-market practices.

What economic path Kuma, and each of us takes, influences the relationship we all have with society and nature. Perhaps what the Radical Economists leave us to think about is how our relationship to society and nature can influence the future course of global economics.

Agency: The phenomenon where individuals make choices independent of structural factors in society like class, religion, gender, ethnicity, nationality, customs, caste, etc. In essence, people are not pawns and can make their own choices.

Antiquity: The historical period before 500 CE that is most often synonymous with the Western civilizations of ancient Greece or ancient Rome. It may also refer to civilizations that predate the Greeks and Romans, such as the Phoenicians, Mesopotamians, etc., in addition to prehistory (before written records).

Capitalism: A system of economics where trade, industry, and the inputs used to produce goods and services are privately owned and used to create profit.

Communism: The theoretical economic system envisaged by Karl Marx and Frederich Engels in which the inputs of production are communally owned. Social classes, money, and the state become obsolete as communism establishes a new social and economic order.

Comparative advantage: the ability individuals, groups, corporations, or states have in contrast with their competitors regarding endowments or advancements in technology. This can involve producing a good or service at a lower cost or the ability to produce more or better quality products and services.

Derg: a term meaning "committee" or "council" in Amharic, it is the short name for the ideological military council that ruled Ethiopia from 1974 to the late 1980s. It attempted to transform Ethiopian society to communism but in practice was more of a dictatorship of the state responsible for the extra-judicial killings of more than 10,000 people.

Double movement: a term coined by Karl Polanyi, it is the shifting governments, lending institutions, and corporations make between practicing laissez-faire and reformist capitalism in order to stave off stagnation in the economy or recession. Although Polanyi believed it was possible to continue a double movement indefinitely, he did not believe its duration was sustainable for both society and nature.

Feudalism: sometimes seen as a social-economic system, other times interpreted specifically as a set of legal and military customs, it was prevalent in medieval Europe from the ninth to the fifteenth centuries. Under feudalism, society was structured around land owners offering protection and access to land to serfs, who in return gave part of their harvests, service, or labor to the land owners.

Fiscal intervention: in order to avoid bust cycles in a capitalist economy, governments spend money in key sectors of the economy to promote growth. When the contrary occurs in an economy and it is booming but inflation is a concern, the government can increase taxes or cut back on spending.

Industrial Revolution: the period in history from 1760 to 1840s when the production of goods transferred from being primarily produced by hand to machine manufacture. Various factors contributed to this, including new chemical and iron production processes, improved efficiency of water power, and use of coal over wood as an energy source.

Invisible hand: the metaphor used to describe how individuals or companies can make profit and maximize the use of profit without government intervention. Adam Smith only used the metaphor three times in his book *The Wealth of Nations*, yet advocates of the free-market system believe that the market can regulate itself without government interference.

Mercantilism: an economic practice from the sixteenth to the eighteenth centuries when European colonial powers intentionally regulated their own national economies for the purpose of augmenting their power against other competing European colonial powers.

Mont Pelerin Society: an international meeting beginning in the 1940s in Switzerland of business leaders, economists, philosophers, and other academics who are committed to political and economic freedom, essentially Neo-Liberalism. Among its founders are Friedrich Hayek, Karl Popper, George Stigler, Milton Friedman, and Ludwig von Mises.

Oil Crisis of 1973: an event in which the members of the Organization of Petroleum Exporting Countries raised the price of crude oil from US$3 to US$12 per barrel. This created a shock for both the global economy and among many countries dependent upon foreign oil for energy supplies.

Organization of the Petroleum Exporting Countries: an economic cartel and international organization that coordinates the policies of oil-producing member countries; also known as OPEC.

Remittances: when a person working in a foreign country transfers money to family or friends back in their home country. It is one of the largest sources of revenue for developing countries.

Subsistence: an economic system that is dependent on the utilization of natural resources through foraging, hunting, fishing, animal husbandry, and agriculture. Industry is absent, and any surplus is used in trade for other basic needs or foods.

Supra-regional organizations: a union of countries that delegate a certain amount of authority to the assembly. A few examples are the European Union, the North American Free Trade Agreement, the African Union, and the Organization of American States.

Stagflation: a term combining the terms stagnation and inflation, it is the phenomenon where the inflation rate is high, economic growth declines, and unemployment remains steady or increases.

World Trade Organization: a meeting where nations discuss the goal and direction of international trade. Its trend in the past was to liberalize the global economy, but this has come under greater criticism since the WTO met in Seattle in 1999 and the latest global recession of 2008.

SUGGESTIONS FOR FURTHER READING

Amin, S. 2008. *The World We Wish to See: Revolutionary Objectives in the Twenty-First Century*. New York: Monthly Review Press.
Bello, W. 2004. *Deglobalization: Ideas for a New World Economy*. New York: Zed Books.
Furtado, C. 1964. *Development and Underdevelopment*. Berkeley: University of California Press.
Harvey, D. 2005. *A Brief History of Neoliberalism*. Oxford: Oxford University Press.

Harvey, D. 2010. *The Enigma of Capital: And the Crises of Capitalism*. London: Profile Books.

Hayek, F. A. 1989. *The Road to Serfdom*. Chicago: Chicago University Press.

Luxemburg, R. 2003. *The Accumulation of Capital*, 2nd Edition. New York: Routledge.

Nugent, W. 2009. *Progressivism: A Very Short Introduction*. New York: Oxford University Press.

O'Connor, J. 1997. *Natural Causes: Essays on Ecological Marxism*. New York: Guilford Press.

Piketty, T. 2013. *Le Capital au XXI Siècle*. Paris: Editions du seuil.

Polanyi, K. 1944. *The Great Transformation*. Boston: Beacon Press.

Ricardo, D. 1984. *On the Principles of Political Economy and Taxation*. Melbourne: Everyman's Library.

Rostow, W. W. 1960. *The Stages of Economic Growth: A Non-Communist Manifesto*. Cambridge: Cambridge University Press.

Stiglitz, J. E. and A. Charlton. 2005. *Fair Trade for All: How Trade Can Promote Development*. New York: Oxford University Press.

Wallerstein, I. 2006. *World Systems Analysis: An Introduction*. Durham: Duke University Press.

Chapter 10

WASTE MANAGEMENT: RETHINKING GARBAGE IN A THROWAWAY WORLD

BY DARRIN MAGEE

WHAT IS GARBAGE? RETHINKING GARBAGE

Perhaps nothing symbolizes humans' troubled relationship with our planet—our truly unsustainable way of existing in the universe—than garbage. Carelessly discarded cigarette butts, piles of household garbage, and truck-loads of toxic waste marked with cryptic warnings are but a few examples of how many humans have come to view consumption as a linear process that begins with a want and ends with away. We want, we buy, we use, we throw away. We repeat. Surely, humans can find a better way of being in the world than this, one that is healthier and grounded in an ethic of stewardship of our planet, not mere ridership. Surely we can shift our actions to be regenerative rather than degrading. What better place to start than with garbage?

We know garbage when we see it, but how might we define it? If we begin by listing characteristics that describe garbage, perhaps that will lead to a useful definition. Garbage is matter that is unappealing, outmoded, worn out, or useless. It can be stinky, noxious, or toxic, or more benign and less offensive yet still unwanted. It may include things that are recyclable or reusable but are often discarded simply because it is cheap to do so and because we do not directly or immediately feel the negative impacts of throwing stuff "away."

In many parts of the world, especially in more developed countries (MDCs), household garbage is often set out for curbside collection by trucks that carry it off to realms unknown to most of us who produce the garbage. In the end, most of us do not care where it goes as long as the garbage is taken somewhere to be thrown "away," which usually means buried in a landfill, burned in an incinerator, or dumped unceremoniously in a vacant lot or down a ravine when no one is looking. As consumers, we are often well aware of the origin of our goods but blissfully ignorant of the final resting place of those goods once they have become garbage. This chapter aims to remove those veils of ignorance by "digging into" our garbage.

It is important to note at the start that garbage is, first and foremost, a symptom of a world economy that is premised on the buying and selling of stuff. In that system, waste is a requirement, if for no other reason than encouraging more consumption of things to replace what is thrown out. Thus, while profligate consumption and discarding is undesirable from a sustainability perspective, it is all but demanded in a capitalist economy where humans—thinking, living, feeling humans—are reduced to consumers who fit or do not fit certain demographics targeted by marketing departments trying to sell us more things. Electronics manufacturers, for instance, have mastered the art of encouraging us to buy more and buy frequently through their use of planned obsolescence, whereby the hottest new digital devices become obsolete, outdated, and out of fashion on their almost predictable new model cycles.

Defining garbage, then, is tricky business. Garbage might be defined as waste, the leftovers of some presumably useful activities. According to the old adage, nature produces no waste, but the same is not true for human societies. Indeed, humans encounter waste in countless daily activities: as packaging for the goods we consume; as the indigestible or less savory bits of our meals; as dirty diapers, socks with holes, last week's newspapers, last year's gadgets. Much of what the developed world's citizens throw away was designed with convenience and expedience in mind. Single-use, "disposable" products fly off the store shelves and across the deli counters, dispensing their contents into our hands and hungry mouths just before we move the residues quickly and effortlessly into the waste stream.

Many so-called disposable products are made of plastics that have a highly concentrated, converted energy content,[1] since they are derived from the very same fossil fuels that power modern industrial and

---

1 Energy content refers to the sum of all the energy stored in the chemical bonds in an item. While it may seem strange to think of an item such as a plastic cup as having a high energy content, one way to measure that energy content would be to carefully measure the amount of heat produced when the cup was burned. The instrument typically used to make such measurements is a calorimeter.

mobile society. Thus, their disposal in a landfill not only means they will no longer serve the purpose for which they were intended (e.g., holding a cup of coffee or a serving of food), but also that the energy stored in their hydrocarbon chains will remain locked up, unable to perform a useful function such as providing warmth or light. Tossing those single-use containers into the recycle bin does not solve the problem, either: despite the ubiquitous three-curved-arrow recycling logo and the numerical code on plastics that lull us into thinking we are doing the right thing, the thermal and chemical processes involved in remanufacturing plastics require lots of energy and create lower-value, lower-quality plastics. As we will learn later in this chapter, the term "downcycling" better reflects what really happens to plastics that go into the recycling bin.

At the start of the twenty-first century, the United States is the world leader in garbage production, yet less than a century ago, many Americans practiced what Susan Strasser (1999) refers to as the "stewardship of objects." Such stewardship, motivated by thrift and, in many cases, outright poverty, led homemakers to find new uses for old items, such as fashioning children's clothes out of the less-tattered fabric of adult clothes and eventually trading the leftover fabric to "ragpickers" in exchange for simple manufactured goods such as tin pots and cups. That thriftiness, however, disappeared as the petrochemical revolution and post–World War II economic affluence in the United States ushered in an era of convenience, disposability, and landfills.

This chapter focuses primarily on one type of garbage: municipal solid waste (MSW), that is, the discards produced by households, businesses, and public entities such as cities. Limiting the definition of garbage in this fashion leaves out other important and sometimes dangerous categories of waste such as sludge from wastewater treatment plants, nuclear waste (high- and low-level), medical waste, ash from power plants, and the like, some of which are often referred to collectively as HAZMAT, or hazardous materials. Even though MSW might contain materials such as paint thinner, waste oil from motor vehicles, and batteries made from toxic metals such as lead and mercury, it is not considered hazardous waste per se since the quantities of such hazardous and toxic components is generally assumed to be small enough to be ignored. For the purposes of this chapter, then, garbage might be thought of as the leftovers of everyday consumption, and except in places where other categories of waste are specifically indicated, the term refers to municipal solid waste.

WASTE MANAGEMENT: MAKING THE GARBAGE GO AWAY

Governments, private companies, and individuals manage garbage through a variety of means, some of which aim to deal with the garbage after it is produced, others of which aim to reduce or prevent the garbage from being produced in the first place. Not surprisingly, there is no International Garbage Authority tasked with policing our discards, though as explained below, numerous international agreements do shape how waste management occurs, including trade in waste (yes, waste is a valuable commodity!).

As the principal intergovernmental forum in the world, the United Nations, with its nearly 200 member states, is the venue where many of those agreements are hammered out. According to the United Nations Environment Programme (UNEP), solid waste management should proceed according to the following hierarchy.

First Priority: Preventing or Reducing Waste Generation

The waste problem shrinks when individuals, families, businesses, and others produce less garbage. The reduction step is fairly straightforward, and anyone with the ability to purchase bulk goods, rather than

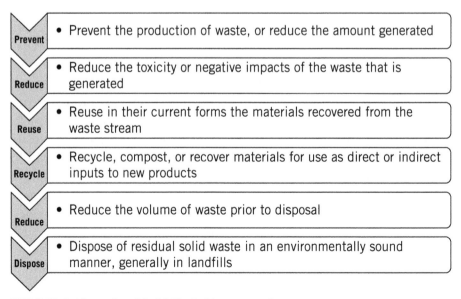

Prevent • Prevent the production of waste, or reduce the amount generated

Reduce • Reduce the toxicity or negative impacts of the waste that is generated

Reuse • Reuse in their current forms the materials recovered from the waste stream

Recycle • Recycle, compost, or recover materials for use as direct or indirect inputs to new products

Reduce • Reduce the volume of waste prior to disposal

Dispose • Dispose of residual solid waste in an environmentally sound manner, generally in landfills

TABLE 10.1: Hierarchy of Solid Waste Management
Adapted from United Nations Environment Programme.

pre-packaged ones, is already taking a step toward reducing waste generation. This is because single servings and smaller retail sizes have a greater percentage of packaging to product. Better still than buying in bulk is buying less. Things that are never produced in the first place cannot, by definition, enter the waste stream. Most packaging materials, aside from bulk containers like forklift pallets, shipping crates, and bulk boxes, are designed to be used one time. Once they are torn off, their next stop is almost always the landfill or incinerator. Moreover, the principal purpose of many packaging materials is to attract consumers' attention, not to protect the package contents.

For instance, how many times have you gone to the store in search of a familiar product—your favorite energy drink, shampoo, or breakfast cereal—only to find yourself puzzled at its apparent disappearance from its usual spot on the shelf? Then, a moment later, you discover it right in front of you, but with a different package with a label that proudly proclaims, "New look, same great taste!" or something similar. Why the gimmick? Manufacturers do this in an attempt to stand out among the overwhelming selection of consumer products that confront us each time we visit the supermarket, products we are told we need to buy in order to feel more energized, look our best, or stay awake longer. The constant attempts to capture consumers' attention both drives and is facilitated by a packaging industry estimated to generate nearly $800 billion in worldwide sales in 2013.[2] Not surprisingly, much of that packaging ends up being discarded rather than reused, landing in either a landfill or incinerator.

It is important to remember, though, that any real progress toward reducing waste requires much more than attentiveness to superfluous packaging. Instead, it requires people—especially those in affluent countries facing a bewildering array of unnecessary products at every turn—to fundamentally rethink our consumer habits. When we think and behave like engaged, critically thinking citizens who care about the future of our planet, we are more likely to examine our wants and needs and question the extent to which buying stuff will make us happier. Conversely, when we think and behave simply as consumers—as data points for advertising agencies and packaging industries—our critical faculties are dulled and our moral conundrums reduced to which flavor of ramen noodles or which color iPhone we will buy.

---

2 Smithers Pira, a packaging industry research firm, put the figure at USD$797 billion for 2013, estimating that number would rise to nearly USD$1 trillion by 2018. See https://www.smitherspira.com/market-reports/packaging/news/global-packaging-industry-market-growth-2018.aspx.

Second Priority: Reducing Toxicity

Even if something is discarded, its impact on the environment—on soil, water, air, and living things—will be drastically diminished if the material is inert or benign rather than toxic. One does not need an advanced degree in chemistry to know, for instance, that an apple core tossed on the ground is less likely to have a lasting environmental impact than, say, an old car battery full of lead and oozing sulfuric acid. According to the US Environmental Protection Agency (US EPA), which sets minimum guidelines for a variety of environmental concerns in the United States, including how wastes are handled, toxicity refers to a substance's ability to do harm or cause death if ingested or absorbed.[3] It is easy to understand, then, why reducing toxicity takes high priority in the waste management hierarchy.

Many items we routinely discard contain toxic components, though we might never refer to those items as toxic waste. For instance, the printed circuit boards (PCBs)[4] comprising the control center of nearly every electronic device, from 1970s console televisions encased in particle board cabinets and weighing over 100 pounds to today's wearable devices such as Google Glass and Bluetooth earpieces, often contain toxic-heavy metals such as cadmium, mercury, and lead. All of these metals have well-understood and well-documented deleterious health effects on humans and other organisms. Still other chemical components, such as the nearly ubiquitous brominated flame retardants (BFRs) found in manufactured goods ranging from electronics to mattresses, are classified as persistent organic pollutants (POPs) due partly to their ability to withstand decomposition in the environment by ultraviolet light, exposure to water, or weathering, and partly to their enduring detrimental effects on the natural systems, such as animal and plant tissues, into which they become incorporated.

Does this mean, then, that the laptops, cell phones, and tablets on which we have come to depend should all be considered toxic waste when we discard them? Nongovernmental advocacy organizations such as Silicon Valley Toxics Coalition (SVTC) and Greenpeace, for instance,

---

3   For more detail, see the US EPA website on "Characteristic Wastes" (wastes that must be handled differently due to their specific properties) at http://www.epa.gov/wastes/hazard/wastetypes/characteristic.htm.

4   In the context of waste, PCB (often in the plural form, PCBs) may also refer to polychlorinated biphenyls, a class of synthetic chemicals that are carcinogenic (cancer-causing) and extremely stable for decades or longer in the environment, a property that makes their toxicity even more problematic.

have campaigned for such a reclassification of electronic waste, so that international agreements such as the Basel Convention on the Control of Transboundary Movements of Hazardous Wastes and their Disposal[5] would then apply to the export from more developed countries (MDCs) of obsolete and discarded electronics. It has become quite common for so-called e-waste to be shipped from MDCs to less developed countries for processing and disposal. More often than not, the working and environmental conditions under which that processing and disposal occur are far less stringent than they would have to be if the processing were taking place in MDCs with stricter regulations and greater enforcement.

Third Priority: Reusing Materials in Their Current Form

In keeping with the old adage, "One man's trash is another man's treasure," it is often possible to divert materials from the waste stream simply by finding ways to continue using them in their original form. Reuse avoids energetically wasteful materials conversion processes, such as melting and re-forming plastics, which occur in chemical and thermal recycling processes. Moreover, reuse exemplifies an ethos of conservation rather than consumption, similar to Strasser's "stewardship of objects" mentioned above.

Frugal parents around the world pass on used children's clothing to younger siblings. Construction site managers who purchase materials such as lumber, insulation, and plumbing fixtures in bulk based on project estimates might find it more cost-effective (in terms of employee time) to simply donate or sell cheaply all those materials to a construction materials resale store, where other customers can then purchase smaller lots of new materials more cheaply than if they were purchasing them new at the original store. Automobile wrecking and salvage yards, while at times unsightly, allow customers to purchase used parts—air conditioner compressors, hubcaps, brake drums, body panels—directly off wrecked or otherwise damaged vehicles, again at a fraction of the cost of new parts. Some cities host "curb days" or similar events where residents may place unwanted household items on their curbs on certain days of the year so that others, to whom those items will be brand new, might find a use for them.

---

5 Note that in this context, "convention" refers to an agreement, not to a meeting. Also, this particular agreement is usually referred to simply as the Basel Convention. For more information, see the Convention website at http://www.basel.int/.

While it may be easy to imagine reusing things like building materials and automobile parts, imagining a second life for food containers, disposable diapers, worn-out bicycle tires, cartons of old CD-ROMs (to say nothing of eight-tracks or cassette tapes from the mid-1900s!), or the CPUs from last year's computer that is now obsolete is decidedly more challenging. The same is true for any number of other everyday discards, most of which were designed for a single purpose.

Fourth Priority: Recycling, Composting, and Materials Recovery

When products or materials cannot be easily reused in their original form and thus enter the waste stream, recovering components of that waste stream so that they may be used as inputs to other processes becomes another effective way of diverting discarded materials from landfills or incinerators and reducing the overall impact of waste on our world. Many parts of the world have active recycling programs for a wide range of materials, including basic commodities like metals, glass, plastics, and paper, as well as more complex engineered products such as cell phones.

Materials Recovery Facilities (MRFs, usually pronounced "murfs" in the waste management industry) employ human labor and modern technology to separate the most economically valuable materials from the waste stream. Technologies such as optical sensors, electromagnets, and electrical eddy currents, along with a host of automation processes borrowed from assembly line manufacturing, are now able to separate so-called single-stream mixed recyclable materials into relatively "pure" streams of glass, plastics, steel, and aluminum. Still other components of the MRF employ focused jets of pressurized air, rollers of different size, and other tools to separate out cardboard and paper. All of these materials can then be sold as commodities (feedstocks) to manufacturers, who then remake those products into new ones.

Complexity is the enemy of efficient and economically viable materials recovery. The more highly engineered an item is, the greater the difficulty of dismantling it in a way that maintains both the purity of the materials and the feasibility (technical and economic) of the process. Nowhere has the challenge presented by complexity been more apparent than in the electronics industry, where product offerings have exploded from simple transistor radios of the mid-1900s to the seemingly endless array of products available today.

Importantly, the business viability of MRFs, and of materials recovery in general except where it is mandated by law, depends largely on the market price of the recycled products compared to that of "virgin" materials (e.g., newly mined and smelted aluminum or paper produced from virgin wood pulp) as inputs into the manufacturing sector. Copper provides an illustrative example. Before the current global economic slow-down, worldwide demand for copper was high, pushing prices for copper to all-time highs and creating demand for scrap copper. As the economic recession set in, however, demand for manufactured goods fell, leading to a fall in demand for raw materials such as copper and a resultant fall in the price for scrap copper. Similar trends occurred for materials such as scrap paper, cardboard, aluminum, and glass.

Fifth Priority: Recovering Energy from Waste

Some components of the waste stream have relatively high energy content and can therefore be burned as fuel to produce heat for industrial processes, electricity production, or indoor climate control. For materials not diverted from the waste stream by the first four steps in the solid waste management hierarchy, then, recovering energy from those materials becomes the next priority.

Waste-to-Energy (WTE) is a catch-all term for various types of facilities designed to recover energy from the waste stream. Two uses in particular are quite common. First, WTE can refer to capturing the copious quantities of methane (CH_4) produced by decomposing organic matter (e.g., yard clippings, food waste, paper) in landfills and burning that methane to produce heat or to power electrical generators and produce electricity. Depending on the size of the landfill, its contents, its moisture level, and the surrounding environmental conditions, methane output can easily reach several hundred cubic meters per second.

Second, WTE can refer to simply combusting the waste materials in an incinerator that serves a dual role as a furnace in a thermal power plant. Petroleum-based products such as plastics tend to have, not surprisingly, a relatively high energy content; if combusted, they produce lots of heat. Since the energy content of much of the rest of the waste stream, however, is far lower than that of fossil fuels like coal or natural gas, WTE incinerators often need to supplement the waste they burn with fossil fuels in order to reach temperatures high enough to produce electricity. This is one reason the EPA's classification of WTE projects as "clean" or "renewable" energy seems more than a little bit problematic.

Sixth Priority: Reducing Waste Volume

Reuse, recycling, materials and energy recovery, and the other higher-priority options listed above all contribute to reducing the total volume of garbage destined for final disposal facilities, generally landfills and incinerators. For the garbage that remains after the above steps have been taken, the sixth priority here refers specifically to reducing the actual geometric volume of a given quantity (mass or weight) of waste. Doing so has implications for everything from the energy used to transport garbage to the useful life of disposal facilities.

For landfills in particular, waste volume is the primary constraint on the life span of a landfill. While operating permits for landfills are generally granted based on tonnages, with daily and yearly limits,[6] a landfill's profitability depends directly on the amount of waste that can be squeezed into the three-dimensional geometry of the landfill. It is easy to understand, then, why operators of modern landfills spend hundreds of thousands of dollars on heavy equipment designed to compact the waste. Maximizing the mass of waste contained in a given volume of space (otherwise known as density and measured in units like kg/m^3) allows landfill operators to accept those daily tonnages for longer periods and has the added benefit of making the waste mass more stable. The less the waste mass in a landfill settles after it has been deposited, the lower the chance that dangerous and unhygienic events such as slope failures (landslides) will occur.

Last Resort: Disposal in Landfills or by Incineration

For garbage already produced, landfilling and incineration—in their technologically primitive or advanced forms—are the most widely used waste management practices around the world. Each has its advantages and disadvantages, some of which are discussed below. Both have a range of environmental and social costs, many of which are treated as externalities and therefore not borne directly by those who produced the garbage or disposed of it. Instead, those costs—increased air pollution, odors, altered landscapes, more truck traffic—are shouldered by society at large. Especially troubling are cases when such costs become environmental justice issues, where low-income or minority communities end up shouldering a disproportionate share of those costs.

---

6   A "mega-landfill" typically has daily limits ranging in the thousands of (short) tons per day in the United States.

In many places, however, reducing the amount of waste generated often comes as the last priority for individuals, businesses, and government agencies acting on incomplete information or, worse, selfish and shortsighted interests that lead them to overlook the true social and ecological impacts of modern consumerist, disposable society. This is especially true when "throwing away" garbage is cheap or unregulated. The primary factors influencing disposal costs include tipping fees,[7] fuel prices (especially for long-distance trash transport), and in the case of landfilling, land prices. It is important to remember, however, that "away" is always somewhere; in many cases, it is "here" for someone else, simply by fault of geography, economic situation (class), political power, race, or ethnicity. Once again, we see that dealing with the leftovers of profligate consumption and modern society is not simply a management problem, but an ethical one with an important social and environmental justice dimension.

Landfills

Long before the advent of single-use plastics and mega-landfills, human societies practiced some version of "out of sight, out of mind" when managing their waste. Some of the richest archaeological digs are often middens, the village waste heaps where animal bones, shards of broken pottery, and scraps of metal and other materials give modern scientists insights into the lives of our collective ancestors. Future archaeologists or alien visitors brave enough to explore the landscape-altering mega-landfills of today may have trouble comparing them to the humble middens of centuries past, but in a very real sense, they are one and the same, differing only in scale, diversity of contents, and complexity.

Modern landfills are highly engineered refinements on the age-old practice of digging holes in the ground in which to bury garbage. In the United States, it was the post–World War II boom in garbage production resulting from the plastics and disposability revolution that led Congress to pass the Solid Waste Management Act of 1965, later amended and renamed the Resource Conservation and Recovery Act (RCRA) in 1976, which laid the groundwork for solid waste management across the country.[8] Among more

---

7 Tipping fees refer to the fee imposed on a hauler to dump or "tip" a load of trash at a landfill or incineration facility. Tipping fees in the United States vary greatly, from free (often in the case of municipally owned landfills in rural areas) to one hundred dollars per ton or more. In Europe, those fees may be roughly three times as much. In a small country like Japan, they may be 10 times as much.

8 RCRA governs six aspects of landfills in the U.S.: location; operation; design; groundwater monitoring and corrective action; closure and post-closure care; and financial

developed countries, the United States is something of an outlier in its high reliance on landfills and low reliance on incinerators as the preferred method for disposing of waste, or at least hiding it, for the medium to long term.

One reason for the preference for landfills over incinerators is the United States' very low population density in many rural parts of the country, which helps minimize political resistance to landfill siting and makes it easy for waste management companies to acquire large tracts of land at very affordable prices. A second reason is that many of the local governments in such rural areas have seen their jobs and tax bases decline dramatically as manufacturing and other blue-collar jobs have been shifted elsewhere, including overseas. Those governments are often cash-strapped and eager to seize any economic development opportunities, including burying trash for their neighbors, even when those neighbors may be hundreds of miles away. Finally, incinerators have faced much more political resistance in the United States than landfills have due to concern over dioxins and furans.

Landfill operators in the United States frequently cite costs on the order of millions of dollars per acre to construct landfills that comply with local and federal regulations. Yet while the costs may indeed be high, burying garbage is certainly profitable, especially as it becomes increasingly difficult to establish new landfill sites due to political resistance or environmental concerns in would-be host communities. While the technical details of landfill engineering are beyond the scope of this chapter, several key elements and their functions are worth mentioning here.

Liner System
One of the principal concerns of landfills is the prevention of groundwater contamination by leachate, the liquid resulting from the waste itself or from precipitation that has come in contact with the waste mass. Modern landfills are required to have a liner that is partly comprised of natural components, partly of synthetic ones. The system includes several barriers designed to prevent movement of liquids (leachate)[9] out of the landfill, beginning with a thick layer of natural clay and ending with a semi-rigid high-density polyethylene plastic directly underlying the waste, all of

---

assurance criteria. For the full text of the portion of RCRA concerning MSW landfills, see http://www.ecfr.gov/cgi-bin/text-idx?SID=0022d174c35bc14366237ccf7ea9ea36&tpl=/ ecfrbrowse/Title40/40cfr258_main_02.tpl.

9   Leachate might be colloquially thought of as "garbage juice." More technically, it is any liquid emanating from the waste mass, whether directly from the waste itself or from liquid such as precipitation that has come into contact with the waste.

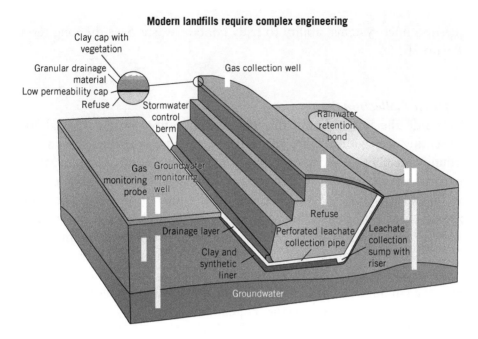

Modern landfills require complex engineering

which is designed to keep liquid in the landfill from escaping through the bottom into the ground and, eventually, the groundwater. The US federal government requires a single-liner system; certain states like California and New York require a second liner to further reduce the likelihood of leachate moving out of the landfill.

While a 60-mil-thick[10] semi-rigid plastic liner may seem like a robust barrier to leachate movement, it is important to keep in mind two points. First, liner systems, like all engineered systems, will eventually fail. How serious an impact that creates will depend largely on the toxicity of the compacted, putrefying waste stored in the landfill, the impermeability of the clay layer, and the local hydrological conditions. In the United States, landfill operators are responsible for the integrity of the landfill, including monitoring the liner system and repairing it if necessary, for 30 years postclosure. Synthetic liners only came into use in the 1990s, and some are already showing signs of failure due to cracking, brittleness, or chemical interactions with caustic leachate. Some scholars have therefore begun to

---

10   One mil is equivalent to 1/1000 (10^{-3}) of an inch, so 60 mil = 0.06 inches.

question liner systems' ability to truly contain waste over the long term (Pivato 2011).

Leachate Collection System

Alongside the liner system, the leachate collection system is vital for preventing seepage of toxins from the waste mass into the surrounding groundwater. Leachate can contain any number of toxins present in MSW, many of which, even in low concentrations, may still have toxic effects on biological systems. Liquid resting on the liner produces hydrostatic pressure that can reduce the integrity of the landfill, and in some cases (such as when it comes into contact with residues from aluminum smelting), it can result in dangerous conditions such as fires.[11] Modern landfills utilize a system of pipes, sumps, and pumps to collect and remove leachate from the landfill in an attempt to minimize the risk of underground fires, groundwater contamination, and slope failures.

Large landfills can produce tens of millions of liters of leachate per year or more, which begs the question: What happens to the captured leachate? In most cases, it is transferred to municipal wastewater treatment plants by truck or pipeline. When that transfer occurs by diesel-powered tanker truck, it creates a further environmental impact in the form of emissions from diesel combustion. In either case, treating leachate in municipal wastewater treatment plants is often controversial, primarily since many municipal plants were not designed to eliminate the myriad chemicals that might be present in leachate, ranging from synthetics such as brominated flame retardants and pesticides to heavy metals and sulfuric acid from batteries.

Some landfills have onsite pre-treatment facilities to reduce the concentrations of such chemicals in their leachate before it is shipped off—usually to municipal wastewater treatment plants designed primarily to handle household sewage—to be further treated. Since the volumes of leachate produced by large landfills can fill several tanker trucks each day, those wastewater treatment plants usually trickle small amounts of leachate into the wastewater influent (rather than dumping it in all at once) so as to avoid disrupting the microbial processes fundamental to effective wastewater treatment. Ironically, the final resting place for the leftovers of wastewater treatment plants, known as sludge, is often the

---

11 For more details on this chemical reaction and the conditions under which it may occur, see Stark et al. (2012).

nearest landfill, thus creating a perverse ecology of waste, leachate, and the toxins contained therein.

Landfill Gas Capture System

As mentioned above, when organic material such as food waste, yard trimmings, and paper products decompose in the low-oxygen conditions inside a landfill, it produces landfill gas (LFG), which is usually about half methane, half carbon dioxide, along with a very small amount of non-methane organic compounds (NMOC). Since both methane and carbon dioxide are odorless, it is the small fraction of other gases that gives landfills their unpleasant odor.

Landfill gas capture systems are comprised of a network of collection wells installed in the waste mass, along with a system of hoses and powerful vacuum pumps that, in theory, keep the entire waste mass under negative pressure. The systems are primarily designed to capture the methane produced in landfills, since it is a highly flammable greenhouse gas and presents both an immediate safety hazard and contributes significantly to climate change.[12] Methane is also, of course, an economically valuable hydrocarbon with wide usage in energy systems around the world, from household heating to vehicle fuel. When functioning well, LFG systems capture or destroy much of the odor-causing fraction of the gas, thereby reducing the nuisance factor of landfills, while directing the methane fraction of the LFG either to gas-powered generators for producing electricity or to pipeline infrastructure where the gas can be used as primary energy for industrial, commercial, or residential heating purposes.

Intermediate Cover

During the time the landfill is in use, the degrading waste mass can be a real nuisance to neighboring communities and ecosystems. The smell of rotting organic matter attracts scavengers such as seagulls, rats, raccoons, and even bears, many of which may then become sick and die from ingesting the leftovers of human profligacy and may spread disease among other

---

12 Climate scientists and atmospheric chemists estimate that methane has roughly 25 to 30 times the heat-trapping potential of carbon dioxide. This is one reason the US EPA requires that landfill methane that cannot be used as an energy source (either for electricity or heat) still be combusted; since the by-products of methane combustion are heat, water vapor, and carbon dioxide, the net effect on climate is less than if the methane were simply released.

animals. Not surprisingly, landfill gases can also cause inconvenience and problems to human residents, ranging from impacts on property values to respiratory ailments. One way of mitigating this type of impact is through the use of intermediate cover.

At its simplest, intermediate cover is material placed on an area of the landfill that is not yet ready to be permanently capped and closed (see below). Intermediate cover might be placed on an active section of a landfill overnight to keep smells down and scavenging animals out, or it might be used for a longer period if a section of a landfill becomes filled but is not ready for final capping. For daily cover, the material, such as a plastic tarp or a layer of soil, is almost always removed first thing the next morning before waste placement (dumping) begins again. Leaving each day's daily cover in place would unnecessarily add expense and take up valuable landfill volume; removing that cover maximizes the volume of the landfill used for actual waste rather than other materials, thereby raising the landfill's economic efficiency. Some landfills are also permitted to use so-called BUD (Beneficial Use Determinant) material such as contaminated soil or chipped automobile tires as intermediate cover. In all cases, covering the waste mass with even a few centimeters of non-waste material helps suppress odors and reduce scavenging by animals.

Final Cap

Once the landfill has reached its capacity, it is capped in a fashion similar to the way it was lined. First, a plastic liner is laid over the waste mass and welded to the liner underneath. In this way, the waste is essentially entombed in a plastic wrapper for the foreseeable future. Some refer to this method of waste management as a "dry tomb" landfill, where dryness promotes stability of the waste mass. On top of the plastic cap, a layer of clay and topsoil are then added, and vegetation is planted in the soil. Large shrubs and trees are avoided, however, in order to avoid potential penetration of the cap by their root systems.

Some closed landfills are repurposed as parks, golf courses, or even sites for photovoltaic arrays, such as the Hickory Ridge Landfill outside Atlanta, Georgia, in the southeastern United States (see Figure 10.2).

One major drawback of landfills is that laptops and Barbies simply do not compost. While it might seem reasonable to assume that waste placed in a landfill will eventually degrade and simply return to the earth, such an assumption is deeply flawed, as the work of scholars, such as the late William Rathje, often known as the founder of "garbology," and others, has shown. As documented in their book *Rubbish: The Archaeology of Garbage* (Rathje and Murphy 2001), Rathje and his collaborators took samples from closed MSW landfills and analyzed them in an attempt to understand both the contents of landfills and the decomposition processes that occur inside landfills.

Some of their findings were quite surprising; others were downright disturbing. Newspapers, for instance, were still legible and were in fact useful in determining the age of various layers of garbage in sampled landfills. Hot dogs were still recognizable as hot dogs, even after decades in a landfill. The reason for this lack of degradation is that landfills lack three vital ingredients that facilitate the breakdown of all sorts of materials: oxygen, water, and sunlight, especially ultraviolet light.

Compressed trash in a landfill has had much of the air (and therefore oxygen) squeezed out of it in order to maximize density of the waste

FIGURE 10.2 Hickory Ridge Landfill with solar photovoltaic array.
Copyright © 2011 by CarlisleEnergy, (CC BY-SA 3.0) at http://en.wikipedia.org/wiki/File:Hickory_Ridge_Landfill_Completed.jpg.

mass. Lack of oxygen means that only anaerobic bacterial breakdown can occur, which is often slower than aerobic breakdown and produces methane gas, a dangerous and potentially explosive substance in landfills unless properly vented or captured, as discussed above. Meanwhile, liquid (leachate), also as noted above, is removed from the landfill through the leachate collection system in order to reduce the potential for liner failure, groundwater contamination, or destabilizing reactions occurring in the presence of water.[13] Finally, just as ultraviolet (UV) light can cause sunburns on unprotected skin and faded paint on automobile hoods and roofs, it also aids in the physical breakdown of most materials one might

---

13 One such reaction is the aforementioned reaction between water and aluminum dross and salt cake, two by-products of aluminum smelting. The reaction is exothermic, meaning it produces heat, which can then lead to difficult-to-control fires in a landfill.

find in an MSW landfill. Lack of UV light, then, means that breakdown no longer occurs.

Incineration

A second common means of disposing of waste is through incineration, or burning. In its most primitive form, trash is simply lit on fire in open pits or rusty backyard burn barrels and left to burn. Such fires are generally poorly aerated and burn at relatively low temperatures, producing lots of smoke and particulate pollution as well as releasing harmful chemical compounds such as dioxins. Dioxins result primarily when plastics are burned. They persist for long periods in the environment—in air, animal tissues, soils, and water—and can cause serious health repercussions, including cancer.[14] Sadly, backyard trash burning is still prevalent in many rural areas in MDCs despite widespread recognition among experts of how harmful the practice can be.

At the other end of the incineration technology spectrum, garbage incineration takes place in furnaces designed specifically to combust MSW or other wastes. Through injection of large volumes of pressurized air, these furnaces burn at very high temperatures, nearing 1000°C, in order to ensure that combustion of the garbage is as complete as possible and that most toxic by-products such as dioxins and furans are destroyed. Additional technologies such as electrostatic precipitators and "bag houses" (essentially, large filter bags that trap fine particulates), obviously absent from backyard burn barrels and pits, further reduce air emissions and take at least some toxins out of circulation.

Incineration has two distinct advantages over landfilling. First, incineration can drastically reduce the volume of the waste, sometimes by as much as 90%. The ash, of course, must then be buried in a landfill or specialized ash monofill (i.e., a landfill designed specifically for waste incinerator ash). In the United States, some states allow so-called beneficial use of ash from incinerators that burn certain types of waste, such as sludge from wastewater (sewage) treatment plants, as industrial inputs for products such as fertilizer and cement.

The second advantage of incineration over landfilling is that some incinerators incorporate WTE technologies that allow the operators to generate high-temperature steam, which can then be used for heating in

---

14   For more on the chemistry and health impacts of dioxins, as well as regulations concerning their release and monitoring, see the US EPA's Dioxins page at http://cfpub. epa.gov/ncea/CFM/nceaQFind.cfm?keyword=Dioxin.

residential, commercial, or industrial settings, or for producing electricity through steam turbine power plants.[15] Depending on the composition of the garbage and its energy content, the waste stream fed into the incinerator may need to be supplemented with a fossil fuel (natural gas, pulverized coal, or petroleum-based fuel oil) in order for it to reach steam temperatures high enough to generate electricity.

Incineration is a much more common means of managing garbage in Europe and Asia than is landfilling. In Sweden, waste management authorities have developed incinerator-based WTE technologies to such an extent, reaching energy efficiencies greater than 90% in some cases through production and utilization of both electricity and heat for district heating, that in recent years, the country has had to turn to garbage imports from elsewhere in Europe in order to keep its WTE facilities running. Once again, geography matters: even though Sweden is a sizable country with large tracts of sparsely populated land, much of that land is heavily forested, frozen for a significant portion of the year, or otherwise ill-suited for landfilling.

While the concept of burning garbage is simple, the workings of a high-temperature industrial incinerator are somewhat more complicated. In general, waste incineration facilities incorporate the following components.

Hopper

Trash trucks arriving at a solid waste incinerator first deposit their loads onto a tipping floor or directly into a large collection basin called a hopper. There, operators use heavy equipment to mix the garbage in order to make it burn more evenly.

Grate

Since garbage has a lower energy content and much higher moisture content than fossil fuels, its combustion, if not aided, will be much less efficient and complete and will release much less thermal energy (heat) than would the combustion of a similar volume, say, of coal. Rather than simply let the trash burn inefficiently and incompletely in a pile on a solid floor, industrial incinerators use a system of moving grates to transport the trash across the combustion chamber. Throughout the transit, the

---

15   For an animated video of how a WTE facility works, see Wheelabrator Technologies USA's "See How Our Plants Work" website at http://www.wheelabratortechnologies.com/plants/how-it-works/. Wheelabrator is wholly owned by Waste Management, which bills itself as "the largest waste environmental solutions provider in North America," at http://www.wm.com/about/index.jsp.

grates are blasted with high-pressure air to increase the efficiency and temperature of combustion. Ash and uncombusted material falls through the grates to the bottom of the furnace, where it is later collected.

Materials Recovery Facility (MRF)

Obviously, not all garbage burns (or burns well), so incinerator operators often perform some minimal degree of sorting to remove non-combustible material from the delivered waste, such as large pieces of metals. Still, some of these materials make it into the incinerator hopper and fall through the grates, where they are collected either for landfilling or recycling. Incinerator operators usually collect economically valuable, non-combustible materials such as metals so that they may be sold to recyclers and remade into new products.

WTE Plant

As noted above, many waste incinerators incorporate facilities that collect and use what otherwise would be waste heat from the incineration process. Facilities that use that heat to produce electricity do so by means of producing steam, which then turns the blades of a turbine linked to a generator, in basically the same fashion as any thermal power plant fueled by fossil fuels, nuclear material, or solar energy. For complex reasons beyond the scope of this chapter, the efficiency of such a process where only electricity (and not heat) is captured as the final product is at best 40%, and often closer to 30%, meaning that roughly two-thirds of the energy contained in the fuel (in this case, garbage) is dumped as waste heat into the atmosphere and the nearby bodies of water used for cooling.

Once again we find an opportunity to rethink waste as a resource here in the case of so-called waste heat. As in the case of Sweden, the overall plant efficiencies may be pushed much higher if the low-temperature steam left over after the electricity-production step, which is still quite hot (near 100°C), is then used to heat nearby buildings or provide thermal energy for industrial processes in nearby factories. Most garbage incinerators worldwide, however, are not designed in such an integrated and strategic fashion. Their principal goal is to dispose of rubbish, and heat and electricity production are simply ancillary benefits whose economic and environmental value may or may not be fully extracted.

Emissions Control

The emissions control unit of an incinerator consists of two principal subsystems: pollution prevention devices and monitoring devices. The complexity, effectiveness, and reliability of these subsystems depend on the level and type of monitoring required in the jurisdiction in which the incinerator operates. Typical monitors will keep track of flue temperature, particulates, and concentrations of target pollutants like dioxins, furans, and toxic metals such as cadmium and mercury.

Pollution prevention devices include bag houses (fabric filters), electrostatic precipitators (ESPs), and scrubbers. Each of these three technologies removes pollutants from flue gases through different mechanisms. Bag houses consist of large suspended filter bags that trap particulate matter (fly ash) of a certain size as the flue gases are forced through them. Meanwhile, the particulates in flue gases passing over ESPs are attracted to charged wires from which they are then collected. Finally, scrubbers function by spraying a scrubbing agent, whose composition depends on the pollutant targeted but may be as simple as plain water, into the flue gases, either neutralizing target pollutants or causing them to precipitate out of the gas and fall to the floor. All three types of systems must be periodically maintained and their components replaced, processes which can expose incinerator workers to high levels of the captured pollutants if proper precautions are not taken.

Flue

The flue is the exhaust chimney or "smokestack" of the waste incinerator, from which the scrubbed combustion gases, waste heat, and any pollutants not removed by the emissions control unit are released into the atmosphere. If smoke is visible coming out of the flue, it is likely an indicator that something is amiss in the emissions control unit and therefore allowing large quantities of particulate to escape. Oftentimes a plume of steam may be seen, resulting from escaping low-temperature steam exhausted from the WTE unit or from the evaporation of scrubber liquid as it is injected into the waste gases exiting the flue. For many living or working in the vicinity of incinerators, the flue and the *unseen* pollutants actually or presumed to be released there symbolize the entire facility's potential to do harm to their health or their surroundings.

Other Waste Management Methods

Scientists, engineers, and entrepreneurs have developed a handful of other methods for getting rid of garbage, but these see very little use worldwide due to their technical complexity or unproven economic feasibility. Two methods worth briefly mentioning here are bioreactors and waste gasification.

Bioreactors are simply landfills that are kept wetter than their "dry tomb" counterparts. The theory behind bioreactors is that increased moisture speeds the rate and increases the completeness of degradation inside the landfill, thereby ensuring that, in the end, nearly all of the biodegradable components of the garbage are decomposed and the remaining mass is as inert as possible. For bioreactor landfills, decomposition is the priority, whereas for traditional "dry tomb" landfills, stability is the priority. An added benefit is that methane production tends to occur earlier and at a greater rate than in drier landfills.

The higher moisture level in bioreactors is maintained either by recirculating leachate as it is collected or by adding additional moisture from outside the waste mass. For instance, the US EPA allows operators to use storm water, wastewater, or wastewater treatment plant sludge to increase the bioreactor landfill's moisture content.[16] Not surprisingly, bioreactors are better suited to wetter climates, where factors such as higher humidity and precipitation would reduce the amount of extra liquid added to the landfill. Some concerns about bioreactors include reduced stability of the waste mass and somewhat greater risk of chemical reactions and leachate migration.

Waste gasification is a more complex process and has not yet been demonstrated to be cost-effective on a large scale. In brief, the process aims to break down garbage into its constituent molecules by essentially vaporizing it in an ultra-high-temperature electrical arc operated in a low-oxygen environment. Doing so allows disassembly and reassembly of the trash at the molecular level, resulting in a synthetic gas usually referred to as synthesis gas or "syngas," which can then be used as a fuel or industrial feedstock.[17] One of the principal hurdles to increasing the use of gasification is the energy balance of the process: at present, more energy is used to produce the syngas than is derived from the syngas, making the entire process an energy loser. Another hurdle is that many see gasification as simply another word for incineration, even when, technically speaking, there is no combustion of the trash since the gasification process takes place in a vacuum. A final challenge is that in order for gasification to

---

16 For more on bioreactor landfills, see the EPA's Bioreactor page at http://www.epa.gov/osw/nonhaz/municipal/landfill/bioreactors.htm#2.

17 In some contexts, "gasification" (especially "biogasification") refers to methane production via anaerobic decomposition of organic material. Here, however, gasification refers to a different process called plasma gasification aimed at treating a much wider range of waste materials. For more on waste gasification, see the US Department of Energy's National Energy Technology Laboratory webpage on the subject at http://www.netl.doe.gov/research/coal/energy-systems/gasification/gasifipedia/westinghouse.

function well, the waste stream must be relatively uniform, composed primarily of materials such as plastics that have high energy content.[18]

One final point on so-called WTE solutions is worth underscoring here, in a textbook on sustainability. While organizations such as the US EPA and profit-driven waste management companies such as Wheelabrator are quick to label WTE technologies as green, renewable forms of energy production and waste management, readers thinking critically about sustainability should not take such statements at face value. All of these methods—landfill methane capture, WTE incineration, and the still-unproven gasification—rely on wasteful consumption patterns of all of us as their fuel source, and those patterns are hardly sustainable from an economic or ecological perspective.

IMPACTS OF GARBAGE ON SOCIETY AND THE NATURAL ENVIRONMENT

A society that produces unparalleled amounts of garbage, much of which (plastics) will not degrade in time frames useful to humans, has a profound impact on the natural systems of the planet on which human societies depend. The various disposal techniques outlined above may mitigate or delay those impacts, but the simple fact is that a modern, Western-style throwaway society is increasingly turning valuable natural resources into items that are used once, discarded, and contribute to what author Adam Minter refers to as our "Junkyard Planet" in a recent book by the same title. Moreover, garbage generation rates have, in general, proven to rise in direct relation to per capita incomes, unlike sulfur dioxide and particulate emissions, which decline as per capita incomes rise and demands for greater environmental quality grow. As Western-style consumption habits are increasingly emulated in emerging economies, the image of a junkyard planet becomes regrettably easy to picture.

---

18 High energy content is a function of the type, number, and strength of molecular bonds in a certain material. When those bonds are broken—for example, through combustion—their energy is released. The bonds in plastics tend to be very strong, which helps explain not only their high energy content, but also their ability to resist degradation in nature.

STASH YOUR TRASH!

It is illegal under U.S. law to dispose of any garbage in lakes, rivers and within three miles of shore.

Do your part!:
- Reduce the use of disposables: switch to re-usable containers, cups, plates and utensils on your boat
- Use trash receptacles and recycling bins on shore
- Stow loose plastics and potential debris below decks
- Retrieve tangled fishing line
- Practice "Plus-One" boating – bring back your own trash PLUS ONE piece of litter from someone else's wasteful wake

Plastic and other garbage fouls props, clogs intakes, entangles animals and destroys the natural beauty of the aquatic environment.
Don't be a polluter!

FIGURE 10.3 Sign near a river in the eastern United States.

The impacts of garbage include environmental impacts on water, air, soil, and landscapes, as well as social impacts such as nuisances (e.g., odors, truck traffic, and noise), depressed property values, and degradation of quality of life. Of particular concern at a variety of scales, from the local to the global, are environmental justice considerations resulting from waste production and disposal practices. The very notion of environmental justice in the United States grew out of the positive momentum toward greater social justice following the civil rights movement in the 1960s, focused particularly on issues of injustice stemming from waste disposal.

In the paragraphs below, we examine in greater detail the environmental and social impacts of garbage.

Environmental Impacts

Ecosystems produce no waste; instead, simply speaking, matter and energy are transferred and transformed from higher levels of organization and utility to lower ones. When a tree dies, its rotting remains on the forest floor become home to countless organisms that break down the tree's complexity—leaves, bark, xylem, phloem—into its molecular constituents such as carbon, nitrogen, and hydrogen, which then form the building blocks of the next generation of forest life.

The modern waste produced by human society, however, is different, and it can yield complex negative impacts on air, water, and soil, threatening the ability of those environmental systems to support human and nonhuman life. As noted above, backyard incineration of waste, unfortunately a widespread worldwide practice, produces numerous toxins that persist for long periods in the atmosphere and can easily enter the food web through the process known as bioaccumulation. From there, those toxins can easily make their way into the bodies, especially the fatty tissues, of virtually all living creatures. No matter how far removed those creatures are from industrial human civilizations, the aquatic and terrestrial food chains eventually connect back to humans. Scientists have documented the presence of dioxins and other by-products of industrial society, for instance, in the blubber of whales and in the breast milk of native peoples living in extremely remote regions of the Arctic.

As mentioned above, organizations such as the US Environmental Protection Agency and their counterparts at the state and local levels are charged with regulating the amounts and types of waste management by-products that enter the environment. The dominant paradigm in the United States is one of risk management based on concepts such as Maximum Contaminant Levels (MCLs) for drinking water and Criteria Pollutants for air. First, scientific studies are used to determine what levels of particular pollutants are "acceptable" from a human health perspective. Next, regulations are established to keep the MCLs at or below that level. Here, "acceptable" means that the likelihood a certain contaminant will have a negative heath impact is below some established threshold.

The problem with this approach, as you may already have guessed, is that it assumes certain levels of pollution are essentially harmless. Those thresholds, in turn, are determined in no small part by the cost of further reducing (or eliminating) the contaminant's presence in the environment. Let us assume, for instance, that the MCL for Contaminant A in drinking water is 15 parts per million (ppm). Does that really mean that consuming drinking water with 14.5 ppm of Contaminant A has no harmful effect on human health? Or that consuming drinking water with only 5 ppm over the course of 20 years is safe? Obviously, it is difficult to answer such questions with absolute certainty lacking long-term, expensive studies with control groups on human subjects, for reasons ranging from cost to ethics to methodologies. But the fact remains that regulatory frameworks and the science on which they are based are at best imperfect tools limited by funding, time, and our ability to fully grasp the complexities of human physiology and the planetary life-support systems that sustain them. A further glaring limitation, of course, is that regulations such as those governing waste management facilities are primarily human-focused rather than ecosystem-focused.

FIGURE 10.4 Each TT combination shown (top photo) can carry. A mega-landfill in a rural area of New York state. Each tractor-trailer combination shown can carry up to 25 tons of garbage, and many travel hundreds of miles one-way to reach the landfill. Middle and bottom photos: View of the landfill from the distance

Photo: Author.

Garbage production and disposal has a wide range of social impacts. Some are obvious and immediate, such as nuisance odors, increased traffic from garbage-hauling vehicles, and depressed property values and quality of life for residents living in the vicinity of garbage facilities. Others are more subtle and pernicious, such as declines in health resulting from long-term exposure to low levels of air, water, or soil pollution. To make matters worse, proving that longer-term impacts on human health are directly related to activities such as leachate treatment and garbage incineration is notoriously hard to do, at least in the United States. This is due to the simple fact that correlation does not equal causation in science or law.

Nevertheless, correlations—for instance, large numbers of ethnic minorities or poor families living near landfills—are highly useful for understanding the social impacts of garbage from an environmental justice perspective. Environmental justice asks whether certain social groups—for instance, marginalized groups who lack cultural, political, or socioeconomic power or status—bear a disproportionate share of environmental "bads" such as dust, noise, pollution, or toxics.

The landmark case that catalyzed the environmental justice movement in the United States involved an attempt to dispose of PCB-contaminated soil in a poor, primarily African American community in North Carolina. Local residents, concerned about impacts on their community and their health, utilized non-violent protest methods by lying down in the streets to prevent the passage of garbage trucks. The event motivated an investigation sponsored by the US government into the correlation between toxic waste facilities and the racial and economic make-up of surrounding communities (General Accounting Office 1983).

The GAO study and subsequent ones demonstrated that the majority of toxic waste facilities in the United States were situated in poor and minority communities with limited access to political, economic, educational, or legal resources with which to resist those facilities (Bullard 2000). Since then, the field of environmental justice has grown substantially, examining questions ranging from noxious facilities (e.g., landfills and power plants) siting to climate change impacts on low-lying coastal communities. In addition, even though environmental justice in its early days tended to focus on whether or not the perpetrators of environmental injustices *intended* to cause harm or injustice, the focus has shifted more recently simply to outcomes, regardless of whether there was intent or not (Pellow 2002). The motivation for this shift is clear: communities and individuals suffering disproportionately from the effects of environmental burdens such as polluting facilities do so regardless of the intent of those who created the facility.

Owners and operators of landfills, incinerators, and transfer stations recognize that attempts to site new facilities frequently invoke the resistance of local residents, even though some of those residents may benefit through employment at the facility, land sales to the operator, or tax revenues (in the case of municipal leaders). In order to counter such resistance, operators may negotiate agreements with the leaders of the host community, sometimes called Community Benefit Agreements (CBAs), which make certain commitments to the community in exchange for the community agreeing to host the facility.

For instance, the CBA between the owner of the landfill pictured in Figure 10.4 in a rural part of the state of New York and the host community commits the company to providing money for firefighting equipment, college scholarships, municipal infrastructure upgrades, buyouts and price guarantees for homes in the landfill's immediate vicinity, and the town's general fund. In exchange, the town leaders agree to host the landscape-altering landfill (one of the largest in the country) on what was once fertile agricultural land, and they will be host to the mountain of waste long after the landfill is closed and the operator has left the area. Not surprisingly, many residents are unhappy with this "cash for trash" arrangement and are campaigning actively to shut down the facility.

TOWARD SUSTAINABILITY: IS ZERO WASTE POSSIBLE?

As we near the end of this chapter, two things should be abundantly clear to readers truly interested in sustainability. First, if you have not been thinking about garbage, you should be. We know where our cars, shirts, toys, and gadgets are made, but in general, we are blissfully ignorant of where they go once we throw them "away." Hopefully, this chapter has helped remind readers that "away" is always somewhere, amidst human communities and non-human systems that suffer from wasteful consumption and careless "disposal" habits. Second, given the staggering amount of information and knowledge produced by the world's societies today, much of which is about ourselves, civilizations of the future will almost certainly *not* have to rely on our trash heaps—our middens—to discern what twentieth- and twenty-first-century human societies were like.

In the United States alone, there are more than 10,000 landfills, with about one-fifth that number active today. Several hundred of those active today are mega-landfills accepting 1,000 or more tons per day of trash, a great percentage of which could have been eliminated by following one or more of the first six waste management hierarchy principles outlined above. A conservative estimate would place the number of landfills worldwide in the hundreds of thousands, each with its own set of environmental and social impacts. It is vitally important, then, that we break the link between affluence and waste production and fundamentally reshape the way so-called developed human societies consume goods and produce "bads" like garbage. Yet world leaders, it seems, are content to stumble toward the third decade of the twenty-first century, mumbling phrases such as "greener future" and "sustainable development" without knowing what they mean or caring enough to demonstrate true leadership on pressing environmental concerns. Is this really how the story ends?

Perhaps not. Forward-thinking leaders in national and local governments around the world—a minority for now, to be sure—have taken some promising initial steps. Recognizing the short life span and limited utility of much flashy packaging, as well as the significance of packaging materials in MSW, South Korea limits the percentage of a product's total mass that can be comprised of packaging. Taiwan, facing a garbage crisis in the late 1990s and finding many construction sites converted to illegal landfills, embarked on a waste reduction campaign and in 10 years cut its per capita MSW generation in half, from 1.1 kg to 0.6 kg per person per day (Ross 2008). Norway, as noted earlier in this chapter, has taken the lead in efficiently utilizing waste for fuel, even as its citizens have one of the highest recycling rates in the world. The US city of San Francisco has set a target of zero landfilled waste by 2020 and is making good headway toward achieving that target. Germany implemented laws in the mid-1990s requiring manufacturers to take back their packaging. As customers began leaving non-essential packaging at the store right after the checkout, both supermarkets and manufacturers got the message.

Going one step further to change the garbage landscape, some activists, academics, and politicians have even begun to ask whether human societies might eventually be able to reach a state of zero waste. Such a scenario reflects how ecosystems function, and while it may seem far off in a world where 25-ton truckloads of garbage have become commonplace, such thinking is gaining traction.

Grassroots groups, academics, municipal leaders, and others who advocate for zero waste believe such a future is possible, but not without hard work. The following are six strategies in various stages of implementation that have inspired innovative people and countries toward zero waste in human society.

Six Strategies for Moving Toward Zero Waste

First, rethinking design from a holistic, systems perspective. Sweden's WTE plants that use trash to generate useful heat *and* electricity are one example of design that is more deliberate and holistic than others where "waste" heat from combustion processes is simply dumped into the environment. Going further would mean ensuring that manufactured items were more modular and could be easily disassembled in a non-toxic, non-destructive fashion, thereby promoting reuse of still-functioning components with as little energy expenditure or pollution as possible.

Second, radically reducing and eventually eliminating the generation of nonbiodegradable waste. Two of the least-traveled places on the planet—Antarctica and Mount Everest—are littered with rubbish, ranging from oxygen bottles to soda bottles, carelessly discarded by human visitors. The vast majority of these materials will remain in place and unchanged for centuries unless they are removed by humans. While it may be a heroic feat to ascend to the summit of the world's highest mountain or traverse the world's coldest continent, it is much more heroic to leave only footprints, not trash. Future innovations in materials and manufacturing for everyday life must move away from synthetic materials that persist and pollute long after their useful lifetimes. Biodegradable packing peanuts made from cornstarch represent one such innovation; insulation made from mushrooms may be another. Surely, human ingenuity, learning from nature's innovations through biomimicry, can find more.

Third, disrupting the business logic of planned obsolescence. The late Ray Anderson, founder of carpet manufacturer Interface, Inc. and vocal proponent of the business logic of sustainability, redesigned his business to radically reuse waste and reduce use of toxic materials. By developing a modular design based on interchangeable tiles of carpet rather than large rolls, his company eliminated the need for replacing entire rooms of carpet by instead allowing damaged or defective tiles to be replaced on an individual basis. In this way, rather than selling rolls of carpet designed to last just long enough to inspire customer satisfaction (or at least complacence) and thereby earn repeat purchases (what industry refers to as planned obsolescence), he built brand loyalty based on environmental values, ease of installation and maintenance, and innovative thinking. This is precisely the reverse of the logic that pervades much of the consumer goods manufacturing sector. While it is most obvious in the high-tech sector, where consumers are trained to upgrade their digital lives every 12 to 18 months, it is increasingly apparent even with so-called durable goods such as refrigerators and washing machines.

Fourth, transitioning from social systems where economic health and individual well-being is irrationally linked to the buying and selling of stuff. Here, perhaps, is where changing—or rather, reclaiming—our identity as citizens rather than consumers is most important. For millennia, humans have found happiness and contentment in actions radically different than the consumption of material goods that we have: in relationships and religion, recreation and meditation, or any number of other pursuits. Dialing back our consumption habits does not mean committing to a life of privation and asceticism, but rather to being more thoughtful and deliberate when deciding our needs, wants, and the sources of our fulfillment.

Fifth, removing subsidies for garbage "disposal" and increasing costs (e.g., tipping fees) to encourage less production of garbage. In the United States, cheap and widely available land, cash-strapped rural governments, powerful waste industry lobbyists, and low fuel prices all contribute to an "out of sight, out of mind" model of waste management centered on burying garbage somewhere else, often far away. Yet the economic logic of that model could be disrupted by a change in one or more variables, such as fuel costs, taxes, or tipping fees, to increase the cost of disposal and send strong price signals to individuals and businesses that produce the garbage.

Sixth, changing the way we talk about materials in order to shift the discourse from one that accepts "garbage" as simply a normal part of modern life to one that instead demands that things be designed simply, purposefully, and in a way that ensures they can be disassembled or reused as completely as possible.[19]

Discourse refers simply to the way we talk about things. In any discursive realm, any topic, boundaries are set by institutions and individuals with vested interests in maintaining the status quo. Shifting the discourse on garbage means pushing the boundaries of how we talk about, and therefore how we think about and act upon, a central component of human society that is at the same time, as this chapter has hopefully shown, a serious stumbling block on our path toward a more sustainable existence on Planet Earth.

In the end, finding a path toward greater sustainability in terms of the materials we produce, use, and cease to use requires shifting our thinking—what energy expert Amory Lovins at Rocky Mountain Institute likes to call "rearranging our mental furniture"—from linear thinking to cyclical thinking. Well-known sustainability and design author William McDonough argues for "cradle to cradle" thinking and action in a book by that same title rather than the current "cradle to grave" paradigm, which has lulled us into thinking that the normal end state of manufactured goods is in some sort of grave, either a fiery one (incinerators) or a cold and dark one (landfills).

---

19 This list is adapted from the Zero Waste Institute's "Principles" page, available at http://zerowasteinstitute.org/?page_id=120.

Bioaccumulation: The entry of a substance (usually a pollutant) into living tissue, where it may then become concentrated in one organism or trophic level or may biomagnify as it moves up the food web into higher-level organisms.

Commodity: Basic materials such as metals, cement, petroleum, rice, or wheat that are vital to large swathes of the economy or to human subsistence. Commodities are usually traded on international markets where prices may vary based on relative surplus or shortages of a given commodity.

Environmental Justice: EJ is the practice of ensuring that all groups of society benefit equally from the protections offered by environmental laws and regulations and that no demographic groups suffer disproportionately from the burdens of modern industrial society, such as polluted air, water, or soil.

HAZMAT: Hazardous Materials, a broad category of wastes that require special handling to prevent release and harm to the environment or human health. Examples include materials such as radioactive and medical wastes, as well as caustic chemicals (strong acids or bases) used in any number of manufacturing processes.

Leachate: Liquid that has come into contact with garbage in a landfill. This includes liquids that originated in the garbage, as well as precipitation, groundwater, or other liquids that have been introduced into the landfill either by natural or human processes.

MSW: Municipal Solid Waste. This term indicates all trash generated by households and businesses but does not include industrial, nuclear, or other specialized wastes.

Planned obsolescence: A business model in which products are designed to cease functioning or lose key functionality after a certain period of time, leading the consumer to purchase a newer, "upgraded" version of the product. Extreme examples in the high-tech industry include printers with internal counters that cause the printer to "fail" after a certain number of pages is printed.

WTE: Waste-to-Energy. Any process that captures and utilizes energy contained in or derived from waste. Examples include capturing methane produced by rotting organic material in a landfill or combusting (burning) garbage to generate heat or electricity.

REFERENCES

Bullard, Robert D. 2000. *Dumping in Dixie: Race, Class, and Environmental Quality.* 3rd ed. Boulder, CO: Westview Press.

Diaz, Luis F., George M. Savage, and Linda L. Eggerth. 2005. "Solid Waste Management." Osaka: United Nations Environment Programme.

General Accounting Office. 1983. "Siting of Hazardous Waste Landfills and Their Correlation with Racial and Economic Status of Surrounding Communities." Washington, D.C.: US General Accounting Office.

McDonough, William, and Michael Braungart. 2002. *Cradle to Cradle: Remaking the Way We Make Things.* 1st ed. New York: North Point Press.

Minter, Adam. 2013. *Junkyard Planet: Travels in the Billion-Dollar Trash Trade.* First US Edition. New York: Bloomsbury Press.

Pellow, David N. 2002. *Garbage Wars: The Struggle for Environmental Justice in Chicago, Urban and Industrial Environments.* Cambridge, MA: MIT Press.

Pivato, Alberto. 2011. "Landfill Liner Failure: An Open Question for Landfill Risk Analysis." *Journal of Environmental Protection* 2:287–297. doi: 10.4236/jep.2011.23032.

Rathje, William L., and Cullen Murphy. 2001. *Rubbish!: The Archaeology of Garbage.* Tucson, AZ: University of Arizona Press.

Ross, Julia. 2008. "Management of Municipal Solid Waste in Hong Kong and Taiwan." In *China Environmental Health Project*, edited by Jennifer Turner. Woodrow Wilson Center China Environment Forum.

Stark, Timothy D., Jeffrey W. Martin, Gina T. Gerbasi, Todd Thalhamer, and R. Edwin Gortner. 2012. "Aluminum Waste Reaction Indicators in a Municipal Solid Waste Landfill." *Journal of Geotechnical and Geoenvironmental Engineering* 138(3): 252–261. doi: http://dx.doi.org/10.1061/(ASCE)GT.1943-5606.0000581.

Strasser, Susan. 1999. *Waste and Want: A Social History of Trash.* 1st ed. New York: Metropolitan Books.

Chapter 11

ECOLOGICAL LANDSCAPE PRACTICES: A SUSTAINABLE MODEL FOR NORTH AMERICA

BY MICHAEL WILSON

INTRODUCTION

When people decide to embrace a sustainable lifestyle, two things they always consider are their carbon footprint and their environmental impact. People first pay attention to their everyday lifestyle, living arrangements, their home and business interior environments. Fortunately, there has been sizable growth in the use of local, environmentally sound materials for construction and interior decoration and in the availability and selection of high-quality food. Increasingly, homeowners are also choosing rooftop solar and other renewable-energy generation technologies, further reducing both their carbon footprint and their family's overall environmental impact. Frequently, though, these same people overlook or give little consideration to the exterior of their homes and the businesses they frequent. Landscaping and yard-maintenance practices adhere to old models and outdated aesthetic ideals. This chapter proposes to the reader that it is time to revisit the assumptions about an attractive landscape and the suitable choices for the exteriors of our homes and to consider the benefits of ecological landscaping practices.

Conventional ornamental horticulture and landscape practices in North America have been developed over time to condition us to accept and believe in a certain normalized standard for our landscapes, with a limited choice of plant material—material that has been selected by the landscape and nursery industry. We have been conditioned to believe that as long as the landscape is aesthetically pleasing and deep green, then it is a healthy system that is in concert with the environment. With good intentions, the nursery trade has selected easy-to-grow ornamental plants that are disease and insect resistant. Part of this was due to the fact that the selection was nonnative plant material; thus, there were few insect predators. This changes over time, and even the hardiest nursery stock attracts all manners of insects, which browse the plants.

Above ground homogeneity and insect vulnerabiity are not the only problems. Conventional practice for housing and office construction usually strips away good topsoil. With the placement of fundamental subterranean infrastructure such as sewage and water pipes, construction exposes nutrient-degraded subsoils. When finishing a construction project and implementing a landscape-maintenance plan, the conventional landscape approach is to then use synthetic fertilizers to adjust pH and synthetic pesticides—both of which are petrochemicals—to combat the insect problems. The conventional approach is environmentally degrading over time. In addition, it has a large carbon footprint and environmental impact. This impact includes ongoing issues with yard waste, pesticide pollution, and non-point pollution from runoff.

The alternative is ecological landscaping, which is a term originally defined by William Cullina in his book *Propagating Native Wildflowers of the Northeast* (Cullina 2000). His approach was "right plant, right place" with the use of local, native plants and choosing the appropriate plants for the individual site conditions. Moreover, resident wildlife populations would benefit from the presence of native species. This would result, for example, in choosing a native wetland perennial to plant in a wet spot in the yard, as opposed to amending the conditions with drainage to accommodate plants that prefer drier conditions, which is the conventional landscape approach.

The concept of right plant, right place is embedded in today's ecological landscaping. The concept is blended with previous approaches that include permaculture, natural gardening, organic gardening, habitat creation, and xeriscaping. Ecological landscaping is a management practice and approach to ornamental horticulture that reduces inputs and outputs, carbon footprint, environmental impact, and supports the local ecology. It is simply integrated with local ecosystems.

When the concept of sustainable development was becoming popular in the early 1990s, one of the concerns was energy use and its measurement, the carbon footprint. Leadership in Energy Efficient Design (LEED), a building certification program, was created to set a standard for the building industry. It uses a point system for rating newly constructed buildings according to their efficiency, measured as their reduction in carbon use. The LEED certification programs led to the formation of a whole educational process to accommodate architects that may design LEED building projects. There was little consideration in the LEED process for the significance of ornamental landscaping around the LEED-certified building, except for some mention of using sustainable landscapes to reduce carbon use and references to the promotion of rain gardens. There was no guidance for achievement of carbon-use reduction through landscaping or creating a rain garden to mitigate runoff from storm events and irrigation.

Through the Lady Bird Johnson Wildflower Garden, a LEED-similar program was developed in 2005 that addresses the issue of sustainable landscape and ecological landscaping. The program is called Sustainable Sites Initiative™ (SITES™) and provides detailed guidance on ecological approaches to landscaping with a point system similar to LEED, with the two programs being able to operate in concert. SITES developed a set of ecological values and their relationship to the landscape, providing a common language for those interested in sustainable landscapes (Christopher 2011). With the educational guidance and resources that are now available, there is no reason for future landscape development to create environmental degradation or be disconnected from the local ecology. Instead, a program like SITES coupled with ecological landscape practices helps new construction to be reintegrated into the landscape and to be supportive of local ecosystems.

THE GREAT AMERICAN LAWN

The concept of the manicured lawn started in the late 1700s when a landscape architect named Capability Brown introduced a design concept that was to create a naturalistic landscape. He did away with the formal, contrived landscape garden that was popular in Europe at the time and instead incorporated large, expansive areas of trimmed grass that began at the back door and expanded out to groupings of trees, berms, and meadows. These were often maintained with a small army of gardeners using scythes or livestock. It was a statement of one's status to be able to afford gardeners as opposed to having to devote acreage to pasture or to grow food crops.

As American landscape practices began to mimic the European approach to landscape, it was determined that the native grasses on the American continent were not as amendable to trimming and cutting. Development of new turf grasses and importation of European seed followed suit.

The creation of the push mower in the 1830s made it possible for the average wage earner and small landowner to also maintain a trimmed lawn and join the ranks of the wealthy in terms of home landscape aesthetics. By the early 1900s, the concept of the lawn became a standard in urban and suburban landscapes and was highly encouraged in gardening magazines and by the US Department of Agriculture. The latter's endorsement served as recognition of the landscape trade as an agricultural industry.

Today, municipalities have ordinances regulating the front lawn and protecting homeowners from the neighbor who may harbor undesirable plants, such as natural meadows, deeming them as weeds and citing weed ordinances. In other words, the government has regulated the cultivated lawn as the approved standard for private property. Across the various zones of the United States and Canada, we have moved far away from anything like a natural landscape around our homes and businesses.

More worrisome than the loss of the natural landscape for one that is simulated naturalistic is that this lawn aesthetic assumes an abundant water supply. "To water the lawn" is a standard phrase referring to an activity that can supplement the rainfall in northern latitudes. However, Europe and, later, the United States exported the lawn aesthetic to where it becomes more problematic—places with insufficient water supply to support green, manicured lawns, such as China, Central Asia, the southwestern United States, South Africa, and other arid parts of the world.

As if concerns over appropriate use of drinking water were not enough, in the last several decades, the lawn has developed into a sink of toxic chemicals, part of our zest for having a manicured, weed- and disease-free landscape. Today, the turf industry has developed into a multibillion dollar industry, and the perfect lawn has become the landscape standard for urban and suburban homes, businesses, golf courses, and corporate and academic campuses. The homeowner can now purchase multistep lawn care products that include synthetic fertilizer mixed with insecticides, fungicides, and herbicides in an effort to control weeds and turf diseases, all with the purpose of creating a standard lawn. The turf industry follows a similar protocol with a spray schedule timed over the course of the growing season.

Academic lab scientists have spent vast sums of research dollars and conducted years of research to develop new turf varieties that work in conjunction with the landscape industry. The average landowner has now been conditioned to believe that a landscape with a lush, weed-free lawn represents a healthy, ecologically fit landscape.

Turf Alternatives

What many gardening professionals realize is that lush, thick lawn with a small grouping of trees and shrubs does not represent a healthy landscape. The push for sustainability has popularized new alternatives to the standard lawn, and the concept of "the lawn" itself is now being reconsidered by landscape professionals with the introduction and use of alternative plants along with acceptance of a different turf aesthetic (Cullina 2008, Christopher 2011, Simeone 2013, Tallamy and Darke, 2014). This new approach has stimulated research into lower-maintenance varieties of turf grass that are disease resistant and more adaptable to different growing conditions, thus requiring less water, fertilizer, and pesticides to maintain a healthy appearance. In addition, slow-growing varieties have been developed so the grass does not have to be cut as often, with some varieties that never grow taller than four to six inches; these may not require cutting all season for some areas in the landscape.

These varieties are perfect adoptions for corporate and academic campuses along with golf courses for areas where pedestrian use and foot traffic are not an issue. Some new turf varieties are bred with the concept of drought tolerance. These new varieties do not require copious amounts of water to stay healthy and alive. When these new varieties are utilized on golf courses and corporate or academic campuses, significant fresh water conservation can be achieved. These new varieties will simultaneously conserve water and reduce the carbon footprint of the standard lawn, yet they still have that acceptable appearance the property owner expects in accordance with the standard set by the conventional landscape industry.

For some areas of a property, there are a number of turf alternatives that can be utilized, such as groundcovers and mosses that do not require cutting and that grow relatively weed-free. Quite often, in fact, a groundcover plant will perform better under certain conditions than a turf plant. For example, the deep shade of a maple tree with its numerous surface roots that use up any available water is a growing condition that turf will simply not perform well in. However, a plant like Japanese spurge (*Pachysandra terminalis)* or Plaintain sedge (*Carex plantaginea*) will thrive here. In some shady areas with a lower pH, moss can colonize into the turf, and in many cases, it may be more beneficial to encourage the moss, even eliminating the turf to produce a moss lawn. This application works best if there is low foot traffic. Third, all groundcovers can be used to minimize the amount of turf by using turf walkways or just smaller areas of turf, combining the two. This groundcover planting can utilize trees and shrubs to make for a more complete aesthetic setting. This approach is often an acceptable way to comply with any local landscape ordinances that require turf in the front yard of a property and can utilize a minimal amount of turf.

At a larger scale than the walkways or the corners of the property, the concept of the meadow has become newly popularized. It is a perfect application for larger suburban properties and corporate and academic campuses. There are numerous benefits to a meadow, and once established, maintenance is greatly reduced compared to lawn care. Meadows provide habitat for beneficial insects, which may prey on other damaging insects, and also provide food for smaller avian species, which feed on a range of destructive insects. On the other hand, it has been found that Canada geese, which have become nuisance species in the northeastern United States on expansive campus lawns, do not fly into meadow areas because the vegetation is too high for the large birds to land and fly out of.

Meadows bring additional benefits that provide ecosystem services beyond those visible aboveground. The large and deep root systems create friable soil that absorbs runoff, thereby helping with water recharge; water conservation makes the meadow more drought resistant. Keeping the meadow healthy includes leaving it alone much of the time. The carbon footprint is lower than for a regular lawn because a meadow only needs to be cut once a year when the plants have developed viable seed to sustain the population. Much of the maintenance comes in the establishment phase with some intentional watering, and then there's yearly maintenance for invasive and woody species removal. The latter maintenance is reduced over time as the meadow matures because invasive species will have difficulty getting established in a healthy meadow. Meadow planting and maintenance introduces a meaningful growth industry within the landscape industry.

The norms for landscaping are changing, but slowly. Even the average homeowner prefers to have some lawn for entertaining. The primary way to introduce change for an average home-size lot is to have a minimal amount of turf, with the balance being trees, shrubs, and groundcovers. More variety provides habitat and addresses storm water runoff, in addition to providing recreational space for the home. Advances have been made with organic lawn care, and the popularity has prompted more research on organic methods.

Organic lawn care works on the principles of developing strong soil health to produce healthy turf plants, and this will help to prevent disease pathogens and insect pests from getting established. The idea is to strengthen the lawn by treating the causes of lawn degradation, not the symptoms.

Selecting Plants

Considering Native and Invasive Species

On the average suburban lot of one acre, or a business lot, the lawn should occupy one-third of the property or less. For the larger suburban yard or corporate academic campus, this can be reduced to a smaller percentage. The remaining part of the landscape could be delegated to **hardscape** like the driveway, patios, and walkways, with adjacent plant material consisting of shrub borders, trees, perennials, and individual gardens, such as a vegetable garden. This selection of plants can wrap around the lawn and follow the edges of the property line with a high percentage of native plants. Often, there is debate over the nativity of the plant material that is used in the landscape, with the purist using only native plant material. Others will argue that there are many useful alien plants that have been developed that are still resource-friendly and exhibit ornamental value without damaging the environment or being invasive.

The conventional landscape practice had made a limited variety of shrubs available to the homeowner and landscape professional. The concept was for selective placement, limited to foundation plantings for the residence or business and a scattering of trees in the yard. There are several issues that arise from this pattern.

First, some of these commonly used species have proven to become invasive species over time. An invasive species is an alien plant that is opportunistic and takes over habitats, displacing not only the surrounding native plant species, but also crowding out the insect, avian, and other wildlife species that may have depended upon the native ecosystem. Nurseries still sell invasive species, and it is best for the consumer to have some education about the growing habits of nursery plants. Second, what is also better known today is that the limited selection of plants used for foundation arrangements provided little benefit to the local ecosystem and were often not suited for the particular site conditions. For example, there is a mismatch between a site's water availability or drainage and a plant's water requirements. This is especially true with turf grasses. Third, nurseries offer a mixed plant selection composed of species, cultivars, and hybrid varieties that are insect resistant and alien, along with a handful of native species. This is because many of the plants are not native and there are no natural predators. Insect herbivores eat the leaves of palatable native species first, sometimes leaving the plants in an unaesthetic state, but nonnative plants are not completely immune to insect damage.

The conventional industry then provides the consumer with fertilizer and sprays to help keep damaged plants alive if an insect infestation should occur. When plants are too aggressive and grow too tall for the site, property owners have been conditioned to prune them and conform bushes to geometric shapes that include spheres and inverted ice-cream cones. Only recently is a new concept taking hold: when suitable plants are chosen appropriately for the site conditions, the composition of plants will thrive with little maintenance. With the appropriate size plant chosen for a particular site, little pruning would be required, and it would simultaneously encourage the plant's natural growth habits.

Choosing Plants that Match the Site Conditions

Adopting an ecological approach is to grow a higher percentage of native plants and, when an alien species is used, to select plants that are drought tolerant or that match the site conditions, require little or no pesticides, and exhibit non-invasiveness. The selection of plants should be based on the concept of the right plant for the right place by placing plants with suitable site conditions; for example, growing wetland species in an area of the yard that may be wet or seasonably wet. The ecological landscape should contain about 60% or more native species, preferably similar plants as those in the surrounding ecosystems. Over time, native plants have adapted to grow in their range and are acclimated to the climate regime and the patterns of water availability that change with the seasons. Therefore, in the correct location, appropriate plants will require little care and few additional inputs. Moreover, because they are native species, they have natural predators among local insect herbivores; thus, the plants become a part of the food chain.

This also means that people need to be educated toward a new understanding of beauty in the landscape. For example, damaged leaves may be a good thing and an indicator that the plant is a healthy member of the environment. By growing native plants that attract insect herbivores, we are providing a food source for insect carnivores, which are beneficial insects. In this way, our plant selection and placement allows for healthy predator-and-prey relationships to emerge. These insects all provide additional benefits as food sources for avian species. A final benefit is that a well-designed garden border will provide nesting habitat (Tallamy 2009).

It is becoming obvious that native plants are an important part of the food chain, and as we remove habitat for construction development, there is a responsibility to mitigate that damage with an ecological landscape. If the planted gardens and shrub borders surround about three-quarters of the standard homeowner lot and the adjoining lots have similar plantings, a continuous row of diverse plantings is formed and can provide a wildlife corridor. If this concept is supported with a high percentage of native plants in adjoining properties across a neighborhood, it allows for Tallamy's theory of defragmenting the suburbs. In short, landscaping with native plants, considering the natural connective features of plantings across adjoining properties as a habitat advantage for local fauna, is more beneficial to the local ecology than a property that has turf growing from corner to corner with similar uniformity across adjoining yards.

Although the choice of plant material for an ecological landscape has different benefits to wildlife and can be matched to site conditions, the design and method of putting it all together is equally important. One concept is to group all the plants that require similar care and site conditions together in that location. Another is to consider the characteristics of the plant. If the plant is easily browsed by insects or provides good nesting for desired bird populations, it is best planted away from high traffic areas like the kitchen door or front entrance to a business due to the unsightliness of insect damage and the fact that birds will never nest close to such high activity. There are a large number of plants to choose from, and something suitable will fill in as foundation plantings. In terms of grouping plants together, it is best to plant on a three-dimensional plane that not only holds visual appeal, but also provides a simulation that is closer to a natural habitat. Representation of the natural layers found in the environment not only completes the visual effect of native plant design, but also creates layers of habitat for wildlife (Burrell, 1997, Simeone, 2013) because some species are ground nesters, while others prefer to nest in shrubs or trees.

The selection and proper use of plant material is critical to the success of an ecological landscape. The unique conditions of each property site challenge the talents of the landscape gardener. Ecologically sound planting is never one design fits all. The ecological approach is to consider surrounding ecosystems and site-specific conditions, with each design a unique project. Ecologically correct design is the final result after suitable selection of plant material. Maintenance and healthy growth of the plantings returns the focus to the soils at the property.

Soils and Plant Health

Conventional landscapers and the landscape industry do consider the soil in terms of pH, chemistry, structure, and nutrients, but they rarely consider the overall health of the soil and the renewal of microorganisms. The landscape industry recommends and provides soil amendments to add when planting shrubs and perennials. This is usually bagged peat moss, sterilized compost, or other organic matter. However, because of the sterilization and the nature of peat moss mining, these additives do not contain the living microorganisms that are necessary for soil health. The industry also sells sifted topsoil, which is usually a mixed soil engineered from localized materials and often taken from construction sites. Again, due to the process of engineering the soil, there is no living matter. Without living matter in the soil in terms of microorganisms, there is no natural defense against pathogens, diseases, and insects for the plant. The conventional landscape industry has a solution for those issues in the form of petrochemicals that will kill off any fungus or insect invasion.

The methods of yard maintenance also disrupt the life of soil. The plantings get mulched to maintain soil moisture, suppress weeds, and as an aesthetic cover because of the expectation for neatness in the yard. When the leaves fall off trees in the autumn and begin to accumulate, they are immediately removed, often with the use of motorized blowers. This practice is environmentally damaging. All the leaves are removed along with a bulk of the mulch that was distributed earlier in the season. Besides the carbon footprint from the combustion engines to power the blowers, there is a great deal of noise pollution and air pollution from the dust. This process is pollutant-laden and also removes any hope of adding organic matter to the soil to maintain it.

When the conventional landscape industry finds a problem with a particular plant's growth and it considers the soil around the plant, the soil is usually tested for pH and nutrients. To correct the problem, the industry recommends the use of synthetic fertilizers in various ratios of nitrogen, phosphorus, and potassium (NPK) or the addition of lime. If moisture is the issue, then landscape professionals recommend the addition of sand, gravel, drainage pipes, or products like Turface that will absorb excess moisture. Chemistry and structure of the soil are considered, but the common landscaper rarely considers general soil health in terms of the presence or amount of microorganisms.

The ecological landscape should contain a good, healthy, living soil. Healthy soil contains microorganisms in the form of fungi, nematodes, worms, and mycorrhiza. All of these feed on each other, and the process of decomposition needs them to keep soil in a loamy condition. Consider the natural process of a forest soil where leaves fall on the ground and have completely broken down to

FIGURE 11.1 Double-ground woodchip mulch piles at the Morris County recycling center.

become the upper layer of the forest floor by the end of the following summer. No one goes out to the woods and blows away the leaves on a yearly basis.

Both new construction developments and existing landscapes contain dead soils. These can be readily renewed with the addition of healthy, composted organic matter, which can be obtained both from commercial sources and from municipal composting operations. The existing soil benefits from liberal amounts of organic matter being added prior to planting. It is then mulched after planting with a two- to four-inch layer of organic mulch. This improvement of the soil layers provides good habitat for microorganisms and encourages their propagation for developing a healthy soil. This augmented soil now contains natural predators for any fungal or pathogen problem that might appear. A healthy soil with good decomposition will break down the layer of mulch, adding more organic matter to the soil. Over time, seasonal mulch additions will help maintain soil health. Leaves that do fall into the plantings can remain; if considered unsightly, they can be covered up with additional mulch.

The key is to find the correct balance of organic matter. If leaves accumulate too thick in one spot, it may be too much for some plants; however, the excess can be removed and put into a compost pile or applied around plants without natural fallen-leaf accumulation. For the lawn, the leaves can be cut with a mulching mower and, again, if accumulating in excess, can be removed to compost. A good example of this process is outlined in the case study at the end of the chapter.

Integrated Pest Management

For some insect and disease outbreaks, the solution is not in the soil, or a natural predator does not exist. The ecological approach is to follow the principles of Integrated Pest Management (IPM). With IPM, the least toxic approach is taken first. In general, IPM is the treatment of a pest population when it is the most vulnerable, often interrupting its breeding cycle. In this approach, insect populations are monitored, and if they require insecticide treatment, the spraying is done when the population is most vulnerable, depending upon the stage in the insects' lifecycle. If a pesticide is necessary, IPM recommends a natural approach with any number of the organic products that have been developed, such as insecticidal soap, horticultural oils, neem oil, pyrethrums, and *Bacillus thuringiensis* (B.t.). As with all chemicals, organic products can still be hazardous to the environment and to the human body. It is only if these approaches are not successful that IPM will recommend a petrochemical. This may be acceptable if a less benign approach was taken first and did not succeed.

In the case of insect predation, greater damage to the nearby ecosystems must also be considered. For example, there is an Asian long-horned beetle that is now affecting natural populations of maple and oak trees throughout the northeastern United States. The ecological landscape approach in this case is to treat the infestation immediately to reduce the impact of the beetle, taking responsibility for not allowing a pest problem to affect the surrounding ecosystems, be it the yard next door or adjacent woodlands.

Another ecological landscape approach is taken when a plant needs continuous care due to insects or a disease; the better treatment is to remove the plant from the landscape. Since ecological landscaping recommends a high percentage of native plants on a three-dimensional plane, this effectively encourages habitat for natural predators such as the downy woodpecker (*Picoides pubescens*) or the yellow warbler (*Setophaga petechia*), whose diet is 60% caterpillars. The ecological landscape approach looks ahead toward potential future environmental impacts and works in harmony with the natural cycles of the seasons, local fauna, and the hydrological cycle for the local area.

Addressing Storm Water

The hydrological cycle is the balance of precipitation and evaporation throughout the year, and in most climate zones, it brings with it the need to manage the moisture that descends from the sky, accumulates as surface water, and must be channeled as runoff into nearby waterways. Before the industrial era, water contained few contaminants and no chemical loads. In residential areas and on commercial campuses, the adherence to the ideal of the great American lawn has changed all that.

Storm water runoff is the greatest contributor of non-point water pollution, with a high percentage of the runoff occurring from landscapes. The chemicals applied to the landscape can be washed away during storm events and enter water sources through drainage systems that are routed to waterways. These chemicals, whether organic or petrochemical, are contributing to algae blooms, eutrophication, and decreased water quality. The conventional landscape with turf growing from corner to corner does not consider storm water runoff and is a contributor to non-point pollution due to its compacted soil and high chemical use allowing for polluted runoff.

Storm Water Regulation

Due to a concern with water quality in the United States, the Water Quality Act of 1987 amended the 1972 Clean Water Act. It was drafted to address non-point pollution of waterways and called attention to runoff. Phase Two of this act in 1999 called for all states to develop a storm water plan and new ordinances to address the non-point source pollution, with compliance required by 2009. The result was that all storm water runoff for new development must be treated either chemically, mechanically, or biologically before being released into an open waterway, with compliance being regulated by each state's environmental agencies.

During this time period, the engineering industry made advancements in the efficiency of detention basins and retention ponds for improving water quality. A detention basin is an excavated area that is usually adjacent to large developments and along highway systems to collect runoff from impervious surfaces to prevent flooding. These basins are connected to stream and river systems. The old standard for detention-system design was to collect and release water to receiving streams. Now the idea is to collect and delay or hold the storm water so the suspended solids, which can clog the gills of fish, among other undesirable outcomes, can settle. Simple measures like changing the orifice size on the effluent end of the drainage pipes in existing basins from the standard twelve inches to four inches reduces the volume of the outflow. This results in a greater amount of the suspended solids settling in the basin, in addition to reducing erosion on the streams receiving the storm water. Another advancement is the use of underground, perforated storage tanks that can be installed under parking lots; in this system, the storm water is slowly percolated back into the ground water system beneath the parking lot, recharging ground water reserves. Since the first half hour of a storm event carries the greatest amount of non-point pollution, some detention systems have a fore bay that collects the initial runoff before releasing it into the detention or retention basin.

Best Management Practices for Storm Water (BMP) is a primary guidance resource for municipal, state, and federal government agencies. BMP is a comprehensive management plan that addresses storm water at its source, through catchment systems, and at collection points. It identifies practices such as biofiltration in retention ponds, detention basins, and using vegetated swales or channels to direct storm water.

BMP relies on a variety of native plants, with an emphasis on wetland plants that normally grow on the floodplain of a river or stream because these plants can handle both inundation and drought. The use of native floodplain plants achieves several goals to improve water quality. First, the long, aggressive root systems of floodplain plants penetrate deeply into the soil, keeping it friable and allowing for ground water recharge. In a high water event, the foliage of the plants slows down the runoff and acts as a barrier to trap suspended solids. The plant material is able to take up nutrients like nitrogen and phosphorous that may be carried by the storm water. Plants like *Typha latifolia,* the common cattail, take up heavy metals and have a phytoremediation effect.

Well-chosen plants provide ecosystem services during the intensity of heavy rains or a flooding event, and they reinforce the value of ecological landscaping. Biofiltration of storm water treats the runoff as it passes through the water systems and helps create new wetlands, which in turn helps create habitat for wildlife. These detention basins can be made into an aesthetic landscape with the use of native trees, shrubs, and perennials.

Capturing Storm Water in Rain Gardens

Storm water management issues have not achieved much public awareness in the past. Unfortunately, landscape and turf chemicals, either organic or conventional petrochemical, still produce non-point pollution to waterways. In recent years, due to the clauses in Phase Two of the Water Quality Act of 1987 that required public education, the concept of the rain garden was promoted by native plant societies and gardening resources like the extension services of land-grant universities, gaining a wider following among smaller landowners. A rain garden is a miniature detention basin for the smaller landscape and fulfills the BMP goal of treating storm water at its source. This makes rain gardens a natural fit for the ecological landscape.

The rain garden is generally located in a low spot in the yard where water naturally accumulates, and in the case where that is not feasible, it is created with a cut-and-fill excavation. The runoff from impervious areas like the roof and driveway is channeled or piped into the rain garden for ground water percolation and filtration, hopefully never leaving the yard but being cleaner if it happens to do so. The rain garden also utilizes floodplain plants that can tolerate periods of drought and inundation. Most of these plants do require full sun, but that does not place a limitation on shady yards. In this case, the appropriate plant materials are based on woodland vernal wetlands and shade-tolerant wetland plants.

One advantage of the rain garden in the suburban yard as compared to the larger detention basins utilized by large-scale commercial development is the capability for a more aesthetic design and greater diversity of plant materials. The homeowner is not limited to official budgets and suppliers. Engineering and commercial restoration firms use specialized nurseries that supply the plant material for habitat restorations and wetland creations. The homeowner is not limited to those sources but can utilize local and ornamental plant nurseries, increasing the diversity of plant choices and ornamental design.

The rain garden has several advantages for an ecological landscape. First and foremost is the ornamental value of a well-designed garden that is a functional addition to the landscape. It also provides habitat for beneficial insects and other species, such as birds. The primary ecological advantage is reduced and cleaner runoff goes into open waterways because the rain garden will absorb the suspended solids from soil and nutrients such as excess nitrogen prior to leaving the yard. The rain garden, together with proper storm water management, resolves a big ecological dilemma resulting from an increased use of chemicals in society over recent decades. There are several other ways of mitigating rainfall, such as rain barrels and shrub borders that encircle the yard. These work well in conjunction with the rain garden.

Putting it All Together

The ecological landscape blends several concepts and designs and cannot be copied over and over from a standard design model like the conventional landscape industry has given us. Every landscape situation is unique in soils, hydration, sunlight, shade, and other influences, which allows for diversity in design and ornamental features. The ecological landscape can also utilize other ecofriendly products that are not plant related into the landscape; for example, the use of rain barrels to capture water for simple irrigation and to fill watering cans. Homeowner and commercial irrigation systems today feature improvements to conserve water, for one with the use of rainwater stored in the barrels, and for another through weather sensors that regulate the amount of water used.

Another way to harmonize the whole project is the use of pervious materials for hardscape sections, such as the recycled material recommended by SITES™. For example, bricks removed from a building demolition can be used for garden edging or as pavers to make a walkway and patio. These are the final steps in individualizing the look of the property and meeting the usage requirements over time. They are only the material objects that are brought into the property, from bricks to sprinkler systems, to keep up the design and the functions of the elements in the landscaping.

There is no product on the market that replaces the importance of laying the groundwork for the ecological landscape through careful observation of the unique features of the property, preparation of the soils, and consideration of the appropriate seeding, placement, and planting of the desired plant materials.

The ecological landscape utilizes many ecological concepts to achieve a successful, low-maintenance and attractive property over the long term. The concept of the right plant for the right place places plants in the conditions that they would grow under in nature to reduce maintenance and to avoid compromising the surrounding environment. Other practices may hold promise for the particular climate zone and interests of the property owner.

Xeriscaping is a popular concept in arid regions in particular, but it can be integrated into landscapes in other regions. Basically, the xeriscape makes use of drought-tolerant plant material to conserve water use, and the choice of plant material does not have to be cacti and succulents, as all regions have certain plants that are less water-thirsty.

Permaculture is the idea of incorporating edible plants into the landscape in an ecological manner and was developed in Australia to reduce the environmental impact from growing food. The organic vegetable garden certainly fits with the design of an ecological landscape. Native plant gardening and habitat gardens can easily be incorporated and are recommended as part of the landscape design.

If all of these principles are brought together into individual, diverse ornamental landscapes, the maintenance of the property will have little or no negative environmental impact over time. More significantly, it will become a critical part of a well-functioning local ecosystem as opposed to producing and contributing to ecological degradation.

CASE STUDY OF AN ECOLOGICALLY BALANCED SUBURBAN YARD

The following case study illustrates how a suburban yard owned by individuals can achieve an ecological landscape over time. The yard presented in the case study had not received any landscape maintenance for almost 10 years prior to purchase by the current owners. The new owners were experienced gardeners who knew what plants they wanted in their yard and produced an ecological landscape without necessarily intending to from the beginning. It was more a combination of practicality, economics, and taking advantage of available materials that produced the ecologically balanced landscape. Their plant selection had to be adjusted to match the site conditions. Over time, it has proven to be a landscape that has no environmental impact, a small carbon footprint, no disease or insect problems, good soil structure, and healthy, thriving ornamental plants.

When these owners of a suburban yard located in the northeastern United States purchased their property 20 years ago, the last thing in terms of landscape that they were thinking about was to create a sustainable landscape. Instead, they were thinking in terms of being practical.

The Front Side of the Property

Soil Degradation and Improvement

As they reviewed their new property through their gardener eyes, they saw a degraded yard that had not been maintained for years. The lawn had become nonexistent, and the front of the property had been compromised by the installation of a new septic system. It was decided that with a nice row of mature sugar maples (*Acer saccharum*) located along the street, traditional turf would never grow well, and it would become a maintenance chore. Therefore, an alternative of growing common *Pachysandra*

FIGURE 11.2 Sugar maples underplanted with Pachysandra terminalis ground cover.

terminalis would be better suited for the site. The first decision already eliminated the standard lawn from consideration as an option.

Compaction had degraded the soil structure, so there also was a lack of microorganisms. This is typical with old, neglected yards. Compaction usually also occurs with new construction, which conventional landscape practices try to improve with the use of chemicals. For this old yard, it was decided to rototill the area from the maple trees to the road because the soil was sandy and lacked organic matter and microorganisms, which would be needed to reestablish a healthy soil. After the area was tilled, a four-inch layer of compost was placed on top and incorporated into the soil with additional rototilling. This accomplished two important goals of providing a food source to attract microorganisms and a loose planting bed for the *Pachysandra*.

The compost was acquired for free from the closest recycling center, operated by the county of Morris in New Jersey. Material comes in from local yards, and they process both compost from herbaceous yard waste and mulch, which is a double-ground wood chip (see Figure 11.2 above). Both of these are allowed proper time to process at the facility. The compost is turned over to ensure the sterility of any weed seeds as core temperatures gauge the rate of decomposition.

This particular facility is a boon to the homeowner. It is a self-sufficient operation because commercial landscapers and municipalities pay a tipping fee to drop off material and can load up on the finished compost or mulch, again for a fee. Taking delivery from the county of Morris, the homeowner also pays a delivery charge. The homeowner may, however, go to the site and shovel as much of the material as he or she wants for free. Some will argue that for organic gardening principles, these are not desirable products for gardening because of the use of chemicals in the landscape industry; however, proper composting methods should resolve those concerns.

Adding Structure with new Planting Beds

The next layer of landscaping came from the realization that the property needed a foundation planting in front, and another bed was made with the same process as described above. The bed was planted with three different species of deer-resistant plant material. These are a pink-flowering rhododendron (*Rhododendron yakusimanum*), mountain fetterbush (*Pieris floribunda*), and Harland boxwood (*Buxus harlandii*). These shrubs were underplanted with hellebores (*Heleborus*), early blooming perennials that are also deer resistant. For a wooded northeastern location where deer populations are large and continue to encroach on suburban gardens, the ecological landscape balances the choice of native (but appealing to deer) with the choice of non-invasive, nonnative plants and the desire to reduce applications of deer repellant. Typical repellants, both chemical-based and organic, work to prevent deer damage through deer-irritating smells but have the downside that they need frequent reapplication. Selecting plants for deer resistance when creating the ecological landscape saves both time and money in the long run and contributes to cleaner runoff.

When the plantings were finished, the bed was mulched heavily with a four-inch layer of double-ground wood chips from the recycling center. This achieved two important maintenance goals. First, it prevented weed growth and made for better aesthetics, and second, it provided the future food source for potential microorganisms to start colonizing. After one year, some of the mulch had to be replaced because of decomposition, a desirable outcome. Decomposition itself renewed the soil, adding to the structure and proving food to the desired organisms. This process of renewal happens on a yearly basis, so fertilizer is not needed except for a few shrubs that require an acidic soil. The latter are treated once a year in the fall with a small handful of Holly-tone, an organically based fertilizer for acid-loving plants.

In addition to these two beds in the front yard, an oval bed was prepared on the side of the front yard to display spring bulbs and perennials. A Chinese dogwood (*Cornus kousa*) was introduced to provide some shade, and sweet woodruff (*Galeum odoratum*) with spring bulbs as a groundcover were added around it. Like the front beds, this planting relied on Asian plant material that is deer resistant. Another bed was placed in the center of the front yard to protect an existing Japanese maple (*Acer palmatum*) and planted with another variety of *Pachysandra*, or Japanese spurge (*Pachysandra terminalis*), called "Green Sheen," an attractive, glossy, darker-colored cultivar.

Much of the front yard was thus reappropriated for attractive plantings of low-maintenance groundcovers, flowering plants, and trees. The lawn was reestablished in the remaining space, and the same basic protocol for preparation was followed with the addition of compost to provide a nice seed bed for turf germination. A contractor's mix that is good for both sun and shade was chosen due to easy establishment under a variety of conditions. As the plants grew and matured, so did the size of the garden beds, and now, 20 years later, the lawn only occupies about one-third of the front yard proper.

The Side of the House

FIGURE 11.3 & 11.4 Cottage garden in fall after mulching. Note the gravel walkway.

Since the house was built in 1866, the property had existing gardens and plantings. The new owners applied the same preparation techniques as in the front yard and landscaped with the same attention to thrift and practicality. There was an old herb and kitchen garden that had become overgrown with tree seedlings. The seedlings were removed, then the space was rototilled, and a thick layer of compost and mulch were applied. Finally, a cottage garden was planted.

The need for a new walkway in the cottage garden brought ecological and economic considerations together with new ideas. The area for a curved walkway was dug to about one foot below grade, and an eight-inch layer of stone dust was put in, which was then compacted. A six-inch layer of ¼-inch pea gravel was applied to create the walking surface, and the walkway was then lined with recycled bricks to give it a semi-colonial appearance and match the house aesthetically. In terms of ecology, this allowed for a pervious surface to absorb storm water while visually harmonizing with the architecture of the house.

When landscaping a property, inevitably, some zones emerge that pose their own challenges and require their own solutions. The paved driveway to the garage bisects the front of the property, leaving a wooded patch to the right of the driveway that is still part of the property. This right side had been more neglected, so there was no lawn left and an overgrowth of plants had taken over. On the plus side, most of these were native species of wildflowers, and the soil health was also in good condition. The rest of the plant material here was diverse, including native decomposers, grasses, forbs, and shrubs. The gardener owners decided to leave the area alone, add to the existing plants, and develop a woodland meadow matching the shade conditions in this location.

The usual protocol of rototilling, then composting and mulching was not followed. Instead, compost was incorporated into the soil as new plants were added. The area was spruced up by introducing new deer-resistant, primarily Asian varietals to form a shrub border with the existing native shrubs. The new bed of shrubs followed the usual protocol of rototilling, then adding compost and mulch.

This part of the yard is a no-mow zone and is only cut once a year in the late fall. The late fall cutting provides two important ecological-maintenance procedures. It provides a deposition area for some of the leaf removal from other parts of the yard, and it helps to spread the seeds from the wildflowers. This section of the property is treated as a woodland meadow, and the addition of a thin layer of leaves on a yearly basis provides the same ecological advantage as mulching. By cycling the leaf

FIGURE 11.5 & 11.6 Wooded meadow.

material through the soil structure, it provides food for microorganisms and helps build soil health. It makes ecological and economic sense.

Conventional landscape practice removes all the leaves from yards, then relies on chemical fertilizers to provide nutrients to the soil and pesticides to handle any disease and insect problems since the natural beneficial insects and bacteria have been eliminated from the landscape. The yard in the case study has few disease and insect problems, and those insects that are present browse on certain native shrubs and provide a food source for neighboring avian species.

The Back Side of the Property

A one-car garage on another section of the property had become dilapidated and one side was overgrown with weeds, while further back were some mature trees surrounded by ferns. This was already naturally shady, so the owners decided to keep these as a background for a shade garden with native and nonnative wildflowers. While digging around, they discovered that there was an old patio made of slates under the weeds and soil surface. The slates were removed to be used elsewhere on the property at a future date, and the same regime of compost and mulch was used to establish the wildflower garden. The center of the new garden got a walkway, and a small sitting area was created with turf. The walkway was again outlined with used bricks to continue with the semi-colonial look to match the house.

Over time, this area provided a learning experience and practice for implementing ecological principles. Grass in this location became a maintenance chore because the turf did not perform well and the cast iron furniture needed to be moved to cut the grass underneath. This area already had a high percentage of moss as an alternative to turf, so the owners decided to encourage the moss and eliminate the grass. This was done with the addition of aluminum sulfate to further acidify the soil and thus encourage the growing conditions for moss. Within one year, a thick, lush moss lawn had formed, and the sitting area has proven itself as a cool place to sit and relax in the shade when hot summer temperatures arrive.

The sloped backyard was already well developed with a diversity of mature trees, including white ash, sugar maple, black walnut, and oak, and shrubs along its border. The border was between 10 and 35 feet wide and included some shrubs that were planted in the same era as the construction of the house. In between were native species that had colonized over the years, with a high percentage of spicebush (*Lindera benzoin)*, a transitional wetland species.

The landscaping began from this well-grown starting point. There were some invasive species like ailanthus and garlic weed that needed to be aggressively weeded out for several years to exhaust the seed base in the soil. More or less in the middle of the back side of the property, a new lawn covered up the installation of a septic system. The tree and shrub borders and both sides of the backyard received additional plantings of native species. A shady perennial garden and a sunny perennial garden were added to take advantage of the natural sunlight patterns. The perennial gardens featured a high percentage of native species, and as they expanded, they further reduced the size of the lawn.

In addition to these two gardens in the backyard, a rock garden was the ecological solution to the elevation problem. Initially, a four-foot drop from the patio behind the house caused safety concerns. The construction of a rock garden from the ground up eliminated the danger of the drop and introduced more variety into the plantings. The owners were able to simulate the soil conditions found in alpine zones, which achieved two results. It allowed for successful cultivation of mountain plants, and it worked in harmony with the intense sunlight on this location in summer since many of these plants are drought tolerant.

Unique Features at the Back Side

A barn at the back of the property is an attractive focal point while also hiding the area in the back allotted for work space, planting equipment, and compost storage. The visitor to the barn area is meant to see and enjoy the native plant garden. The plantings here are primarily from the northeastern United States, which are well adapted to the four seasons and potentially harsh winters. The walkway through the native plant garden is woodchip mulch, again allowing for a permeable surface that facilitates good drainage and storm water runoff. The native plants often seed themselves on the walkway, providing free additional plants for transplanting.

The beds and spaces devoted to plantings have grown over the years. The side of the barn that faces the house also has a mixed bed of shrubs and perennials with a high percentage of native species. This twelve-foot-wide bed further reduces the size of the lawn as it expands. The lawn area in the backyard had now been reduced to less than half of what it was. The wide diversity of plantings (a ratio of 60% native species to 40% exotic species) and the increase in deer populations made a fence advisable despite the attention paid from the beginning to choosing deer-resistant plants. A deer fence was installed to protect the plants from being eaten and to reduce the use of repellants.

All the gardens and plantings in the backyard followed the same protocols as the front yard, except for the rock garden, which required a special soil preparation. If treated with the same maintenance regimen as conventional landscape practices, in time the soil would become degraded again and would not retain the living soil characteristics that the initial rototilling with compost and mulch protocol encouraged. Maintenance is an important issue, and the concept of a no-maintenance landscape does not exist. By following this ecologically balanced method of yard maintenance, the soil conditions can be preserved. Except for the few ericaceous shrubs that require acidic conditions, the front yard and backyard in this case study are never fertilized.

During the growing season, most of the maintenance is weed removal in the gardens and cutting the lawn. The lawn is cut at a height of three inches with a mulching mower so the clippings are incorporated back into the soil. The weeds are gathered in the compost pile. The bulk of the maintenance and soil renewal occurs in the fall with leaf removal. The leaves that fall onto the lawn are cut weekly with the mulching mower. The leaves that fall into the garden beds remain. If the leaves accumulate too heavily in certain areas of the yard, they are reduced to avoid damage from a biological oxygen demand (BOD) overload, which can create anaerobic conditions and smothering of plant material. These leaves are also placed on the compost pile. The leaves that accumulate on the *Pachysandra* beds are raked into the bed to allow the evergreen leaves of the *Pachysandra* to emerge above the fallen leaves so the plants do not become smothered. The leaves decompose and further renew the soil since these beds are not mulched. The perennials are cut back and the cuttings placed on the compost pile. After the bulk of the leaves have fallen from the trees and any excessive spot accumulations are addressed through redistribution, the formal garden areas are mulched with a two- to four-inch layer of double-ground wood chips from the recycling center. This mulch is placed on top of the leaves that were left to remain in the garden beds. By the following fall, this additional layer of organic matter will be completely broken down into humus, providing food for the microorganisms that maintain a living soil.

CONCLUSION

The fact that the property owners were both full-time gardening professionals enhanced the success of the ecological landscape project. They knew how to take advantage of special features of their home, and they also knew how to shape the garden as it grew and reproduced itself. Although it was not their intention initially to develop an ecological landscape, it is evident from the above case study that an ecological landscape can be achieved over time and does not have to occur at once.

A novice can produce excellent results by paying attention to the principles outlined in this chapter. Older properties have the advantage of pre-existing mature trees but need more consideration for integrating new plantings with healthy older plants. For new construction, an ecological landscape can literally be built from the ground up. Time and effort spent in the beginning lays the groundwork for a beautiful landscape, less maintenance, and less degradation over time. It can take time for a healthy soil to develop and for the ecological interaction in the food chain that includes microorganisms and larger wildlife to occur. A well-designed landscape requires just enough maintenance to provide the property owners with regular exercise, as many of the benefits accumulate and some aspects of the garden become self-regulating.

The twenty-first century is the beginning of a new era. We must address the challenges of mitigating greenhouse gases, global warming, and climate change. All property owners, gardeners, and landscape professionals now face droughts, water restrictions, and concerns about increased runoff of chemical-laced storm water. Most homeowners and landscape professionals rarely think about the resource and energy use related to conventional landscape practices. Fortunately, LEED and SITES provide guidance and a set of standards to follow.

William Cullina, in *The Propagation of North American Wildflowers*, has defined the term Ecological Horticulture, a concept of matching plants to their suitable environments. This simple practice alone helps to integrate sound ecological decisions with the given habitat and limits excessive resource use. By making intelligent choices with plant selection, hardscape materials, utilizing plants to address runoff, and taking the holistic approach to ecological landscaping, ornamental landscapes will practice conservation that promotes ecology, biodiversity, and responsible land stewardship.

Biofiltration: A method of biologically filtering water, sewage, or storm water utilizing hydric plants to separate solid particles and impurities with a created wetland.

Biological oxygen demand: The amount of dissolved oxygen needed to decompose organic matter.

Carbon footprint: The amount of carbon dioxide and possibly other greenhouse gases that an individual or organization produces through their activities.

Cultivar: A variety of a plant species originating in cultivation and continuing in cultivation, which has a proper name in modern language.

Ecosystem services: The important benefits for human beings that arise from healthily functioning ecosystems, notably production of oxygen, soil genesis, and water detoxification.

Effluent: The outflow of a sewage system, water treatment facility, or storm water system.

Friable: Having the ability to break-up and crumble.

Groundcover: Any of the various low, dense-growing plants used for covering the ground, as in places where it is difficult to grow grass.

Hardscape: Non-plant material part of an ornamental landscape, such as patios, walkways, and driveway.

Invasive species: Non-indigenous plants that are capable of "invading" natural plant communities, where they displace indigenous species, contribute to species extinctions, alter the community structure, and may ultimately disrupt the function of ecosystem processes.

Loam: Soil that contains an equal amount of sand, silt, and clay.

Non-point pollution: Toxins and pollution that come from an unknown source.

Phytoremediation: A process of decontaminating soil or water by using plants and trees to absorb or break down pollutants.

Right plant/Right place: The concept of matching appropriate plant material with specific growing conditions.

Xeriscape: Landscape or garden that utilizes plants that are structurally adapted to be grown under dry conditions.

REFERENCES

Burrell, C. Colston. 1997. *A Gardeners Encyclopedia of Wildflowers: An Organic Guide to Choosing and Growing over 150 Beautiful Wildflowers.* Emmaus, PA: Rodale Press, Inc.

Christopher, Thomas. 2011. *The New American Landscape.* Portland, OR: Timber Press, Inc.

Cullina, William. 2000. *The New England Wildflower Society Guide to Growing and Propagating Wildflowers of the United States and Canada.* New York, NY: Houghton Mifflin Company.

Cullina, William. 2008. *Native Ferns, Mosses, and Grasses.* New York, NY: Houghton Mifflin Company.

Darke, Rick, and Douglas W. Tallamy. 2014. *The Living Landscape.* Portland, OR: Timber Press, Inc.

Simeone, Vincent A. 2013. *Grow More with Less: Sustainable Garden Methods.* Minneapolis, MN: Cool Springs Press.

Tallamy, Douglas W. 2009. *Bringing Nature Home.* Portland, OR: Timber Press, Inc.